NEW YORK'S
BEST-KEPT
SECRETS

NEW YORK'S BEST-KEPT SECRETS

Mike Michaelson

PASSPORT BOOKS
a division of *NTC Publishing Group*
Lincolnwood, Illinois USA

Editorial writer: Michael Sweeney
Editorial research and production:
  Glynis A. Steadman

Published by Passport Books, a division of
NTC Publishing Group, 4255 West Touhy Avenue,
Lincolnwood (Chicago), Illinois 60646-1975.

Manufactured in the United States of America.

Library of Congress Catalog Card Number: 93-83801

3 4 5 6 7 8 9 ML 9 8 7 6 5 4 3 2 1

CONTENTS

INTRODUCTION

Would you like to discover a spot in New York where you can visit a real neighborhood that seems like a New England fishing village? Or where you can find a lovely private park in the middle of Manhattan? Or the restaurant where the term *power breakfast* originated? How about a church where services break for jazz interludes? Or saloons where you can roll bocce balls and find out all you ever wanted to know about rugby football? Or a McDonald's with a grand piano? Or simply the best spot to sit and watch the river go by?

This sampling of distinctive and intriguing attractions summarizes what this book is all about—showing off a wide range of "bests" that New York has to offer. Not just the classic things and familiar places in this colossus of a city (although, of course, they are included here...sometimes presented in a new way), but also the unique, the offbeat, and the irreverent—in short, a fascinating collection of intriguing things to do and places to see in and around New York, including restaurants, hotels, shopping, entertainment, sports (to watch *and* participate in), museums, cultural diversions, and much more.

This book will direct you to the finest and most elegant restaurants in New York...as well as more casual spots for ethnic or regional cooking of nearly every stripe—from Turkish to Jamaican, seafood to soul food. We'll show you a restaurant run by a protégé of the late James Beard, dean of American food critics; we'll direct you to the leanest pastrami, the most refreshing egg creams, and plumpest pancakes, to diners that dish up diner food, and diners that serve gourmet food. And we'll steer you to a variety of pizzas, including Chicago-style and New Orleans-style—with visits to the favorite pizza parlors of celebrities, and to the best pizza place with "Ray's" in its name. We'll point out literary bars and taverns where O. Henry wrote many of his classic short stories and where Dylan Thomas inspired the myriad tales of his eventually fatal overindulging. You'll read about concert halls offering some of the finest classical music in the world, as well as a pub where a famous comic actor and director likes to spend his nights off playing the clarinet. We pinpoint the "chic-est" boutiques and the funkiest bargains—often only a block or two apart!

These contrasts—and many more—are what make New York such a vibrant, challenging, and exciting travel destination. And this book shines its whimsical spotlight on all of the diverse facets of the sprawling, cosmopolitan "Big Apple."

As you may have guessed, this is not your standard guidebook. Think of us as a well-informed friend—the kind you wish you had in every city you visited. Wouldn't it be great to have a friendly native New Yorker (no, that's not *necessarily* a contradiction in terms) to steer you to all of the worthwhile (and even unusual) sites, while avoiding the overrated or past-their-prime spots? Wouldn't it be fun to learn the real inside gossip and fascinating history about the sights you're seeing? We aim to do that—and more. Our thorough chapter selections and comprehensive index make this a practical book to use—but our innovative suggestions make it *fun* and (we think you'll come to agree) indispensable to use.

Looking for historic sights? You'll find the expected here, often examined in a new light...Rockefeller Center, the Staten Island Ferry...but we'll also introduce you to the unexpected. We'll tell you why the Bronx's Little Italy is more authentic than the same-named (and more-often visited) neighborhood in Manhattan, we'll direct you to the best travel bargains in the city, and we'll show you a house only 10 feet wide that has been home to some famous people.

And, as is apparent from some of these samples, not all of these city treasures are confined to the bustling, busy island of Manhattan. We'll also uncover some of the best-kept secrets in the other four New York boroughs. We'll show you the Bronx's rich heritage, prove that Brooklyn is more than Coney Island and tract housing, explore sports and museums in Queens, and uncover the often-bucolic splendor of Staten Island.

Bringing the kids along? We'll direct you to an entire chapter of attractions keyed especially to families visiting New York—the best storytellers and puppeteers, ice-cream parlors and parties. Ditto for lovers—and honeymooners—with the special selections in our "Romantic" chapter, such as a shop that sells only heart-themed merchandise, a wholesale flower market, and charming restaurants and cafés for every romantic occasion.

And if you venture beyond New York's five boroughs? We've even got you covered there. Head for our "Environs" chapter for a brief sampling of special places in the surrounding area, such as a whaling museum where you can take a class in scrimshaw and learn to make a ship-in-bottle, a close-in ski resort, and one of the largest and best-equipped planetariums in the country.

This is a book to browse through. You may find yourself chuckling at some of the folly revealed within. (Is it true that business actually picked up at a Manhattan steakhouse after a well-known mobster was rubbed out in front of it?) But it is also a solid reference guide—we let you know not just what's out there, but *why* it's worth a visit. And, while this book strives to be a good, lively read, full of fun as well as fact, it is also a completely practical volume, giving full addresses and phone numbers for attractions, so you'll have all the information you need for a delightful trip close at hand.

Our team of travel experts and expert travelers have prepared this book for the first-time visitor and the New York veteran alike. We'll help the first-timer find the unexpected treasures that can literally make a vacation. As for veteran travelers,...we'd be hard-pressed to believe that anyone (even an immensely curious native New Yorker) has journeyed to *all* of the 500-plus sites we've surveyed in this book. This means, of course, that we can help seasoned visitors get even *more* out of a trip to New York by helping them discover hidden gems that may have escaped them on previous trips or by pointing out new worthwhile restaurants or attractions that have opened since they last visited. (And, in New York, "new" is a major part of the restaurant and enter-tainment scene!)

Let's face it—it can be hard work having a great vacation or even a stimulating weekend in the city or a night out on the town. Well, we've attempted to take some of the work out of your playtime by tracking down everything you might want to do in and around New York,...not to mention the things you *didn't know* you wanted to do, but *will* after reading about them!

So, what this book offers is both the famous *and* the should-be-famous,...both the expensive *and* the inexpensive (and—in price-notorious New York—even the free!). But, overall and most importantly, it offers a unique and entertaining perspective on one of the most popular vacation destinations in the world.

If you can make it there you can make it any-where, as Sinatra would remind you about the Big Apple....And, our perspective (with equal touches of history and humor) is designed to help you "make it there"—or, at the very least, help you make your visit there a fun, full, and memorable one.

DINING

Best Pizza Where There's an Axe

John's Pizzeria

In *Broadway Danny Rose*, Woody Allen is held captive by two hoods. One directs the other to watch the prisoner while he goes to fetch the axe. "There's an axe?" asks a wide-eyed Woody. This amusing line is acknowledged in the "Woody Allen Room" of this Village pizza parlor with an axe mounted on the wall—along with photographs and other memorabilia relating to John's most famous patron. The older front room, though, has more atmosphere with big bands and Sinatra on an ancient jukebox, knotty-pine walls, large wooden booths carved with graffiti, a scarred, chipped black-and-white tile floor, and a dilapidated high tin ceiling with churning fans in various states of disrepair. The excellent thin-crust pizza baked in a coal oven comes in 54 combinations. From the same oven comes calzoni, a half-moon-shaped pocket of dough stuffed with fresh ricotta and mozzarella cheese and pieces of sausage. There are a few spaghetti selections, plus homemade stuffed shells, manicotti, and ravioli with accompaniments of fresh pork sausage and meatballs. Wash down your pizza with domestic or imported wine, draught beer, or soda.

John's Pizzeria, 278 Bleecker St, New York, NY 10014, 212/243-1680. Mon-Thu & Sun 11:30 am-11:30 pm, Fri & Sat 11:30 am-12:30 am.

Best Pizza Place with "Ray's" in the Name

Famous Ray's Pizza in the Village

This is the perfect place for "a slice" (as New Yorkers like to buy and eat their pizza), serving up thin-crust pizza with tons of gooey mozzarella. So what's the big deal about *this particular* "Ray's"? The Byzantine story of the city-wide proliferation of Ray's started with the spread of the legend of great pizza available at a little joint called Ray's. As quick as you could say "Gimme a slice!" New York was gripped with an epidemic of pizza places named "Ray's" (or some permutation thereof). Among these were or are Ray's Pizza, Ray's House of Pizza, Ray's Real Pizza, Original Ray's, Original Famous Ray's, Ray's Original Pizza, Ray's Famous Pizza, and even a Ray Bari Pizza (someone obviously neglected to inform Mr. Bari that a last name was not necessary in this game). In short, there are plenty of "Ray's"—and many sources get the genealogy of this elusive non-chain "chain" wrong. Just for fun, while researching this amusing story, we looked at a few guidebooks that mentioned Ray's—and found that most treat all the Ray's as if they were part of a larger whole. One even went as far (in the wrong direction) as to recommend some locations from "the Ray's chain," but said this one (the *real* one) wasn't to be confused with the others and *wasn't* included in the recommendation. Still other sources ignore the weighty "Ray's" question altogether, instead sticking with a "safe" endorsement of John's Pizzeria (which *is* very good—see separate listing). But, there's no fooling many savvy New Yorkers who know the *real* Ray's from all the pretenders. They flock here, usually meaning there is a line in front of the place. But, at a slice here, a slice there, and the occasional whole pie (all at reasonable prices), the line moves fairly quickly, as real-Ray's radicals rally 'round what may well be the best pizza in the city!

Famous Ray's Pizza in the Village, 465 Sixth Ave (at W 11th St), New York, NY 10011, 212/243-2253. Sun-Thu 11 am-2 am, Fri & Sat 11 am-3 am.

Best Chicago Deep-Dish Pizza

Pizzeria Uno Restaurant & Bar

Back in 1943 in Chicago, Ike Sewell started making the hefty deep-dish pizzas that since have become a legend, creating a successful chain with clones across the country as well as in Australia and Canada. This Manhattan branch (one of several) is handy to the American Museum of Natural History (see separate listing) and is the spot to get a fix of Chicago-style pizza, made with a thick crust, a gooey layer of cheese, a wide choice of toppings, and a layer of tomatoes and tomato sauce. Baked in an oven-blackened pan (6" or 9" sizes), it takes longer to cook than a flat pizza (baking times, up to 20 minutes, for each type of pizza are listed on the menu). A deep-dish pizza also is more filling. Appetizers include garlic bread and toasted raviolis; soup choices are cheese minestrone and cream of broccoli. There are burgers, sandwiches, half a dozen salads, and chili—but pizza is the thing here. Desserts, mostly ice cream concoctions and cheesecake, are pictured in a book. This attractive eatery has black-and-white checkerboard tiles and matching tablecloths, a tiny patio, and a comfortable room called "the study" with brick walls, hardwood floors, and vintage posters.

Pizzeria Uno Restaurant & Bar, 432 Columbus Ave, New York, NY 10024, 212/595-4700 (and other locations). Mon-Thu 11 am-1 am, Fri & Sat 11 am-2 am, Sun noon-1 am.

Best Cajun Pizza

Two Boots

A business executive transferred to Chicago observed that one of the things she missed about New York was her favorite pizza. But how can that be, she was asked incredulously, now living in a city famous for its pizza. Yes, she said, but not *Cajun* pizza. And that is what makes this East Village eatery one-of-a-kind. Many who try its delicious pizza declare it is among the best—and certainly the most unique—in the city. The pizza is the thin-crust kind with a piquant tomato sauce and top-quality Romano and mozzarella cheeses. Louisiana-style toppings include barbecued shrimp, crawfish, andouille sausage, and jalepeño peppers—along with such Italian favorites as calamari, roasted peppers, eggplant, artichokes, and peppery-garlicky soppressata sausage. Other Louisiana-Italian hybrid dishes include jambalaya served over pasta, ravioli with jalepeño pesto, crabmeat minestrone, and linguine Dominique, featuring blackened chicken, julienne vegetables, and a light cream sauce. The menu also features unadulterated Italian and Cajun dishes. To go with the food are wine and Italian beer (Peroni and Moretti) and Louisiana brews (Dixie and Blackened Voodoo). An eclectic jukebox selection includes lively zydeco tunes as well as blues and rock. Across the street is Two

Boots to Go, with a newer take-out, Two Boots to Go-Go, at 74 Bleecker Street. There is a second restaurant in Brooklyn.

Two Boots, 37 Ave A, New York, NY 10009, 212/505-2276. Tue-Sun noon-midnight.

Best Bet for Bar Pies

R.H. Tugs

Across from the popular cultural attractions of Snug Harbor (see separate listing), this restaurant and bar, with a high tin ceiling, shiny black tables, and framed watercolors of tugboats, is a handsome reclamation of an abandoned waterfront building. It is noted for its grilled meats and fish, but also offers a selection of imaginative bar pies—mozzarella and tomato, pepperoni pizza, crab pizza, Texas beef, and broccoli, garlic, and oil. Windows and a small patio overlook the busy harbor. During the day, there is an entertaining procession of tugboats; after dark, the unsightly storage tanks of oil refineries on the Jersey shore are transformed by twinkling lights. For starters, there is chowder made with shrimp, crab, and fish, and fried seafood dumplings. Entrées include seafood fettucine, shrimp sautéed in a spicy sauce and served over rice, flavorful seared ribeye steaks, and large slabs of tasty ribs. Finish with ice cream pie. In summer, the adjacent Outback Grill fronts on the water and features an entirely different menu with a Caribbean emphasis. On Thursday evenings a Caribbean band performs.

R.H. Tugs, 1115 Richmond Terrace, Staten Island, NY 10301, 718/447-6369. Sun-Thu noon-midnight, Fri-Sat noon-1 am.

Best Italian Muffaletta Sandwich

Cucina & Co.

On trips to New Orleans, food fanciers often schedule a visit to Central Grocery or one of the other Italian delis across from the French Market. The attraction is a muffaletta sandwich, a large circular loaf filled with layers of olive salad, meat, cheese, and sausage—large enough to feed two. This specialty of the Big Easy is available in the Big Apple at a 100-seat European café and take-out food shop in the lobby of the Pan Am building. Other signature sandwiches include pan *bagnat* (basically a tuna niçoise sandwich) and es*calivada*, a Spanish-style sandwich filled with roasted vegetables. For traditionalists, a triple-decker club features smoked turkey, bacon, and avocado. Specialty dishes include cannelloni with ricotta and porcini mushrooms and orzo with scallops and mussels. Desserts feature miniature fruit tarts, key lime pie, and spun-sugar cookies. Modeled after an old-style European country kitchen, the restaurant features terra cotta floors, an attractive oak-and-glass pantry, and imported Italian wall tiles.

Cucina & Co, 200 Park Ave, New York, NY 10166, 212/682-2700. Mon-Fri 7 am-9 pm, Sat 8 am-5 pm.

Best Restaurant with the "Chairman of the Board" on Its Side

Patsy's

This family-owned Midtown restaurant has been serving up Southern-Italian cuisine for more than 45 years, using recipes that have been in Pascuale "Patsy" Scognamillo's family for more than twice as long. But a momentary dark cloud passed overhead a few years ago, when an influential *New York Times* reviewer downgraded this popular eatery. Quickly springing to Patsy's defense was none other than Frank Sinatra, a longtime Scognamillo confidante and passionate fan of Patsy's cuisine (and, it must be noted, no fan of the press). This storm blew over, without seeming to affect this restaurant's popularity. Favored starters include hearty escarole soup and a hot antipasto platter. Follow these with a selection from the well-regarded daily specials; Thursday's chicken contadina and Saturday's homemade stuffed manicotti are long-running favorites. Also good are linguini with clam sauce, sausages with peppers, veal and pork chops, a variety of great homemade pastas and sauces, and traditional Italian desserts such as zabaglione, cannoli, and gelatos. Don't be surprised if the background music is Sinatra—probably singing "New York, New York"—Patsy knows what side his (crusty, Italian) bread is buttered on!

Patsy's, 236 W 56th St, New York, NY 10019, 212/247-3491. Sun-Thu noon-10:30 pm, Fri & Sat noon-11:30 pm.

Best Italian Restaurant with Its Own Bocce Court

Il Vagabondo

This restaurant isn't trendy or daring. It is a comfortable neighborhood spot to spoon your traditional Southern Italian favorites (read: red sauces galore), and to try your hand at the leisurely—and somewhat addicting—Italian pastime of bocce (more about which later). Il Vagabondo is a longtime favorite of residents of this East Side neighborhood. It serves good veal dishes (a rich veal stew, popular parmigiana, and a special "Veal Vagabondo" with eggplant, prosciutto, and wine), homemade cannelloni and gnocchi, chops, chicken, and steaks—as well as pastas in simple, but rich and tasty sauces. But the pleasant dining is only part of the story here. The other is bocce, a game similar to lawn bowling, which involves trying to toss/roll croquet-sized clay balls close to a target ball, while trying to also knock your opponent's shot out of the way. Sip a few glasses of post-dinner wine and try your hand at this fun game—or watch the resident experts, trying to pick up pointers for your next visit. Il Vagabondo's dirt-floored (for the real outside feel) bocce court is believed to be the only indoor court in New York.

Il Vagabondo, 351 E 62nd St, New York, NY 10021, 212/832-9221. Mon-Fri noon-3 pm, 5:30 pm-midnight; Sat 5:30 pm-midnight; Sun 5:30-11:30 pm.

Best Italian Restaurant in Greenwich Village

Il Mulino

Behind this restaurant's run-down exterior is a dark, often crowded interior. But beyond these unpretentious appearances is a restaurant whose reputation is growing as a hole-in-the-wall spot that happens to serve some of the best Italian food in the Village—perhaps in the entire city. Among Il Mulino's favored appetizers are a truly transcendent lightly fried zucchini (perhaps the definitive of this often-tasteless finger food) and a well-balanced antipasto plate. Its most popular entrées include a variety of excellent pastas (especially the delicate spaghettini bolognese and the hearty spaghetti carbonara), stuffed mushrooms, several seafood dishes (such as breaded clams, salmon with porcini mushrooms, and mussels sizzling in garlicky butter sauce), and a number of good veal specials. It also offers the basic Italian specialties for dessert—or a homemade-daily chocolate mousse sure to please even the most discerning chocoholic. *A note to the potentially claustrophobic:* Il Mulino can get very crowded, especially at dinner; lunch is a better bet to avoid masses of people and long waits for tables. A couple of other good Village choices for Italian are Ennio & Michael (539 La Guardia Place; 212/677-8577), which has a comfortable outdoor patio, and Il Cantinori (32 E. 10th Street; 212/673-6044), for Tuscan specialties in a rustic, antique-filled setting.

Il Mulino, 86 W 3rd St, New York, NY 10012, 212/
673-3783. Mon-Fri noon-2:30 pm, 5 pm-midnight; Sat
5 pm-midnight.

Best Italian Restaurant in the Bronx Without a Menu

Dominick's

It stands to reason that an authentic ethnic neighborhood would include a few terrific ethnic restaurants. A good case in point is the Bronx's Little Italy,
known locally as Belmont (see separate listing). In
the heart of the Bronx, this neighborhood is centered
around Arthur Avenue, where in-the-know diners
from throughout the boroughs head for authentic
Italian cooking, usually opting for either Dominick's
or Mario's (see separate listing). Family-run
Dominick's is a popular eatery with a bit of a difference—it has no set menu. While at first this can
be a bit disconcerting, it can really lead to a liber-
ating dining experience. Simply ask your waiter for
whatever Italian specialty you crave, and, barring
the rare lack of a crucial ingredient, the inventive
and experienced kitchen at Dominick's will whip up
their version of it for you. These choices can include
pasta, meat (good steaks and chops), fish, and
chicken, mostly rendered with a Southern-Italian
slant. But don't let that discourage you from asking
for fettucine Alfredo or another non-red-sauce
pasta—when it comes to pasta, Dominick's delivers.
It also attracts big crowds, and may even have a line
in front. But don't let a potential wait discourage you
from trying a singular Italian dining experience. *Note
for the potentially shy or unsure:* Dining here doesn't
have to be from a completely blank slate of choices—
Dominick's patient and helpful waiters are usually
more than willing to make their own nightly suggestions of appetizers and entrées.

Dominick's, 2335 Arthur Ave, the Bronx, NY 10458,
212/733-2807. Wed-Mon noon-10 pm.

Best Italian Restaurant in the Bronx with a Menu

Mario's

Good Italian cuisine in the Bronx's Little Italy isn't
confined to the unstructured choices at Dominick's
(see separate listing); if you prefer, you can head
across the street to this restaurant, where they *do*
have menus. Mario's has been a well-loved staple of
Little Italy/Belmont since 1919. Its friendly, casual

atmosphere attracts happy, noisy crowds—including a large complement of neighborhood families.
Basic pastas and sauces are faultless—the ravioli is
a consistent crowd-pleaser. Popular choices include
pasta fagioli, hearty homemade gnocchi, and several
veal entrées, including a standout version of osso
buco. Some lesser-known and perhaps more adventurous items also are worth sampling, including
octopus salad, a tasty deep-fried mozzarella sandwich, and a bountiful seafood antipasto platter.
Mario's is not a trendy trattoria or ristorante—just
a good old-fashioned family eatery, full of Old-Coun-
try charm and hearty food at reasonable prices.

Mario's, 2342 Arthur Ave, the Bronx, NY 10458, 212/
584-1188. Tue-Sun noon-11 pm.

Trendiest Trattoria

Bice

As with its counterparts in Chicago and Beverly
Hills, this trendy trattoria (with the original in Milan
and a branch in Paris) is a place to see and be seen.
Show biz celebs pop in, but this is a serious stamp-
ing ground for fashion gurus Bill Blass and Calvin
Klein and various garment-district nabobs. Expect
to find excellent Tuscan bean soup and reliable
risotto at this pricey restaurant. Pasta dishes also
are good—try fettucini or a medley of ravioli as a
starter—or choose from a good selection of hot and
cold antipasti. Entrées include broiled veal chops,
roast rack of veal, grilled chicken, lamb chop with
a pepper sauce, veal stew, and a selection of grilled
fish that includes salmon, snapper, and swordfish.
Considering the restaurant's Milanese antecedents,
the dessert of choice here is gelato (although all-
American cheesecake is surprisingly good). This
elegant restaurant, with a long bar of white marble,
stunning floral arrangements, and attractive contemporary art has seating on several levels.

Bice, 7 E 54th St, New York, NY 10022, 212/688-
1999. Daily noon-midnight.

Tastiest Tiramisu

Arqua'

This is a moderately trendy—but not stiflingly so—
SoHo restaurant that is known for its nicely accomplished presentation of simple, yet satisfying food of
Venice and its surrounding area. (It takes its unusual name from Arqua' Petrarca, a village not far
from Venice, which was home to its owner-chef.) It
offers a pleasantly muted art deco interior (nice and

spacious) and dishes made with fresh ingredients and homemade pasta (the gnocchi is a crowd-pleaser). For starters, try the stuffed artichoke, a rich fish soup, or, when available, fresh octopus. Top entrées include a black-ink risotto, excellent liver (like your mother never used to make—unless she hailed from a tiny village near Venice) with onions and polenta, and a variety of fish, chicken, and, especially, veal dishes. Homemade cheesecake, chocolate cake, and fruit tarts are all good dessert choices—but the now-ubiquitous Italian dessert of tiramisu is a "must." Its blend of creamy and nutty flavors provides a delicately delightful end to a nicely rendered meal. Arqua' also offers a decent selection of Italian wines, which, as with the food, are fairly moderately priced.

Arqua', 281 Church St, New York, NY 10013, 212/334-1888. Mon-Fri noon-3 pm, 5:30-11 pm; Sat 5:30-11:30 pm.

Best British Pub Grub

North Star Pub

It's somewhat contrived, and it is in the touristy South Street Seaport area...but this busy watering hole has the look and feel of a London pub. There are imported British ales to quaff and a good selection of single-malt Scotch. On tap is Bulmer's Wood-pecker cider—a wonderfully refreshing drink on a warm day—and on the tables are malt vinegar and the ubiquitous HP brand black sauce. Traditional simple ploughman's lunch consists of a wedge of cheese (cheddar or Stilton) with chutney, apple, pickled onion, Branston pickle (a popular English relish), and bread and butter. Add a slice of pâté forestière for a similar plate cutely labeled "ploughman's boss." Starters include Scotch egg, sausage-and-onion roll, and grilled Cumberland sausage. Entrées feature such Brit favorites as shepherd's pie, bangers and mash, sausage, beans, and chips (the lorry driver's special!), fish and chips with peas, and Madras-style chicken curry with rice and mango chutney. Desserts include deep-dish apple pie with custard sauce and raisin scone with double Devon cream and raspberry jam. Contribut-ing to the pub-like ambience are etched-glass pan-eling on a bar equipped with ceramic pump handles and a brass foot rail. Decorations include Royal Navy hats bearing the insignia of historic ships the HMS *Ark Royal* and HMS *Phoebe*.

North Star Pub, 93 South St, New York, NY 10038, 212/509-6757. Mon-Sat 11:30 am-10:30 pm, Sun noon-10:30 pm.

Best Black Beans (Cuban Style)

Sabor

On a gray New York day, the food and atmosphere of the tropics is as close as this small storefront restaurant, which offers a range of Cuban specialties and a friendly, welcoming ambience. Start with chilled gazpacho, the traditional Spanish soup that Cuban restaurants seem to do so well. You can get a decent rendering of *ropa vieja*, the Cuban-American-concocted beef stew, regarded by knowledgeable foodies as the Cuban equivalent of chop suey—not quite authentic, but representational and popular. For more authentic fare, try the roast suckling pig (a great feast for groups), fish such as red snapper or swordfish in *salsa verde*, sizzling sautéed shrimp, mussels in garlic sauce, or a terrific Cuban version of Spanish paella. Hearty black beans with rice accompany the entrées, and it is a winning rendition of this simple, yet soul-satisfying combination. Our favorite way to enjoy this dish is the Spanish style—spooning the beans over the rice and seasoning it with the garlicky seafood broth accompanying the aforementioned mussels. Popular beverages are fruity rum-based cocktails made with fresh tropical fruits. For dessert, there are fried plantains, flan, key lime pie, and various Cuban/Spanish/Mexican desserts. Another popular Cuban spot in Manhattan is Victor's Café 52 (236 W. 52nd Street; 212/586-7714), the latest outpost of a long-established, authentic restaurant (formerly on Columbus Avenue); this is a convenient place for a bowl of black bean soup—also very good here—or other Cuban specialties before a night at the theater.

Sabor, 20 Cornelia St, New York, NY 10014, 212/243-9579. Daily 6-11 pm.

Best Black Beans (Brazilian-Style)

Via Brasil

This restaurant is located in the tiny midtown enclave dubbed "Brazil Row"—a mere two blocks of West 46th Street between Fifth and Sixth avenues that is sprinkled with Brazilian businesses. The owner and chef hail from Brazil and fellow Brazilians sometimes stop by the bar to watch televised soccer games. Toward the end of the week there's moody live bossa nova music. Of course, the real test of ethnic authenticity is cuisine, and this stylish restaurant does admirably on that count. The signature dish of Brasil—the restaurant and the country!—is *feijoada*, a stout, stew-like blend of black beans, sausage, beef, bacon, and pork, that is heaped onto rice and served with garnishes on the side. Also typically Brazilian are a range of grilled poultry and meats and substantial herbed seafood casseroles flavored with tomatoes and coconut milk. As a lighter repast, order an omelette stuffed with shrimp or with a mixture of garlicky sausage, peppers, and hearts of palm. Starters include tiny meat pies, codfish fritters, fried squid, and, of course, an authentic rendition of black bean soup. A simple flan or some fresh fruit is an appropriate dessert. As an aperitif, choose a cocktail made with rum and fresh lime juice that is the Brazilian national drink. Finish with superb Brazilian coffee.

Via Brasil, 34 W 46th St, New York, NY 10036, 212/ 997-1158. Sun-Tue noon-10 pm, Wed & Thu noon-11 pm, Fri & Sat noon-midnight.

Best Black Beans (Elegant)

The Coach House

This Greenwich Village restaurant is the antithesis of the sort of down-home eatery where one might expect to find black bean soup, warm corn bread, pecan pie, and other representations of Southern cooking. Probably, it is because this elegant establishment more represents the genteel South populated by the O'Haras and their plantation-house coterie. Named after the quarters it occupies—a brownstone coach house, circa 1843—the restaurant has strict dress codes, gracious—some say aloof—service, and a loyal following of patrons, some of whom have been coming here to dine over more than two decades. The elegant ambience runs to red-leather banquettes and brick walls adorned with oil paintings depicting landed gentry at play. Be sure to sample the standout thick black bean soup and impeccable crab cakes, and don't pass up the chance to select one of the restaurant's ambrosial desserts, such as chocolate mousse cake. Standards such as rack of lamb and poached salmon also are reliable. The tab can run high here—particularly if one makes a selection from a pricey wine list.

The Coach House, 110 Waverly Pl, New York, NY 10011. Tue-Sat 5:30-10:30 pm, Sun 4:30-10:30 pm.

Best Bet for Greek in Manhattan

Periyali

There are many Greek-run restaurants in Manhattan, but, curiously, few restaurants offering authentic Greek cuisine. Among the dozens of Greek-run coffee shops on corners and in lobbies throughout the city, most offer a few token Greek dishes (usually salads, souvlaki, gyros, or spinach pie). For a full menu of fine Greek specialties in Manhattan—including some unusual, innovative dishes—head to this popular, crowded, and often noisy Chelsea restaurant. Top dishes at Periyali (it means seashore) include fresh fish (flown in nearly every day from Greece), plus excellent lamb entrées (especially the grilled, rosemary-seasoned chops), charcoal-grilled octopus, herbed grilled shrimp, tasty *gigantes* (a peasant dish of white beans stewed in a tomato and garlic sauce), and other Greek standbys, such as moussaka, spinach-and-cheese pies, and crackling-skinned broiled chicken. For dessert there's rich and gooey baklava, of course, but also lighter fare, such as phyllo-dough-based pastries and *diples*, strips of fried dough sweetened with honey. Finish with strong Greek coffee, and you've got a meal fit to yell "Opaa!" over. Other Manhattan spots offering Greek fare include Molfetas (307 W. 47th Street; 212/840-9537) and New Acropolis (767 Eighth Avenue; 212/581-2733), around the corner from each other, just off the Theater District, both popular for their good food at reasonable prices.

Periyali, 35 W 20th St, New York, NY 10011, 212/463-7890. Mon-Sat noon-3 pm, 6-11 pm.

Best Bet for Greek in Astoria

Roumeli Taverna

While the oft-repeated claim that the Astoria neighborhood in Queens has the third-largest Greek population in the world (after only Athens and Salonika) may be spurious, it is definitely true that this neighborhood's Greek population is substantial and quite evident. The streets between Broadway and Ditmars Boulevard are lined with Greek groceries, restaurants, shops, cafés, and more than 10 Greek Orthodox churches. Some of the best food served up in this tight-knit enclave is found at Roumeli Taverna, a popular restaurant named after a Grecian mountain range. Try the taramasalata and tzatziki dips for openers; main courses include baked lamb with artichoke, lemon chicken with garlicky vegetables, rich moussaka, a variety of fresh grilled fish dishes, and excellent traditional stuffed grape leaves, all washed down with a glass of retsina or rod)tys. Roumeli is a bit fancier than some of the other neighborhood spots; it draws strong crowds of locals and visitors alike—many of the latter also taking in the nearby Museum of the Moving Image (see separate listing). Other good spots in Astoria for

Greek cooking are George's Hasapotaverna (28-13 Twenty-third Avenue; 718/728-9056), widely hailed for its sublime spinach pie; Taygetos (30-11 Thirtieth Avenue; 718/726-5195), offering a good selection of vegetarian dishes along with the usual Greek fare; Salonika Restaurant (31-17 Twenty-third Avenue; 718/728-5829), noted as a romantic spot; and Taverna Vraka (23-15 31st Street; 718/721-3007), a sometimes haunt for Hellenic celebrities since Aristotle Onassis favored it in years past (some entertaining folk dancing, too).

Roumeli Taverna, 33-14 Broadway, Astoria, Queens, NY 11106, 718/278-7533. Daily 11:30 am-1:30 am.

Best Borscht Near the Boardwalk
National Restaurant

These days, the Russian expatriates who gather on weekends at this lively Brooklyn eatery to meet *tovariche* from the old country (and new American friends, too) have plenty to talk about—and sing and dance about. It is for good reason that the Brighton Beach neighborhood has been dubbed "Little Odessa-by-the-Sea." Russian grocery stores, gift shops, and bookstores line the main street, Brighton Beach Avenue, where this restaurant draws a lively crowd. Those who saw the Robin Williams movie *Moscow on the Hudson* may recognize this as the restaurant where Soviet defector Robin Williams drank and danced with his Russian friends. Go for a boisterous good time, rather than remarkable food. A Russian dance band plays authentic music, the vodka and wine flow, and a rowdy crowd tucks into a procession of hot and cold appetizers, pickled mushrooms, smoked fish, borscht, stewed chicken, baked eggplant, and lamb, chicken, and beef kebabs. Other Russian eateries along this strip include Odessa and Primorsky.

National Restaurant, 273 Brighton Beach Ave, Brooklyn, NY 11235, 718/646-1225. Fri & Sat 8 pm-3 am, Sun 8 pm-1 am.

Best Bet for *Bigos*
Odessa

Now that we're fully into the post-Cold War, post-Soviet Union era, a bit of information about this restaurant's region of origin is in order: Contrary to years of references otherwise, the large southwestern region of the former USSR is simply "Ukraine," not "*the* Ukraine." If you want to know more about this region, the friendly patrons of this restaurant, located in the Little Ukraine section of the East Village, which is home to some 30,000 residents of Ukrainian descent, is a good place to start. Odessa resembles a typical diner or corner restaurant, with red vinyl booths, white tabletops, and a central counter. In addition to a variety of Eastern European-flavored entrées, such as goulash, roast pork, pirogen, blintzes, and borscht, this is the best spot to try *bigos*, a favored Ukrainian dish of sliced kielbasa sausage (sometimes referred to as *kobasa* sausage in Ukrainian restaurants or markets) and sauerkraut. For dessert, try the homemade cheesecake, rich and delicious. Like most of Manhattan's Eastern European eateries, Odessa is a remarkably good bargain, and it attracts a variety of Lower East Siders, from punk rockers to Puerto Ricans. Not far away—and open 24 hours—is the Kiev International Coffee House and Restaurant (117 Second Avenue; 212/674-4040), another Ukrainian-style establishment that serves up big portions at small prices (it's big with students and other budget-watchers); the challah-based French toast and excellent soups are winners here.

Odessa, 117 Avenue A, New York, NY 10009, 212/473-8916. Tue-Sun 7 am-11 pm.

Happiest Haven of Hungry Hungarians
Mocca Hungarian

This comfortable, homey restaurant is part of what's left of a small Hungarian neighborhood in once-German-dominated Yorkville (which was transported there from a turn-of-the-century Hungarian enclave in the East Village's Alphabet City area). It offers large portions of stick-to-your-ribs food at low prices—Mocca's meals typically include soup (especially cold fruit soups), salad, an entrée (the best of which include goulash, roast loin of pork, roast duck, a Hungarian version of Wiener schnitzel, calf's liver, stuffed cabbage, and a sublime chicken paprikash), and dessert (the great authentic strudel is the top pick). During the week, the three-course set lunch is another great bargain; on weekends, dining here is accompanied by that Hungarian staple, the roving Gypsy violinist. Choose a robust red "bull's blood" wine to accompany this solid fare. For other choices in Hungarian dining, a few blocks south are both Red Tulip (439 E. 75th Street; 212/734-4893), offering more hearty eating in an Old World atmosphere (plus violinists every night), and Csarda (1477

Second Avenue; 212/472-2892), well-known for its
generous portions.

Mocca Hungarian, 1588 Second Ave, New York,
NY 10028, 212/734-6470. Daily 11:30 am-11 pm.

Best Jewish/Roumanian "Soul Food"

Sammy's Roumanian Restaurant and Triplet's
Roumanian

The usual spelling may be "Rumanian," but both of
these authentic restaurants choose to spell it
"Roumanian"—so who are we to argue with "u"?
Especially when these somewhat-funky, always-
rollicking establishments offer such terrific spreads
of old-world Jewish (if not always kosher) cooking.
For lack of a better description, both of these good-
time places may well remind you of stumbling into
someone's bar mitzvah; if this sounds entertaining,
these are for you. Sammy's is on the once-Jewish,
now-mixed Lower East Side, near the Bowery. The
kibitzing and hearty eating only *seem* like they have
been going on here since the turn of the century—
in reality, Sammy's has been around since 1975.
This dark, cluttered—some say tacky—storefront
restaurant (with live music that is as often Broadway
tunes as Yiddish songs) serves up chopped liver with
onions, a sure-to-cure-whatever-ails-you chicken
soup (with kreplach noodles, motzah balls, or both),
potato pancakes, and tender Roumanian-style steak
and dumplings, all in suitably large portions. A fun
touch is that each table is equipped for patrons to
create their own egg creams—with a container of
milk, a spritzer of seltzer, and—this is key among
aficionados—a jar of the hard-to-find Fox's U-Bet
brand of chocolate syrup. Dining here can be cheap,
can be expensive—it all depends on what (and how
much of it) you have; head here with a group for
sharing to get the best bargains. Triplet's offers more
of the same (if a little more uncluttered), with an
even more interesting background story—it's run by
triplet brothers who were separated at birth and
reunited in their late teens. Catch one of the three,
and he'll spin his tale while you sample stuffed
cabbage, liver-and-onions, veal chops, brisket, and
thick and hearty soups. Triplet's also offers good egg
creams—but, unlike at Sammy's, they make 'em, not
you.

Sammy's Roumanian Restaurant, 157 Chrystie St,
New York, NY 10002, 212/673-0330. Sun-Fri 4-10 pm,
Sat 4 pm-2 am. Triplet's Roumanian, 11-17 Grand
St, New York, NY 10013, 212/925-9303. Daily 5-1 pm.

Best Spot Where the Czech Comes Before the Check

Vasata

Never as numerous nor as obvious as New York's leading ethnic groups, the Czechoslovakians none-theless managed to carve out a niche for themselves in the city, first in a "Little Bohemia" area on the Lower East Side, and, by the turn of the century, in a same-named neighborhood on the East Side, near the river. All that is tangibly left of this later enclave are a few old-time residents, the handful of shops and churches that they patronize, and this pleasant, Old-World-style restaurant. Vasata has been family-run for nearly 40 years, and offers a hearty menu of Czech favorites. These include roast duck; fresh game in the fall, such as goose, hare, or venison; tender roast loin pork with dumplings in gravy; and satisfying Czech soups, including a favored cream of mushroom that puts to shame anything you've ever heated out of a can. Dessert is the traditional *palacinty*, a crepe-like concoction, filled with fruits, nuts, or chocolate, rolled, and dusted with powdered sugar (or, if you prefer, flambéed in liqueur).

Vasata, 339 E 79th St, New York, NY 10021, 212/ 988-7166. Tue-Sat 5-10:30 pm, Sun 11 am-9:30 pm.

Fondest Fondue

La Fondue

Although the fondue fad has faded, this busy res-taurant continues to feed the flame (and light the Sterno). Fondues run the usual gamut of cheese (blending Swiss gruyère and emmenthal with chablis), steak, and seafood (featuring stuffed crab claws), plus chocolate dessert fondue blended with honey, almonds, sweet cream, and brandy with fruit and cake for dunking. The main dining room of this popular after-theater spot is at street level but has the feeling of a ratskeller with its arched ceiling, white stucco wall, and cracked bricks. Soup selec-tions—suggested as a main dish with a salad and sourdough bread—include onion gratinée, Swedish green pea, cheddar cheese, vegetable with pasta, and gazpacho. In various versions of England's re-nowned ploughman's, the restaurant offers cheese and sausage boards served with crusty breads, Dijon mustard, and assorted relishes. Pairings include English cheddar with German Black Forest smoked pork, Italian fontina and salami, French brie and pâté, and Danish gröddost with Polish kielbasy. Another specialty is quiche—available in ham, ba-con, spinach, and broccoli versions.

La Fondue, 43 W 55th St, New York, NY 10019, 212/
581-0820; fax 212/246-4316. Mon-Sat 11:45 am-
midnight, Sun 11:45 am-11 pm.

Best Turkish Delight
Divan

For an authentic taste of Turkey, step into the stark
interior of this Village restaurant with its bare-brick
walls, white stucco arches, and wooden tables. Start
with red lentil soup, or a cold appetizer such as
eggplant dip, red caviar with olive oil and lemon
juice, or the ubiquitous *humus* (mashed chick peas).
For those who like their appetizers spicy, there is
acili ezme, a fiery combination of walnuts, red bell
peppers, garlic, and spices. Hot appetizers include
börek (pan-fried phyllo stuffed with feta cheese) and
lahmacun (a sort of Turkish pizza made with ground
beef, tomato sauce, and onions). Entrées include
mixed grill, a variety of kabobs, and grilled lamb
patties and lamb chops. Desserts run to sticky
baklava, chocolate cake, and ice cream. Of course,
there is sweet, thick Turkish coffee as well as Turkish tea. There is a sidewalk alfresco area in front of
the white stucco building with its wood-framed
windows and green-and-white striped awning.

Divan, 102 Macdougal St, New York, NY 10012,
212/598-9789. Sun-Thu 1 pm-1 am, Fri & Sat 1 pm-2
am.

Peerless Pierogi Purveyor
Christine's

Whenever you're in the mood for some hearty fare,
this mini-chain of three Polish eateries has a number of things going for it. The food is filling, of the
robust, stick-to-the-ribs variety. And when the check
arrives, you might be surprised to receive change
from a twenty. The quality is reliable and even. If
you're unfamiliar with that basic of Polish cuisine,
the pierogi, this is the spot to give it a try. These
sturdy dumplings come filled with all manner of
goodies, including various combinations of chicken,
beef, veal, pork, cheese, and vegetables. Also on the
menu are the likes of stuffed cabbage, blintzes,
borscht, *kopytka* (potato dumplings), and *placki*
(potato pancakes). Sausage aficionados will find a
good version of smokey kielbasa. Ambience ranges
from basic luncheonette, to something a little fancier, depending upon location. An inexpensive house
wine is available by the glass and by the bottle.

Christine's, 344 Lexington Ave, New York, NY 10016,
212/953-1920, Daily 11 am-9 pm. Other locations:
438 Second Ave (212/684-1879); 208 First Ave (212/
505-0376).

Best Restaurant Where You Eat the Plate, Too

The Blue Nile

Sharing is the thing at this Upper West Side Ethiopian eatery, preferably with companions you're comfortable with, since there are no utensils and dining
tends to get a little messy. Combination plates offer
samplings of the main menu items. Mounds of meat
and vegetables are set on a platter covered with thin,
pancake-like slices of Ethiopian bread, called *injera*,
with extra bread on the side. Simply break off a piece
of bread for use as a scoop. Finish by eating the host
bread, by that time soaked with flavorful juices.
Some entrées are seasoned by berbere sauce, a hot
red-pepper sauce traditionally made by mixing up to
15 different spices with water in a jug and then
burying it for three days. *Tib wot*, for example,
consists of beef cubes simmered in a blend of hot
berbere, onions, aromatic fenugreek, garlic, and
other spices. *Kitfo*, Ethiopia's national dish, is a
spicy version of steak tartare—raw chopped lean
beef seasoned with spiced butter and topped with
hot chili powder. It can be ordered hot or mild.
Vegetarian dishes featuring lentils, kale, potatoes,
yellow split peas, broiled green beans, carrots, tomatoes, onions, and romaine lettuce, dominate the
menu, along with a handful of lamb, beef, poultry,
and even a couple of fish entrées. Beer is a good
companion drink, with domestic brands available,
plus Club brand imported from Ghana. Seating is
at three-legged stools set at low straw tables.

The Blue Nile, 103 W 77th St, New York, NY 10024,
212/580-3232. Mon-Fri 5 pm-midnight, Sat & Sun
noon-midnight.

Purveyor of Perfect Paella

Harlequin

A friend who is a dyed-in-the-wool Neopolitan
puckishly calls paella "Spanish deep-dish pizza." Of
course, it does arrive at the table in a deep, pizza-
type pan with an array of "toppings" on its bed of
saffron-tinted rice. In Valencia, the region of Spain
where this dish originated, there are virtually as

many recipes for paella as there are chefs. In New York, an excellent rendition is served at Harlequin. Opened in 1985 by Ileana and José Bárcena, it is regarded by many as the city's finest Spanish restaurant. Harlequin's sizzling paella skillet is filled with its base of golden rice (flavored with saffron, garlic, and other spices), and topped with generous portions of pork, chicken, spicy sausage, game in season (such as venison or rabbit), and a brimming array of seafood, including lobster, mussels, clams, shrimp, and crayfish. This reasonably priced favorite is a perfect dish to share among two, three, four, or more people (especially when accompanied by a few selections from Harlequin's list of starters, such as a bowl of chilled gazpacho). Harlequin also offers the city's most complete selections of Spanish wines. Perhaps after sampling Chef Bárcena's unforgettable and incomparable handiwork, our friend will start calling pizza "Italian paella."

Harlequin, 569 Hudson St, New York, NY 10014, 212/255-4950. Daily noon-3 pm, 5:30-11 pm.

Tops in Tapas Tasting

The Ballroom

Contrary to 1980s opinion, the culinary practice of "grazing"—dining on small, appetizer-sized portions of a variety of different dishes—didn't originate with Yuppies, but instead has roots in the Spanish tapas that are traditionally consumed as a light supper, usually accompanied with plenty of wine (as well as in Chinese Dim Sum meals—see separate listing). Tapas at this Chelsea restaurant include traditional bite-sized cold or hot portions of cheeses, chorizo, marinated meats, mussels, clams, snails, anchovies, squid, and smoked ham, as well as more unusual ingredients, such as frogs' legs and pigs' ears. Bone-dry fino dry sherry or a sangria make the perfect complement to these offerings—as do wines from Rioja and Navarra. Like Dim Sum, platters of individual tapas are priced reasonably, but separately, meaning you can (almost without realizing it) eat your way to quite a bill. This is a fun place to visit with a group, since these appetizer-sized portions of food are ideal for sampling and sharing. The Ballroom also features a menu of regular entrées, including several varieties of paellas; it claims to have been the first tapas bar in the U.S. (Cabaret-style entertainment is also offered.)

The Ballroom, 253 W 28th St, New York, NY 10001, 212/244-3005. Tue-Fri noon-1 am, Sat 4:30 pm-1 am.

Super Spot to Say Sköl
Aquavit

Scandinavian specialties and a selection of eight kinds of fiery aquavit from Sweden, Denmark, and Norway are attractions at this elegant restaurant— as is a two-course pre-theater menu priced at $19. A walk-down enclosed by a black wrought-iron fence provides entry to a pair of townhouses built in 1896-97 in a Renaissance-inspired style. At the rear, an eight-story atrium that encloses the former back-yard is attached to an office building on 55th Street. On the first level, a café decorated with watercolors by Swedish artist Peter Dahl has a takeout display of smoked salmon and caviar. The formal downstairs dining room incorporates the atrium, with a water-fall tumbling down one wall, a 16-foot live birch tree, and colorful canvas mobiles. Starters include Swed-ish pea soup with salt pork, warm Baltic herring, and smoked Arctic venison served with horseradish cream and bleak roe. A smörgasbord plate includes various herring, salmon, whitefish caviar, liver pâté, and Västerbotten cheese. Swedish specialties include meatballs with cream sauce, lingonberries, cucum-ber salad, and meat hash with pan-fried eggs and beets. Scandinavian desserts feature Swedish pan-cakes with raisin ice cream and cheesecake with cloudberries, lingonberries, and whipped cream.

Aquavit, 13 W 54th St, New York, NY 10019, 212/307-7311. Mon-Fri noon-10:30 pm, Sat 5:30-10:30 pm.

Best Bet When You're Fit to Be Thai-ed
Bangkok House

A friend who travels relentlessly on business, some-times, when confronted with the uncertain culinary choices of an unfamiliar city (especially foreign cit-ies), opts for what appears to be the best Thai place— explaining that even though quality can vary, she's never had a disappointing Thai meal. She shouldn't be disappointed at Bangkok House, which is per-haps New York's finest Thai restaurant. Spring rolls, beef satay (kebobs of marinated meat cooked in the ubiquitous Thai peanut-based sauce), or spicy shrimp make good openers, as does a shared entrée of pad Thai, the deceptively simple but tasty and filling national dish of rice noodles stir-fried with vegetables, meat, tofu, and peanuts. Also excellent are spicy chicken breast slices with bamboo, green curry pork, many great seafood choices (scallops with scallions and ginger, spicy sizzling shrimp with shredded vegetables), and a wide variety of beef, pork, chicken, and vegetarian dishes. Bangkok House's menu is voluminous and varied, showing off the diversity and versatility of Thai cuisine—also, helpfully, the dishes are noted as to their level of spiciness. Contrary to some opinions, unspicy Thai dishes *do* exist and are not bland—while, at the other end of the spectrum, the hottest dishes will test even the most fire-loving taste buds (with Thai-brand beers available to douse the flames).

Bangkok House, 1485 First Ave, New York, NY 10021, 212/249-5700. Daily 5-11 pm.

Best Vietnamese Vittles

Indochine

This authentic ethnic restaurant has received a bit of trendy attention of late (celebrities are spotted here from time-to-time), but it is still a comfortable place for some fine Southeast Asian food. Start with such appetizers as fried pork balls, delicate spring rolls, a Vietnamese version of ravioli stuffed with seasoned tofu, or some good soups—including hot and sour soup, thick beef soup, and fish soup with thin noodles. Seafood dishes—especially steamed or fried shrimp or steamed whole bass—are good, as are traditional chicken with lemon grass and sizzling filet of beef in a subtle sauce. More adventurous patrons may want to try the frogs' legs in coconut milk or the unusual stuffed chicken wings. Wine is available, but Vietnamese beer goes best with this cuisine. One complaint is that the staff—which has been compared to a coterie of attractive actresses between parts—isn't as acquainted with the ins and outs of the menu as they could be....But some persistent questioning can overcome this deficit. The bar downstairs is open late—and may be the best place to run into one of Indochine's celebrity patrons (or, for those so inclined, its pretty waitresses after hours). Another Manhattan restaurant offering fine Vietnamese cuisine is Saigon (60 Mulberry Street; 212/227-8825); its seafood dishes are universally cheered.

Indochine, 430 Lafayette St, New York, NY 10003, 212/505-5111. Daily 6 pm-12:30 am.

Best Upscale Sushi

Hatsuhana

This popular restaurant has long been regarded as Manhattan's finest spot for sushi (check out the confirming number of visiting Japanese business-people who dine here), and has been known to attract big crowds during lunch hours, often for "power lunches," one suspects. Hatsuhana is split into two floors, each with seating at tables or at long sushi bars. The traditional raw (and, in some cases, lightly cooked) offerings of tuna, flounder, fluke, salmon, eel, caviar, and other fin- and shellfish, garnished with seaweed, spinach, cucumber, and other vegetables, are excellently rendered, as are the restaurant's tempura and teriyaki dishes. Accompany these choices with saké, green tea, or Japanese beer. The sushi bar's à la carte items can add up to a substantial bill; the *prix-fixe* lunch can therefore be a satisfying—and money-saving—choice (although this can be a bustling spot during lunch hour). Since its popularity has grown, Hatsuhana has opened a second restaurant, at 237 Park Avenue (212/661-3400).

Hatsuhana, 17 E 48th St, New York, NY 10017, 212/355-3345. Mon-Fri 11:45 am-2:30 pm, 5-10 pm; Sat 5-10 pm.

Dandiest Dim Sum

Hee Seung Fung and Shun Lee Café

Dim Sum restaurants are perfect for visiting with large groups—the better for passing and sharing. This style of dining consists of small pastries, egg rolls, dumplings, spare ribs, and dozens of other varieties of appetizer-sized portions of light Chinese food. These little delicacies are selected à la carte from trolleys rolled from table to table. Commonly known by its initials, Hee Seung Fung (HSF) is one of Chinatown's best and most popular spots for Dim Sum. It's huge and noisy, but offers authentic food, as its large contingent of Chinatown locals will attest. HSF claims the largest selection of Dim Sum choices in the city—some 75 items, which are made easier to choose from by a photographic menu you can point to....Or, of course, you can select items the usual way—waiting for the cart to roll by with something that looks good. (A regular dinner menu offered after 5 p.m. isn't as accomplished or as popular as the morning and afternoon Dim Sum.) HSF also has a branch Uptown, at 578 Second Avenue (212/689-6969). Shun Lee Café, adjacent to the more formal Shun Lee West (which is a branch of the elegant Shun Lee Palace—see separate listing), also offers a delightful selection of Dim Sum to Lincoln Center-area diners. It is a great, convenient spot for pre-theater dining.

Hee Seung Fung, 46 Bowery, New York, NY 10013, 212/374-1319. Daily 7:30 am-midnight (Dim Sum

served until 5 pm). Shun Lee Café, 43 W 65th St,
New York, NY 10023, 212/769-3888. Daily 5 pm-
midnight.

Best Upscale Chinese Cuisine

Shun Lee Palace and Canton

As these two fine dining establishments prove,
Chinese restaurants are not all formica tabletops
and cardboard carryout cartons! Shun Lee Palace is
attractive and subdued—albeit a little cramped—
appearing more as a European or American restaurant than a Chinese one. It offers a menu of mainly
Hunan and Szechuan specialties, including some
very good appetizers—an excellent wonton soup, an
interesting Chinese take on frogs' legs (in a black
sauce)—and such entrées as Peking duck (also a
spicy Hunan duckling), orange beef, whole sea bass,
tuna steak, and beggar's chicken. As Chinese dining
goes, this is expensive, but the quality of the dining,
the service, and the surroundings justify it. Shun
Lee has another branch on the West Side, which
includes a delightful Dim Sum café (see separate
listing). Canton is far from the typical Chinatown
restaurant. When dining here, opt for the daily
specials, or, better yet—as many of the regulars do—
let the proprietors, Eileen and Larry Leang, create
a custom meal for you. Seafood—including bass,
pike, lobster, shrimp, and scallops—is one of the
consistent winners at Canton. No liquor is served,
but patrons are welcome to bring their own.

Shun Lee Palace, 155 E 55th St, New York, NY
10022, 212/371-8844. Daily noon-11 pm. Canton, 45
Division St, New York, NY 10002, 212/226-4441. Wed-
Fri & Sun noon-10 pm, Sat noon-11 pm.

Top Tandoori

Darbar

A friend who travels to London frequently and delights in the abundance of fine Indian restaurants
there, claims that this midtown restaurant serves
northern Indian food that is just as good. It is attractive, adorned with gleaming hammered copper,
exquisite tapestries, and fine carpets, and offers
dining on two floors of a duplex connected by a
curved staircase. A number of booths are screened
to provide optimum privacy. It is convenient enough
to the theater district to qualify as a pre-curtain
dining stop. It also is an economical luncheon choice,
offering an all-you-can-eat buffet that allows the

sampling of a variety of Moghul specialties. Tandoori dishes are a good choice, as is the extremely popular *josh vindaloo*, pungently curried lamb stew cooked with potatoes. Start with spinach or onion fritters and be sure to sample the excellent array of breads that, along with a well-rendered crunchy *pappadam*, include a tandoori bread stuffed with cheese and an onion-flavored flatbread. Imported Indian beer is an appropriate accompaniment; fig ice cream is a good choice for dessert.

Darbar, 44 W 56th St, New York, NY 10019, 212/432-7227. Daily noon-10:30 pm.

Best Indian Lunch Buffet
Bombay Palace

Many Manhattan Indian restaurants are well-known for bargain all-you-can-eat lunch buffets (including Dawat and the East Village Indian restaurants on E. 6th Street—see separate listings), and this Mid-town restaurant is another notable contributor. A nice tone is established for an elegant and pleasant lunch by the turban-clad doorman who ushers guests inside, where the $9.95 lunch buffet is the popular choice. Buffet selections vary from day-to-day, but, in general, include a good variety of Indian favorites, such as lamb curry, tandoori chicken, prawns and other seafood dishes, mixed grills of kebab meats, vegetable dishes, salads, samosas, papadams, and other nibblers. The flavors here are tasty and complex, but are generally more mild than the flaming spiciness found in some other Indian restaurants. Accompany your meal with an Indian beer and follow with a mango ice cream or rice pudding flavored with sweet rose water for dessert, and you've got an affordable lunch fit for a Raj. Bombay Palace is across the street from the venerable 21 Club (see separate listing).

Bombay Palace, 30 W 52nd St, New York, NY 10019, 212/541-7777. Mon-Sat noon-3 pm, 5:30-11 pm; Sun noon-3 pm, 5:30-10 pm.

Indisputedly Incomparable Indian Repast
Dawat

Dawat is stylish and comfortable, dominated by its glass-walled kitchen. It offers a fine selection of traditional Indian fare—curries, tandoori dishes, mulligatawny soup—but also some more inventive and/or daring dishes, such as a piquant *reshmi kebab* (of marinated chicken and vegetables), tender goat served on a bed of spiced rice, and any of a number of excellent seafood entrées, including a spiced shrimp dish. Carnivores can sample the variety of Dawat's meat dishes by ordering the mixed grill. For vegetarians, there is a wide variety of spicy and flavorful vegetable-based dishes, including coconut-flavored green beans, an acclaimed baked eggplant, and shredded cucumber with a yogurt base. Run by Indian food writer and actress Madhur Jaffrey, this restaurant's Urdu-language name means "an invitation to feast"—a fitting invitation, indeed. This fine Midtown restaurant is probably the city's best—and most attractive—Indian restaurant and is also a bargain (especially at lunch, when a fine buffet is presented); for a variety of other Indian dining in the East Village, try the many restaurants along East 6th Street (see separate listing).

Dawat, 210 E 58th St, New York, NY 10022, 212/355-7555. Mon-Sat 11:30 am-3 pm, 5:30-11 pm.

Best Bet for Most Indian Restaurants
East 6th Street

What started out in the 1970s as a venture in community cooking by a group of homesick N.Y.U. students from India has grown into a delightful little neighborhood of inexpensive and varied Indian restaurants in the East Village. The stretch of East 6th Street between First and Second avenues (with a little spillover on to the avenues themselves) is home to more than a dozen small Indian restaurants, which can all trace their pedigree back to the aforementioned students, who started cooking group meals for themselves and their friends, and eventually moved, one-by-one, into the restaurant business. By acclamation, this strip's two brightest culinary lights are Mitali (334 E. 6th Street; 212/533-2508) and Anar Bagh (338 E. 6th Street; 212/529-1937). Mitali is a little more expensive than the rest of these (and it offers a full bar—most of the others are B.Y.O.B.), but its Northern Indian specialties are, generally speaking, considered a cut above the rest; the traditional tandoori chicken and lamb *dupiag* are among the best selections offered. Anar Bagh is most successful with its appetizer items, making a grazing meal of its *samosas* (crispy pastries filled with meat or veggies), hot *vindaloo* meats, curries, and puffy *poori* and other light Indian breads a winning choice. Also worth noting on (or just off) this block are Shah Bagh (320 E. 6th Street; 212/677-8876), one of the street's first Indian restaurants (and owned by the same brothers who run

Anar Bagh); Sonali Restaurant (326 E. 6th Street;
212/505-7517), often crowded and offering bargain
prices; Ghandhi (345 E. 6th Street; 212/614-9717);
and Gaylord (87 First Avenue; 212/529-7990).

Tiniest French Bistro

Chez Brigitte

It's easy to miss this diminutive white-painted brick
storefront restaurant in the heart of the Village. Look
for a window bursting with flowers and potted plants
sporting a sedate neon sign that declares, simply,
"Brigitte LUNCH DINNER." And expect some hearty
French fare at budget-stretching prices. For example,
beef bourguignonne and *ragout de veni* are priced at
around $7, and hearty, flavorful split pea soup at
$1.40 cup, $1.85 a bowl. There are just a dozen
stools gathered around a horseshoe-shaped counter
where you can watch the chefs at work, a la short-
order cooks. The bill of fare features basic Provençal-
accented cooking and includes French onion soup,
mushroom, cheese, and other omelette creations,
filet of sole meuniére, and daily specials such as
gigot de mouton and *veal blanquette*. For dessert, this
inexpensive homey luncheonette serves up a variety
of homemade pies. There are, of course, no reservations taken—it's strictly first-come-first-served for
the handful of counter seats.

Chez Brigitte, 77 Greenwich Ave, New York, NY
10006, 212/929-6736. Mon-Sat 11 am-9 pm.

French Bistro with the Best French Fries

Café Un Deux Trois

Good, simple, French-accented food, in a location
that makes it ideal for pre- or post-theater dining,
are among the assets of this Times Square area
restaurant. It's a cavernous Parisian-style brasserie,
dominated by Corinthian columns, accented by
Tiffany glass, and populated by flurrying waiters in
white aprons. You can't go wrong ordering a small
steak accompanied by French fries good enough to
gladden the heart of the most unabashed francophile.
Other reliable choices include grilled chicken or
mixed grill (matched, of course, with those great
pommes frites), a variety of omelettes, quiche, pepper steak, roast duck, and well-rendered calf's liver.
Choose a pâté (the duck pâté is excellent) as a starter
and finish with profiteroles or poached pear with ice
cream and chocolate sauce. Kids—and adults with
artistic bent—enjoy the butcher-paper cloths and
supplied crayons. A *prix-fixe* brunch offers good
value.

Café Un Deux Trois, 123 W 44th St, New York, NY 10036, 212/354-4148. Mon-Sat 11:30 am-midnight, Sun 11:30 am-11 pm.

Best Fine French Restaurant That Isn't as Expensive as It Sounds
Montrachet

Confidently steered by Drew Nieporent, its devoted and passionate owner, this nouvelle French restaurant in TriBeCa offers inventive cuisine in an unpretentious atmosphere. Montrachet is found in a dismal neighborhood behind an unassuming storefront and inside a high-ceilinged, former industrial space. Nieporent's young (but already acclaimed) chef, Debra Ponzek, works her magic with three fixed-price menus, which range from bargain to moderate to still-not-very-expensive (relatively). Items within these menus vary, but often include such dishes as mostly roasted, sometimes grilled fowl—duck, squab, pigeon, pheasant, and quail; a variety of almost-universally excellent fish, most notably moist and lemony red snapper and whole sea bass; and some top-notch pasta, game, and grilled or roasted meat dishes. (Montrachet's à la carte menu also has its merits—but can push your tab considerably higher than the reasonable prix-fixe options.) The crème brûlée is a leading light among dessert choices, which also include special soufflés and other made-in-house pastries and sweets. The wine list is excellent, and continues to evolve. Patrons regularly reserve weeks ahead for this pleasure, because at as (relatively) little as $100 per couple (including a decent wine), this is a popular dining destination. A note of warning: Montrachet also offers a Friday-only lunch, but, in a bit of a reverse from most of the city's fine restaurants, this is an à la carte-only affair; it isn't exorbitantly expensive, but it can definitely be more expensive than the lowest-priced option of the superior dinner menu.

Montrachet, 239 W Broadway, New York, NY 10013, 212/219-2777. Mon-Thu, Sat 6-11 pm; Fri noon-3 pm, 6-11 pm.

Best French Food in a Hotel Dining Room (with a Chef from Brooklyn)
Maurice

After being dark for almost a year, this highly regarded French restaurant off the glittering marble lobby of the Parker Meridien reopened in 1991 with a new chef (from Brooklyn!), a new menu, a new outlook, and lowered prices (by as much as 40 percent). French-trained chef Marc Salonsky, who moved over from the Petrossian, has stepped away from classic Gallic cooking and introduced a menu emphasizing regional American (and often unusual) ingredients prepared simply, but with a French approach. Pairing the familiar with the unusual is evidenced in such dishes as golden skate wing with sweet cabbage and grilled sausage, and ravioli of fresh sweet peas, bacon, and tarragon. Creative appetizers include cream of caramelized shallots, silky saffron mussel soup with Provençal vegetables and roasted garlic, and scallops with avocado tartare, olive oil, and lemon juice. Entrées include grilled chicken breast with artichoke ragout and creamy polenta and salmon with spiced salt, mustard greens, and cardamom lime juice. Seating is in comfortable banquettes, some romantically tucked away, with tables dressed with peach napery.

A *prix-fixe* lunch and pre-theater dinner is offered for $28.

Maurice, Le Parker Meridien Hotel, 118 W 57th St, New York, NY 212/245-5000. Mon-Fri noon-11 pm, Sat & Sun 5:30-11 pm.

Best French Restaurant in Greenwich Village

La Tulipe

On the ground floor of an attractive Village brownstone you'll find this casual, romantic bistro with an intimate interior that is uncrowded and appropriately hushed. As of this writing, it offers only a pair of prix-fixe set dinners, with choices among several nightly specials. For openers, these might include zucchini fritters, cream of wild mushroom soup, rich fish soup with bits of lobster, or a creamy soufflé lightly flavored with Parmesan cheese. The entrées that follow (accompanied by nightly vegetables) include roast chicken with garlic, grilled lamb chops, various game in season, and some nice fish choices, including red snapper and filet of cod. The next course is salad, in the Continental style, to clear the palate for cheese and dessert. The favorites among La Tulipe's finales include warm apple (or other fruit) tart, fresh from the oven; hot soufflés; and homemade ice creams and sorbets. Some decry the prices (in the $150-and-up per couple range)—but, in this neighborhood, among similar restaurants, they seem

more than fair for the overall package of food, atmosphere, and crisp, pleasant service.

La Tulipe, 104 W 13th St, New York, NY 10011, 212/
691-8860. Daily 6:30-11 pm.

Steak House People Are Dying to Get Into

Sparks Steakhouse

Here's a helpful hint to those who like to order what
celebrities get at restaurants: Don't ever ask for
"What Paul got" at this steak house. "Paul" was
mobster Paul Castellano and what he got was
"whacked"—Mob parlance for killed. In December of
1985, Castellano, the head of the city's notorious
Gambino crime family, headed to this restaurant
(one of his favorites) for a meal. He never made it—
he was shot out in front of Sparks, allegedly on the
orders of the man who succeeded him as Gambino
boss, none other than the "Dapper Don" himself,
John Gotti. Amazingly, this gory event seems to have
actually helped business, making Sparks more popular than ever (albeit, in a bit of a macabre way).
Besides the curiosity factor, this steak house pulls
crowds in for its excellent steaks (naturally) and
pork, lamb, and veal chops. Sparks is also known
for some nice, usually light fish selections, good
lobsters, and an especially thorough and thoughtful
(especially for a steak house) wine list. Good desserts, too, led by that steak house standard, cheesecake. Overall, a package virtually guaranteed to
provide a *much* more enjoyable night than the one
Mr. Castellano had here!

Sparks Steakhouse, 210 E 46th St, New York, NY
10017, 212/687-4855. Mon-Thu noon-3 pm, 5-11 pm;
Fri noon-3 pm, 5-11:30 pm; Sat 5-11:30 pm.

Best Spot for Steak Dinners and Horse Lovers

Gallagher's

You know this is a serious spot for carnivores when
you enter past a glass-encased cold-storage locker
hung with aging prime beef. And you know you may
eavesdrop on some racing talk, when you look
around at the framed portraits of jockeys and race
horses. During the day, this is a business-luncheon
spot. At night, its near-Broadway location attracts

pre- and post-theater crowds. Dating back to the 1920s, this former speakeasy has staid, traditional wood-paneled walls covered with photos of show-biz and political celebs—in addition to the equine portrait gallery. Red checkered tablecloths and sawdust-covered floors complete the trappings of a traditional New York steak house. Standard appetizers include oysters and clams on the half shell. Baked potatoes, onion rings, and spinach are popular sides. The hickory-grilled sirloin steaks are hard to beat for serious meat lovers. Prices are fair for the quality and quantity of food served.

Gallagher's, 228 W 52nd St, New York, NY 10019, 212/245-5336. Daily noon-midnight.

Best Steaks After Midnight
Christo's Steak House

This old New York-style steak house, with traditional wood and brass, Kelly green booths, and a gallery of signed photographs of celebrities, has been around more than 65 years. It also *stays* around 365 days a year, serving its customers until two in the morning. Perhaps it is these long hours, along with solid cuisine and a warm ambience, that attracts entertainment and sports stars, such as Lawrence Taylor and Phil Simms of the New York Giants; actors Sylvester Stallone, Michael J. Fox, and Richard Gere; and Hulk Hogan, who has been known to consume a steak or two. Along with a selection of broiled steaks and chops is the house specialty, pan-fried steak smothered in onions. The menu also features a number of Italian veal dishes (plus schnitzel à la Holstein and broiled double veal chop) and a half-dozen seafood entrées. Also featured are prime rib, beef Stroganoff, capon parmigiana, and Long Island duckling. Starters include stuffed baked clams, scampi with garlic butter, and homemade cannelloni. As part of a recent renovation, the restaurant's 35-year-old bar was sanded down to its original finish.

Christo's Steak House, 143 E 49th St, New York, NY 10017, 212/355-2695. Mon-Fri noon-2 am, Sat & Sun 4 pm-2 am.

Biggest Steak and Lobster
The Palm

Although it lacks a formal menu and its wait staff display a contrived lack of gentility, this is one of New York's top spots for carnivores. There's sawdust on the floor, walls densely covered with caricatures of comic-book characters as well as famous (and not so famous) patrons, and a club-like ambience. Dry-aged prime beef steaks are perfectly prepared and can be paired with large lobsters that weigh in at four pounds or more. Sweet-tasting onion rings and cottage fries are a good accompaniment to crusty-on-the-outside, tender-on-the-inside steaks (pass on the undistinguished vegetables). With everything à la carte, tabs can run high, but portions are large enough to share. Most people go for the steaks (and the lobster), but rib roast, veal chops, and lamb chops also are good choices. When this steak house gets overly busy, as it frequently does, neighboring Palm Too is a close facsimile that is ready to take the overflow.

The Palm, 837 Second Ave, New York, NY 10019, 212/687-2953. Mon-Fri noon-10:45 pm, Sat 5-11 pm.

Best Brooklyn Beef

Peter Luger Steak House

This historic steak house is located in the Williamsburg neighborhood of Brooklyn, just beyond the Williamsburg Bridge (and predating it!). This large, bi-level restaurant resembles—in appearance and in atmosphere—a Bavarian beer hall, and is big with the business crowd at lunch and families and tourists at dinner. They all come here for Luger's famously huge steaks—regulars sagely suggest that you split single steaks between two people and be prepared to take leftovers home if you order the offerings listed on the menu as serving two. These juicy aged meats are butter-basted and come on the rare side—yes, this is one of those steak houses where employees may literally frown on those who order steaks well-done, well-well, or "burnt." Also served are great lamb chops and hearty slabs of dripping prime rib. Luger's sides are the steak house standbys of thick French fries, hash browns, buttery spinach, or simple salads; for dessert, it's cheesecake or a few varieties of pies, cakes, and pastries. Grazers with a bent for exploring may wish to skip dessert and head to Junior's, which is relatively nearby and serves some of the best cheesecake in all of the boroughs (see separate listing). *Transportational note:* Be sure to valet park your car or take a taxi—the neighborhood is not the best.

Peter Luger Steak House, 178 Broadway, Brooklyn, NY, 718/387-7400. Mon-Thu 11:45 am-9:45 pm, Fri & Sat 11:45 am-10:45 pm, Sun 1-10:45 pm.

Best Big Mac with a Large Order of Chopin

McDonald's

The arches were never like this! This McDonald's has a white-gloved doorman, classical background music from a grand piano (complete with candelabra), cappuccino on the menu, and fresh flowers in the washrooms. Its location in the financial district assures that this upscale McDonald's attracts Wall Street players who study the market as they munch on Quarter Pounders. Expect prices a little higher than elsewhere in Manhattan, maybe a buck more than in the hinterland. But this ritzy Mickey D's is worth a visit for curiosity's sake—if only to have a hostess in black velvet hat and tie seat you at a marbletop table decorated with a fresh carnation, slipping a paper place mat under your diet coke. There's a gift boutique upstairs (near the loft where a pianist renders show tune and other requests), and an ambience of dark paneling and chandeliers. A digital ticker tape keeps diners informed of stock market prices as they sip espressos and nibble on fruit tarts and Danish baked at the well-regarded Dumas bakery. There's delivery on orders received by fax.

McDonald's, 160 Broadway, New York, NY 10038, 212/227-7916, fax 212/385-2959. Mon-Fri 6 am-11 pm, Sat 7:30 am-9 pm, Sun 8 am-9 pm.

Best Non-Franchise Hamburger

Hamburger Harry's

If you're doing a theater evening on the cheap, pick up some half-price tickets at the Times Square Tkts booth (see separate listing) and stop at Hamburger Harry's (colloquially known as "Ha Ha's") for one of the most flavorful hamburgers you'll find in Manhattan. Of course, by fast-food standards, these burgers are priced on the high side. But they're worth it. Thick patties of lean beef are broiled over mesquite and are served with toppings that you'll never find under the arches—close to a dozen and a half combos that include béarnaise, pungent gorgonzola cheese, chili, guacamole, and caviar and sour cream. Alternatives to hamburgers include steaks, grilled seafood, and fajitas. Accompany your meal with a soft drink, beer, or wine. There is piano entertainment in the evenings and a special menu, crayons, and baseball-themed cups for kids. Finish with an ice cream, a sundae, or mud pie. Wall Street types

wander over to a second branch of Harry's, downtown at 157 Chambers Street.

Hamburger Harry's, 145 W 45th St, New York, NY
10036, 212/840-0566. Daily 11:30 am-11 pm.

Most Expensive Hamburger

"21" Club

You could treat a dozen or more friends and col-
leagues to hamburgers under the arches for the
price of a single "21" burger. But, of course, that isn't
the point. For those anxious to see and be seen—
as was the Gecko character and his protégé-in-sleaze
in the movie *Wall Street*—the famed "21" Club is *the*
spot. Though not, in fact, a private club, "21" does
have a clubby (some say snobby) feel when it pam-
pers to regulars and falls over itself to give Frank his
usual table. The downstairs bar is the spot frequented by movers and shakers, as evidenced by the
miniature cars and other corporate toys festooned
from the ceiling in tribute to the CEOs who bunch
and munch there. Along with the pricey hamburger,
popular items on the bar menu include the
restaurant's signature chicken hash, excellent oysters on the half shell, crab cakes, and a variety of
grilled meats and fish. Those who may not have
visited "21" in some years may be surprised at the
spruced up appearance and gentrified menu that
resulted from a change in management and major
remodeling in the late 1980s. Located in a brownstone mansion that was a Prohibition-era speakeasy, the spruced-up restaurant is an institution
that continues to draw New York's elite—as it once
attracted members of the famed round table of the
Algonquin (see separate listings).

"21" Club, 21 W 52nd St, New York, NY 10019, 212/
582-7200. Mon-Sat noon-midnight.

Best Crab Cakes North of Chesapeake Bay

The Sea Grill

For authentic Maryland crab cakes and other Chesa-
peake Bay seafood dishes, this popular upscale
Rockefeller Center seafood house is a good bet. For
openers, try the signature Sea-Grill chowder, which
features a rich combo of clams, shrimp, and lobster.
Other standout dishes include fresh raw oysters and
clams, charred filet of salmon, Dover sole, seared
yellowfin tuna, lightly grilled swordfish, and red

snapper seasoned with ginger and accompanied by Oriental vegetables. The moist, tender, and crumbly crab cakes are offered as an appetizer or entrée. They can be accompanied by traditional sweet and tangy tartar sauce or, for a change, a lobster-based herb sauce. The Sea Grill offers basic seafood-spot dessert choices; tops among these are key lime pie and the rich Prometheus chocolate cake, topped with a golden dusting to match the hue of its name-sake statue outside Rockefeller Center. The view from the restaurant is of the Center's skating rink, making this a pleasant winter spot; in summer, there are alfresco tables in the rink area. Another good spot for crab cakes—or nearly any other varia-tion of crab—is Sidewalkers (12 W. 72nd Street; 212/799-6070), named not for the sidewalks of New York but for the peculiar gait of its featured seafood.

The Sea Grill, 19 W 49th St, Rockefeller Plaza, New York, NY 10020, 212/246-9201. Mon-Fri 11:30 am-3 pm, 5-11 pm; Sat 5-11 pm.

Best Crab Cakes West of MoBay

Tropica Bar and Seafood House

Crab cakes in Jamaica? Shouldn't that read Mary-land? Well...a friend with an office within walking distance of this Caribbean-theme restaurant in the Pan Am building concourse eats here regularly and almost invariably orders crab cakes. They're served with mustard beurre blanc and they *are* that good. Although little more than a clamshell's toss from the famous Oyster Bar, this light, whimsical restaurant, decorated with colorful native Caribbean art, is in bright contrast to the dark-paneled seafood land-mark. And its offerings, while nowhere near as extensive, are every bit as good and generally more imaginative. Try roast cod with sake wine and Chinese black bean sauce or seared sea scallops with salsa, plantains, and guacamole. Starters in-clude sashimi and conch chowder. Maine lobsters are available, as is a wide selection of grilled fish, ranging from amberjack and pompano to bluefish and tilefish. Desserts feature coconut flan, tart key lime pie, and tropical fruit soup served with sorbet and ginger. Adding to the tropical ambience are rattan chairs and tables and pretty tiles with a Caribbean fruit motif. Crowded at lunchtime, this is a good spot for a quiet dinner.

Tropica Bar and Seafood House, 200 Park Ave, New York, NY 10017, 212/867-6767. Mon-Fri 11:30 am-10 pm.

Best Traditional Spot to Catch Seafood

Oyster Bar & Restaurant

Opened in 1913 in the bowels of landmark Grand Central Station, this restaurant was a favorite with such celebrities as Lillian Russell and Diamond Jim Brady. It remains a popular—and perhaps New York's best—spot for fresh, simply prepared seafood. With vaulted ceilings, tiled arches, and periodic rumbling of trains, the cavernous, noisy main dining room sometimes gives the impression of being in the business part of the station. Quieter choices are the saloon, its paneled walls decorated with model ships and paintings of schooners and steamships, and even the adjoining diner-style room with a long lunch counter. Usually, there are more than a dozen kinds of oysters (try the house shallot sauce), and more than three dozen fresh fish selections. Specialties include bouillabaisse, coquille St. Jacques, and mako shark piccata. Stews and panroasts feature oysters, clams, shrimp, lobster, scallops, and mussels. A large cold buffet includes squid salad with avocado and halibut flakes on fresh spinach with lemon mustard dressing. You can get Maryland crab cakes, Florida stone crab claws, and Maine lobster. Desserts include lemon-lemon tart, open-faced peach tart, and red currant sorbet. An impressive list features more than 100 American white wines, from Anderson champagne to Zaca Mesa chardonnay.

Oyster Bar & Restaurant, 42nd St & Vanderbilt Ave, New York, NY 10017, 212/490-6650. Mon-Fri 11:30 am-10:30 pm.

Best Contemporary Spot to Catch Seafood

Docks Oyster Bar & Seafood Grill

With high ceilings, art deco lighting, smart black-and-white tiles, and a wooden bar with a brass footrail, this bright seafood restaurant (with a twin at 2427 Broadway) is the antithesis of the dark fish house. There are ichthyological prints and original nautical art, a wood-and-brass railing separating two dining levels, and a Dow Jones ticker. Starters include chowder, steamers in beer broth, crab cakes, calamari, and mussels in tomatoes and garlic. There is a selection of grilled fish; steamed lobsters that range from one to nine pounds; and cold entrées, such as poached salmon, chilled stuffed lobster, and grilled tuna niçoise salad. A clambake on Sunday and Monday nights features lobsters, mussels, clams, new potatoes, corn on the cob, salad, and dessert. There are daily blackboard specials, a daily pasta (plus linguini with red or white clam sauce), and a raw bar offering clams, shrimp, and four kinds of oysters (selections change daily). Dessert choices include hot fudge sundaes, key lime pie, mud fudge, and chocolate mud cake.

Docks Oyster Bar & Seafood Grill, 633 Third Ave, New York, NY 10017, 212/986-8080. Mon-Thu 11:30 am-11 pm, Fri 11:30 am-midnight, Sat 5-11 pm, Sun 10:30 am-3 pm.

Best Bet for Lobster 22 Different Ways

Lobster Box

Even though the rehabbers have gotten to City Island, this nautical enclave in the Bronx, poking its bony finger into Long Island Sound, remains reminiscent of a New England resort. Sailboats glide across Eastchester Bay, sleek yachts and charter fishing boats bob at anchor, and streets are lined with old frame houses, restaurants, and antique shops. The Lobster Box, owned by the Musacchia family since it opened almost 50 years ago, maintains this New England image. It served as a U.S. Coast Guard station during World War II, and at its core is a small white frame house built in 1812—greatly expanded to create a restaurant that serves up 2,000 pounds of lobster a week. Lobster is prepared in almost two dozen different ways. Variations range from basic steamed-and-split lobsters (the crustaceans are never boiled, as patrons can see for themselves by viewing an open kitchen), to thermidor and au gratin preparations, and such dishes as saffron-flavored paella, which marries lobster with shrimp, scallops, mussels, and clams. Other shellfish—oysters, clams, shrimp, and scallops—is noteworthy, as is fresh finfish—swordfish, snapper, trout, and flounder. Fresh seafood is bought directly from the local commercial fishing fleet. Desserts include lemon chiffon pie, as well as apple and various other all-American fruit pies served with mounds of ice cream.

Lobster Box, 34 City Island Ave, Bronx, NY 10464, 212/885-1952, 800/924-1181, fax 212/885-3232. Late Mar-Oct, noon-11 pm.

Best Seafood by Gaslight

Gage & Tollner

Wood paneling, mahogany tables, elegant mirrors, a stamped tin ceiling, and original gaslight fixtures create the warm atmosphere of this Brooklyn land-mark restaurant, which opened its doors in 1879. Crabmeat Virginia, lobster Maryland, excellent crab cakes, and a variety of dishes made with fresh clams, bay scallops, shrimps, and oysters are among the acclaimed fresh seafood offered at this arresting Vic-torian eatery. Noted chef Edna Lewis came here from South Carolina, so it is not unexpectedly that excel-lent renditions of Low Country favorites such as she-crab soup show up on the menu. Starters include shrimp and crab gumbo, lobster bisque, oyster stew, and clam chowder. The daily fish selection is reli-able, while, for meat eaters, the classic English-style mutton chop is recommended, along with excellent steaks and lamb chops. Waiters wear insignia to signify the number of years they have been waiting on the mix of Brooklyn power brokers, local regulars, and tourists who wander in from Manhattan.

Gage & Tollner, 372 Fulton St, Brooklyn, NY 11217, 718/875-5181. Mon-Fri noon-9:30 pm, Sat 4-10:30 pm.

Poshest Seafood in Manhattan

Le Bernardin

This excellent eatery started as the New York off-shoot of brother/sister team Gilbert and Maguy Le Coze's highly praised Paris restaurant of the same name. However, the American version has become so successful—and the Le Coze's preferred style is so intensely hands-on—that they sold their Paris Le Bernardin to concentrate full-time on the New York restaurant. Seafood is the draw. When a menu states offhandedly that there *are* non-seafood dishes avail-able, but only upon request, there is no doubt about the focus of the kitchen's energies and talents. Lunch and dinner menus are prix fixe, with dishes varying day-to-day, depending on fresh provisions that are obtainable and meet the restaurant's demanding standards. Starters may include black-bass seviche, a sampler of mollusks, and simple but sublime raw oysters and clams on the half-shell; these may be followed with baked sea urchins (a Le Bernardin original now found at other top seafood restaurants), carpaccio tuna, codfish in red-wine-and-shallot sauce, poached halibut, or roast monkfish with savoy cabbage—another signature dish that truly raises monkfish far beyond its station as "poor man's lobster." The crowd at Le Bernardin may contain such luminaries as Warren Beatty and Annette Bening, Mick Jagger and entourage, and Dustin Hoffman. Tables are usually booked solid a month in advance—but, for such sublime offerings of the sea, the wait can be more than worth it.

Le Bernardin, 155 W 51st St, New York, NY 10019, 212/489-1515. Mon-Thu noon-2:15 pm, 6-10:30 pm; Fri & Sat noon-2:15 pm, 5:30-10:30 pm.

The "Power Breakfast" Place

540 Park Avenue Restaurant at the Regency Hotel

Fastidiously cooked eggs, faddish heart-healthy grains, and British-style kippered herring. Freshly squeezed orange juice, a selection of market-fresh fruits, perfectly brewed coffee, and assorted bakery goods not long from the oven. Take all of the above, present them with panache and serve them with the proper degree of haughty subservience in the most elegant surroundings. You then will have the perfect backdrop for the so-called power breakfast, where corporate moguls and other movers and shakers meet over early morning vittles to cut deals, position stock, and decide the futures of those who labor for—or against—them. Certainly, Manhattan has many such suitable settings for power breakfasts. It also has *the* definitive venue for power breakfasts— the elegant dining room of the Hotel Regency, where the term is said to have been coined! During the breakfast hour, The 540 Park Avenue Restaurant (its address also is its name) is where you'll find executives inside, their chauffeurs at curbside. The Regency, flagship of the Loews chain, attracts jet-setters, show biz folk, and assorted captains of industry to its opulent Regency-period premises gleaming with gilt and marble and furnished with French antiques.

540 Park Avenue Restaurant, Regency Hotel, 540 Park Ave, New York, NY 10021, 212/759-4100. Breakfast daily 7-9 am.

Best Business Breakfast to Please the Controller

Palace Restaurant

This restaurant makes heroes! No, not the sandwiches, but out of the business people who enjoy budget breakfasts and turn in expense reports that bring smiles to the faces of controllers. Choose from a variety of omelettes or wheatcakes with Virginia ham, bacon, or sausages—all for less than $4. A ham-and-egg breakfast sandwich costs little more than $2, as does French toast, thick-yet-light (and served with four strips of bacon for an extra buck). Nor does the ambience suffer because of the low prices. This two-level restaurant is a cheery spot, with glass-covered mauve tablecloths and fresh flowers on tables, many booths, and fast counter service. The pleasant main dining room is decorated with four small chandeliers. For those who make it a luncheon stop, there are burgers, triple-decker sandwiches, cold salad platters, and diet plates, plus entrées such as broiled sirloin steak, turkey with stuffing, honey-dipped chicken, breaded veal cutlet, and eggplant parmigiana—all at budget-stretching prices (and even a cocktail for those who desire it). Temptingly on the counter are large homemade chocolate-chip cookies and freshly baked donuts.

Palace Restaurant, 122 E 57th St, New York, NY 10022, 212/319-8989. Daily 6 am-10 pm.

Best Luncheon Bet for Bankers, Bulls, Bears, and Beef

The Bull and Bear

If you need to know about the prime rate or other banking matters, the bar of this masculine restaurant is the place to hang out. Many bankers are among the regular customers who lunch here every day. With heavy dark paneling, etched glass, and an electronic stock market monitor, this restaurant looks every inch the private men's club that it once was. Centerpiece is a four-sided mahogany bar with bronze statues of Wall Street's symbolic bull and bear and monogrammed glasses of long-time patrons. The menu runs to basic meat and seafood—aged sirloin, double rib lamb chops, filet mignon, baked red snapper, grilled salmon, shrimp, lobster, gray sole, and broiled centercut swordfish with lemon chive butter. Appetizers include crab cakes, fettucine carbonara with vegetables, and oysters and clams on the half shell. For dessert, many regulars choose deep-dish apple pie. Other choices include veal stew with sautéed spaetzel and several salads. For a secluded spot to cement a business deal, request seating in the alcove known as "the Library."

The Bull and Bear, The Waldorf-Astoria, 301 Park Ave, New York, NY 10022, 212/355-3000. Daily 10 am-1 am.

Politicos' (and Other High-Rollers') Preferred Restaurant

Le Cirque

As the name so prophetically proclaims, this is, indeed, owner and impresario Sirio Maccioni's trend-setting dining "circus"—universally regarded as one of the city's top few restaurants and as *the* leading place for the city's political and financial movers and shakers to gather. An ever-evolving range of specials—plus the delightful experimentation that goes on in the kitchen—makes suggesting dishes almost moot. Many of Maccioni's devoted regulars let the peripatetic and detail-oriented owner (or one of his equally attentive captains) select their meal; other patrons simply order whatever they have a taste for, and, fresh ingredients allowing, see what Le Cirque's minions come up with. In any case, you cannot go wrong with such longtime favorites as a sublime pasta primavera (not on the menu, but one of Le Cirque's pioneering dishes and always available), sea scallops black tie (with delicate truffles as the seafood's elegant "neckwear"), or a simple—but no less accomplished—grilled filet of sole with a bounty of fresh vegetables in a delicate wine sauce, or the tenderest baby lamb. Desserts also are highly regarded—most foodies believe the "craze" for crème brûlée in top restaurants across the country in recent years can be traced back to Le Cirque's signature handling of this dessert (the pastries are also top-notch). Le Cirque is expensive, to be sure, but, surprisingly, it is not as costly as many lesser lights...and its *prix-fixe* lunch is a terrific bargain.

Le Cirque, 58 E 65th St, New York, NY 10021, 212/794-9292. Mon-Sat noon-2:30 pm, 6-10:30 pm.

Best Culinary Landmark

The Four Seasons

The cuisine at this landmark restaurant is a successful blend of American, French, and Continental. As its name implies, the restaurant's menu changes four times a year, taking advantage of seasonally fresh game, fruits, and vegetables. Entrées include such standards as Dover sole, highly praised lamb chops, and pheasant, along with more contemporary dishes, such as a number of venison entrées (with crabmeat and artichokes, for example), and a delicate crayfish ravioli. Straddling the line between expected and unexpected are entrées such as sautéed soft-shell crabs and sublime chicken pot pie. The venerated Four Seasons also offers excellent service (which, alas, is not always the case among some of New York's older top restaurants), including theatrically charming tableside presentations and preparations. In the Pool Room (the Four Season's main area), try to get seating near the fountain, the most impressive and romantic spot; the separate Grill Room offers a lighter menu of health-conscious items, such as grilled fish and chicken, inventive salads, and specially trimmed meats. This is a prime power-lunch and -dinner spot (especially among the publishing industry and with Japanese executives), and tends to be expensive, but the pre-theater meal is a comparative bargain. The restaurant's striking decor includes walnut paneling, chain draperies, a white marble pool, and a massive Picasso tapestry. *Trivia note:* The Four Seasons is located in the innovative steel-and-glass Seagram Building, architect Mies van der Rohe's only New York building.

The Four Seasons, 99 E 52nd St, New York, NY 10022, 212/754-9494. Mon-Sat noon-2:30 pm, 5-11:30 pm.

Best "Expensive, But Worth It" Spot

Chanterelle

Comfortable and sophisticated (without being stuffy) this downtown restaurant is run by Karen and David Waltuck. This, however, is not a case of a Yuppie couple dallying in restaurateurship—David, a graduate of the Culinary Institute of America, had worked under some of the best chefs in France before opening his own place; Karen runs the dining room with a friendly style, while David masterminds in the kitchen. Chanterelle recently moved from its comfy SoHo digs to the landmark Mercantile Exchange Building (built in 1884) in TriBeCa—after which, its ratings dropped. But devotees say the food has maintained its extraordinary high quality and plenty of professional surveyors have tended to agree. The new spot is bigger (but not huge—it seats about 60, or about three times as many as the old location), but is still understated and elegant, perhaps even stark. The menu changes frequently, depending on the seasonal availability of ingredients and the discoveries and whims of the kitchen. Accordingly, the choices are not usually extensive—but this is by design to concentrate on depth of quality, rather than on breadth of quantity. For appetizers try the always-available grilled seafood sausage (a signature dish), the light calamari, or the rich foie gras. Among entrées, fish dishes are tops—including a singularly accomplished salmon in a surprising beet sauce,

grilled swordfish steaks, and a piquantly sweet fric-
assee of shellfish. Other winning selections include
fresh game in season, such as rabbit, venison (nicely
roasted with a cream of sundried tomatoes), and
squab; and inventive versions of veal, lamb, and
pork chops. Chanterelle's cheese tray—included in
the meal—is one of the city's most acclaimed, and
its dessert cart offers fresh fruit pies and tarts, rich
cakes, and homemade ice creams and sorbets. Even
with moderate wine choices, it's easy to end up with
tabs of $100 and more per person—but, as a culi-
nary treat and an all-around pleasurable experience,
a night at Chanterelle is definitely worth it. A fixed-
price lunch added since the move is a comparative
bargain—but the consensus is that the kitchen is
really at its best at dinner.

Chanterelle, 2 Harrison St, New York, NY 10013,
212/966-6960. Tue-Sat noon-2:30, 6-10:30 pm.

Best Top-of-the-Line Restaurant for Lunch

La Côte Basque

Dedicated budget gourmets know that fine dining at
a top restaurant becomes infinitely more affordable
for lunch rather than dinner. Perhaps nowhere is
this more true than in Manhattan, where nearly all
of the fine restaurants that are open for lunch offer
some sort of *prix-fixe* midday meal (pre-theater meals
can also represent savings over traditional dinners).
A good place to put this knowledge to use is La Côte
Basque, a restaurant that is neither cutting edge nor
nouvelle, but has long been successful with its menu
of classic French cuisine. This restaurant has been
around for more than 30 years and its reputation
may have dimmed slightly with the passing of time
and coming and going of new dining trends—but it
is still highly thought of by its loyal crowd of regulars, which sometimes includes Donald Trump, Bill
Blass, and Paul Newman. La Côte Basque presents
great soups and other starters (especially the foie
gras and crab-and-lobster salad), and, among its
entrées, the grilled sole is popular, as are chef Jean-
Jacques Rachou's special cassoulet and the delicate
renderings of veal chop, filet mignon, and steak au
poivre. These meals are rounded off with a fine
selection of desserts (best of these include chocolate
mousse flavored with Grand Marnier, soufflé featuring the same liqueur, and freshly baked apple tarts),
and truly transcendent espresso. Dinner attracts
crowds, but bottom-line-watchers appreciate La Côte
Basque's *prix-fixe* three-course lunch, which is *nearly
half the cost of the set dinner.* This restaurant has

an excellent wine list—choices from which can *considerably* up the price of a (relatively) bargain lunch!

La Côte Basque, 5 E 55th St, New York, NY 10022, 212/688-6525. Mon-Sat noon-2:30 pm, 6-10:30 pm.

Best Restaurant Turnaround of the Last Decade

Gotham Bar and Grill

When this restaurant opened in the northwestern quadrant of the Village in 1984, it was nearly swamped in a tidal wave of hype as a trendy, see-and-be-seen spot. Consequently, when its "flavor-of-the-month" fame passed away as the trendoids of the 1980s moved on, it was thought sure to fail soon afterward. But, under the guidance of chef Alfred Portale, the reputation of Gotham's food soon outstripped its opening fame, and a completely successful restaurant emerged. (One constant has been the huge, multi-level restaurant's visual appeal; its postmodern look of high ceilings and dramatic lines won a prestigious design award soon after the restaurant opened—and Gotham, with a dramatic, pink-accented decor, is still a treat for the eyes.) Best bets from the eclectic menu of American and Italian specialties include a generous seafood salad or a portion of one of the homemade pastas for starters, and such entrées as golden-brown roasted chicken (seasoned with rosemary), a variation on steak au poivre, rack of lamb (seasoned with mustard), grilled shrimp in tomato sauce, and veal carpaccio. Wine is featured by the bottle or the glass (with the care and devotion of a good wine bar; not just from a few open bottles of house red and white); excellent desserts include lemon tart, homemade strudel with ice cream, and warm, rich chocolate cake. Dining here isn't cheap (Gotham offers the archetypal $12 Manhattan hamburger, for example), but neither is it unwarrantedly pricey—an average tab, with wine, can run around $50-$75 per person.

Gotham Bar and Grill, 12 E 12th St, New York, NY 10003, 212/620-4020. Mon-Fri noon-2:30 pm, 6-11 pm; Sat 6-11 pm; Sun 5:30-9:30 pm.

Best Restaurant Run by a James Beard Protégé

An American Place

This good-looking art deco restaurant, named (pretentiously, some would say) after photographer Alfred Stieglitz's one-time noted gallery, is a celebration of

American cooking, from Colonial time to the ever-exploring present. Run by Larry Forgione, a student of the late James Beard (the connection is prominently mentioned on the restaurant's menu), An American Place offers a varied and inventive menu. This menu includes some excellent seafood, such as grilled salmon with light potato pancakes or Key West shrimp in a piquant mustard sauce, sweet-potato ravioli, excellent roasted chicken with fresh green beans and creamy mashed potatoes (gourmet comfort food!), and wild game that varies from season to season. The wine list is also, naturally, all-American—heavy on California choices, but including a few homegrown New York State selections. The dessert choices are equally good, with chocolate-based items dominating; the fudgy devil's food cake seems to be the reigning winner among chocoholics (an alternative is rich bread pudding, spiked with a smooth bourbon sauce). Prices are not low—but neither are they anywhere near the wallet-busting range of other restaurants of this caliber (with savings on *prix-fixe* dinners for early diners). This restaurant's newer (since 1989) location is much larger than the old Lexington Avenue space it once inhabited, admitting more customers without creating a crowded feeling.

An American Place, 2 Park Ave, New York, NY 10016, 212/684-2122. Mon-Fri 11:45 am-2:30 pm, 5:30-11 pm; Sat 5:30-11 pm.

Most Elegant Early Bird Dinner Bargain
Lafayette

An open kitchen, festooned with copper pans and with white-suited chefs cooking up a storm, somehow imparts this elegant, 72-seat restaurant with an air of informality. Adding to the warm ambience is wrought-iron ornamentation—gates and swan-shaped sconces—crafted by an artisan from Strasbourg, and an antique French provincial hutch—handsome enough to prompt more than one collector to inquire about buying it. Presiding over the kitchen is Marybeth Boller, one of America's rising young chefs. A convenient (and relatively inexpensive) way to sample her creative cookery is an early-evening dinner, served 6-7 p.m. and priced at $32.50. It includes soup or salad, a choice of salmon, veal, beef, or tuna entrée, and coffee or tea. Choices include the likes of shitake-studded salmon with braised Savoy cabbage and porcinis; veal filet with a farce de veau, spinach, and pancetta; tournedos with a garlic-and-shallot confit; and grilled tuna with black and white beans. This is a perfect pre-theater meal. Popular with regulars, and an ideal accompaniment to a glass of wine, are palate-perking complimentary appetizers, such as miniature vegetable-goat-cheese tarts. The restaurant is a pretty spot for a romantic dinner, with fresh flowers in silver single-bud vases on tables and a stunning central floral display in a black ceramic vase. For an aperitif or after-dinner drink, an intimate private bar is equipped with well-padded comfortable stools.

Lafayette, The Drake Swissôtel, 66 E 56th St, New York, NY 10022, 212/832-1565. Tue-Fri noon-10 pm, Sat noon-10 pm.

Most Interesting Combinations of Cuisines (and Perhaps the Most Expensive!)

The Quilted Giraffe

The cuisine at this Midtown restaurant is a spectacularly successful hybrid, adroitly blending French, Japanese, and American dishes and ingredients. Examples include grilled salmon with crisp Japanese-style vegetables, rack of lamb in a hot Chinese mustard sauce, a savory duck cassoulet, and fresh-from-the-coast-of-Maine scallops in a vinaigrette. Here is a menu on which sushi coexists with confit of duck and chocolate chip Napoleon. Excellent desserts come in such tempting arrays that the bet-hedger's choice may be the Grand Dessert, which offers tastes of *all* current dessert specials. The Quilted Giraffe is also well known for its outstanding selection of wine (the prices of which can make the list seem more like a readout of government defense contracts), which is updated daily. Overseen by inventive chef Barry Wine and his wife Susan, this restaurant was formerly housed in a brownstone on Second Avenue but has moved to the AT&T Building (Philip Johnson's controversial Chippendale-highboy-style edifice). No mincing of words: Dining here can be *very* expensive—you can expect to pay $125 to $175 per person for that unique privilege (these prices are for dinner; the costs are lower at lunch...and can be much more with the selection of a top-notch bottle of wine or two)—but, for the dedicated gourmet, this is a splurge that can well be worth its considerable price tag. (Chef Wine was a practicing lawyer before he became a restaurateur—and the joke goes that it was in his previous profession that he learned to charge prices like those found at The Quilted Giraffe!)

The Quilted Giraffe, 550 Madison Ave, New York,
NY 10022, 212/593-1221. Tue-Fri noon-2:30 pm, 5:30-
10 pm; Sat 5:30-10 pm.

Best Spot to Reserve a Month Ahead For

Lutèce

The kitchen of this exquisite restaurant is run
somewhat like a French (or, to be more exact,
Alsatian) boot camp by its exacting chef/owner André
Soltner—and while this can be tough on his
employees, the results are indisputedly good for his
patrons. For more than 25 years, Lutèce has seemed
to defy many of the "rules"—it is small (almost
cramped), with rather nondescript decor, not much
pizzazz, and a menu that seldom varies. But the
results transcend these elements, creating a
restaurant that in-the-know people (who include
regulars Jackie Onassis and Lee Iacocca) reserve
many weeks (or even months, for special occasions)
ahead to experience. Soltner's standards are exacting
and his connections legion—the ingredients for his
dishes are almost universally the finest and freshest
available. The consensus is that nearly everything
here will delight—but definite established winners
include trout in a light cream sauce, crab-and-potato
pancakes, lobster ravioli, veal with succulent morels,
and a delicate roast chicken; in general, Soltner's
fish dishes, such as snapper in red-pepper sauce,
are unilaterally terrific. One small complaint is that
Lutèce's wine list is a bit lacking—but its dessert
selections are not, with tarts and pies primed with
the freshest seasonal berries and other fruits; the
soufflés and homemade cakes are very nice, as well.
This is consistently picked among the city's top few
restaurants—but it is also consistently friendly
(rather than snobby) to its patrons, even first-timers.
Mark your calendar early and prepare to be
impressed.

Lutèce, 249 E 50th St, New York, NY 10022, 212/752-
2225. Tue-Fri noon-2 pm, 5:30-9:45 pm; Mon & Sat
5:30-9:45 pm.

Most Elegant Restaurant for Three Squares

Mark's

This elegant restaurant doesn't wait until dinner to
strut its stuff. It starts at 7 a.m., when diners can
sit down to homemade yogurt-granola parfait, duckling hash with poached eggs, strawberry pecan

waffle, and kitchen-smoked salmon with toasted bagel chips and cream cheese. In a short time, this restaurant in the new Mark hotel has established itself as one of New York's top hotel dining rooms. The assertive cuisine of Normandy native, executive chef Philippe Boulot, has created a dining destination for non-guests. The stylish English club-like decor features burgundy, rose, and teal furnishings in velvet and silk, floral carpets, rich mahogany and lacquer furniture, and antique prints. The luncheon menu focuses on light cuisine—red orange and roast pepper salad, Caesar salad with lobster and scallion quesadillas, and a lobster-and-avocado club sandwich. Dinner choices include sautéed red snapper served with a succotash of lima beans and smoked lobster, barbecued striped bass on creamed savoy cabbage, and sautéed breast of guinea hen with cider sauce, wilted spinach, and braised baby turnips.

Mark's, The Mark, 25 E 77th St, New York, NY 10021, 212/879-1864. Mon-Sat 7 am-10 pm, Sun 8 am-10 pm.

Most Artistic Food

Bouley

Like an artist choosing complementary—or purposefully discordant—colors from his well-worn palette, this French provincial restaurant's chef-owner David Bouley blends familiar and surprising ingredients for both taste and appearance. The results are at once eye- and palate-pleasing. Now ensconced in his own classy-looking TriBeCa establishment, Bouley learned his trade among the fine chefs of France— and earned his New York reputation at Le Cirque and Montrachet (see separate listings). Among his signature dishes are crisp-roasted duckling in nine spices, venison in wine-and-pepper sauce, braised pigeon wrapped in cabbage, lobster with asparagus and black truffles, seared sea bass swimming in a pool of flavors (including a touch of curry), and roasted halibut or salmon. To get a good overview of the Bouley experience, try the eight-course tasting menu that explores the depths and breadths of the chef's visual and victual imagination. The complementary appetizers beforehand and petit fours afterward are nice touches, as if acknowledging the special bond between patron and chef. Prices are what you would probably expect for this level of accomplishment—which is to say they are high—but cost-conscious patrons can check out the lunch for a better bargain. One complaint: Service can be a bit slow here—perhaps to make the presentations of the attractive dishes all the more dramatic?

Bouley, 165 Duane St, New York, NY 10013, 212/
608-3852. Mon-Fri noon-3 pm, 6-11 pm; Sat 6-11
pm.

Best Rooftop Restaurant

Terrace Restaurant

Although this restaurant is located on the top floor
of a Columbia University residence hall, typical dorm
dining this ain't! A mere 16 stories high, it, nonetheless, offers an excellent southern view of Manhattan, including both rivers. (The views to the west—of
the Palisades—and to the north—of the George
Washington Bridge—are less dramatic, but still striking.) The restaurant offers a soft, romantic atmosphere (including live harp music) and serves a basic
menu of French-flavored cuisine. Lightly grilled fish
entrées (tuna, red snapper, swordfish) are good, as
are inventive game dishes and homemade pastas.
Top dessert choices are great fruit tarts and a knock-
out chocolate mousse. In summer, an outdoor terrace (the Terrace's terrace?) is the place to be for
open-air dining with a view. This restaurant is located on the eastern edge of the Columbia campus,
in a neighborhood that is far from the best; patrons
are advised to take a cab or use the restaurant's free
valet parking service.

Terrace Restaurant, Butler Hall, Columbia University,
400 W 119th St, New York, NY 10027, 212/666-9490.
Tue-Fri noon-3:30 pm, 6-10 pm; Sat 6-10 pm.

Top Spot for Scribes

Extra! Extra!

This funky restaurant-cum-bar off the lobby of the
art deco Daily News Building is decorated with a
newspaper theme (framed headlines, ink spattered
on the floor)—the sort of spot where you might expect
to find Clark Kent and Lois Lane hanging out. Lois
probably would experiment with the grilled alligator
sausage served with Louisiana hot sauce, spicy
chicken wings, or a Jamaican-inspired peppery
chicken sandwich served on a toasted brioche bun.
Kent, well, he probably would stick to the turkey
club, eight-ounce burger, or grilled chicken salad.
This lively, friendly bar *is* a scribes' hang-out, not
only for *Daily News* reporters, but for staff of a
number of magazines located nearby. The eclectic
menu has a selection of tacos, burritos, and
quesadillas, with well-made margaritas as popular
accompaniments. A standout appetizer is tender fried
fresh calamari, served with the sauce of the day.

Rounding out the menu are pizzas, pasta, and such
entrées as chicken scallopini, crab cakes, and stir-
fries. There is live music on Fridays and Saturdays,
ranging from rap to rock 'n' roll. Brooke Shields is
reputed to hang out here. Afternoon parties are held
for kids, who also enjoy peeking at the giant revolving globe in the lobby (see separate listing).

Extra! Extra! 767 Second Ave, New York, NY 10017,
212/490-2900. Mon-Fri 11:30 am-10 pm.

Tearoom That Might Have Pleased
Izaak Walton

Anglers & Writers

The river that flows near this café is not exactly a
pristine stream, but, with its walls festooned with
rods, reels, creels, and an assortment of other vintage fishing tackle, there is a definite appeal to those
who pursue piscatorial pleasures. Offering a peek
through its large picture windows at the distant
Hudson River and of minuscule James J. Walker
Park, this Greenwich Village café entices with its
spread for afternoon tea. Served daily (3:00-6:00
p.m.) are sandwiches, scones, teacakes, cookies,
buns, and various homemade pies and pastries.
With sturdy oak furniture, mismatched china, fresh
flowers, and shelves of books, this comfortable café
offers a feeling of the country in the midst of the city.
A writing desk and the works of Hemingway, Dos
Passos, Fitzgerald, and other literary giants of the
"Lost Generation" account for the second group noted
in the name.

Anglers & Writers, 420 Hudson St, New York, NY
10014, 212/675-0810. Mon-Fri 9 am-11:30 pm, Sun 11
am-6 pm.

Best Mixture of "Greenwich Village
Cool" and "New Orleans Hot"

Sazerac House

Where to find a bit of the Big Easy in the Big Apple?
Head down to Greenwich Village, where this restaurant has been long known for serving up some of the
best "Nawlins"-style eats to be found anywhere in
the city. With its pronounced New Orleans feel, the
Sazerac almost seems to be from a different place—
but it is definitely a popular part of the Village. It
is housed in the oldest building on Hudson Street,
which dates back to 1826, when it was a farm
structure. Today, it offers a pleasant decor of antiques and a roaring fireplace under a classic

pressed-tin ceiling; throughout, it is accented with mementoes of New Orleans, including photos of the city and of some of its most famous musicians. The local crowd that flocks here enjoys the menu of gumbo, jambalaya, oysters, crayfish, *pain perdu* (New Orleans-style French toast), and some inventive, out-of-this-world egg dishes worthy of a famous New Orleans breakfast spread. The weekend brunch is a great time to join the Sazerac's regulars and take a brief culinary trip down to the Bayou. *A namesake note:* "Sazerac" comes straight from the Crescent City, where it is the name of a hotel restaurant *and* of a famous New Orleans drink invented there.

Sazerac House, 533 Hudson St, New York, NY 10014, 212/989-0313. Nightly until 2 am.

Best Texas Barbecue in Manhattan
Dallas B-B-Q and Wylie's Ribs

What's the difference between so-called Southern barbecue and truly Texan barbecue? The answer, in a word, is *beef*. While southern barbecue can include beef (along with pork and chicken), it is definitely the Lone Star meat of choice. (Which is not to say you won't find pork ribs or barbecued chicken—but beef is the star.) And while the atmosphere at these restaurants isn't as non-stop "Texas" as at the funky Lone Star Roadhouse (which also offers some good Texas eats—see separate listing), the food *is*. Dallas B-B-Q seems almost as huge as its namesake city, with literally hundreds of diners packed into its West Side (just off the park) warehouse-style space every night. The huge and hearty beef ribs they flock here for are moist and tender, with the deep-barbecued meat practically falling away from the bone. Dallas also offers good pork spareribs, barbecued and fried chicken, corn bread, skin-on potato planks, and loafs of onion rings. This is not an expensive spot—but come early (before 6:00 p.m.) for dinner specials that are both bountiful and even cheaper than the regular prices. Dallas also has a popular (if smaller) branch in Greenwich Village, at 21 University Place (212/674-4450), where N.Y.U. students head to munch the reasonably priced fare. Another Texas-themed barbecue restaurant is Wylie's, on the eastern edge of Midtown, not far from the United Nations. It serves up large portions of juicy, slow-cooked beef and pork ribs, and never-dried-out barbecued chicken, all accompanied by tasty sauce (extra pitchers of it are provided on each table to supplement your entrée or for pouring over fries or rings). A branch of Wylie's, at 59 W. 56th Street (212/757-7910) offers more of the same, plus a nice outdoor garden for fair-weather dining.

Dallas B-B-Q, 27 W 72nd St, New York, NY 10023, 212/873-2004. Sun-Thu noon-midnight, Fri & Sat noon-1 am. Wylie's Ribs, 891 First Ave, New York, NY 10022, 212/751-0700. Daily noon-midnight.

Best Southern Barbecue in Manhattan

Brother's Bar-B-Q

This fun and funky SoHo diner serves up some of the city's finest barbecue, and some of the best Southern-style eats south of the famed Sylvia's up in Harlem (see separate listing). Fans of this food order up heaping platters of slow-cooked pork ribs, slathered with a smoky, sweet, tangy sauce; fried or barbecued chicken; beef brisket on a plate or in a sandwich, with more of that perfect-for-dipping sauce; and good ole sides such as collard greens, crumbly corn bread, and creamy mashed potatoes. The place is a little more calculated and less authentic than Sylvia's, but it is inexpensive and the food hits the mark. The soul music playing constantly in the background makes a good accompaniment to this soulful dining. Not far away in SoHo is another good southern restaurant, Tennessee Mountain (143 Spring Street; 212/431-3993), which is a little more upscale—and, with it, more expensive—but also offers up hearty portions of authentic Southern barbecue, fried chicken, and plenty of tempting sides; good chili, too.

Brother's Bar-B-Q, 228 W Houston St, New York, NY 10014, 212/727-2775. Mon-Fri 11:30 am-11 pm, Sat 6 pm-midnight, Sun 5:30-11 pm.

Hottest Spot for Five-Alarm Chili

Manhattan Chili Company

Should you order the Texas Chain Gang chili, you may want to keep a cold brew handy—perhaps an Anchor Steam or a Dos Equis. The menu describes it as "hot hot" and it doesn't exaggerate. Seven chilis, available by the pint or quart, offer varying degrees of heat and include lamb, turkey, and meatless versions. Fixings (extra) include sour cream, red or white onions, scallions, diced tomatoes, cilantro, mixed jack and cheddar cheeses, and jalapeños. The Tex-Mex/Southwestern menu also features chicken or vegetable tortilla pie, fajitas, and barbecued baby back ribs. There are a number of salad combinations, plus burgers (try a topping of bacon and guacamole) and sandwiches. Appetizers include spiced chicken wings and mini chimichangas; soups feature gazpacho and spicy black bean with smoked ham. Desserts include apple-raisin-walnut bread pudding, chocolate banana tortilla cake, and margarita pie (lime pie spiked with tequila and triple sec). Decor is pink and green with a bare-brick wall. There is extra seating at a small bar and alfresco dining (April-October) at a green-trellised patio with a brick floor.

Manhattan Chili Company, 302 Bleecker St, New York, NY 10014, 212/206-7163. Mon-Fri 11:30 am-10:30 pm, Sat & Sun 5:30-10:30 pm.

Most Elevated Low-Country Cooking
Jezebel

This theater-district eatery is itself brashly theatrical (and somewhat bordello-like), transporting diners to a cloistered bit of the old South. Heavy floral drapes cover windows. Shawls in a variety of colors and fabrics hang from the ceiling. Small round tables draped with floral cloths sport white candles and bouquets of fresh miniature daisies. In some cases, seating is provided by suspended porch swings. Framed vintage posters, some in French, and pictures of black celebrities such as Lena Horne and Muhammad Ali, complete the ambience. Owner Alberta Wright, who hails from Charleston, South Carolina, opened this restaurant in 1984 and uses her own recipes for upscale soul food and Low Country cooking. Starters include she-crab soup and chicken livers (a large bowlful, plenty to share), lightly breaded and sautéed in a sauce that is hot and sweet. Popular entrées include pan-fried catfish, honey chicken, curried lamb, and ham steak prepared with carrots, raisins, and caramelized honey sauce. Entrées come with a choice of two side dishes—grits, black-eyed peas, yams, collard greens, and the like. Desserts include a wonderful combination of light cake, banana pudding, and whipped cream, plus such standards as pecan pie and bread pudding. "We don't get tourists, we get travelers," said our waitress. She might have added yuppies, we thought, eyeing the upscale couple who had stopped at the small bar area for a drink and appetizer—an unlikely combination of champagne and chicken livers. There is a pianist after 8:00 p.m., taped jazz prior to that.

Jezebel, 630 Ninth Ave, New York, NY 10036, 212/582-1045. Daily 5:30 pm-midnight.

Most Inventive Southwest Cuisine
Arizona 206

Southwestern-style cooking need not mean warmed-over Americanized attempts at Mexican cooking or the mesquite-barbecuing of anything that moves. Predictably, this restaurant and bar presents a casual, noisy atmosphere, with plenty of bright Southwestern colors, adobe-and-pine, fireplaces, and loud rock 'n' roll (some good singles-bar type mingling, too). But it also offers a menu of pleasant surprises, adding distinctive touches to food from cultures thousands of miles from the nearest cactus. Southwestern-style Peking duck, for example, is as spicy and deeply flavorful as it is moist and crispy; lightly grilled salmon is complemented nicely by corn pudding. Other taste-blending offerings might include juicy seared salmon with a fruity-hot salsa, rich venison chili, black-bean cakes with crawfish, and tostada salad with chunks of lobster. These inventive dishes are accompanied by a list of primarily American wines, but they are also nicely complemented by Arizona 206's great sweet and salty frozen margaritas. Next door, at 204 E. 60th Street, is the restaurant's casual side, the Arizona 206 Café, which serves tapas-style grazing portions of the type of Southwestern fare served in the main restaurant.

Arizona 206, 206 E 60th St, New York, NY 10022, 212/838-0440. Mon-Sat noon-3 pm, 6-11 pm.

Longest Taste of Tijuana
Benny's Burritos

As you'd expect from a corner/storefront Mexican joint, the food here is cheap—two can stuff themselves for less than $15. But, as you might not expect from this slight-cut-above-fast-food type of place, the food is also very good. The decor at Benny's is sort of retro-cheesy, with gurgling Lava Lamps, a jukebox full of oldies, and various Tex-Mex artifacts. It attracts a big, boisterous crowd for its menu of quesadillas, tacos, beans and rice, enchiladas, and, of course, its namesake, burritos. Of these, the restaurant cheekily boasts that "Ours are bigger than yours." At least a foot long, these homemade flour tortillas are filled with combinations of chicken, beef, steak, beans, and vegetables—with the requisite accompaniments of a cool dollop of sour cream and the thick creamy tang of homemade guacamole. Wash them down with a choice of Mexican beers, and leave with the satisfied glow that comes with good food at low prices. There's another Benny's at 93 Avenue A in the East Village (212/254-2054).

Benny's Burritos, 113 Greenwich Ave, New York, NY 10014, 212/633-9210. Mon-Thu 11:30 am-midnight, Fri 11:30 am-1 am, Sat 11 am-1 am, Sun 11 am-midnight.

Best Louisiana Cooking Far from the Bayou

Great Jones Café and Gulf Coast

Great Jones Café, which is located on and named-after our favorite-named street in the East Village, started off as a neighborhood bar a few years ago, but the food (originally a limited menu to accompany drinks) started drawing more of a crowd than the bar. Today, it is loud and crowded, with tables close together, creating a party atmosphere. Good Cajun (and/or Southern) food at good prices include blackened fish (especially bluefish and redfish) and chicken, hearty gumbo, good half-pound burgers, and flavorful, fiery chili; on weekends, try what the menu describes as an "Elvis-style" breakfast—your choice of eggs, served with homemade biscuits, rich country gravy, and black-eyed peas. Great Jones may have moved beyond its roots as a bar, but the joint's signature specialty remains alcoholic: a powerful jalapeño-spiked "Cajun martini" of straight gin or vodka (you may want a cold beer—crisp, clear Rolling Rock is the brew of choice here—on hand to chase down this fiery and potent potable). Combine dining here with a trip to La Mama E.T.C., just down the block, for some of the best experimental theater in the city (see separate listing). For Cajun eats farther west in the Village, try Gulf Coast. Its popularity often means a wait, but that gives patrons a chance to try some of the fine appetizers at the bar, such as crayfish, oysters, and crispy fried vegetables. Top entrées include catfish, mesquite-grilled shrimp or chicken, alligator steaks, and an excellent rendering of simple red beans and rice (seasoned with bits of spicy andouille sausage). Gulf Coast is big with the after-work crowd, who eat, drink, and bop to the oldies on the jukebox. It also offers a good Louisiana-style Sunday brunch, and live zydeco music on Monday and Tuesday nights.

Great Jones Café, 54 Great Jones St, New York, NY 10012, 212/674-9304. Mon-Fri 5 pm-1 am, Sat & Sun noon-2 am. Gulf Coast, 489 West St (at W 12th St), New York, NY 10014, 212/206-8790. Mon-Thu 5-11:30 pm, Fri & Sat 5 pm-1 am, Sun 12:30-11:30 pm.

Restaurant with the Least-Aspiring Slogan (but Great Down-Home Cajun Cooking)

Acme Bar & Grill

Although the Acme self-deprecatingly bills itself as "An Okay Place to Eat," it consistently proves it is much more. This is a big place, fixed up in an old Southern style (featuring pitted metal advertising signs in a mixed garage/barn-like interior with ceilings of corrugated tin), and offering a good mixture of Southern/Cajun/basic bar eats. Tops among these are authentic jambalaya and gumbo, tasty barbecue, hearty burgers, oyster po' boy sandwiches, excellent catfish and trout dishes, plump grilled pork chops, and such sides as black-eyed peas, collard greens, homemade corn bread, and crispy-on-the-outside, soft-on-the-inside corn fritters. In addition to dining, Acme's other claim to fame is its truly taste-bud-burning collection of hot sauces, claimed to be the largest in the world (the Guinness people have apparently yet to sanction this category—and there are counterclaims from Chicago and Iowa). Try a few of these to spice up your meal, including such fiery little-known brands as Cureau's Cajun Sauce, Tiger Sauce, Trappey's Pepper Sauce, Cajun Power Spicy Hot Sauce, and (our incendiary favorite—we have a friend who regularly brings this brand back from New Orleans) Gib's Bottled Hell. There is a music/pool room downstairs, offering blues, R&B, and zydeco music; when Rolling Stones guitarist Keith Richards is out on the town, he has been known to stop in downstairs. Acme also offers a weekend brunch, where, quite frankly, you are *not* likely to spot Keith—he prowls at night.

Acme Bar & Grill, 9 Great Jones St, New York, NY 10012, 212/420-1934. Sun-Thu 11:30 am-midnight, Fri & Sat 11:30 am-1 am.

Queen of Harlem Soul Food

Sylvia's

This Harlem soul-food establishment grew from a luncheonette and now boasts a second dining room and an outdoor patio. Even if you're not up to black-eyed peas and collard greens with ham, give the barbecued slabs of spare ribs a chance. Tangy with Louisiana hot sauce and satisfyingly meaty and fall-off-the-bone tender, they draw diners from downtown to join the Harlemites who frequent this popular spot that has earned owner Sylvia Woods the sobriquet, "Queen of Soul Food." Fried chicken and spicy smothered chicken are specialties, along with pork chops and baked ham. Candied yams (baked with nutmeg and vanilla seasonings) are a tasty side dish; home fries a "must." This is a good spot to go with a bunch of companions willing to sample down-home cooking by ordering a number of different dishes and sides. Peach cobbler is Sylvia's renowned dessert, but sweet-potato pie and carrot cake also are worth their weight in calories. Belt-busting breakfasts with eggs, spicy sausages, griddle cakes, home-made biscuits and corn bread, and, of course, the inevitable grits, are another draw. Following Sunday brunch, there is live entertainment.

Sylvia's, 328 Lenox Ave, New York, NY 10027, 212/996-0660. Mon-Sat 7:30 am-10 pm, Sun 1-7 pm.

Best Bet for Soup and Salad

Camelback & Central

This is a casual and popular East Side eatery—the sort of comfortable, affordable, and friendly place that every neighborhood could use (but that, alas, many do not have). It is spacious and minimally decorated, featuring wide windows and grey-brick walls; copious flowers and well-placed candles enhance its uncluttered atmosphere. The acclaimed soups and salads are good, fresh, and quick. These range from simple, yet satisfying basic soups (tomato, mushroom, baked onion, consommés) and side salads to satisfying meals that combine hearty chowders and cheese soups with substantial, entrée-sized chef, Caesar, and Cobb salads; there is also an excellent bouillabaisse. Among more substantial entrées, the variety of light fish (swordfish specials are top-of-the-line), chicken, pasta, and grilled chops (pork and lamb, especially) are highly praised; the hefty burgers are also good. The dessert choices are mostly chocolate-based and include creamy chocolate silk cream pie and tasty ice cream-and-fruit sundaes drizzled with thick chocolate fudge sauce. Camelback & Central offers a set pre-theater menu, including the excellent soups and salads with a choice of entrées (with vegetables), desserts, and beverages; a weekend brunch presents a buffet of egg dishes, salads, soups, fresh fruits, and tempting baked goods. The restaurant's unusual name comes from an intersection in Phoenix, Arizona, where one of the owners hails from.

Camelback & Central, 1403 Second Ave (at E 73rd St), New York, NY 10021, 212/249-8380.

Theatergoers' Favorite Outdoor Dining
Barbetta

Opened in 1906, this restaurant's northern Italian cuisine has become one of the Theater District's longest-running hits. Specializing in the food of Piedmonte, in northwestern Italy, it incorporates into its unique dishes truffles gathered by Italian hunters it keeps on retainer. Barbetta is housed in a pair of late-19th-century town houses, decorated elaborately with 18th-century Italian antiques. When weather permits, there is dining in a charming, tree-shaded and flower-accented garden. Specials include delicate fettucine with its signature shaved white truffles, cold minestrone, pasta primavera, fresh game (roasted, with pasta, and in combinations) in season, and a variety of fish (especially salmon and sole). The wine list complements the entrées with a good variety of Italian selections. This restaurant's location makes its pre- and post-theater menus very popular—but, for best service and time to linger in the garden over dessert and cappuccino, in-the-know diners (including Elizabeth Taylor and Robert Redford) visit during the mid-evening lull between curtain and curtain calls. Located across the street from another Theater District dining hot spot, Orso (see separate listing), Barbetta is believed to be the oldest restaurant in the city still owned by its founding family.

Barbetta, 321 W 46th St, New York, NY 10036, 212/246-9171. Mon-Sat noon-2 pm, 5 pm-midnight.

Best After-Theater Spot for Scrambled Eggs and Irish Bacon
The Ginger Man

After the theater, grab a cab to this eatery a block west of Central Park, across from Lincoln Center. This large, rambling restaurant has a variety of seating choices, including a glass-enclosed sidewalk patio, the dark-paneled saloon, covered with paintings and prints and with a room-length bar, a white-tiled anteroom with a curved, corrugated-iron ceiling, and a room with plank floorboards, blue floral tiles, and Parisian-style, art-wrapped pillars. An after-eight supper menu offers thick, juicy hamburgers (and a veal burger) dressed with fontina cheese, bacon, mushrooms, and onions. There are light entrées, such as chargrilled warm chicken salad and fusilli pasta with tomato, cream, and Parmesan cheese. Scrambled eggs are paired with Irish bacon and omelettes incorporate watercress with sour cream, imported cheese, and smoked salmon with dill. Posted daily specials include an excellent gazpacho. Good dessert choices are walnut chocolate torte and chocolate mocha terrine with caramel sauce. Black bean soup and lobster ravioli are their standards.

The Ginger Man, 51 W 64th St, New York, NY 10023, 212/399-2358. Mon-Fri 8 am-midnight, Sat-Sun 10 am-midnight.

Most Likely Spot to Spot the "Saturday Night Live" Cast

Orso

This northern Italian restaurant is noted for its delicious thin-crust pizzas and celeb patrons. On Tuesdays when *Saturday Night Live* is taped, executive producer Lorne Michaels often brings in the cast for dinner. Other famous patrons include Al Pacino, Glenn Close, and Gene Hackman. The engaging decor features parquet floors and rough-finished walls painted a sandstone color and decorated with wrought-iron sconces and black-and-white photos of Italian peasants, movie stars, and village scenes. There are large clay pots filled with red, yellow, and orange peppers, and an open kitchen at the back. Food is served on colorful dishes, hand-painted in individual patterns. Crusty bread is brought to the table for dipping in olive oil seasoned with rosemary and thyme. Recommended are beef carpaccio with asparagus and Parmesan, and whole-wheat spaghetti with white beans, caramelized onions, grappa, and tomato sauce. Pizza toppings include artichokes, eggplant, spinach, prosciutto, roasted peppers, and ricotta. Finish with gossamer-light tiramisu and a double espresso. This is a hot spot with the pre- and post-theater crowd, where the friendly trattoria atmosphere is enhanced by the philosophy of international restaurateur Joe Allen to let patrons pour wine refills for themselves.

Orso, 322 W 46th St, New York, NY 10036, 212/489-7212. Daily 11:30 am-11:45 pm.

Most Unlikely Restaurant for Star-Grazing

Conservatory Restaurant & Café

While it certainly can't be considered a luxury-class hotel, the pleasant Mayflower frequently is chosen as a location for movie and television productions and for commercials and fashion shoots. As a result, its restaurant attracts many entertainment celebrities. It also is probable that a neighboring table may be occupied by a cellist from Carnegie Hall or a soprano from the Met, since both of these venues are virtually close enough to hear the orchestra tune up. The restaurant overlooks Central Park. Its chef, formerly of Maxim's, presides over dinners that feature fresh snap pea soup with thyme, endive-and-dandelion salad, peppered salmon filet, red snapper with pernod sauce, and grilled sirloin steak with peppercorn whiskey butter. Pasta selections include gnocchi with gorgonzola, black linguini with mussels and clams in lobster sauce, and porcini stuffed ravioli. Sunday champagne brunch, with entertainment by a pianist and cabaret-style singer, offers pasta, seafood, salads, and traditional breakfast dishes such as eggs Benedict and eggs Florentine, plus homemade pastries, cappuccino, and international coffees.

Conservatory Restaurant & Café, The Mayflower Hotel, 15 Central Park W, New York, NY 10023, 212/265-0060. Daily 7 am-2 am.

Happiest Spot for Pizza and Star-Gazing
Allegria

Two landscapes painted by Tony Bennett grace the walls and a pizza oven produces some unusual combinations at this trattoria, which may have Midtown's largest alfresco dining area (April-mid-October). Although it opened only in December 1991, the restaurant is attracting such celebs as singer Bennett, superstar-model Cindy Crawford, and band members of the Gypsy Kings. The restaurant's name translates to "happiness," a theme continued in a wraparound hand-painted fresco of joyous scenes of the sea, countryside, and carnival festivities. The decor features blue-tile ceiling, salmon-colored walls, and tiled floor. On a list of a baker's dozen pizzas, the most popular combines tomato, mozzarella, and spicy salami. Other topping combinations include grilled radiccio, smoked mozzarella, and tomato, and a blend of grilled zucchini, eggplant, fennel, and carrots. Pastas include spaghetti with fresh peas, rigatoni with diced eggplant and ricotta cheese, and spaghetti with seafood in a light tomato sauce. The spinach salad with pancetta and ricotta is meaty, sweet, and crisp; a simple hot main course is grilled breast of chicken topped with artichokes and a touch of tomato.

Allegria, 66 W 55th St, New York, NY 10019, 212/956-7755. Daily 11:30 am-1 am.

Wackiest Hollywood-on-the-Hudson Dining Experience

Planet Hollywood

There are no explosions, broken glass, or erupting Uzis at this hot new eatery owned by a beefy triumvirate of box-office stars. But this restaurant, owned by Arnold Schwarzenegger, Bruce Willis, and Sylvester Stallone is adorned with a mega-dose of movie memorabilia. It includes a *Terminator 2* Arnold-look-alike cyborg and a motorcycle once owned by James Dean and features a stunningly dramatic decor (by the designer who created the dark look of the first *Batman* movie). This is a restaurant that is as fun to browse as it is to graze. The menu offers a credible mix of light, semi-nouvelle specialties (the inventive California-style pizzas are winners), along with more traditional meat and fish dishes; for dessert, there's apple strudel, made from Mama Schwarzenegger's own recipe. This is somewhat of a Hard Rock Cafe (see separate listing) for an older, movie-oriented crowd—however, the ambience is quieter, the food is more upscale, and the possibilities of spotting celebrities (at least at this early stage of the restaurant's life) are fairly good. The souvenir situation is (for now, anyway) *quite* different than that at the Hard Rock: Those ultra-hot Planet Hollywood baseball-style caps (seen in candid, *People* magazine shots of such celebrities as Mel Gibson, *Home Alone* director John Hughes, and Madonna—while jogging, no less) are harder to come by than hen's teeth. By the way, this hot, new celebrity hangout is located next door to a hot, old celebrity hangout, the Russian Tea Room (see separate listing).

Planet Hollywood, 140 W 57th St, New York, NY 10019, 212/333-7827. Daily 11 am-2 am.

Best Bet to "Send a Salami to Your Boy in the Army"

Katz's Delicatessen

Although there no longer is patriotic fervor to ship salamis to GIs, Katz's famous World War II slogan remains. So does the production of salami at this deli, established in 1888. You'll see aged salamis hanging in the window as you enter, take a ticket, and give it to the person behind the counter (pay as you leave). New deli hands discover that egg cream is made with neither namesake ingredient. The deliciously refreshing beverage combines milk, Fox's U-Bet chocolate syrup, and "selza." Corned beef, made on the premises the old fashioned way—dry cured with no injected additives—is a popular sandwich meat, as is hot pastrami, and brisket of beef piled high. Popular combinations pair pastrami or tongue with eggs. From the griddle you can order potato, spinach, and broccoli knishes; side dishes include homemade cole slaw, potato, and macaroni salad. Thick puddings—rice, tapioca, chocolate—are popular desserts. A cavernous dining room is filled with formica-topped tables and illuminated by fluorescent lights (many of them failed). Look for movie stills from *When Harry Met Sally*. Katz's claims that the famous restaurant scene, filmed there, owes the realism of its orgasmic sound effects not to acting but to its corned beef.

Katz's Delicatessen, 205 E Houston St, New York, NY 10002, 212/254-2246, fax 212/674-3270. Sun-Thu 7:30 am-11 pm, Fri & Sat 7:30-1 am.

Leanest Pastrami and Corned Beef
Carnegie Delicatessen & Restaurant

Legend and *institution* are terms associated with this busy deli—as are *pastrami* and *corned beef*. These warm, smoky meats piled high on rye form sandwiches so large that there is a "sharing charge." The comedian-narrators in the movie *Broadway Danny Rose* congregated here to nosh on sandwiches and discuss the life and times of the title character. Honoring that movie, the "Woody Allen" sandwich piles on corned beef *and* pastrami. Carnegie attracts many out-of-towners along with local celebs, its cramped seating conducive to neighborly dining. An archetypical New York deli, it has wiseacre waitresses, indifferent waiters, hanging salamis, and sometimes lines outside. A huge menu lists everything, and more, you'd expect in a deli—brisket of beef, beef tongue, pot roast, goulash, chopped liver, lox, latkes, kishkas, herring, smoked whitefish, bagels, and bialys. There's a wide range of egg dishes, as well as sautéed chicken livers, and corned beef and pastrami hash. The blintzes and the cheesecake are, as they say, "boffo." And where would a deli be without homemade chicken soup—served with matzoh balls, noodles, kreplach, or rice? It is difficult *not* to enjoy an eatery that provides fat, crunchy pickles on its tables and alliteration on its menu, to wit: "dispensing delectable deli daily from dawn to distraction."

Carnegie Delicatessen & Restaurant, 854 Seventh Ave, New York, NY 10019, 212/757-2245, fax 212/757-9889. Daily 6:30-4 am.

Best Deli When the Line's Too Long at Carnegie

Stage Delicatessen Restaurant

Because of its celebrity hype, the Stage probably is generally better known than the Carnegie Deli, and certainly is not much more than a bagel's toss away. But, for the discerning deli fancier, it should remain second choice to the superior Carnegie, particularly since both are equally convenient to the midtown hotels. For those who enjoy the passing scene of New York street life, the Stage does have the advantage of providing some seating in a glassed-in sidewalk café—and it certainly does serve two-fisted combo sandwiches, plus the perennially popular pastrami and corned beef on rye. It just somehow seems a little more contrived and a little more touristy than its neighborhood rival. Nonetheless, it is worth going to, for the mountainous sandwiches named after comedians and other celebrities, and for such standards as chicken soup, matzoh-ball soup, salami, chopped liver, borscht, brisket of beef, lox, latkes, herring, bagels, blintzes, and cheesecake. Corned beef and beef tongue are good choices, since both are pickled in house.

Stage Delicatessen Restaurant, 834 Seventh Ave, New York, NY 10019, 212/245-7850. Daily 6 am-2 am.

Best Deli on the Block Near the Block

Kaplan's

Just around the corner from Christie's, the New York branch of the renowned London auctioneers, this is the quintessential unheralded New York deli. This basic, spacious eatery is what Carnegie and Stage might be like if they hadn't become famous! It has faux-wood-paneled walls, tables with an autumn motif matched with solid Colonial-style chairs, and a large menu that includes around 60 sandwich and burger selections. Along with standard corned beef, pastrami, tongue, brisket, and salami, are specialty sandwiches such as hot roast beef with melted mozzarella cheese on garlic bread. Entrées include chicken in the pot served with matzoh ball, noodles, carrots, and peas, and stuffed cabbage with mashed potatoes and vegetables. There are cold-cut platters, salads, and a variety of egg dishes (try the Hungarian omelette—deli meats, sautéed peppers, and onions), plus appetizers such as pickled herring and chopped liver. Traditional deli nosh includes cheese blintzes, potato knishes, and bagels with Nova Scotia salmon, sable, and sturgeon. Soups feature split pea, mushroom barley, Russian cabbage, matzoh ball, borscht, kreplach, and, inevitably, various chicken-soup combos. Orders are accompanied by glistening, crunchy pickles and thick-cut cole slaw. The wait staff is helpful—my waitress cheerfully accommodated a substitution of potato pancakes for fries.

Kaplan's, 59 E 59th St, New York, NY 10022, 212/755-5959, fax 212/755-5152. Daily 7 am-10 pm.

Best Egg Cream in Town

Gem Spa

Above all else, there may be a surefire way to pick New Yorkers of a certain age out of a mixed crowd: Simply say the words "egg creams" and look to see whose eyes glaze over nostalgically. For the uninitiated, egg creams are a particularly New York treat bearing a bit of a resemblance to an ice cream soda. Egg creams are frothy drinks made with neither eggs nor cream. They are concocted with ice-cold milk, a generous squirt of chocolate syrup (or strawberry or other flavorings—but chocolate is the traditional flavor, Fox's U-Bet Chocolate Syrup the preferred brand), and a bubbling spritz of seltzer. Once-upon-a-time these drinks *did* include raw eggs; these were first included at the fountains, but, later, as the price of eggs rose, they were sent along with the kids who loved these treats by their health-conscious moms. Eventually, eggs dropped out of the recipe, but the evocative name stuck. Today, you can still get egg creams at many of the city's best delis (try Katz—see separate listing) and at some family-run ice cream shops. But for the real deal, head to the East Village—near the corner of Second Avenue and St. Mark's Place—and the Gem Spa, a newsstand/smoke shop that has been serving some of the city's best egg creams since this was a heavily Jewish neighborhood earlier this century. Today, the Gem Spa is cheerfully run by a family of East Indians, but that hasn't detracted from its status as an egg cream mecca. Besides its sublime egg creams, Gem Spa also carries an impressive selection of out-of-town newspapers, obscure periodicals, and foreign cigarettes, cigars, and loose tobaccos.

Gem Spa, 131 Second Ave, New York, NY 10003, 212/529-1146. Daily, 24 hours.

Top Island Eats

Pete's Eats

Its name suggests comfort food, and certainly the menu of this eatery does feature good old Yankee pot roast. But the informal dining room of this rather noisy, bustling local watering hole comes up with some pretty creative cooking at reasonable prices. Grilled duck salad, for example, features nicely seasoned slices of duck paired with a spinach-and-lettuce salad and a sweet vinaigrette dressing. Other recommended entrées are shrimp in a parsley-based sauce served with angel hair pasta and sautéed salmon with basil cream sauce. Starters include a variation on a shrimp cocktail, where the iced shrimp have been lightly grilled and are accompanied by a piquant remoulade. Other menu items, in addition to daily blackboard specials, include baby back ribs, blackened sirloin tips, stuffed jalapeños, and crab cakes. Desserts also feature some basic American cooking, such as homemade apple crumb pie. This Travis restaurant is under the same ownership as lively R.H. Tugs, which is across the island (see separate listing).

Pete's Eats, 4026 Victory Blvd, Staten Island, NY 10310, 718/494-5161. Sun-Thu 10:30 am-11 pm, Fri & Sat 10:30 am-midnight.

Best Diner for the Glitterati

Empire Diner

If this was in Jersey, it would be a real diner! Certainly, this West Side 24-hour eatery *looks* like a diner, with its traditional gleaming railway-car exterior. If you've a craving for breakfast at 3:00 a.m., this art deco spot is where you'll more likely find stylish nightclubbers returning from a round of the latest hot spots than bus drivers, night-shift workers, and others with nocturnal occupations. It dishes up diner-style food that includes omelettes and other egg dishes with all of the usual sides, plus French toast, club sandwiches and a good range of other sandwiches, burgers, solid soups (including chili), pasta, and steaks. For the sweet tooth, there are the expected varieties of pie plus excellent brownies and hot-fudge sundaes. Other nondiner attributes at this stylish Chelsea all-night eatery include full bar service, live entertainment—there usually is a pretty good piano player—and alfresco dining at sidewalk tables. As well as a favorite of dance-club patrons, this diner seems to be a hangout of artists and designers.

Empire Diner, 210 Tenth Ave, New York, NY 10011, 212/243-2736. Daily 24 hrs.

Best All-Night Diner with a French Accent

Brasserie

A friend who is a hotel executive transplanted from Pennsylvania swears by this all-night Midtown bistro for a drink in the wee small hours or a meal when hunger pangs overtake her at some ungodly hour. The French-accented menu offers such standards as quiche Lorraine, escargot, duck pâté, omelettes, and a variety of grilled meats, fish, and fowl. If you don't plan to go to bed for a while, it may be well worthwhile to try the choucroute garni, rich with meat, sausages, sauerkraut, and potatoes. Onion soup gratinée is reliably good and European-style steak and fries are a popular choice. The customer mix here is likely to include an entertainment celebrity or two among the night owls seeking late-night sustenance. There is raw bar fare for starters and rich desserts. Ambience includes a long counter, comfortable booths, Picasso art, and a location in the stylish Seagram building.

Brasserie, 100 E 53rd St, New York, NY 10022, 212/751-4840. Daily 24 hrs.

Best Fifties-Style Diner—Pretend

Stardust Diner

It does *look* like an authentic diner, with shiny round metal counter seats, glittery vinyl seating at formica tables, lots of pink neon reflecting onto pale green painted ceilings and walls, and '50s music in the background. And yes, you can get malts and thick shakes with homemade ice cream, plus a chicken salad, tuna club, or BLT sandwich. Or meatloaf, chicken pot pie, and lasagna. Despite its studied pretense, this is a pretty good spot to go for breakfast—where coffee comes in heavy-duty mugs and cereal comes to the table in a family-size box with a carton of milk (just like home!) and you can order a variety of croissants, rolls, and muffins, and blintzes, waffles, pancakes (try cinnamon-apple-raisin) and three-egg omelettes (with cutesy names). Or stop in to order up an egg cream, a black cow (root beer float), or a half-pound burger served with the diner's signature crinkly whiffle-ball fries. While you're waiting, you can entertain yourself examining a collection of plastic radios, a row of "Miss Subway" pinups, and the obligatory movie posters and stills of Elvis and Lucy and Desi.

Stardust Diner, 1377 Sixth Ave, New York, NY 10019, 212/307-7575, fax 212/489-5656. Mon-Thu 7 am-11 pm, Fri & Sat 7:30-12:30 am, Sun 8 am-11 pm.

Best Fifties-Style Diner with Gourmet Aspirations

Lil's Eatery

Take a ride on the Staten Island ferry (see separate description), still one of New York's best travel bargains at 50 cents each way. Leaving the Island terminal, walk uphill to Stuyvesant Place (look back for spectacular views of the Manhattan skyline). Lil's Eatery is a '50s-style diner decorated with a neon clock and pictures of Judy Garland, James Dean, and Elvis, and posters from such movies as *Some Like It Hot*. Black booths have white formica tables mounted with original individual jukeboxes, and the menu features a wide range of well-prepared diner-style food—soups, salads, sandwiches, sides, and hearty daily specials. The food is good because the owners like to cook, and food aficionados know that they especially like to cook on Friday and Saturday evenings. This is when Lil's offers special meals that elevate this eatery way above diner level. These festive, four-course dinners (a bargain at $7.95 to $14.95) feature such dishes as leek soup, broccoli and cheddar soup, escargot, mussels marinara, veal chop with port wine, and beef Wellington.

Lil's Eatery, 95 Stuyvesant Pl, Staten Island, NY 10301, 718/273-9555. Mon-Fri 6:30 am-3 pm, Sat 7:30 am-1 pm (special dinners Fri, Sat 6-10 pm).

Most Heroic Eatery

Manganaro's Hero Boy

Take a fresh, crusty loaf, slather it with olive-oil dressing, pack it with imported cold cuts and cheeses, garnish it with fresh lettuce, tomatoes, olives, peppers, and other vegetables, sprinkle it with seasonings, and you have...well, the name varies. Lately, it is popular to call this meal-in-a-sandwich a submarine. In New Orleans it's known as po' boy or muffaletta. This basic blue-collar-style eatery sticks to an earlier designation, *hero*. The term was said to have been coined in the 1940s by a food writer who declared you'd have to be a hero to finish one of these monsters. The ultimate monsters are the six-foot-long versions of these sandwiches which are perfect for parties. But, if you are a party of one, you can get a manageably sized sandwich stuffed with smoked mozzarella, provolone, prosciutto, bologna, smoked salt pork, Genoa salami, and other Italian meats and cheeses and prepared by a family restaurant that has been in the food business (with a grocery as well as the eatery) since before the turn of the century. Other fare includes excellent pasta salads, meatballs and ziti galore, as well as roasted peppers, marinated mushrooms, and a variety of pastas.

Manganaro's Hero Boy, 492 Ninth Ave, New York, NY 10018, 212/947-7325. Mon-Sat 7 am-7:30 pm.

Best Spot for Late-Night Noshing

Lox Around the Clock

Some wags have declared this almost-always-open eatery a "punk deli," no doubt both for its late-night club-going clientele (a number of nightclubs are nearby, and after closing, many of their patrons end up here) and for its funky-junky decor, topped off by numerous TV monitors playing the latest from MTV or various video artistés. So, Carnegie or Katz it isn't—but it *is* open at times when other pastrami purveyors have long been shuttered for the night, and it does offer a good selection of sandwiches, soups, blintzes, bagels, and other munchies. What about the lox, you ask? It's as good as you'd expect in a place named after it; try some with the deli's fresh-baked bagels. Sandwiches run the basic deli gamut and full dinners include fish, chicken, and brisket entrées. This is a usually noisy, often crowded, but fun spot—and, anyway, where else are you going to go to quell a hankering for a slice of nova on a fresh poppyseed bagel with a smear at 3:30 in the morning?

Lox Around the Clock, 676 Sixth Ave, New York, NY 10010, 212/691-3535. Sun-Wed 7 am-4 am, Thu-Sat 24 hours.

Best Spot for Chicken Pot Pie

Oscar's Coffee Shop

A restaurant in the sumptuous Waldorf-Astoria might seem an unlikely spot to find good and inexpensive comfort food, but this pleasant coffee shop offers both. Home-style meals include chicken pot pie, pork tenderloin with country gravy, pot roast, macaroni and cheese, meatloaf with mushroom gravy and mashed potatoes, and liver, bacon, and onions. Most entrées are around the $10 range. This is as an attractive coffee shop as you'll find. You can sit at a big tiled counter area decorated in pretty pink and green, or in a dining room with wood-topped tables, a huge floral canopy, and impressionistic paintings along one wall. Choices for starters include black bean soup, onion soup, salad niçoise, Thai beef salad, and tortellini with fresh tomato sauce. Sandwiches run the gamut of burgers, club, Reuben, BLT, and tuna melt, but also include more creative choices, such as grilled turkey with cheddar and cranberries on pumpernickel, and charbroiled breast of chicken with mozzarella and roasted red peppers on focaccia. Lighter fare includes grilled chicken and Cobb salads—and the famous Waldorf salad.

Oscar's Coffee Shop, The Waldorf-Astoria, 301 Park Ave, New York, NY 10022, 212/355-3000. Daily 7 am-11:45 pm.

Best Top Dog

Nathan's Famous

When I stepped off the BMT Broadway Express at the Coney Island subway stop, it was like stepping into the 1940s. Women wore long print dresses; men favored jackets and ties. The newsstand carried *Collier's* and *Look*, the street signs were made of wood, and Nathan's—well it was Nathan's. It turned out that a movie crew was filming *Enemies, A Love Story*. Not that Coney Island has changed a great deal over the years—apart from becoming worn and tired. You can still head for Astroland amusement park to ride the famed wooden roller coaster, the Cyclone, and you can still stop at Nathan's for an all-beef hot dog. Nathan's has been dispensing franks here since Nathan Handwerker hung out his shingle in 1916, when the dog and the ride from Manhattan each cost a nickel. Although it built its reputation off its spicy hot dogs, this fast-food emporium also serves hamburgers, fried chicken, pizza, corn on the cob, and assorted seafood including fried clams and deep-fried soft-shelled crabs, There is a branch of Nathan's at Times Square, but tradition dictates a trip to Coney Island to soak up the atmosphere, albeit seedy, as you munch on a link and an order of crinkly fries.

Nathan's Famous, Surf Ave at Stillwell, Brooklyn, NY 11224, 718/946-2202. Sun-Thu 8 am-2 am, Fri & Sat 8 am-4 am.

Best Local Chicken Mini-Chain

Chicken Kitchen

When Manhattanites get a hankering for convenient chicken, but decide that the Colonel and his franchised cohorts won't fill the bill, an option is to visit (or call) an outlet of this locally popular chain. It offers a simple menu of quick-and-tasty chicken and side dishes. The birds here are chargrilled over an open flame to crispy-on-the-outside, moist-and-juicy-on-the-inside perfection, and can be adorned with a variety of fresh, homemade sauces, including smoky and tangy barbecue, spicy salsa, honey mustard (with a touch of curry), and sweet cranberry. The chicken is available in half and whole portions, all for not much more than the cost of a frozen bird at the supermarket. Each order comes with fresh pita bread; sides of flavorful rice (several varieties), green salads, cole slaw, and potato salad are also available (and inexpensive). Chicken Kitchen offers only minimal seating, which makes sense, since it does mostly takeout or delivery business; it guarantees delivery to anywhere in Manhattan in 30 minutes or less. The 80th Street location is a little larger and more comfortable than most of the others.

Chicken Kitchen, 301 E 80th St, New York, NY 10021, 212/517-8350. Locations also at: 982 Second Ave, New York, NY 10022, 212/980-5252; 1177 Second Ave, New York, NY 10021, 212/308-9400; and 461 Sixth Ave, New York, NY 10011, 212/980-1100. Hours vary by location.

Best Café for Coffee and Dessert

Café Lalo

Head here for cappuccino and espresso, shakes, specialty coffee drinks, and European and American desserts. This European-style café has marble-topped tables, bentwood chairs, bare-brick walls with still-life Monet prints, and elegant tall windows with brass latches. The menu features 15 tarts, ranging from hazelnut to apricot-cranberry; 8 kinds of cheesecake; and 15 pies, including strawberry-rhubarb, sweet potato-pecan, and sugarless apple-raisin. Italian desserts include chocolate cannoli, tiramisu, and zuppa Inglese, while a brass-and-glass display case is filled with tempting fruit-laden and creamy cakes that include key lime mousse cake, mocha hazelnut cake, lemon bundt, Grand marnier cake, and fresh-fruit supreme. You can order ice cream and frozen yogurt with fresh berries or with liqueur, and have your coffee splashed with brandy, peppermint schnapps, amaretto, and a variety of other cordials and liqueurs. There's also wine by the glass and imported beer. Out front are park benches under a sidewalk tree.

Café Lalo, 201 W 83rd St, New York, NY 10024, 212/496-6031. Mon-Thu noon-2 am, Fri-Sat noon-4 am, Sun 11 am-2 am.

Cream of the Crop of Cheesecake
Junior's

Following a performance at the Brooklyn Academy of Music (see separate listing), concertgoers stop for a mountainous slice of what many claim is the world's best cheesecake. This huge, bustling, family-style restaurant that seats 425 (and also is a caterer and baker), offers a wide range of meals with lots of made-on-the-premises accompaniments. Choices vary from southern-fried chicken, lamb, ravioli, and sautéed lemon chicken on a bed of spinach to lobster or shrimp Newburgh, beef Stroganoff, and Chinese pepper steak. A full-service deli offers well-stuffed sandwiches, and a variety of homemade salads include, shrimp, lobster, chicken, cucumber, tuna, egg, and pasta salad primavera. But it is the cheesecake, made with cream cheese, fresh eggs, cream, flour, sugar, and vegetable shortening, that is a major attraction. If you're splurging on dessert, other considerations might be a slice of cream pie, miniature Danish pastries, or one of the tall soda-fountain creations that come in a tempting variety. Cheesecakes to go (that may be shipped to any destination in the United States) come in 6-, 7-, 8-, and 10-inch sizes that produce from 6 to 20 slices. For patrons with youngsters there is a children's menu and crayons.

Junior's, 386 Flatbush Ave Ext, Brooklyn, NY 11201, 718/852-5257. Sun-Thu 6:30 am-1:30 am, Fri & Sat 6:30 am-3 am.

Tastiest Homegrown Ice Cream
Peppermint Park/Serendipity 3

Modern ice-cream shops, such as those offering the inventive combinations available at Ben & Jerry's (see separate listing) seem a world away from the classic bright lights, mirrored walls, and delicately fluted glass dishes of the ice-cream parlors of generations past. But, for traditionalists, there remain in Manhattan a few classic ice-cream shops. Tops among these is Peppermint Park, which offers up to

50 flavors (a sop to the big franchises) of *homemade* ice cream, yogurt, and sherbet. Flavors range from the Big Three (vanilla, chocolate, and strawberry) to Dutch-apple, rocky road, and, of course, peppermint. This East Side shop is decorated in peppermint-inspired green-and-white stripes, and also offers homemade chocolates, cakes, cookies, and a menu of light sandwiches, salads, and quiches; there are additional Peppermint Park locations at 666 Fifth Avenue and in Penn Station. Serendipity 3 is more than an ice cream shop—it's also a toy store and all-around hangout for the young and the young-at-heart, who sit in classic wire-backed chairs at marble-topped tables to enjoy huge sundaes, sodas, and splits. The menu includes good burgers, hot dogs, salads, and other light fare, as well as egg creams and "frozen hot chocolate" (a house specialty). For those interested in art history—or simply celebrity kitsch—Andy Warhol used to hang out here during the wild and wacky 1960s.

Peppermint Park, 1225 First Ave, New York, NY 10021, 212/288-5054. Mon-Thu 10 am-midnight, Fri 10 am-1 am, Sat 10 am-2 am, Sun 11 am-midnight. Serendipity 3, 225 E 60th St, New York, NY 10022, 212/838-3531. Mon-Thu 11:30 am-12:30 am, Fri 11:30 am-1:30 am, Sat 11:30 am-2 am, Sun 11:30 am-midnight.

Tastiest Ice Cream Direct from Vermont

Ben & Jerry's

This ice-cream shop provides all of the necessary—and delicious—information about how Ben Cohen and Jerry Greenfield became Vermont's most famous counterculture capitalists with the help of such delectable (and sometimes strange) concoctions as Heath Bar Crunch, Chocolate Chip Cookie Dough (with chunks of dough in vanilla ice cream), and Cherry Garcia (more about which in a moment). This fun shop has all of the familiar flavors of Ben & Jerry's ice cream that can be found in pints in supermarket and convenience store freezer cases, plus a variety of new, "limited-edition," and experimental flavors and other sorts of goodies—banana splits, ice-cream cakes, malts, and shakes—that you'd expect in an ice-cream store. Newer varieties of low-fat frozen yogurt include lower-calorie versions of their top ice-cream flavors, plus such new fruit flavors as Raspberry, Blueberry Cheesecake, and Banana Strawberry. Cherry Garcia—cherry ice cream with bing cherries and bits of chocolate (named after Grateful Dead guitarist Jerry Garcia)—

is still one of the chain's most popular flavors; it's one of our favorites as well, along with more subtle seasonal flavors such as Wild Maine Blueberry and Fresh Georgia Peach. There are Ben & Jerry's branches at the World Trade Center and at various suburban locations.

Ben & Jerry's, 41 Third Ave, New York, NY 10003, 212/995-0109. Sun-Wed 11 am-midnight, Thu-Sat 11 am-2 am.

ACCOMMODATIONS

Best Hotel with a Phone Number You May Already Know

New York Penta Hotel

As famous phone numbers go, 736-5000 may not ring a bell (as it were)—but when you convert it back to the way phone numbers were known a few decades ago, before area codes, when numbers had lettered exchanges, it becomes "PEnnsylvania 6-5000," which many will recognize as the title of one of big-band-leader Glenn Miller's most popular hits. Back then, this was the stylish Pennsylvania Hotel, designed by noted turn-of-the-century architect Stanford White, and a popular stop for big bands (hence Miller's commemorative song). Since metamorphosed into the New York Penta (in the interim it was the Statler), this remains a popular lodging destination with a desirable and convenient location—directly across the street from the Penn Station/Madison Square Garden complex and a few blocks from the sprawling Javits Convention Center (in fact, the 1,700-room Penta is the closest large hotel to the Center and a shuttle bus regularly runs between it and the hotel). The Penta has been recently renovated at a cost of $20 million; additions include a modern business conference center, secretarial and support services for visiting businesspeople and/or conventioneers, and a full health club. *Tip for budget-conscious visitors:* A few very small (but still attractive and comfortable) single rooms are available at the Penta for less than half the regular room rate.

New York Penta Hotel, Seventh Ave & 33rd St, New York, NY 10001, 212/736-5000.

Best Beds for the Beatles
Warwick Hotel

Back in the 1960s during one of the Beatles famous American tours, the Fab Four stayed at (and perpetrated some of their trademark zany antics at) this European-style hotel. (Linen used by the Liverpool lads during their stay was cut up and sold in tiny swatches to fans.) Built in 1927 by William Randolph Hearst, this well-maintained, 500-room hotel has a handy midtown Manhattan location and a rich club-like lobby. Once famous for its Raleigh piano bar, this flagship hotel of the Warwick chain still attracts actors and scribes to its paneled bar and lounge. Refurbished guest rooms are large, with high ceilings, large closets, thick carpeting, mini-bars, and an arresting English-style decor. Services include an on-premises barbershop and beauty salon, plus interpreting and babysitting. The imposing Sir Walter Raleigh restaurant, serving continental cuisine, is a popular business-lunch venue.

Warwick Hotel, 65 W 54th St, New York, NY 10019, 212/247-2700, 800/522-5634.

Best Hotel to the Manor Borne
Westbury Hotel

British travelers feel at home in this charming, European-style Trustehouse Forte hotel located in a chic East Side residential and shopping area. Built in 1926 by Max J. Kramer, an American polo player, the hotel has undergone a $12-million renovation. Its ambience is reminiscent of an English country manor, its 231 guest rooms and suites decorated in warm tones of tan, red, and forest green, providing a rich backdrop for gleaming mahogany furniture, striking Oriental carpets, and classic prints. Amenities include writing desks, safes, mini-bars, and two-line telephones adaptable for PCs and fax. Bathrooms are equipped with hair dryers, scales, telephones, makeup mirrors, terry cloth bathrobes, and imported toiletries. Suite have VCRs, with a tape library available for guest use. The English clublike atmosphere continues in the Polo restaurant, done in mahogany and leather and decorated with equestrian prints and a portrait of Prince Charles. The Polo offers excellent (but pricey) French-accented contemporary American cuisine with good value on prix-fixe luncheons, brunches, and dinners. There is piano music Tuesday through Saturday.

Westbury Hotel, 15 E 69th St, New York, NY 10021, 212/535-2000, 800/321-1569.

Right Rooms for Writers

The Algonquin Hotel

A writer friend who hails from West Virginia visited New York frequently and loved to stay at the Algonquin. His favorite divertissements were breakfast of creamed finnan haddie and spending the cocktail hour surrounded by some of New York's literary elite (and, would he admit it, a goodly number of wannabes) in the storied lobby bar (see separate listing). He did admit, though, that the rooms were on the small side and way past their prime and that the single elevator provided painfully slow access. My friend doesn't travel to New York any more. If he did, he might enjoy the Algonquin even more, now that this 160-room Gothic landmark hotel, founded in 1902, has been refurbished and restored. For guests and non-guests alike, it remains a better spot for drinking than for eating—and is popular for a pre-theater cocktail and perhaps a light repast. For the most part, adequate but undistinguished fare is served in the Rose Room (home of the famous round table of Dorothy Parker and fellow critics and wits) and in the dark-paneled Oak Room. The latter is well worth a visit for its first-class cabaret entertainment, which features top vocalists. The Algonquin probably remains a hotel to stay at because of its nostalgia and mystique rather than its comfort quotient.

The Algonquin Hotel, 59 W 44th St, New York, NY 10036, 212/840-6800.

Best Touch of Paris in NYC

The Plaza Athénée

As French as a croissant, this hotel might stand out as a premier and elegant representation of French stateliness even in *France*. In New York, it provides classy and comfortable lodgings (although some complain that it is haughtily formal) that are a cut above—and a world away—from most hostelries in town. The lobby offers a Versailles-like confluence of marble and glass, tapestries and antiques, accented by huge plants and floral arrangements. The staff is efficient and responsive—there are three concierges to attend to various needs and it is claimed that most of the staff members are bi- or trilingual (or beyond), to best serve the many European guests who are regulars. This relatively new hotel (housed in what was the 1920s Hotel Alrae) offers just 160 rooms and suites on 17 pleasant floors—but the accommodations are very attractive and comfortable, albeit with rooms that are on the small side. The dining room, Le Régence, is known for its authentic and fine—if pricey—French cuisine.

The Plaza Athénée, 37 E 64th St, New York, NY 10021, 212/734-9100.

Most European of New York Hotels
The Mayfair Regent

This stately hotel has been called "European" for its quiet efficiency, discretion, and overall atmosphere of understated elegance. Rather than the leather-jacket-and-jeans rock performers or flashy movie stars that frequent other top-notch New York hotels, at the Mayfair Regent you are more likely to catch glimpses of dukes, duchesses, diplomats, and dowagers (which is not to say that celebrities don't stay here—they do, but usually not ostentatiously). Its relatively small size—around 250 rooms and suites—allows management and staff to maintain (seemingly effortlessly) the Mayfair Regent's high standard of quality. This level of excellence is continuously and assiduously maintained through an ongoing, multi-million-dollar refurbishing plan, designed to keep accommodations at their peak. Rooms are tastefully decorated in antiques and pastel colors; many rooms have fireplaces and Jacuzzis. The attractive sunken lounge just off the lobby is a great spot for breakfast, tea, or cocktails; for fine dining guests need not look farther than—but should definitely reserve well ahead for—the famed Le Cirque, one of the city's top restaurants, which is located in the hotel (see separate listing). For an uncommon, if costly, treat, guests may order sumptuous room service from Le Cirque during hours when the restaurant is open.

The Mayfair Regent, 610 Park Ave, New York, NY 10021, 212/288-0800.

Best Touch of Europe in Brooklyn
Bed & Breakfast on the Park

One expects to find bed-and-breakfast inns in the Hudson Valley and along the Jersey shore. But in Brooklyn? In reality, this B&B nestled among a row of brownstones in leafy Park Slope, is more European. Proprietor Liana Paolella has restored this four-story brick-limestone and patterned it after the best B&Bs she encountered growing up in France and Switzerland. A one-time antique-store owner, Paolella has furnished her five-guest-room Victorian inn with collections of antique furnishings, lace, china, and glassware collected on her travels. Amid period secretaries, vintage lamps, and antique lace-canopied beds are original classical and contemporary oil paintings, part of her family's extensive art collection. Breakfast, too, is a European delight, with fresh-baked bread, German pancakes, quiche Lorraine, bacon, ham, and homemade preserves. Adding to the grand style of this inn—which attracts business and professional travelers from overseas— are Victorian antiques, Oriental carpets, rococo armoires, and wood-burning fireplaces. Noted as one of the borough's top 10 Victorian landmark buildings, it features handsome stained glass, intricate oak moldings, African mahogany, and bird's-eye maple.

Bed & Breakfast on the Park, 112 Prospect Park W, Park Slope, Brooklyn, NY 11215, 718/499-6115.

Best Little-Known Hotel (Where You Don't Have to Be Female to Stay Anymore)

Barbizon Hotel

This little gem originally gained fame as the exclusive Barbizon Hotel for Women, a short- and long-term residence at which parents could entrust their daughters to New York. In that incarnation, it hosted up-and-coming women such as Grace Kelly, Liza Minelli, and Candice Bergen. Since 1981, when it became the full-service hotel it is today, it has not been necessary to be a member of the fairer sex to stay here, but, perhaps nostalgically, women seem to still make up a discernable majority of the Barbizon's guests. Rooms are small, but pleasantly decorated and homey (without seeming "lived in"); there are more spacious accommodations in a dozen tower apartments, roomy suites with large windows and terraces offering gorgeous city vistas. Recent renovation has spruced up this beckoning spot; plans are afoot for further changes, including, perhaps, conversion of the hotel by its owners (the cutting-edge types who radically remade Morgans—see separate listing) into a full-time spa. *Art trivia:* The

Barbizon has been a famous vantage point for painters and photographers, most notably Samuel
Gottscho (who photographed the city's skyline from
the roof) and Georgia O'Keeffe (who did some of her
Spartan city studies from rooms here).

Barbizon Hotel, 140 E 63rd St, New York, NY 10021,
212/838-5700.

Best Hotel for Non-Smokers

Omni Berkshire Place

If burning butts burn you up, this may be a perfect
lodging spot. This hotel dates from the 1920s, which
was somewhat of a "Golden Age" for solid, medium-
sized hotels in the city; many remain as converted
apartment buildings along the edges of Central Park
or on the posher avenues. It was renovated to the
tune of $10 million a decade or so ago. Part of this
renewal was the establishment of five floors of
rooms—a large and commendable amount—that are
set aside for non-smoking guests (perhaps the largest concentration of such rooms in the city). The
rooms here are appointed in a comfortable and not
disconcerting mèlange of modern (mini-bars, stereo
units) and classic (antique furnishings). The Berkshire has a concierge level for the pampered business or vacation traveler, and, in general, an
excellent and attentive staff. Other amenities include
health club privileges and complimentary coffee and
newspaper each morning. Located smack in the heart
of Midtown, this is a pleasant and affordable find—
all the more so for non-smokers.

Omni Berkshire Place, 21 E 52nd St, New York, NY
10022, 212/753-5800.

Best Lodgings in Town Houses

Box Tree

For jaded travelers who have experienced
Manhattan's top hotels and are ready for something
new—or for the first-time visitor who enjoys something different—this unique hotel represents a nice,
small, change-of-pace lodging, without giving up
elegance or comfort. Housed in two side-by-side town
houses, the very European-seeming Box Tree offers
only 12 small but comfortable and lavishly decorated
suites (including two penthouses—one on top of each
unit) in a good Midtown East location. ("Small" is
relative here—these interesting L-shaped rooms are

small as suites go, but are large and comfortable compared to most standard hotel rooms.) Decor is eclectic—some rooms are furnished in an Oriental manner, others bear French or Egyptian touches. Yet, what could be a disconcerting hodgepodge, works charmingly, making the Box Tree a bona fide underdiscovered (if not outright "undiscovered") treasure. The homey, private-inn-type rooms do not come cheaply—but the mid- to upper-level rates become a delightful bargain when you factor in the $100 credit at the Box Tree restaurant (which serves well-regarded French cuisine) included with every room. This is definitely a one-of-a-kind New York find.

Box Tree, 250-252 E 49th St, New York, NY 10017, 212/758-8320.

Best Hotel That Asks What It Can Do for You

Hotel Carlyle

JFK stayed here—as have many other celebrities and dignitaries. But perhaps the style and grace of this exquisite hotel and its classy clientele is best exemplified by its most famous public face—that of Bobby Short, the pianist-singer who regularly holds court in the hotel's Café Carlyle (see separate listing). His silken renditions of Cole Porter and George Gershwin favorites conjure an image of a celluloid black-and-white New York, with streets full of sophisticated ladies and their top-hatted gents—who, of course, would stay at the Carlyle when in town. This hostelry attracts plenty of old-money Americans and Europeans, as well as the cream of the corporate crop, relaxing between meetings and deals. About half of the rooms, suites, and apartments in the hotel are for nightly stays (a large percentage of these have kitchens, terraces, and other pleasantly unexpected features); the rest are long-term residences. While this is a discreet, elegant hotel, it is part of the modern world—and this juxtapositioning is illustrated by the fact that not only are the rooms furnished with French and English antiques, but that they also have convenient fax machines and VCRs. Rumor has it that when President Kennedy stayed at the Carlyle, he dallied discreetly (although perhaps not *that* discreetly, since there are rumors) with a certain blond bombshell.

Hotel Carlyle, 35 E 76th St, New York, NY 10021, 212/744-1600.

Best Former Host to Mark Twain, Dylan Thomas, and Sid Vicious (Among Many Others of Note)

Chelsea Hotel

In the eyes of the world, this offbeat hostelry may well be New York's second- or third-most-famous hotel, after only the Plaza and the Waldorf-Astoria (see separate listings). But while those other two hotels are as equally well-known for their style and comfort as for the continuing array of glittering celebrity guests who stay there, the Chelsea is better known for its casual world-weariness and the list of famous people (some more gritty than glittering) who *have* stayed there in the past. And what a list of artists—of varying stripes and types—it is: Mark Twain, Arthur Miller, Dylan Thomas (who staggered here after his final bout of overimbibing), O. Henry, and Thomas Wolfe; lower down on the evolutionary scale of "artists" is punk rocker Sid Vicious, who may or may not have killed his girlfriend in their room at the Chelsea (the matter was never settled before Vicious himself shuffled off this mortal coil). Today, the Chelsea's clientele are still artsy-looking—though, to be sure, there are probably as many studied and affected poseurs in the crowd as there are "real" writers, painters, and actors. The decor is simple, but rooms are spacious and comfortable and have been spruced up with new furnishings and carpets. Many feature full kitchens and working fireplaces. An additional plus are the Chelsea's thick, soundproof walls—all the more appreciated should some noisy spiritual heir of Vicious occupy the next room down the hall.

Chelsea Hotel, 222 W 23rd St, New York, NY 10011, 212/243-3700.

Best Quiet Hotel Near Grand Central

Doral Tuscany Hotel

Although it is convenient to the hustle-bustle of Grand Central station, this European-style hotel might as well be worlds away. Located on a quiet Midtown tree-lined backwater in the classy Murray Hill neighborhood, the Tuscany is popular with many travelers who enjoy its handy locale while preferring the civilized charms of a smaller hotel. Amenities include in-room refrigerators, exercise bicycles, recliner chairs, butler's pantries, original art, free shoe shines, and a health club with racquetball courts. As a spot for quiet conversation in a lavish setting, the Time & Again Restaurant, with rich paneling and comfortable upholstered chairs, is a destination restaurant in and of itself with French-accented American cuisine (well-prepared veal chops or beef tenderloin are good choices, along with excellent soups and seafood salads). With close to 150 rooms, the Tuscany is smaller than sister Doral Court Hotel located next door (see separate listing) but is a little more sophisticated and a little more pricey.

Doral Tuscany Hotel, 120 E 39th St, New York, NY 10016, 212/686-1600, 800/847-4078.

Best Quiet Hotel's Sister

Doral Court Hotel

In an area of shady trees, one-of-a-kind shops, and turn-of-the-century mansions, this smart but rather old-fashioned hotel offers quiet, sunny guest accommodations. Located in the fashionable Murray Hill district, it is just three blocks from Grand Central station. The hotel's 248 guest rooms are over sized and include private-entry foyers, walk-in closets, separate dressing alcoves, and refrigerators. Amenities include VCRs, premium movies, writing desks, bathrobes, and the availablity of exercycles. All 50 suites have living rooms with sleep-sofas, club chairs, dining areas, and fully equipped kitchens. Many have outdoor balconies. The lobby, with paneling, checkered floor, and simple white ceiling, is clublike. The delightful Courtyard Café & Bar (see separate listing) offers seating indoors and in a secluded garden. It is a romantic spot, open for breakfast, lunch, dinner, cocktails, and Sunday brunch. Next door is the sister Doral Tuscany Hotel (see separate listing).

Doral Court Hotel, 130 E 39th St, New York, NY 10016, 212/685-1100, 800/624-0607.

Best Swiss High-Tech Hotel

The Drake Swissôtel

There is the traditional bowl of Swiss chocolates at the reception desk and a staff that seems uncommonly warm and friendly in such a large—552 rooms and suites—hotel. But this old, 21-story hotel, dating back to 1926, also is the ultimate in high tech. A $52-million dollar renovation has transformed the hotel into a sleek, elegant hostelry in the manner of the handsome new generation of European hotels. Yet, somehow it retains its earlier style—in, for example, its remade 1930s-era bar. The new lobby epitomizes the concept of blending contemporary and classic styling. It combines wood paneling, Oriental carpets, crystal art deco wall sconces, and a centerpiece chandelier with brass and contemporary crystals. State-of-the-art, high-speed elevators whisk guests 26 stories in 22 seconds. All guest rooms have been refurbished and feature marble bathrooms, individual safes, three telephones with call waiting, and jacks for fax machines and computers. The newly reopened Café Suisse has European bistro-style decor accented by ink drawings of Swiss village scenes, pewter steins laden with floral arrangements, and a marble-and-brass pastry cart. A range of business services are available, along with complimentary morning transportation to Wall Street.

The Drake Swissôtel, 440 Park Ave, New York, NY 10022, 212/421-0900.

Best Luxury Hotel with a Dance Named for It

Essex House Nikko Hotel New York

Since its debut in 1931, when it was designed to be New York's tallest and largest hotel, the Essex has gone through many changes and seen many celebrity guests. It has hosted presidents and entertainers, such as opera star Lily Pons, who kept a pet jaguar in her rooms; and Sammy Kaye, who broadcast from the hotel during the big-band era and who added a new song, "Essex Hop," to his repertoire. The most recent change culminated with the reopening of the hotel in September 1991 following a $75-million renovation. In restoring the hotel to its art deco splendor, the Nikko people reduced the number of accommodations to 516 rooms and 77 suites to allow for larger quarters. Rooms feature Louis XVI- or Chippendale-style furnishings and such modern amenities as VCR players, outlets for personal fax machines and computers, and dual-line phones on desks, at bedsides, and in bathrooms. This elegant hotel with its nonpareil views of the celebrated urban greenery of Central Park across the street, offers top-flight restaurants, a state-of-the-art business center (with fully equipped private offices available for rent), and The Spa, a training floor filled with exercise equipment, steam rooms, sauna, and private treatment rooms for massages.

Essex House Nikko Hotel New York, 160 Central Park South, New York, NY 10019, 212/247-0300.

Best Luxury Hotel Where Escoffier Cooked

The Pierre

August Escoffier, the "father of French chefs," attended the 1930 gala opening of the glittering hotel that quickly became the toast of high society. Later, he served as guest chef. Although the hotel suffered Depression woes that led to bankruptcy, and although some of its rooms were sold off as cooperatives, it survives as a shining example of high style and stunning Georgian architecture that incorporates a gleaming copper tower. Now managed by the Four Seasons group, the landmark hotel offers a high ratio of suites—46 of 205 guest accommodations. Included are 15 one- and two-bedroom Grand Suites that formerly were private apartments and feature such distinctive touches as Frette linens and Lancôme toiletries as well as accommodating guest preferences for magazines, flowers, and other amenities. All of the guest rooms are highly individualistic with elegant furnishings that run to Chippendale, Chinoiserie, and fabrics of muted tones. The Café Pierre, with distinctive trompe l'oeil walls and ceiling murals, provides innovative touches to classical French cuisine. The hotel overlooks Central Park and is close to the famous stores of Fifth Avenue and the galleries and boutiques of Madison Avenue.

The Pierre, Fifth Ave at 61st St, New York, NY 10021, 212/838-8000.

Best Luxury Hotel Where Scott and Zelda Stayed

The Lowell

This 1928 landmark hotel once was home to F. Scott and Zelda Fitzgerald, Dorothy Parker, Nöel Coward, and other literary elite, American and British. It remains popular with visiting Brits, perhaps because it is small, quiet, and private. It has only 62 guest rooms (including 48 suites) and is located on a tranquil tree-lined street. Suites are decorated with French tapestries, Oriental period pieces, 18th- and 19th-century prints, wood-burning fireplaces with elegantly restored mantlepieces, large writing desks, marble bathrooms with brass fixtures, hair dryers, and make-up mirrors, and fully equipped kitchens with well-stocked mini-bars. Amenities include plush bathrobes, down comforters, feather pillows, complimentary shoe shines, and the delivery of newspapers of choice. Business-related extras include multi-line telephones, fax machines, VCRs, and round-the-clock multi-lingual concierge service. Afternoon tea is served in the English-styled Pembroke Room. This intimate, European-style hotel, regarded by many of its guests as a *pied-à-terre*, is the sole NYC member of the prestigious Relais & Chateaux group. One critic declared: "The Lowell would scream class, if class did that sort of thing!"

The Lowell, 28 E 63rd St, New York, NY 10021, 212/838-1400.

Best Luxury Hotel for Gallery-Goers

The Mark

Located in the heart of Manhattan's fashionable shopping and gallery district, a short walk from Museum Mile, this glitteringly remade hotel is perfect for visitors to the Guggenheim, Whitney, and Metropolitan Museum of Art. In 1989, the East Side hotel (formerly the Madison Avenue) underwent a $35 million renovation and became the U.S. flagship of the Rafael Group. It has a handsome art deco facade and landmark copper tower. In front are four brass flagpoles that are lit at night; lacy ginkgo trees and flower boxes flank the entrance. Its 120 rooms and 60 suites are furnished with overstuffed chairs, upholstered sofas, and tasteful prints, and equipped with videocassette players (with a rental library available), double-line telephones, pantries with refrigerator, Italian-made Frette sheets and bedside mats, and feather pillows. Marble bathrooms feature twin vanities, soak tubs, separate glass shower stalls, heated towel bars, hair dryers, decanters of bath crystals, and Molten Brown of London toiletries. Guests are provided with plush terry robes and umbrellas. Afternoon tea is extremely popular (see separate listing), as are after-theater drinks in the intimate bar. Mark's restaurant (see separate listing) is gaining a reputation as a dining destination.

The Mark, 25 E 77th St, New York, NY 10021, 212/744-4300.

Best Hotel That Includes Admittance to a Private Park

Gramercy Park Hotel

This is a pleasant, comfortable, and reasonably priced hotel, that happens to have a park as a perk! Guests have key privileges at the gated-in Gramercy Park across the street (see separate listing), the city's last private park. Admittance is limited to residents on the streets surrounding the park and guests of this hotel. The few-block area around the park has been designated the Gramercy Park Historic District, and is a nice area for walks and sightseeing. By word-of-mouth (and not least because of its rates), this hotel attracts a large contingent of English and other European visitors, giving the Gramercy Park an almost continental feel. The hotel's best rooms face the park. Because recent (and ongoing) renovating has left some rooms more desirable than others, prospective guests may wish to ask to see a few available rooms before making their choice. *An etymological note:* The unusual name of the park and the hotel comes from an anglicization of *crommessie*, a word formed by combining two Dutch words which mean "crooked knife" and were used to describe a stream that once flowed here.

Gramercy Park Hotel, 2 Lexington Ave, New York, NY 10010, 212/475-4320.

Hotel with the Hugest Lobby (and Tallest Guests)

Grand Hyatt

Knowing that Hyatt hotels seem to have a penchant for excessive, glittery chrome-and-glass-and-whatever-else-is-eye-catching lobbies, it should come as no surprise that New York's largest Hyatt should sport such an extravaganza. Wandering its cavernous—yet comfortable—expanse, you'll find a roaring waterfall, a virtual jungle of trees and flowers, and, maybe, Michael Jordan or Karl Malone waiting for a team bus to the stadium or the airport (the Grand Hyatt is a favorite New York spot for visiting sports teams). Rooms are large and comfortably decorated and the service is a cut above what you might expect from a hotel of this size (more than 1,400 rooms in a 30-story structure). It also has a Hyatt-signature club level, with sparkling service and various complimentary amenities; and a gorgeously huge presidential suite with four separate bedrooms. In general, this agreeable, if sometimes overwhelming spot, is popular with business travelers and tourists alike. *Trivia note:* This was originally the Commodore Hotel, and was renovated beyond recognition in the late 1970s (including a gutting that made possible the trademark lobby).

Grand Hyatt, Park Ave at Grand Central, New York, NY 10017, 212/883-1234.

Newest Hotel-Within-a-Hotel

Sheraton New York Hotel & Towers

Although not "new" in the strictest sense, a $143-million renovation has remade this Sheraton flagship property virtually beyond recognition. Refurbished in time to serve as headquarters for the 1992 Democratic National Convention, this massive Midtown hotel offers 1,750 rooms, including 213 Towers rooms and 25 hospitality and VIP suites with parlors. The Towers has been expanded from five to seven floors and now occupies the 44th through 50th floors, offering dramatic views of the Manhattan skyline. Towers' guests enjoy such services and amenities as buffet breakfast, a bar, cocktail hour, pantry, butler and concierge service, business library, and a private boardroom. The Penthouse Suite is a bi-level duplex with upper and lower sitting rooms, wet bar, guest bath, study, two to four bedrooms, and a baby grand piano. Streeter's New York Café, a large, glass-enclosed restaurant, offers views of Seventh Avenue. The Lobby Court serves cocktails, hors d'oeuvres, and afternoon tea, and offers nightly piano entertainment.

Sheraton New York Hotel & Towers, Seventh Ave & 53rd St, New York, NY 10019, 212/581-1000, 800/223-6550.

Best Hotel Around a Mansion

The Helmsley Palace

In midtown Manhattan, amid the gilded, ostentatious trappings of this Helmsley extravaganza of a hotel, is an historic piece of Italian Renaissance architecture. When the soaring glass tower of this 900-plus-room hotel was built, it was designed to incorporate the Villard mansion, a brownstone built in 1882 and modeled after the Palazzo della Cancelleria in Rome. Full of stained glass and art treasures by LaFarge, Tiffany, and Saint-Gaudens, this old-world mansion has been converted into magnificent meeting rooms. They contain marble fireplaces, coffered ceilings, frescoes, mosaics, and intricately carved moldings. Designed by the celebrated firm of McKim, Mead & White, these public spaces, lavish with bronze, crystal, tapestries, murals, painted ceilings, and plush carpeting, are worth a peek, even if you're not staying at the hotel. If you are a guest, expect lavish rooms and suites (and prices to match) with period-style furnishings, marble-topped furniture, and opulent bathrooms.

The hotel's ultimate when-cost-is-no-object accommodations are tri-level suites with their own elevators and grand terraces overlooking Manhattan. High tea in the Gold Room, with Fortnum & Mason teas, excellent sandwiches and cakes, and gentile background music provided from a minstrel's balcony, is an English-style treat worth attending.

The Helmsley Palace, 455 Madison Ave, New York, NY 10022, 212/888-7000.

Best Hotel for Workouts

Hotel Inter-Continental New York

When the Inter-Continental folks spent $32 million restoring the landmark Barclay Hotel, built in 1925, they installed a 2,500-square-foot state-of-the-art health spa. Complimentary to guests, it provides circuit training, Lifecycles, treadmills, Stairmasters, saunas, and a steam room. There are the services of a masseuse or masseur, grooming areas, and earphone outlets to allow exercisers to plug into any of three central video monitors equipped with cable and VCR. Joggers may borrow portable tape players with earphones for use inside or outside the hotel, and select cassette tapes from the club's library. The official Roadrunners Club of New York Central Park jogging map is available for purchase. The Midtown hotel has 691 rooms (including 82 suites) with amenities and services that include Caswell-Massey toiletries, weekday delivery of *The New York Times*, complimentary HBO movies, and direct-dial telephone with personal message retrieval. Dining is in the club-like Barclay Restaurant or in the informal Terrace, overlooking the main lobby. There is live piano music in the Bar One Eleven cocktail lounge. The striking lobby features an authentic Federal-style Tiffany skylight and an enormous latticed brass bird cage that has become a signature of the hotel since its installation in 1945.

Hotel Inter-Continental New York, 111 E 48th St, New York, NY 10017, 212/755-5900.

Best Hotel Rooms Where You Sleep on the Floor

Kitano

You don't need to visit Tokyo to experience the serenity of a well-run Japanese hotel—but you *do* have to book well ahead at this hotel to get a real taste of the Orient. Located in the quiet Murray Hill neighborhood, the Kitano is a Japanese-owned and -managed hotel with 95 rooms; however, most are Western-style rooms, with mere touches of the Far East (in the form of artwork, some pieces of furniture, and multilingual menus and instructions). For a real change of pace—and a taste of a different culture—guests can book one of the hotel's popular Japanese-style suites. These peaceful and pleasant rooms are decorated with traditional rice-paper screens, tatami sitting mats, and roomy Japanese-style bathtubs (which are more akin to California hot tubs than to the usual hotel tubs). To complete the Japanese experience, guests can dine at the hotel's well-regarded restaurant, Hakubei, which serves sushi and other Japanese specialties (the Japanese-style breakfast of salmon, cold noodles, rice, and soup is unique to the city). As you might expect, the Kitano is very popular with visiting businesspeople and vacationers from Japan. Crowds of Japanese visitors in the lobby may make you feel as if you are in Tokyo after all.

Kitano, 66 Park Ave, New York, NY 10016, 212/685-0022.

Best Bet to Find the Convention Crowd

Marriott Marquis

When out-of-town hardware salespeople or electronic retailers amassing at the Javits Convention Center say "I'll see you back at the hotel," chances are they are referring to this large and popular hotel. The Marquis is spread out over 50 floors, with nearly 1,900 rooms, and packs in crowds of visiting conventioneers, businesspeople, and tourists. Built in 1985, it looms over the Theater District-Times Square area as a highly visible sign of the area's ongoing renewal. Above a lobby that begins on the eighth floor, the Marquis has a huge, 47-story atrium (one of the tallest in the world) of glittering steel and glass, filled with lush greenery. (Below the lobby are levels of meeting rooms, halls, and the Marriott Marquis theater, the most recent addition to Broadway and the city's only theater located in a hotel.) Rooms are among the largest in the city, and are furnished comfortably, if not lavishly. The Marquis also offers a health club with all the usual facilities—weight machines, sauna, and Jacuzzi—plus available personal trainers to help you set a pace to feel that burn. The View, the hotel's rotating restaurant and lounge, may seem like a hokey spot, but, since this is the only revolving restaurant in Manhattan, it is worth a visit, if only for drinks at the adjacent bar and a few panoramic looks at the city.

Marriott Marquis, 1535 Broadway, New York, NY 10036, 212/398-1900.

Favorite Hotel for Lincoln Center Artists

The Mayflower Hotel

With Lincoln Center and the Met just a couple of minutes walk from this Upper West Side hotel, and with Carnegie Hall also within strolling distance, it is not surprising that it is the choice of many concert artists. Movie actors also have taken up residence here—the likes of Robert DeNiro, Joe Pesci, and Mickey Roarke. Located across the street from Central Park, the hotel has 577 rooms, most with serving pantry and refrigerator. Many of its 200 suites have views of the park and of the New York skyline rising above the park greenery; many penthouse suites have terraces overlooking the park. Rooms are spacious, with high ceilings, thick carpeting and heavy drapes in jade green, and reproductions of American cherrywood furniture. Amenities include voice mail, cable TV, a video-rental library, and complimentary early-morning tea, coffee, and newspapers in the lobby. A well-equipped exercise room has a juice bar, large-screen TV, and lounge area with leather furniture. In addition to attracting entertainment-industry notables, the hotel itself has become something of a celebrity, providing the location for such movies as *Raging Bull*, *Superman II*, and *The Pope of Greenwich Village*, and for TV shows "Equalizer" and "Miami Vice."

The Mayflower Hotel, 15 Central Park W, New York, NY 10023, 212/265-0060.

Best Avant-Garde Hotel for Show-Biz Folks

Morgans

While a hip and postmodern look, style, and attitude is something you might expect at a new and/or exclusive dance club or bar, these elements also characterize this hotel in the Murray Hill neighborhood (just south of Midtown). Where else but at a hotel designed by the founders of the classic 1970s disco Studio 54 would you expect to find high-tech stereo systems and stainless-steel bathroom sinks in each room, celebrities casually wandering the halls, and a staff that prides itself on fulfilling nearly every whim of its guests ("You want six Nathan's with kraut, a magnum of Mumm's, and videocassettes of the three most recent Scorsese movies? No problem!"). This was formerly the Executive Hotel, and, way back when it opened in the 1920s, the Duane. Today, it offers just more than 150 small, but stunningly decorated (most often in shades of black and grey) rooms—which are usually booked solid by the likes of Cher, Oprah Winfrey, Billy Joel, Julia Roberts, and other music, movie, and television celebrities. (You're not likely to find many buttoned-down business types—business guests are more likely to be the latest mid-twenties whiz kids running their own computer software biz or independent movie production company.) All rooms come equipped with VCRs (there is a vast library of films available), multiple phone lines, and well-stocked mini-bars. Make sure you know the address when looking for Morgans; its owners consider the place so "cool" that they have never bothered with a sign or awning out front to direct guests to the hotel's understated front door. Not for everyone, but definitely a New York original.

Morgans, 237 Madison Ave, New York, NY 10016, 212/686-0300.

Best Hotel Art Collection

New York Hilton Hotel

While a multi-million-dollar art collection might be commonplace at a corporate headquarters or private gallery, you would probably not expect to find it at a bustling mega-room hotel. However, at the New York Hilton, you can roam the halls taking in sights that, while less lofty than those found at the Guggenheim, are definitely a considerable cut above the basic sea- and landscapes that adorn the walls of many hotels. The Hilton has more than 2,100 rooms—but still manages to establish its own personality beyond that usually found in such sprawlingly massive hotels. Its rooms are large and softly decorated and furnished, creating a soothing atmosphere; two floors are set aside for non-smoking guests (these are popular—request well in advance to assure choice of rooms on one of these floors). As you would expect in a property of this size, the Hilton offers a city-unto-itself array of bars, shops, restaurants, and other amenities; at times, this can seem like a *world* unto itself, especially when you consider that the hotel boasts that, among various staff members, no less than *30* different languages are spoken. Business travelers can avail themselves of the special services of a *Wall Street Journal*-sponsored office center, with secretarial service, business equipment (computers, fax machines, photocopiers, etc.), and the latest stock quotes and business news; additionally, a multi-media teleconferencing center can link the hotel with other sites across the country or around the world for two-way video meetings. For the top experience this hotel has to offer, book a huge room or suite in the Executive Towers, where amenities include around-the-clock concierge service, complimentary breakfast and evening hors d'oeurves, and a private lounge—perfect for conducting business during the week or planning sightseeing outings on weekends.

New York Hilton Hotel, 1335 Sixth Ave, New York, NY 10019, 212/586-7000.

Hotel with Best Views of Central Park

Helmsley Park Lane

When an important criterion in making a lodging choice is the view—particularly a view of the greens or golds of Central Park (or even its starkly beautiful wintertime vistas)—then this hotel of fairly recent vintage may be your best bet. Opened in 1971, it reaches 46 stories over the south end of Central Park and offers some truly stunning views. The lobby has a profusion of glass, marble, and plants; its 600 rooms and 30 suites are comfortably sized and elegantly furnished (they have recently undergone complete remodeling). Upper-level suites provide some of the best views of Central Park to be found in any city hotel—making the Park Lane a longtime favorite for honeymooners and others who cherish stunning Manhattan views. Alas, not all rooms face the park—and the price differential shows it. Be sure to ask for a north-facing room, as high up as possible—the effort and the splurge are worth it. The service here is sharp (from a top-notch and very attentive multi-lingual staff)—perhaps because this Helmsley property is the one that Leona and Harry Helmsley favored for city stays before she ran afoul of the feds.

Helmsley Park Lane, 36 Central Park S, New York, NY 10019, 212/371-4000.

Best French High-Tech Hotel

Le Parker Meridien Hotel

About 10 percent of the guests who stay at this French-managed luxury hotel are from France, and its restaurants serve French-accented food and drink. It also is American high tech, with fax machines, rentable portable telephones, videocassette players in 88 of its rooms (a special convenience for the numerous entertainment-industry guests who patronize the hotel), and voice mail, which allows guests to leave outgoing messages and receive recorded incoming messages from remote locations. A dual-line telephone service provides immediate access to a Japanese interpreter. Many of the rooms of the 700-room, 42-story hotel overlook Central Park (available by request), and it is close to Broadway theaters, museums, and Fifth Avenue shopping. Guest room furnishings include dressing areas, desks, coffee tables, overstuffed couches and armchairs, and limited edition French lithographs. Airing continuously is an in-room video aerobic exercise program. Fitness buffs enjoy the complimentary membership in Club La Raquette athletic club with squash and racquetball courts, a wide range of exercise equipment, Jacuzzi, sauna, and exercise classes. There are indoor and outdoor sun decks, an outdoor jogging track, and a rooftop heated swimming pool enclosed by a vaulted skylight.

Le Parker Meridien Hotel, 118 W 57th St, New York, NY 212/245-5000.

Best Belle Époque Hotel

The Peninsula

High-tech know-how and painstaking renovation have transformed the old Gotham Hotel into a grand showcase—albeit an extremely user-friendly one. Featuring a sweeping staircase of imported Italian marble, a European crystal chandelier, and art nouveau artworks and furnishings, The Peninsula, acquired in 1988 by the Hong Kong-based group, evokes the grandeur and elegance of the Belle Époque period. Dominating the lobby is a magnificent art nouveau armoire featured at the 1904 Exposition des Beaux Arts in Paris. Throughout the lobby, reception area, and waiting salons are original pieces by art nouveau master Louis Majorelle, including sofa, Bergere arm chairs, and gallery tables. The 250 luxurious guest accommodations (including 30 suites and a presidential suite) feature custom-designed furnishings, including cast bronze Belle Époque messagere lamps and hardwood headboards that replicate French art nouveau design. Amenities include oversize marble bathrooms furnished with robes and slippers. Bedside consoles use infrared technology for remote control of lighting, room temperature, and TV, and feature a two-line telephone and a data port for computer or fax hookup. The hotel offers a luxurious health spa, the romantic Adrienne restaurant, and spectacular views from the Pen-Top Bar and Terrace (see separate listings).

The Peninsula, 700 Fifth Ave, New York, NY 10019, 212/247-2200, 800/262-9467.

Best Art Deco Masterpiece

The Waldorf-Astoria

It took five years and $150 million, but this hotel, built in 1931 (to replace a hotel built in 1893 at the site where the Empire State Building now stands) has been restored to its art deco splendor. This landmark hotel, which has hosted every president since Herbert Hoover, has 1,410 guest rooms and suites, all decorated, no two alike, with original art deco features. Restoration uncovered many treasures hidden by the streamlining trend of the 1950s and 1960s. Hidden beneath a carpet in the Park Avenue lobby was a 148,000-piece mosaic depicting the Wheel of Life by the French artist, Louis Rigal. Heavy draperies concealed 13 allegorical oil murals by the same artist. Even if you're not attending a banquet, well worth a peek is the restored four-story, two-tiered Grand Ballroom. A textbook of art deco design, it resembles an Old World opera house. Take a look, too, at the nightclub on the 18th floor, where broadcasts once came "direct from the Starlight Roof." This legendary home of the big bands had a retractable roof. Restoration has added recessed lighting to create the illusion of a starlit sky. Permanent residents of the Waldorf Towers, the luxurious "hotel within a hotel" that occupies the 28th through 42nd floors, have included President Herbert Hoover (after leaving office), Cole Porter (whose suite was taken over by the Sinatras), and General Douglas MacArthur (whose widow still lives there).

The Waldorf-Astoria, 301 Park Ave, New York, NY 10022, 212/355-3000.

Best Hotel That Even Detractors of "The Donald" Have to Admire

The Plaza Hotel

In 1988, when Donald Trump was still financially riding high (but was already starting to attract such denigrating epithets as *Spy* magazine's oft-quoted "short-fingered vulgarian"), he bought this most famous of New York hotels and put his wife, Ivana, in charge of running it. At the time, the much-loved Plaza was far from decline, but had definitely lost some of its legendary luster. Yet, most spectators cringed at the thought of the brash developer pouring money into the old place without regard for taste or history. Amazingly, their fears proved pointless, for the now-separated Trumps turned out to be the best thing that happened to the Plaza in years. Mrs.

Trump oversaw a multi-million-dollar refurbishing of the hotel, from the cobblestones outside the Plaza's front door to the fixtures in bathrooms. The result is a return to elegance for this gem overlooking Fifth Avenue and Central Park. The hotel's 800-some rooms have been recently restored and tastefully furnished (at a cost of $100 million) with antiques, artwork, and crystal. The most expensive and desirable rooms, of course, are those with views of the park, but all have their own style and elegance, as befits the only hotel in the city to be named a National Historic Landmark. The Plaza is also home to several notable restaurants—the Oyster Bar, where fresh bivalves are shucked to order; the elegant, tweedy Oak Bar and Restaurant; and the staid but classy Edwardian Room.

The Plaza Hotel, Fifth Ave at 59th St, New York, NY 10019, 212/759-3000.

Best Hotel Suite

Regency

This top-drawer hotel attracts a wide variety of celebrities (particularly from the worlds of music and movies), corporate types, and jet-setters. They enjoy rooms that combine a past-era elegance with modern amenities, such as bathrooms that offer phones and televisions. The Regency has been upgraded and renovated at a cost of more than $15 million, highlighting its gorgeous Regency-style decor; also renovated was the ornate marble-and-glass lobby, replete with tapestries and a huge chandelier. Top-drawer comfort and opulence can be found in the hotel's lavish presidential suite—which is not only spacious and exclusively cloistered, but also boasts a sprawling terrace offering a breathtaking view above Park Avenue. One of the most lavish suites in the city, this is a perfectly decadent spot for a leisurely breakfast and the newspaper before facing the day or for skyline-lit cocktails and dancing to end it. Businesspeople have long savored the hotel's comfort and charged atmosphere—in fact, the Regency Hotel Restaurant was the spot where the term *power breakfast* originated last decade (see separate listing); today, you can still find movers and shakers carving out fortunes and mapping out strategies over their eggs and croissants there.

Regency, 540 Park Ave, New York, NY 10021, 212/759-4100.

Best Hotel Make-Over

Sheraton Manhattan

If the name seems unfamiliar, wait until you see the surroundings. Business travelers who remember staying at the old City Squire—which had humble beginnings in the 1960s as a motor inn and a reputation for brusque, no-nonsense, move-'em-in-and-out service, won't recognize the place. It has emerged with a startling new identity after a $47 million metamorphosis completed in 1992 (in time for the National Democratic Convention). With a prime Midtown location and a stylish new restaurant, Bistro 790, the 650-room *new* Sheraton Manhattan is making an end-around run to score with upscale corporate travelers. In addition to redesigned guest rooms (equipped with desks stocked with office basics and featuring telephone data ports with PC and fax hookups), it offers a two-floor executive level, plenty of new meeting rooms, expanded convention facilities, and a business center offering secretarial services. High-tech touches include electronic voice mail, computerized guest history, and video check-out (in six languages). Also introduced are expanded concierge services and such amenities as complimentary newspapers. Fitness buffs enjoy a well-equipped health center that includes sauna, locker rooms (equipped for the disabled), and a generously sized four-lane lap pool with a deck area and adjacent terrace. Fitness programs include Aquajogging, said to deliver the same benefits as running, but without the impact.

Sheraton Manhattan, Seventh Ave & 52nd St, New York, NY 10019, 212/581-3300, 800/223-6550.

Best Hotel Where You Can Be the Judge

Sheraton Park Avenue

This hotel is a pleasantly personable find behind the oft-times predictable and impersonal Sheraton name. Long a standout, this was still the Sheraton Russell (named after Judge Horace Russell, whose home was once on the site of this hotel) when we first stayed here a few years ago; it satisfied then, and does even more so now, after a recent refurbishment. The tone is established with a warm, oak-paneled lobby that seems more like a stately home library—indeed, there are shelves of books and beckoning overstuffed chairs there as well. This elegance is carried through the hotel's 150 comfortable, non-cookie-cutter rooms, many of which offer great views above wide, toney Park Avenue; some even have fireplaces. Additionally, the Park Avenue offers a good level of service (it has been likened to that at a private club), an on-site health club, and a bar and restaurant; the latter was the locale of a scene in the Paul Newman movie *The Verdict*. This Sheraton property is definitely a cut above what you might expect.

Sheraton Park Avenue, 45 Park Ave, New York, NY 10016, 212/685-7676.

Most Attentive and Discreet Hotel Staff

The Sherry Netherland

It may sound like a paradox, but the ideal hotel staff is much like the best movie soundtracks—they are best serving their purpose when you don't notice them, when they are such a part of the whole (be it the movie or the hotel) that they blend in. Such is the case at this elegant hotel, whose staff is ready to cater to the various whims and needs of the hotel's guests—which include a large contingent of long-term residents (in fact, these permanent or semi-permanent guests outnumber the hotel's "traditional" short-term guests, creating a high-class, home-like atmosphere). The Sherry's large, pleasantly appointed rooms (which number more than 100, plus 20 suites) are appointed with antiques and other classy, muted furnishings. They range from small-ish, but comfortable singles and doubles through handsome suites overlooking the green splendors of Central Park. This old dowager of a New York hotel, housed in a 38-story baroque landmark building, attracts discreet celebrities who love the attentive service (which you need not be a royal to receive) and are often seen in the Sherry's bar and dining room.

The Sherry Netherland, 781 Fifth Ave, New York, NY 10022, 212/355-2800.

Most Cosmopolitan Hotel

The United Nations Plaza Hotel

What could be more cosmopolitan than a hotel adjoining the headquarters of worldwide, multicultural cooperation? Guests can play a fascinating game of "Where are they from?" while watching the passing parade of diplomats, delegates, and other dignitaries from around the world who make up a large portion of the United Nations Plaza's clientele. The hotel begins on the 28th floor of 1 United Nations Plaza (below the hotel is office space), and rises above the East River. Rooms are comfortable, well-appointed, and, since they start high in the building to begin with, offer great views. The hotel features a popular health club on its upper floors (another spot for grand vistas of Manhattan), which includes an indoor swimming pool and several tennis courts. The appropriately named Ambassador Grill offers a well-regarded menu of American-Continental cuisine; its weekend brunch is popular with guests and U.N. regulars alike. As you would expect, the United Nations Plaza is staffed with a cosmopolitan, multilingual staff. And even if you are not an international diplomat, you can still travel like one—the hotel offers complimentary limousine service to addresses on Wall Street, in the Theater District, and to various other business and pleasure spots in Manhattan. This hotel is run by the Hyatt International sub-group of Hyatt Hotels; appropriately (since this part of New York is so internationally flavored), it is the only Hyatt International property in the U.S.

The United Nations Plaza Hotel, 1 United Nations Plaza, First Ave at E 44th St, New York, NY 10017, 212/355-3400.

Homiest Hotel Near the U.N.

Beverly Hotel

Across from the opulent Waldorf-Astoria, this small, comfortable, privately owned hotel is its antithesis. Only four blocks from the U.N. and popular with its delegates, its reasonably priced homey accommodations might seem more likely to attract delegates from Senegal than from Sweden. Popular, too, with budget-conscious business travelers, it has just about everything one would need for basic comfort. Most guest rooms are one-bedroom or junior suites—spacious, comfortably furnished, and equipped with kitchenettes, pull-out sofas, and cable TV. The Georgian and Edwardian meeting rooms offer amenities for groups from 10 to 100. There are generous room service hours, and the personalized services of a concierge. Off the high-ceilinged, paneled lobby is Kenny's, a basic and reliable steak house that also serves a substantial breakfast, a lounge, and a convenient 24-hour drugstore (an increasing rarity in Manhattan).

Beverly Hotel, 125 E 50th St, New York, NY 10022, 212/753-2700, 800/223-0945.

Best Bet for Business

New York Vista

In the heart of the downtown business district, close to Wall Street, this 23-story hotel is the flagship of Hilton's Vista International group, offering an array of amenities for business travelers. These include a business center with secretarial and translation services, business machines (including telex, fax, photocopiers, and portable PCs), and a travel agency. Executive floors have express check in and a private clubroom with complimentary continental breakfast, cocktails, and canapes. The 821 rooms and suites have work desks and seating areas; a health club features pool, fully equipped gym, sauna, racquetball courts, and jogging track. The hotel is directly connected to the World Trade Center and the World Financial Center, with access to the acclaimed Windows on the World and Cellar in the Sky restaurants (see separate listings) 107 floors above New York. The American Harvest Restaurant has a menu designed to showcase American regional cooking. Afternoon tea and evening cocktails with piano music are served in the Vista Lounge; the Tall Ships Bar, with a clipper ship theme, is a casual spot for lunch, dinner, and cocktails. There is indoor parking for 124 cars.

New York Vista, 3 World Trade Ctr, New York, NY 10048, 212/938-1990, 800/258-2505.

Best Mid-Level Hotel for Business

Loews Summit

By necessity or prudent choice, not every businessperson to roll into New York blazes a trail to one of the city's most elegant—and, therefore, most expensive—hotels. Many bottom-line-conscious execs eschew puffery and ostentation and instead stay at this comfortable and pleasant hotel. Moderately priced and located in the heart of Midtown on Lexington Avenue, the Loews Summit is definitely geared to the business traveler—it is more accommodating and efficient than touristy (plus, nearly a quarter of its rooms and suites are on the hotel's Executive Level floors). All rooms have been recently remodeled in satisfyingly muted tones and offer streamlined layouts, mini-bars, and multiple phone lines. The hotel also includes a fully equipped health club, including sauna and Jacuzzi (which gets quite a workout from the power-deal business types here), and the Lexington Avenue Grill, a favored meeting and eating spot (its weekend buffet is a popular bargain). You may also spot professional athletes at the Loews Summit, as many pro teams (especially basketball teams) favor its low-key atmosphere and convenient location.

Loews Summit, 51st St & Lexington Ave, New York, NY 10022, 212/752-7000.

Best "Upscale Bargain" Hotel
Holiday Inn Crowne Plaza

If the words *Holiday Inn* still conjure only visions of roadside motels and garish neon signs, you have doubtless yet to try this chain's upper-end "Crowne Plaza"-designated properties. This Theater District-Times Square hotel (helping anchor renewal there, along with the Macklowe and the Marriott Marquis—see separate listings) is large, attractive, and flexible, offering three different types of lodgings at reasonable rates. In ascending style and price, these choices are: Handsome doubles, standard-looking, but a cut above the doubles to be found in a traditional chain room; the "King Leisure" rooms, which offer comfortably appointed sitting areas and desk space along with a king-size bed; and large, multiroom suites. Changes of pace (for a Holiday Inn property) include premium-amenity Concierge Floors, a full health club (including indoor pool), and a passel of pleasant bars, lounges, and restaurants beyond the usual "theme" motel dining rooms. Ask for lodging near the top of the hotel if you like a room with a view; at that height, all four sides offer pleasant vistas. *Trivia note:* This hotel was built on the exact site where Irving Berlin's music publisher was located. And, of course, Berlin wrote the music for the movie *Holiday Inn*...which is the source that entrepreneur Kemmons Wilson tapped for the name of the hotel chain.

Holiday Inn Crowne Plaza, 1601 Broadway, New York, NY 10019, 212/840-8400.

Best Affordable Non-Chain Hotel
Dorset Hotel

Staying in Manhattan on a budget need not mean settling for some cookie-cutter franchise hotel or a cheap room in a questionable neighborhood. Take, for example, this very affordable hotel, located just off Fifth Avenue, with the enviable location of being the closest hotel to the Museum of Modern Art (it's just around the corner). Recently renovated, the Dorset offers a stylish and understated lobby and common areas and comfortable, modern rooms (200 rooms and 60 suites, mostly on the large side). Rates—especially for this level of quiet, unassumingly upscale service at a prime Midtown location—are moderate, providing more comfort and elegance for your buck than comparably priced chain-hotel lodgings. The Dorset attracts a loyal following of regular guests and also houses a sizable population of permanent residents. It is also home to a bar and restaurant—the Dorset Room (great seafood choices)—that are both popular with guests and neighborhooders alike.

Dorset Hotel, 30 W 54th St, New York, NY 10019, 212/247-7300.

Best Rock-Bottom Room Rates at a Non-Scary Hotel

Pickwick Arms

Certainly, the rooms at the Pickwick Arms are nothing special and you have to pay every day in advance to stay at this hotel, but accepting these conditions can be well worthwhile for travelers on a budget, since this may be just about the only acceptable (i.e., clean and non-scary) Midtown hotel offering single rooms for under $50 a night and doubles from around $80. For these prices, you may expect just a locked door and a bed, but the Pickwick also provides some bang (in the way of amenities) for your buck—including telephones, air conditioning, and cable television in every room, and affordable room service from an on-site deli; there is also a rooftop garden for sightseeing or suntanning. The hotel's 200 rooms range from (at the absolute rock-bottom end) those with shared baths to small-apartment-sized rooms with built-in kitchenettes (allowing in-room cooking, another good money-saver for budget-conscious visitors); additionally, all of the Pickwick's affordable doubles have their own baths. This hotel fills up on a regular basis with people looking to squeeze the most from their New York travel dollar.

Pickwick Arms, 230 E 51st St, New York, NY 10022, 212/355-0300.

Suitest Lodging Deal

Off Soho Suites Hotel

A luxury suite for two for $66! In New York City? Opened in October, 1990, this 38-suite hotel bills itself as the "traveler's alternative to New York's overpriced, undersized hotel rooms." So what's the catch? Well, the neighborhood, east of Soho and Little Italy, near the Bowery and Houston Street, isn't exactly chic. But it has convenient access by bus to the financial and theater districts. Some of the windows look out onto a rather grubby street scene; some take in a huge mural of a naked woman and embryo painted on a facing building wall. Accommodations are spacious and comfortable, with beautiful hardwood floors, smart light oak furnishings, and Oriental-type throw rugs. A living room has an attractive seating area with couch and color TV, a full kitchen is equipped with stove, refrigerator, microwave, cookware, silverware, and dishes. There is a marble bath, linen closet, air conditioning, private telephone, and 24-hour self-service laundry room and free fitness center. A suite for four goes for $99. A second location is in the East Village on East 12th Street off Third Avenue.

Off Soho Suites Hotel, 11 Rivington St, New York, NY 10002, 800-OFF-SOHO, 212/979-9808.

Best Renovated Affordable Hotel (Which Used to Be Apartments)
Milburn Hotel

In reverse of usual New York practice (and, indeed, that found in many big cities), this was originally an apartment building, and was recently completely overhauled and turned into a hotel. Spending several million dollars, owners converted about half of the Milburn's rooms into hotel lodgings, giving the lobby, common areas, and all of the rooms a considerable sprucing up at the same time. The result is 70 rooms, furnished in a modern, upbeat style, looking very new. Not only do these rooms offer cable TV, air conditioning, and new phones, but also fully equipped kitchens, which include new microwave ovens, utensils, and appliances. The Milburn also offers 24-hour concierge service, and, in general, a very good and attentive staff. Rooms are moderately priced and discounts are often available for the asking (but book ahead and don't be surprised if it's crowded—word is getting around about the Milburn, especially among longer-stay corporate clients). *A location note:* The Milburn is located on the north end of the West Side, an area where apartment buildings predominate—there are not many other hotels in this part of town.

Milburn Hotel, 242 W 76th St, New York, NY 10023, 212/362-1006.

Best Budget Hotel for In-Room Snacking

Salisbury Hotel

This former apartment building provides modest lodgings at prices to match. Well located—across from Russian Tea Room, near Carnegie Hall, Lincoln Center, and Central Park—it offers large rooms equipped with dinettes. With ample cabinet and counter space and half-size refrigerators, the spacious accommodations in this 320-room hotel are ideal for families or for budget-conscious business travelers who wish to keep handy soft drinks, cold cuts, fresh fruits, and other snacks. Complimentary continental breakfast is served in a pleasant, but not fancy, room on the second floor. It includes croissants, pastries, fresh fruits, and various juices, and provides morning newspapers and tables decorated with fresh flowers in bud vases. More substantial breakfasts are available at the Stardust Diner (see separate listing) just half a block away.

Salisbury Hotel, 123 W 57th St, New York, NY 10019, 212/246-1300.

One of the City's Best Hotel Values (Provided You Secure a Renovated Room)

Shoreham Hotel

You can find less expensive rooms than those offered at the Shoreham—and you can certainly find more luxurious lodgings. But, all things considered, the combination of price and style that *many* of this hotel's rooms offer places the Shoreham in a special pantheon among Manhattan hotels. (The important qualifier in that statement is "many," since not all of the rooms are up to the same level of quality— more about which below.) The Shoreham offers a gleamingly renovated—if smallish—lobby and a convenient location (just off Fifth Avenue), which is great for shopping expeditions. More than half of the hotel's comfortable, decently sized rooms have been recently restored—these rooms are very nice for the price and offer coffee makers and mini-bars...but, to guarantee getting one of these new rooms, it is necessary to specify such when making reservations. Unfortunately, if the hotel is heavily booked, you can end up in one of the old, noisy, pre-renovated rooms for the same price. So, we strongly suggest that you inquire well ahead, and ask to see a room before agreeing to take it. (Also—even some of the new

rooms can be haunted by noise from 55th Street;
light sleepers should further specify a new room
away from the street.) Ironically, on the premises of
the affordable Shoreham is La Caravelle restaurant,
once more highly rated, but still estimable. Dinner
and lunch tabs there could easily wipe out any
savings from a hotel stay.

Shoreham Hotel, 33 W 55th St, New York, NY 10019,
212/247-6700.

Best Budget Bet for Travelers Who Ask Y

de Hirsch Residence, 92nd Street Y

There are no chocolates on the pillow or newspaper
at the door. But, for rooms that cost only $24 a night
(double occupancy) and $35 a night (single), the
absence of frills is understandable and overlookable.
However, the Y's newly renovated de Hirsch Residence does feature a 75-foot swimming pool; complimentary privileges to the Center for Health,
Fitness, and Sports; and access to the Tours & Talks
department, offering a wide variety of walking and
sightseeing tours. Most residents stay four weeks or
longer in furnished dorm-style rooms with shared
kitchen, bathroom, and laundry facilities. Weekly
maid and bed linen services are included, and there
is round-the-clock security. Men and women are
accommodated on separate floors. The residence is
just a short walk from six of New York's finest
museums, including the Guggenheim and the Metropolitan Museum of Art. It is three blocks from
Central Park. The residence also is one of New York's
finest (and oldest) cultural and community centers,
where guests receive discounted admission to a
variety of concerts, lectures, poetry readings, classes,
and membership programs. For travelers on a budget, this undoubtedly is one of New York's best
lodging buys, providing a cosmopolitan setting for
visitors from around the world.

The 92nd Street Y, 1395 Lexington Ave, New York,
NY 10128, 212/415-5450.

NOTABLE POTABLES

Best Bar to Meet Yuppies

Amsterdam's on Amsterdam

The 1980s are gone—junk bonds are just junk again, Donald Trump has been humbled, and Ronald Reagan has retired to his California ranch....But a prominent part of the last decade lives on: The yuppie life-style is apparently here to stay. And if you're looking for a prime nightspot to mingle with a boat-shoes-and-Dockers-wearing crowd while you sip your Corona (with a slice of lime wedged in the neck, of course), this popular establishment will serve your purpose nicely. It attracts a young, upscale crowd, with a heavy concentration of West Side yuppies. Amsterdam's has a pleasant bistro-style decor under high ceilings, and is usually crowded—meaning that food and drink service can be slow....But who cares when you're a Bright Young Thing seeing and being seen by other BYTs? This spot offers a good selection of above-average bar eats, including hefty burgers with heaps of fries, great baskets of roasted or fried chicken, hearty ribs, and a tempting array of desserts. There is also a branch of Amsterdam's in SoHo (454 Broadway; 212/925-6166), which attracts pretty much the sort of yupster crowd as the original (rather than the "typical" SoHo area patrons).

Amsterdam's on Amsterdam, 428 Amsterdam Ave, New York, NY 10024, 212/874-1377. Sun-Thu noon-midnight, Fri & Sat noon-1 am.

Most Likely Bar to *Avoid* Yuppies
Jean Lafitte

This bar is pleasant, comfortable, and stylish, without being "hot" or "in." At first blush, it may seem, with its faux art nouveau decor and front windows that slide open to create an airy bistro-style bar, to be a trendy take-off of a Parisian-style bistro. But it quickly becomes apparent that this truly is a neighborhood bar frequented by regulars, many of whom the French mâitre d' appears to know by name. This definitely is not yuppie territory. Its mature patrons seem to be primarily martini and Scotch drinkers (but the bartender, who also is a fixture who seems to know everyone and their history, makes a great spicy Bloody Mary). There are small, round tables, a few booths, and stools around an L-shaped bar, all of which are bathed in yellow-hued lighting. Dark wall paneling adds to the relaxed, friendly atmosphere. A dining room at the back serves up reliable but not especially notable French fare. Its Midtown location is close to Carnegie Hall.

Jean Lafitte, 68 W 58th St, New York, NY 10019, 212/751-2323. Mon-Fri noon-midnight, Sat & Sun 5:30 pm-midnight.

Most Likely Bar To *Really* Avoid Yuppies
Downtown Beirut II

While not *exactly* devastated by bombs and mortars (as its namesake city has been), this club is a rugged, disheveled, somewhat-dangerous (more in attitude than in reality), not-for-the-meek sort of place. Downtown Beirut II is a rough, in-your-face club, decorated with barbed wire and other punkish trappings. And the throbbing, rough-'n'-ready, fast-'n'-loud music that blasts through this establishment is usually as out-there as the club's clientele. Patrons opt for ripped, slashed, or otherwise abused denims and/or leathers—or, failing those, any sort of black clothing—to fit in with the enthusiastic, hard-rocking crowd that is usually found here. The smaller, original location of this punky club (at 156 First Avenue) is also a lively—if somewhat sleazier, if that is possible—outpost of hardcore music and severe fashion. Although both Downtown Beiruts are located in and around the Village area, these are *not* the sorts of clubs where you can expect to find the typical Village yupsters.

Downtown Beirut II, 157 E Houston St, New York, NY 10002, 212/614/9040. Daily noon-4 am.

Best Authentic New York Saloon

P. J. Clarke's

Even if you haven't been to this historic Midtown tavern, you may have *seen* it, since P. J. Clarke's was one of the taverns frequented by Ray Milland's self-destructive character in the 1945 Academy Award-winning film *The Lost Weekend* (both the movie and Milland won Oscars). Housed in a 19th-century brick structure nestled among towering skyscrapers, this classic New York tavern is popular with neighborhood residents and visitors alike. It dates from before Prohibition and features an attractive wood-and-cut-glass bar, a great jukebox with '40s and '50s prerock oldies (including a heavy concentration of Sinatra selections), and a wide and varied assortment of imported beer. The crowd at this particularly friendly bar runs from executives in suits to students in jeans, and often includes more than a sprinkling of politicos, newspaper people, and assorted celebrities. If you're looking for a taste of what a "typical" New York bar is like (if, indeed, there *is* one), this would be a good place to start.

P. J. Clarke's, 915 Third Ave, New York, NY 10022, 212/355-8857. Daily 10 am-4 am.

Best Jazz Club Where Woody Allen Sits in with the Band

Michael's Pub

In *Annie Hall,* Woody Allen repeats a Groucho Marx joke about not wanting to "belong to any club that would have someone like me for a member." But, apparently, a club that would have someone like him as a member of a *band* is a different story. Fans of Allen's films know of his love for music, especially jazz. Both the action and the soundtrack of many of his movies prominently feature music, such as the breezy, New Orleans jazz of the Preservation Hall Jazz Band, which was featured in *Sleeper.* And Allen himself plays a similar brand of traditional jazz at this club, with his New Orleans Funeral and Ragtime Orchestra. This loose aggregation of mostly nonprofessional musicians (including a college professor and a stockbroker, as well as Allen) plays every Monday night, as it has done for close to 20 years. Allen shows up more often than you might expect (nearly every week—in fact, he was at Michael's the night *Annie Hall* won four Academy Awards), and plays either clarinet or, occasionally, soprano saxophone, instruments he has played since his Brooklyn childhood. During the rest of the week, this dark,

atmospheric club offers old-fashioned jazz and cabaret performers; Michael's also features a full continental menu.

Michael's Pub, 211 E 55th St, New York, NY 10022,
212/758-2272. Mon-Sat 4:30 pm-1 am, sets at 9 &
11 pm.

Best Bar Owned by New York's *Other* Woody

Woody's

Most New Yorkers know that Woody Allen has been
known to play clarinet at Michael's Pub (see separate
listing) on Monday nights, but is this the namesake
joint he hangs out at the rest of the week? Not likely,
for this club *isn't* named after the famed filmmaker,
but rather for a British import of some notoriety
himself—Rolling Stones guitarist (and, of late, acclaimed painter) Ron Wood. But, alas, don't show up
with high expectations of seeing the craggy-faced,
rooster-haired rocker tending bar here—his visits
are occasional, at best. Luckily, this rollicking joint
has more to recommend it than its celebrity owner.
Woody's offers a good mix of rock, blues, folk, and
other music in a friendly atmosphere. The mostly
unknown bands that play here are usually accomplished and eager-to-please, the crowd is generally
young and boisterous (but not uncontrollably so),
and the spirits are plentiful. Plus, you never know
when the reclusive Mr. Wood may just decide to
shake off the musical cobwebs between infrequent
Stones' tours and offer some of his slash-and-grunge
bluesy rock onstage. An adjoining art gallery shows
off interesting works by Wood and other rockers-
turned-painters.

Woody's, 84 E 4th St, New York, NY 10003, 212/982-
3686. Daily 9 pm-4 am.

Best Bar with a Name That Describes What It Is

Landmark Tavern

While perhaps not bearing a gilded plaque proclaim-
ing its heritage, this old-time bar certainly does live
up to its name—it has been slaking the thirst of New
Yorkers since just after the Civil War. The Landmark
is a classic tavern in the Irish manner, full of dark
wood and mirrors, with a pressed-tin ceiling. Its
blazing fireplace and cheery potbelly stove invite

cozying up with a fortifying beverage on a brisk day. In general, this is a nice spot to sit and soak up a bit of the history that has seemed to permeate the bar's walls; along with McSorley's Old Ale House (see separate listing), this is one of the prime examples of an "Old New York" tavern. Its near-the-Hudson location made the Landmark a one-time long-shoremen's and dockworker's hangout. One has to wonder what those long-ago patrons would make of the bar's current lively mix of Javits Center conventioneers, Westsiders, theatergoers, and curious tourists. There are some good—if uncomplicated—eats. The consensus favorite is the hearty Irish-style oatmeal pancakes, available at the bar's weekend brunch.

Landmark Tavern, 626 Eleventh Ave at 46th St, New York, NY 10036, 212/757-8595. Daily noon-2 am.

Probably the Oldest Tavern in New York City

McSorley's Old Ale House

A few years ago, when a friend told me about having been to a very old bar in the city, she couldn't immediately remember the name, but she *did* remember the ancient tavern's crusty ambience. It sounded familiar. "McSorley's" I asked helpfully. "Yes—that was it!" she replied with a smile. (Since I didn't want to dim her enthusiasm for the old place, I didn't tell her that her visit would've been impossible only two decades before; until 1970, McSorley's was a males-only bastion of drinking and socializing.) Dating from 1854, and almost certainly the oldest tavern in town, McSorley's has attracted literary types such as Brendan Behan and presidents (or campaigning presidents-to-be) such as Lincoln, both Roosevelts, and Kennedy. These days, it is usually crowded with neighborhood regulars, as well as with generous complements of tourists and tweedy-looking college students. There are simple bar eats such as sandwiches and boiled eggs, as well as McSorley's own brand of creamy draft ale (also available at Lion's Head—see separate listing). This is a perfect spot to pull up a chair around the bar's sooty potbellied stove to share a frosty mug and lively talk with friends or with McSorley's opinionated (about sports, politics, etc.) retinue of regulars.

McSorley's Old Ale House, 15 E 7th St, New York, NY 10003, 212/473-9148. Mon-Sat 11 am-1 am.

Best Rooftop Potables

Pen-Top Bar and Terrace

As New York skyscrapers go, the 23-story Peninsula Hotel is a midget. Yet this newly and elegantly re-furbished New York branch of the famous Hong Kong hostelry is home of the Pen-Top Bar and Ter-race, overlooking Fifth Avenue and offering a dra-matic view of the Manhattan skyline. This intimate cocktail lounge, with curved glass-topped bar and good-looking chrome-and-black-leather seating, is almost totally glass-enclosed, providing a feeling of height and a view of neighboring buildings from almost any seat in the house. In warm months (around the beginning of April through October), the adjoining terrace becomes busy with those who enjoy their cocktails under the stars. This pleasant rooftop terrace also offers a light menu—smoked salmon, shrimp cocktail, and cheese platter—and for special occasions, such as July 4th, it fires up a barbecue and produces grilled meats and fish along with other buffet-style food. With green carpeting, patio-style chairs, and pretty flower boxes, the terrace is as close as you can come to resort-style outdoor enter-taining in the heart of midtown Manhattan.

Pen-Top Bar and Terrace, The Peninsula Hotel, 700 Fifth Ave, New York, NY 10019, 212/247-2200. Mon-Thu 5 pm–midnight, Fri & Sat 5 pm–1 am (open 1 hr earlier in summer).

Best Bet for Beers

Peculier Pub

If your tastes in beer run more to Pilsner Urquell and Christian Moerlein Dark than to Budweiser and Miller Lite, this is the place for you. (On the other hand, if you find yourself stuck for decisions when faced with large numbers of choices, perhaps this bar *isn't* for you.) This small, often crowded bar offers more than 250 different types of brews—far more beer on tap and in bottles than any other bar or restaurant in the city. These myriad choices repre-sent the best brews from some 35 different coun-tries. Located in the Village, just south of Washington Square Park (see separate listing), this is a comfort-able place that attracts a usually quite friendly cli-entele who, at the drop of a bottle cap, are ready to debate the merits of barley versus wheat or double brewing versus cold finishing. The all-around pub atmosphere includes a good jukebox of oldies and a couple of dartboards that get serious workouts. As for the bar's peculiar (or should that be "peculier"?)

name, it's from—surprise!—a beer: English Old
Peculier Ale, the owner's favorite brand.

Peculier Pub, 145 Bleecker St, New York, NY 10012,
212/353-1327. Mon-Sat, until 2 am.

Best Wine Bars

Lavin's Restaurant and Wine Bar and Tastings
Restaurant

If you enjoy fine wines by the glass at a restaurant
or bar—but don't consider yourself a committed
oenophile—you may not be aware of the device that
allows you to best enjoy wine in this way. Called a
cruvinet, it sort of vacuum seals the remaining wine
in an open bottle with nitrogen (which does not react
with the wine nor affect its taste). Lavin's is said to
have been the first in the city to use this method
(Tastings was not far behind), greatly improving the
quality of wine poured by the glass. Lavin's is housed
in what was once a private dining room built for
Andrew Carnegie; it was converted into its current
attractive space in 1980. The offerings tend toward
California wines, with good selections of European
vintages available as well. The mid-level dining here
is reliable—mostly semi-nouvelle cuisine, with the
light fish and pasta dishes shining through as definite winners; lunch is popular. Tastings is another
nice spot to enjoy a fine wine or two, with or without
a meal. The list here is extensive and seems to fit
all tastes and budgets. If you're at a loss to decide,
the staff's suggestions are worth listening to—they
have all been trained at the International Wine
Center's school, located above this restaurant. (This
school also offers open-to-the-public classes and
tasting events; info is available at the restaurant.)
Dining at Tastings is perhaps not as highly thought
of as at Lavin's, but the wine list is beyond reproach.

Lavin's Restaurant and Wine Bar, 23 W 39th St,
New York, NY 10018, 212/921-1288. Mon-Fri noon-10
pm. Tastings Restaurant at the International Wine
Center, 144 W 55th St, New York, NY 10019, 212/
757-1160. Mon-Fri noon-midnight, Sat 5:30 pm-
midnight.

Best Bar for Over-Imbibing Welsh Writers

The White Horse Tavern

Fans of *Under Milk Wood* or *A Child's Christmas in
Wales* may want to stop here and raise a toast to

both the genius and the folly of Dylan Thomas (we suggest whiskey, to follow the salutee's unfortunately excessive example). This venerable, yet unpretentious tavern was once a Village speakeasy, but is perhaps best known as one of Thomas's favorite drinking stops during his final days. The not-even-40-year-old writer drank himself to death, and was supposed to have been here, downing copious amounts of whiskey, just days before his demise in 1953. For this reason, the White Horse has become popular with tourists, and is often crowded with the equivalent of literary groupies, swapping stories of the often-larger-than-life Welsh writer's debaucheries. However, the bar isn't always packed, and during slower times can make an interesting stop, especially for a drink while pondering the twinned muses and demons of the man who is considered one of the greatest poets of the 20th century. *Conversational note to toss at the literary snobs:* Norman Mailer also used to hang out and drink here—but, of course, he managed to survive doing so.

The White Horse Tavern, 567 Hudson St, New York, NY 10014, 212/243-9260. Sun-Thu 10 am-2 am, Fri & Sat 10 am-4 am.

Best Bookish Bar Booth

Pete's Tavern

If genius is inspired by location, it would certainly behoove any would-be writer to hie himself or herself over to this venerable Gramercy-neighborhood bar and plop down with pad and pen in the first booth in the front of the bar. Legend has it that this is the very spot where O. Henry wrote his classic Christmas tale of ironic love and sacrifice, *Gift of the Magi*. This is one of the oldest bars in the city—it's of the same era as McSorley's (see separate listing), except, back then, it was known as Healy's Bar. Under any name, it has more history on its side than just O. Henry—Boss Tweed (of Tammany Hall infamy) was a regular here, and other famous visitors include Butch Cassidy and the Sundance Kid (allegedly) and John F. Kennedy (definitely). Pete's dark, authentic look has mostly remained unchanged since the repeal of Prohibition, and has been featured in numerous movies, television shows, and commercials (most notably in a scene from *Ragtime* and in many of the Miller Lite sports-oriented spots of the 1970s and 1980s). The food here is basic, but good—burgers, steaks, pasta, and the like; the desserts get high marks, especially the cheesecake and pecan pie. A weekend brunch is also offered.

Pete's Tavern, 129 E 18th St, New York, NY 10003, 212/473-7676. Daily, 8 am-2 am.

Best Lobby Libations with the Literati

Lobby Bar, The Algonquin Hotel

When James Thurber was daydreaming Mitty-like scenarios and drawing his outrageous cartoons for *The New Yorker*, and when its offices were populated with the likes of Harold Ross, Alexander Woolcott, and Robert Benchley, it was convenient to slip next door for libations in the bar of The Algonquin Hotel. It was here that Dorothy Parker and other literary wits and sages held forth at the famous Round Table. This also was a popular spot for theatrical types such as Irving Berlin and Nöel Coward. Doubling as a bar, the club-like, paneled lobby, with inviting sofas and overstuffed chairs grouped around small tables, continues to attract luminaries from the New York publishing scene. They begin gathering on weekday evenings between 5 and 6, when the talk of book contracts and movie options is interrupted only by the tinkling of little service bells that are placed on each table (along with bowls of peanuts) to summon waiters. This club-like lobby is a pleasant, sophisticated spot for afternoon tea, cocktails, and conversation, with a piano player to tempt the crowd to linger until the dinner hour. Some things never change: The offices of *The New Yorker* remain in convenient proximity.

Lobby Bar, The Algonquin Hotel, 59 W 44th St, New York, NY 10036 212/840-6800. Daily 11 am-1 am.

Best Literary Bars

Chumley's and Lion's Head

Since New York is—and has been—home to so many writers, it's not surprising that the city is also home to a number of bars with interesting literary pedigrees. And, also not surprisingly, most of these bars are concentrated in the artsy enclave of Greenwich Village. Chumley's, tucked away on a hard-to-find side street of the Village, has attracted such literary luminaries as James Joyce, Ring Lardner, John Steinbeck, and John Dos Passos. These authors— and others—are celebrated with such literary mementoes as dust jackets and photos. Even considering its somewhat obscure site, this bar attracts crowds of curious bibliophiles and imbibers. Easier to find is Lion's Head, a comfortable, dimly lit tavern on Christopher Street. It attracts journalists, poets, and other writers—as well as those who would just like to *fancy* themselves as authors. It, too, offers a musty crop of dust jackets lining its walls, as well as a popular jukeboxful of oldies and a back room offering a varied menu of sandwiches and complete dinners. Other Manhattan bars with reputations as literary watering holes are Pete's Tavern (129 E. 18th St.), which includes a booth where O. Henry is supposed to have written his Christmas classic *The Gift of the Magi*, and the White Horse Tavern (see separate listing).

Chumley's, 86 Bedford St, New York, NY 10014, 212/675-4449. Mon-Fri 5 pm-1 am, Sat & Sun noon-1 am. Lion's Head, 59 Christopher St, New York, NY 10014, 212/929-0670. Daily noon-4 am.

Best Irish Pubs

Rosie O'Grady's South, Tommy Makem's Irish Pavilion, and the Eagle Tavern

You say you're looking for an "authentic" Irish pub to while away your next St. Paddy's Day (or even *any* day worth celebrating)? New York may not wear its Gaelic heart on its sleeve the way that Boston and Chicago do, but it has its share of Irish drinking establishments. Heading the list is Rosie O'Grady's South, a crowded, popular joint at the southern tip of Manhattan. This is a prime spot for lively Irish music, since the likes of the Clancy Brothers often play here. It's a good spot to dance a jig—or to just down a heady black-and-tan (a mixture of dark Guinness stout and light Harp lager). Tommy Makem's is a basic Irish pub, located just south and east of Central Park. It has been around since the late 1960s—which is a near-eternity compared to some of the "authentic" ethnic bars which have appeared in the last decade or two. Makem's is known for the live bands it offers and the heavy concentration of Irish pols and other notables it attracts. The Eagle Tavern is another old, authentic Irish pub in a real Irish neighborhood (which has seen some recent renewal and gentrification). All three of these are lively spots any time of the year—but especially so on March 17th!

Rosie O'Grady's South, 211 Pearl St, New York, NY 10038, 212/424-7912. Tommy Makem's Irish Pavilion, 130 E 57th St, New York, NY 10022, 212/759-9040. Eagle Tavern, 355 W 14th St, New York, NY 10014, 212/924-0275.

Pub Where the Most Cockney Is Spoken

Drake's Drum

If you hear a couple of chaps talking "football" in this bar, chances are they are not debating the relative merits of the Giants and the Jets. They are more likely to be handicapping the chances of Arsenal or West Ham United winning Britain's FA Cup. This is a great hangout for soccer/football fans, local rugby players (the owners used to play), and expatriated Brits in general. Drake's Drum offers a dark, Old World/Old New York sort of decor—ornate wood-and-metal bar, huge oil paintings on the walls, and sawdust on the floor. In warmer months, the bar's few outdoor tables are nice spots to watch the world rush by. Even if you don't know a scrum from a scrimmage, just relax and enjoy the atmosphere— you can't go wrong by joining the regulars in a dark, thick pint of Guinness. Drake's Drum offers some good and inexpensive pub grub, including hearty burgers, steak sandwiches, omelettes, and such British specialties as toad-in-the-hole (sausages encased in Yorkshire pudding), shepherd's pie, fish and chips, and bangers and mash. This bar also features a number of simple, but nice brunch items on Saturdays and Sundays. *Note:* This place gets packed to the rafters when the World Cup or any other important international football (the round kind) event is available on television. At other times it is a nice, quiet spot for a glass of pig's ("pig's ear" = beer in Cockney rhyming slang).

Drake's Drum, 1629 Second Ave (between 84th & 85th sts), New York, NY 10028, 212/988-2826. Open nightly until 4 am.

Hottest Hut

Bamboo Bernies

If you're looking for a kitschy (and very popular) bit of island-style fun, head to this Upper West Side haunt. There's no sign out front, but you can't miss it—it's the only hut with a corrugated tin overhang on the block. Probably, there'll be a line out front, with just about every other person standing in it seeming to be still working on a bottle of beer from the *last* bar they were at. Bernies is that kind of place, attracting a young, looking-for-fun sort of crowd. Young? Well, even those who can't remember the last time they were asked for proof of age, may wish to carry an ID if they want to visit here. "Let's see proof; everybody needs proof," was the cry of the doormen—even to a friend who, while fumbling through her purse, tried to shame the bouncer by telling him that she could, *theoretically*, of course, be his mother. Inside, the decor is faux-thatched-straw and conch shells, the music is steel drums and reggae, and the beverages are large and fruity (unless, of course, they are sweating longneck bottles of beer—some of which, no doubt, are fated to be carried to the line outside the night's *next* stop). Happy hour is usually hopping, with freebie snacks and drink specials—but pretty much any time of the night is as crowded as any other. As you might expect, Bernie is a made-up character; this is the flagship of a burgeoning chain of high-concept bars, with an outlet already open in Chicago (and other cities to follow).

Bamboo Bernies, 2268 Broadway (at 81st St), New York, NY 10024, 212/580-0200. Daily noon-4 am.

Classiest Piano Bar

Café Carlyle

As opposed to the "typical" image of many piano bars, you won't hear a "mellow" (read: nearly coma-tose), marginally talented singer warbling "Feelings" at this high-class establishment. Instead, the musical entertainment at the Café Carlyle (located in the Carlyle Hotel) is usually provided by the legendary New York saloon performer Bobby Short. The mellifluous and suave Short tickles the ivories at this sophisticated hangout, backed by a bassist and drummer, as he has for nearly 25 years. He is a vibrant showman, who works the Carlyle's small, comfy, and usually crowded room with endearing and enduring style and grace. His twice-a-night sets, Tuesdays through Saturdays, are great chances to hear-as-they-should-be-heard renditions of classic Gershwin and Porter (and other, similar) tunes. When Short (who was featured performing in Woody Allen's *Hannah and Her Sisters*) isn't in residence, the Café Carlyle has offered such jazz-pop greats as George Shearing.

Café Carlyle, The Carlyle Hotel, 35 E 76th St, New York, NY 10021, 212/744-1600. Nightly shows at 9:30 pm & 11:30 pm.

Piano Bar Reaching the Greatest Heights

The Hors D'oeuverie

If you're looking for a bar that soars as high as the clear, pure jazz notes it also provides, this is your spot. Towering some 107 stories above Manhattan, this classy cocktail bar offers well-mixed libations, top-notch appetizers (such as raw shellfish, sushi, and other savory munchies), and, of course, stunning panoramic views of New York (and New Jersey and Connecticut, etc.) The music here leans to smart jazz combos and atmospheric piano, and, generally, sets an understated, cosmopolitan tone. This is an upscale, dress-up sort of place, which regularly attracts a large and stylish crowd. It's a perfect spot for expense account patrons. Cocktails with a view are also available at the neighboring City Lights Bar (see separate listing).

The Hors D'oeuverie, 1 World Trade Cntr, 107th Fl, New York, NY 10048, 212/938-1111. Daily 3 pm-1 am.

Best Parisian-Style Piano Bar

Bar Montparnasse/Le Patio

The patron seated at one of the tables in this Parisian-style piano bar is persuaded to sing and stylishly belts out a song. Her performance surprises no one, inasmuch as her name is Ella Fitzgerald. Many entertainers, from Cher to Tom Berringer, are guests at the French-managed Le Parker Meridien, conveniently located near Carnegie Hall and Radio City Music Hall (home of the Grammy Awards). The Bar Montparnasse and the adjoining Le Patio provide a pleasant spot for a cocktail-hour libation or evening hors d'oeuvres. From September through June a jazz trio performs in this fashionable bar on Tuesday through Saturday from 9 p.m. to 1 a.m. During the summer, a pianist takes over. Le Patio has a jazz brunch on Sundays (and a French country buffet Mon-Sat) and is nicknamed "the LA Lounge" because of the producers, directors, and other motion-picture types who frequent it. The bar, off the lavish glittering marble courtway that incorporates the hotel lobby and connects 56th and 57th streets, is hung with Aubusson tapestries that a curator travels in from Washington, D.C. to clean.

Bar Montparnasse/Le Patio, Le Parker Meridien Hotel, 118 W 57th St, New York, NY 212/245-5000.

Best Spot Where You May Feel Dizzy *Before* the Drinks Are Served

City Lights Bar

Before its more recent (and, unfortunately, more dangerous) connotations, the phrase "getting high" used to refer to the giddy, soaring feeling one could get from having a few (or a few *more*) drinks. And we can't think of any other place where the twin pursuits of "getting high"—with the help of both alcohol *and* an elevator—can be as appropriate and as entertaining as at this sky-high bar. Basically, the ambience of this nightspot is both classy *and* expected—it pretty much looks the way you might expect *any* bar 107 stories above Manhattan to look. Of course, the interior of the bar is not nearly as important as the vistas on display through its windows. This is a relaxing and timeless spot to enjoy a cocktail while taking in what must be called—somewhat hyperbolically, but fairly indisputedly—unparalleled views of the city. (For similar views, plus live jazz music and usually inventive morsels, try the neighboring Hors D'oeuverie—see separate listing.) It may sound like a touristy clichè, but this is a great spot to bring a friend, date, or client from out of town. The heady views from this Olympian vantage point may help cement whatever deal you're trying to pitch!

City Lights Bar, 1 World Trade Cntr, 107th Fl, New York, NY 10048, 212/938-1111. Mon-Sat 3 pm-1 am, Sun 4-9 pm.

Best Hotel Bar for Broadway Hits

Drake Bar

In other lives it was a shoe store and a trendy '60s disco, but the new street-level bar at the corner of Park Avenue and 56th Street is a comfortable spot to listen to the mellow sounds of pianist-composer Jimmy Roberts. Over a period of six years at the old Drake Bar, Roberts gathered a loyal following, regulars who have trailed him here. He intersperses Chopin and Mozart with Gershwin, Porter, and Sondheim and also performs his own original works, including pieces from *The Velveteen Rabbit*, a show he wrote for children, and an environmental song called *Love Canal.* A colleague who stays at the Drake comments: "This bar has a very comfortable, safe feeling for women—I feel that I don't need to go elsewhere to find a bar for an evening cocktail." The bar is paneled in elm burl and bleached walnut with brass accents and beveled mirrors. Richly textured fabrics and touches, such as lizard skin lampshades and surrealist 1930s and 1940s fashion photographs by renowned German-born Horst (now in his 80s), give the two-level bar an art nouveau feel. Some regulars choose to eat right at the free-standing octagonal island bar, the room's focal point, spread with burgundy cloth placemats.

Drake Bar, Drake Swissôtel, 440 Park Ave, New York, NY 10022, 212/421-0900. Daily noon-2 am.

Best Bar with a Museum of Rock 'n' Roll

Hard Rock Café

Here's your one-stop shopping spot for burgers, beers, T-shirts, and glimpses of various rock memorabilia. This is yet another outpost of this loud-music-and-sweatshirts chain, which started in London in 1971. It remains popular with a young, (mostly) suburban or out-of-town clientele, and can seem a bit distracting and frenetic to the thirty-something-and-older crowd. However, the burgers and shakes are hard to beat, the desserts are huge, and there *are* some interesting artifacts on display, such as Chubby Checker's made-to-Twist-in boots, a guitar that Jimi Hendrix played (but didn't end up burning or smashing), and Prince's signature purple jacket. And the occasional celebrity can also be seen here. The lines can be long, especially on weekends, but...if you've got kids along, they'll probably insist on going here. *Directional note:* You can't miss the entrance—it's directly under the fins of the tail end of a 1950s Caddy.

Hard Rock Café, 221 W 57th St, New York, NY 10019, 212/489-6565. Daily 11 am-4 am.

Best Bar for Classic Soul Sing-Alongs

Raccoon Lodge

Here's another bar—along with Amsterdam's and Bamboo Bernies (see separate listings)—that is big with a young crowd that combines yuppies with college students into a big, beer-fueled, amorphous good time. Which means that customers can feel comfortable whether they've simply loosened tie and rolled up shirt sleeves after a day at the office *or* whether they're decked out in baggy shorts and Red Hot Chili Peppers T-shirts after a day of avoiding work. Both groups are attracted to this Upper West Side establishment for the inexpensive drinks and frequent specials, an interesting singles scene, a popular and well-worn pool table, and a jukebox stocked with plenty of oldies (especially Stax/Volt soul hits from the 1960s). Our diversion is the jukebox, which usually ends up leading the crowd in fun sing-alongs—one night the whole place is screaming along with Wilson Pickett, the next night everyone's soulfully crooning with Otis Redding. If you prefer to get your kicks closer to the East River than the Hudson, there's another Raccoon Lodge at 1439 York Avenue (212/650-1775).

Raccoon Lodge, 480 Amsterdam Ave (at 83rd St), New York, NY 10024, 212/874-9984.

Best Bar for Sports Fans

Sporting Club

What are expatriated Chicago Bulls, Los Angeles Dodgers, or Washington Redskins fans to do in opinionated, local-sports-heavy New York? Other than pretending to root for the Big Apple's home teams, they could head to this TriBeCa sports mecca, where, at any given moment, there could be up to *six* "home" teams on TV to cheer for. The Sporting Club is dominated by a 10-foot-tall video screen perched above the bar, which shows whatever is determined to be the "marquee" sports event going on at that time. But there are also video monitors all over the place, allowing this bar to show up to six different sporting events at a time. (You can call ahead with a request for a certain professional or college game; if it's floating around up on a satellite, they'll try to pull it in for you.) And, even if your favorite team's game isn't available on TV, you can keep track of the score on the continuously updated digital scoreboard, which also hangs above the bar. The Sporting Club offers good, reasonably priced food, albeit with sports-themed monikers. For example, you don't just get a bowl of chili and a steak—it's a "Super Bowl" and a "Steak LaMotta" (as in boxer Jake of *Raging Bull* fame). The crowd *is* heavy with high-fiving groups of men, but a large number of female sports fans also hang out here, making the Sporting Club a pleasant meeting and mixing spot. Another decent sports spot is Mickey Mantle's (42 Central Park South; 212/688-7777—see separate listing), also full of TVs and a video library of historic sporting events...and, perhaps, the chance to meet the tavern's Baseball Hall of Fame namesake.

Sporting Club, 99 Hudson, New York, NY 10013, 212/219-0900. Open daily until 2 am.

Best Nightclub/Singles Bar Housed in a Former Church

The Limelight

The 1980s seem further removed—not just in time, but in *attitude*—every day. But some relics symbolizing that decade still remain in the, well, limelight—such as this nightclub, which had its heyday during the go-go '80s, when it more or less pioneered the huge-club concept in New York. Housed in a former 19th-century Episcopal church, the Limelight sprawls over three noisy and lively levels and makes good use of the various trappings of its building's original function. Tired of high-energy dancing? You can take a seat in a pew. Want a bit of privacy and (relative) quiet? Head for one of the isolated chapels off the main floor. (For those who may be worried about the theological implications of partying here, rest assured the church *has* been deconsecrated.) The Limelight attracts a widely mixed clientele—from arty types to the so-called bridge and tunnel crowd; it even hosts occasional celebrities—although perhaps not as many as it did a few years ago. The club also hosts live—or Milli Vanilli-style lip-synched—musical performances, fashion shows, and other special parties. Above all, this nightspot remains a heavy-duty spot for singles to meet and dance.

The Limelight, 47 W 20th St (entrance on Sixth Ave), New York, NY 10011, 212/807-7850. Tue-Sun 10 pm-4 am.

Best Singles Bar to See and Be Seen In

Jim McMullen

The phrase "single and looking to mingle" may be a bit of bumper-sticker philosophy leftover from the disco-and-party scene of the 1970s, but it could well be the unofficial motto of many of the patrons of this lively, no-nonsense establishment. Not *every* person you run into at this classic singles bar is a model, a sports star, or an actor or actress—but many of them would like you to *believe* they are. (And the fact that McMullen *does* attract its share of genuine celebrities doesn't hurt the illusion.) On most nights, you will find the joint packed with (mostly) young, (relatively) good-looking, and (presumably) single folks eyeing each other with a mixture of cool detachment and warmer interest. McMullen also has three dining rooms for retiring from the bar area for a little nourishment—or for less-frenzied conversation when flirter and flirtee have made a desired match. *Note to the ochlophobic:* This is no place for those who fear crowds; this bar often gets jammed—especially during the after-work rush.

Jim McMullen, 1341 Third Ave, New York, NY 10021, 212/861-4700. Daily 11:30 am-4 am.

Best Faux-West-Coast Singles Bar
Lucy's Home for Retired Surfers

For bleached-blond, surf's-up sorts of good times, one need not travel all the way to the West Coast—you can merely journey to the West Side and this theme bar, which mixes a California beach atmosphere with more than a touch of Gulf Coast, Tex-Mex-style spice. There's often a line for this popular spot—a convenient time for the club to peddle its Lucy's T-shirts and other souvenirs (when did things change so that nearly *every* bar or club set up its own souvenir stand?). Once inside, try one of the excellent margaritas (or other neon-colored blender drinks) or a frosty beer—the brands of choice are, of course, Dos Equis and Corona. Or, if you're up for a bit of college-age tomfoolery, try a jello shot—paper cups of colorful, jiggly gelatin made with vodka instead of water. Lucy's also has some surprisingly good and authentic Mexican food—the fajitas, burritos, and tostadas are the best of these offerings. Sure, this is pre-packaged fun—and, as you might guess, is big with a young crowd—but it *is* a lively good time, whether you've ever "hung ten" or not.

Lucy's Home for Retired Surfers, 503 Columbus Ave (near 85th St), New York, NY 10024, 212/787-3009. Daily until 3 am.

Best Gay and Lesbian Bars
Among American cities, New York's gay scene is perhaps second only to that of San Francisco. The bars are as varied as the individuals who frequent them—some are sedate, with a quiet, neighborhood ambience, while others are absolutely wild and definitely not for the meek. There seems to be an abundance of bars for most "types"—leather bars, drag bars, disco-dance bars, quietly sophisticated bars, and so on. A good way to sort out what the city has to offer is to contact the Lesbian and Gay Community Center (208 W. 13th Street; 212/620-7310) or the popular A Different Light Bookstore (548 Hudson Street; 212/989-4850). Both sources can give detailed suggestions on bars, parties, and other gay-themed social events. In general, while Christopher Street is no longer *the* "Main Street" of

Gay New York (as it was during the 1970s and early 1980s), there are still a number of notable bars located on—or just off—it, including Badlands (388 West Street), Clyde's (340 Bleecker Street), Two Potato (145 Christopher Street), and Ty's (114 Christopher Street). Other bars to check out are The Eagle's Nest (142 Eleventh Avenue), Julius (159 W. 10th Street), Kelly's Bar (46 Bedford Street), Rounds (303 E. 53rd Street), The Spike (120 Eleventh Avenue), and Uncle Charlie's (56 Greenwich Avenue). New York's gay scene does seem to lack true lesbian bars—Crazy Nanny (21 Seventh Avenue S.) is somewhat popular, and, of the gay men's bars, Kelly's Bar and Uncle Charlie's—which is kind of the *Cheers* of N.Y. gay bars—welcome gay women and actively solicit their patronage. Lesbian house parties or special club nights can be tracked down through the above-mentioned community center and bookstore, as well as through a local Lesbian Switchboard (212/ 741-2610).

MUSIC, ENTERTAINMENT, & NON-PUB NIGHTLIFE

Best Bet for Free Concerts

The World Financial Center Arts & Events Program

Consider dancing to the swinging sound of the Count Basie Orchestra, enjoying a performance by the National Dance Institute, and listening to a poignant performance by members of the Boston Symphony Orchestra of works by Czech Jewish composers interned in the Theresienstadt concentration camp. And consider that all of these experiences can come your way by visiting a financial-district office building. And that they are all free! The World Financial Center and its stunning Winter Garden (see separate listing) provide some of the most attractive public spaces in Manhattan, areas designed specifically to provide venues for performing and visual arts. Year around, there are concerts under a canopy of palm trees (provided by 16 towering royal palms) in the Winter Garden. There is also dancing on the plaza to the likes of the Spinners and Kay Starr with the Woody Herman Orchestra. Other performances run the gamut from flamenco and Latin dancing, comedy, music, dance, theater from Indonesia, and chamber music, to Cirque du Soleil, poetry readings, an Independence Day patriotic sing-along, pop concerts, reggae, and blues. Seating is limited and on a first-come, first-served basis.

The World Financial Center Arts & Events Program, 200 Liberty St, New York, NY 10281, 212/945-0505.

Best Bach and Beethoven on a Coffee Barge

Bargemusic Ltd.

This floating concert hall is permanently moored in the East River at the historic Fulton Ferry Landing at the foot of the Brooklyn Bridge. It is the largest presenter internationally of chamber music performances, with a twice-weekly, year-round program. The venue, a 102-foot-long, 75-year-old Erie-Lackawana coffee barge, might seem quirky, but it works extremely well. The interior of this plain white barge is cozy, resembling a large living room, with seasoned cherrywood panels, a working fireplace, and a magnificent panoramic view of Manhattan. Its size, acoustics, and ambience lend well to an atmosphere of warmth, good fellowship, and quality music. On the program you'll find such talent as a solo violist who has appeared with the New York Philharmonic, the principal violist of the Toronto Symphony, a piano soloist with the Berlin Symphony, and a cello soloist from the Chinese National Philharmonic. One of the missions of Bargemusic is to provide a showcase for young American talent. It now retains a roster of more than 100 musicians, many of whom have attained international honors and status as world-class performers.

Bargemusic Ltd., Fulton Ferry Landing, Brooklyn, NY 11201, 718/624-4924.

Best Place to Hear the Fat Lady Sing

Metropolitan Opera House

This is the largest and grandest—and the most criticized—of Lincoln Center's main halls. It is decorated with Marc Chagall tapestries, crystal chandeliers (which dramatically rise with the curtain), plush red carpeting, and gold ceilings; some think the appearance is a bit over-the-top tacky, while others find it a perfectly appropriate setting for grand opera. It is the home base of the world-famous Metropolitan Opera and plays host to the top names of the opera world—Luciano Pavarotti, Placido Domingo, and Kiri Te Kanawa have appeared regularly. Tickets are expensive and sometimes hard to come by (especially for season openers, special performances, or notable debuts). Standing room tickets are more readily available and go on sale every week for the following seven days' performances, for anyone willing to line up before dawn on a Saturday morning for the privilege. The Met is often the target of criticism for its conservative and stately ways, and, indeed, opera fans who crave more adventurous and less predictable stagings may prefer those offered by the New York City Opera or even the occasional avant-garde opera at the Brooklyn Academy of Music. But, for traditional opera with big-name stars, the Met is as close to a national opera as this country has to offer. The Metropolitan Opera House also hosts the American Ballet Theater's season—and is a touring stop for dance companies such as the Royal Ballet and the Bolshoi. Due to the prodigious size of this hall (3,800 seats), not all of the outlying seats provide good (or even, in some spots, *adequate*) sightlines—however, the acoustics are amazingly good. Daily one-and-a-half-hour backstage tours include a warren of rehearsal and dressing room space, as well as the vast stage and auditorium itself (reservations required, 212/582-3512).

Metropolitan Opera House, Lincoln Center, W 64th St & Broadway, New York, NY 10023, 212/362-6000. Metropolitan Opera season runs approx. Sept-Apr.

Best Lower-Priced, English-Language, Less-Stuffy Opera Company

New York City Opera

Perhaps it's just because the Metropolitan Opera is so big that seems to make it such an appealing target to critics. Whatever the reasons, the curious fact remains that the New York City Opera—by far the smaller and less prestigious (and, the above-mentioned critics might add, less stodgy) of the city's two major opera companies—tends to garner better press and is more fondly thought of than its well-established cousin. Without expectations to be the grand opera of record, this scaled-down company does just fine, offering a slate of lower-priced (City Opera tickets can cost half as much as the Met's), but still high-quality opera during summer and early fall—the season when the Met is dark. (It has also recently successfully mounted some classy revivals of famous musicals, such as *The Sound of Music* and *South Pacific*.) Continuing the policy set by the company's last director, famed soprano Beverly Sills, City Opera features only American singers usually performing operas that are sung in English. When foreign-language performances are presented they are accompanied by English subtitles projected above the stage. This "less is more," smaller-scale approach is not without its detractors, but, in general, City Opera is a well-liked, well-attended complement to the grand designs of the Met.

New York City Opera, New York State Theater, Lincoln Center, W 64th St & Broadway, New York, NY 10023, 212/870-5570.

Most Casual, Affordable Concert Series
Mostly Mozart Festival

Each July and August, the vastly popular Mostly Mozart Festival blows into Avery Fisher Hall, like a welcome summer breeze. Although it was originally conceived as merely a fill-in for the months when the hall was unused after the conclusion of the Philharmonic's season, this festival has grown to widespread acceptance. The reasons are rather simple—great music (usually by Mozart, always performed by world-class ensembles and soloists), low prices (every seat is priced the same and available on a first-booked basis), and a general atmosphere of casualness that matches that of the festival's season (you are far more likely to see shirtsleeves—and even shorts—worn by Mozart Festival patrons, rather than the more formal attire of a Philharmonic crowd). Established in 1966, this has become a delightful summer tradition for the city's classical music fans. Discount ticket booklets (offering seats for eight concerts and coupons for savings on parking and refreshments) are available by mail from Mostly Mozart Coupon Books, Lincoln Center, 140 West 65th Street, New York, NY 10023.

Mostly Mozart Festival, Avery Fisher Hall, Lincoln Center, W 64th St & Broadway, New York, NY 10023, 212/874-2424. Jul & Aug.

Best Live Symphonic Music Hall
Avery Fisher Hall

Of course, this famous hall is known the world over as the home to one of the country's top orchestras (as well as its oldest), the New York Philharmonic (see separate listing). But, even among classical music fans, the questions often remains, "Who is Avery Fisher?" The answer, at its simplest, is a monied music fan who appreciated good sound.

When the Philharmonic left Carnegie Hall for Lincoln Center in the '60s, it moved into this 2,700-seat theater, then called Philharmonic Hall. But, alas, from the start, the acoustics were notoriously poor. Enter Mr. Fisher, who donated a total of $10 million to remodel the hall and drastically improve its sound quality (it took several attempts before this work was done satisfactorily—the hall as it stands now was finally deemed finished in 1976). Thus, and henceforth—Avery Fisher Hall. You can admire the results of both Mr. Fisher's largesse *and* the incomparable Philharmonic each September through May. During summer, Avery Fisher Hall hosts two popular annual musical events, the Kool Jazz Festival and the Mostly Mozart Festival (see separate listing), as well as the occasional "upper-level" pop or rock concert—featuring such artists as Paul Simon or Sting—where the crowd is likely to be discerning and classy, rather than rowdy.

Avery Fisher Hall, Lincoln Center, W 64th St & Broadway, New York, NY 10023, 212/874-2424.

Oldest—and Perhaps Best—Symphony Orchestra in the Country

New York Philharmonic

Born when John Tyler was president (and the United States itself was only 66 years old), the Philharmonic is both a national treasure and a fiercely loved part of New York. History abounds in this orchestra, which spent some 70 years ensconced in Carnegie Hall before moving to Avery Fisher Hall in Lincoln Center. Toscanini, Stokowski, Bernstein, and Mehta, among others, have led this fabled ensemble, and virtually every important solo performer of the last half-dozen generations has played with it. Today, the Philharmonic offers a varied program of concerts each September through May, featuring a stellar array of top-level classical soloists and visiting conductors. Whether your tastes in composers run to Beethoven (whose Eighth Symphony was debuted in the United States by the then-two-year-old Philharmonic) or Boulez (another of the Philharmonic's distinguished former musical directors), you'll find numerous performances each season to delight you. This is a highlight of cultural New York, and also one of the best entertainments in the city. Ticket prices and availability vary, depending upon a variety of factors, but a nice budget treat can be had by dropping in on the Philharmonic's open-to-the-public rehearsals, which are usually held on Thursdays at 9:45 a.m. During summer, the Philharmonic plays

a number of free outdoor concerts (at such locations
as Central Park's Great Lawn), attracting a multi-
tude of fair-weather concertgoers.

New York Philharmonic, Avery Fisher Hall, Lincoln
Center, W 64th St & Broadway, New York, NY
10023, 212/874-2424. Season runs approx. Sept-
May.

Best Overall Entertainment Center (with a Behind-the-Scenes Peek)

Lincoln Center

This is, quite simply, the capital of performing arts
in the city—if not in the entire country. This sprawling, modern complex of buildings and theaters is
home to (among others) the Metropolitan Opera, the
American Ballet Theater, the New York City Ballet,
the New York City Opera, the Kool Jazz Festival, the
Mostly Mozart Festival, and the mighty New York
Philharmonic, the country's oldest symphony orchestra. Built in the '60s, Lincoln Center has served
as the anchor for the artistic and spiritual rebirth
of the Upper West Side, which now flourishes with
restaurants and shops, and is home to a variety of
musicians, dancers, and other performing artists.
The center's main halls are well-known—the Metropolitan Opera House, Avery Fisher Hall, and the New
York State Theater (see separate listings). Lincoln
Center also offers a number of smaller venues and
lesser-known programs, including Alice Tully Hall
(in the Julliard building), said to have the best
acoustics in the Center, which hosts a variety of
chamber concerts, and, each September, the New
York Film Festival; the Julliard School's theaters,
which showcase performances by the famous
conservatory's talented students (and also various
productions by the City Ballet's acclaimed School for
American Ballet); the Guggenheim Bandshell (at the
Center's southwestern corner), offering free outdoor
concerts ranging from Bach to rock; and a branch
of the New York Public Library, which houses extensive dance, music, and theater research materials
and an intimate auditorium for concerts, recitals,
and readings. Various free events are offered year-
round, ranging from light concerts to student recitals; in summer, many of these events move outside,
to the Center's plaza, around the large fountain
(itself a favorite brown-bag lunch spot during fair
weather). Daily one-hour tours of the entire complex
are available; these sometimes coincide with rehearsal time in one of the theaters, giving you a full

behind-the-scenes view into the workings of this massive art center.

Lincoln Center, W 64th St & Broadway, New York, NY 10023, 212/877-1800.

Best Place You Need to "Practice, Practice, Practice" to Get To

Carnegie Hall

According to the hoary old joke, a young out-of-town musician with a violin case under his arm approaches a native New Yorker for directions. "How do you get to Carnegie Hall?" he innocently asks, evoking the classic punchline, "Practice, practice, practice." Jokes aside, Carnegie Hall has long been considered the pinnacle of the world of American classical music. It also symbolizes a peak in other types of entertainment—the nonclassical artists who have played here range from Isadora Duncan to Groucho Marx to the Beatles. The old hall was inaugurated by Tchaikovsky himself in 1891—others who conducted and/or played their own works here include Rachmaninoff and Gershwin—but it was almost torn down in the early '60s when the New York Philharmonic fled to what is now Avery Fisher Hall. A concentrated effort of music buffs and preservationists (led by violinist Isaac Stern) saved the old hall, preserving it for future generations of music buffs. The word among the cognoscenti is that Carnegie's acoustics haven't been quite the same since its $50 million remodeling in 1986, but this still is a great, historic spot that truly represents some of the best that the city has to offer. On Tuesdays and Thursdays, an interesting backstage tour is available.

Carnegie Hall, 154 W 57th St, New York, NY 10019, 212/247-7800.

Best Ballet Theater

New York State Theater

What do you get when you construct a theater with input from two of the foremost names in dance? Not surprisingly, the result is a theater that may be the best place around to see fine dance. The State Theater was designed as the home of New York City Ballet by noted architects Philip Johnson and Richard Foster, with advice and suggestions from New York City Ballet's illustrious founders, Lincoln Kirstein and choreographer *extraordinaire* George

Balanchine. The result is a theater that is comfortable and intimate for its size (2,800 seats), with good sightlines even from the very topmost seats. (One problem that the architects and/or dancemeisters created is the lack of a center aisle on the main floor, resulting in patrons with seats in these long rows having either to climb over, be climbed over, or both.) The ballet's two seasons run November through February and April through June; both offer can't-miss mixes of new dances and classics (with the latter often being from the voluminous catalog of the late, great Balanchine). City Ballet's *Nutcracker* is a delightful Yuletide tradition—but can be a hard ticket to obtain. Summer sees the State fill the slack for the off-season Met by featuring the well-regarded New York City Opera (see separate listing).

New York State Theater, Lincoln Center, W 64th St & Broadway, New York, NY 10023, 212/870-5570.

Best and Most Challenging Musical Entertainment Outside of Manhattan

Brooklyn Academy of Music

It certainly is fitting that this lively performing-arts center is often referred to by its sound-effect-like acronym "BAM"—since many of its performances carry the startling firepower of the avant-garde. Although BAM is the oldest performing arts venue of its type in the country (Mary Pickford, Edwin Booth, and Mark Twain performed here; it is where Enrico Caruso is said to have sung his last professional concert), the emphasis these days is on the new. This center consistently offers some of the most exciting and innovative music, dance, theater, and performance art to be found anywhere in the city (and this in an *outer borough*, much to the bewilderment of some culturally and geographically chauvinistic Manhattan dwellers!). A prime—and popular—example of BAM's offerings is the Next Wave Festival (presented each fall), which showcases the best in avant-garde performances from individuals and groups from around the world. The Academy's three theaters have also played host to such artists as composer-performer Philip Glass, multi-media performance artist Laurie Anderson, the Twyla Tharp Dance group, and former Velvet Underground rockers Lou Reed and John Cale, whose recent "Songs For Drella"—a song cycle about the late Andy Warhol—was commissioned by BAM and premiered onstage there. In 1987, BAM acquired the shuttered Majestic Theater (two blocks away at 250 Fulton Street) and rechristened it with a lavish production of the nine-hour Indian epic, *The Maha-bharata*. Special productions are often offered at this intimate, historic theater.

Brooklyn Academy of Music, 30 Lafayette Ave, Brooklyn, NY 11217, 718/636-4100.

Worst Jazz Club for Casual Conversations

Sweet Basil

Entering this pleasant, yet serious jazz club, you may be lured by the comfy-looking area you first see. Out front is a glass-enclosed sidewalk terrace, usually offering plenty of seats. But this is for a good (or bad, depending on your point of view) reason: Unfortunately, you can't see the performers from this little café area. Instead, our suggestion is to opt for the larger (but still often crowded) wood-and-brick back room, which offers perfect sightlines to the performers onstage, as well as better sound than the café area. Sweet Basil is not only one of the city's top spots among jazz aficionados—it is also considered to be one of the more pleasantly decorated jazz clubs in the city. It is lightly filled with plenty of glass and plants, but this is no mere fern-bar-with-a-combo. Sweet Basil offers a good variety of serious jazz for appreciative and knowledgeable fans, ranging from tight trios to booming big bands. One note of caution, however: If you're looking for background music to chatter over, look elsewhere—Sweet Basil's management actively enforces an unofficial (yet very real) shut-up-and-enjoy-the-music-or-get-out policy. A basic dinner menu is also offered.

Sweet Basil, 88 Seventh Ave (at Bleecker St), New York, NY 10011, 212/242-1785. Music nightly at 10 pm.

Best Jazz Club Where You Might Actually Feel Like Dancing

The Village Gate

A *New Yorker* cartoon, playing on the title of a best-selling book about a corporate takeover, called *Barbarians at the Gate*, depicted a couple of spike-haired, safety-pinned punks storming this famous Greenwich Village jazz hangout. The caption read: "Barbarians at the Village Gate." While patrons of this classic jazz spot need not worry about being overrun by "barbarians" of any stripe, there are some nights when ardent fans have piled into the old place, as if attempting some sort of takeover of their own. The Village Gate is, of course, known for its jazz offerings, but it also presents a variety of musical performances, the cream of which include off-Broadway-style mini-revues and inventive pairings of top Latin salsa bands with like-minded jazz stylists. The club offers a trio of public areas, led by a large, darkish performance space downstairs, which includes a rare (for a jazz club) spacious dance area; this gets its heaviest use during the jazzified salsa nights. Upstairs is more piano-bar-like, with a small combo playing background music for the singles-bar and casual-café set; even *further* upstairs is the so-called Top of the Gate, an intimate cabaret area.

The Village Gate, 160 Bleecker St, New York, NY 10012, 212/475-5120. Nightly 9:30 pm-2:30 am.

Best Club for Dining Upstairs and Jazz Downstairs

Fat Tuesday's

To enter this jazz club (located below the popular Tuesday's restaurant), you pass through a nondescript-looking side door, traverse a beat-up mirrored hallway, and descend a flight into a semi-claustrophobic, but comfortable, room filled with perhaps just a touch too much red velvet and mirrors. But, decor criticism aside, this is yet another of the city's top jazz clubs. It offers one of the best small-club sound systems in the city and features an interesting variety of performers. For example, in one given week, the club offered shows by jazz great McCoy Tyner and Brazilian vocalist Astrud Gilberto (of "Girl from Ipanema" fame) within a few days of each other. In addition to its always changing schedule, Fat Tuesday's Monday nights are the regular preserve of Les Paul, the nearly 70-year-old inventor of the electric guitar, who leads a crisp jazzy trio. Jazz is also offered upstairs at Tuesday's during its weekend brunch.

Fat Tuesday's, 190 Third Ave (at 17th St), New York, NY 10003, 212/533-7902. Music begins at 8 pm nightly.

Best Jazz Club That Sells Belt Buckles

The Blue Note

At first glance, the pairing of art (in the form of pure, unadulterated jazz) and commerce (represented by T-shirts, coffee mugs, and, yes, even belt buckles) at this club may seem, at best, unseemly. But you can't fault management for trying to cash in a bit on the club's storied cachet. After all, this *is* the club that has brought (and *continues* to bring) audiences such talented performers as Dizzy Gillespie, the Modern Jazz Quartet, Herbie Hancock, and Wayne Shorter, among many others. In general, this long-standing institution attracts big-name jazz artists and bands. No matter who is on the schedule, a visit here is almost always a certain winner. The Blue Note advertises itself as the "Jazz Capital of the World," a boast that perhaps the Village Vanguard (see separate listing) and Ronnie Scott's in London (among others) might dispute, but...this *is* one of the definite highlights of New York's lively jazz scene. This club also offers dining, including a pleasant light-jazz brunch on weekends. As for those belt buckles, they can be found among other club-related souvenirs at the Blue Note's popular gift shop.

The Blue Note, 131 W 3rd St, New York, NY 10012, 212/475-8592. Music nightly from 9 pm.

Best Bet for the Blues

Chicago B.L.U.E.S.

Even the most chauvinistic New York music fans would probably grudgingly defer to Chicago's pre-eminence as a blues mecca. And while such established clubs as Tramps (45 W. 21st St.) and the Dan Lynch Blues Bar (221 Second Ave.) offer a steady diet of blues artists from New York and other parts of the country, this club concentrates on importing the genuine Chicago sound. This relatively new blues showcase promises to feature only Chicago performers (importantly, playing with their regular bands, rather than with hired sidemen), offering such Windy City blues luminaries as Fenton Robinson, Jimmy Dawkins, and the legendary Son Seals. (For a real treat, keep an eye open for bookings by the current king of the Chicago scene, Buddy Guy; Eric Clapton has called Guy his favorite guitarist.) The club's decor hasn't much changed since this was the blues-oriented Abilene Cafe (meaning it still looks as grungy as a blues joint *should* look), but a few of the additions indicate the shift in the club's focus; in particular, look for the authentic purloined street sign for "East Muddy Waters Drive," honoring a stretch of South Side Chicago's 43rd Street that is home to a number of blues clubs that were frequented by the late blues great.

Chicago B.L.U.E.S., 73 Eighth Ave, New York, NY 10014, 212/255-7373. Music begins nightly at 9 pm.

Best New-Old Spot for Blues, Rock, and Zydeco

Tramps

Trying to transplant the ambience and atmosphere of a longtime club to a new location is, at best, a tricky proposition. However, the last few years have seen a number of longtime New York favorites make successful moves. Along with the Duplex and the Lone Star Roadhouse (née Café), this popular blues-rock joint has also survived the uprooting of its karma, and continues to attract lively partying crowds. The new location is a large, comfortable loft-like hall. The pillars in the open area don't harm the sightlines too much (unless, of course, you get stuck right behind one!), but the sound system is not the most reliable (although work continues to clear up its glitches) and it can make those near the speaker stacks wish they'd remembered to bring earplugs. Along with the new location has come some slightly new bookings. This is still a great place for swinging bluesy rock (or hard-rocking blues), but it also offers some newer alternative rock acts, as well as some hot zydeco dance parties. The old East 15th Street location of this club was perhaps best known as the launching spot and resident stage of Buster Poindexter and his blistering blues-rock-salsa-etcetera combo, the Banshees of Blue. This band, which had a big hit with the old island song "Hot Hot Hot," used to pack `em in at the old Tramps. In the eats department, this club is known for its good burgers—and now offers some satisfyingly authentic Creole cooking, too.

Tramps, 45 W 21st St, New York, NY 10010, 212/727-7788. Music begins nightly around 8 pm.

Best Bar to Drive You Batty

Le Bat Bar

Although Bruce Wayne and Dick Grayson (aka Batman and Robin) don't own this hot midtown discotheque, you'll probably not find a watering hole more reminiscent of their alter egos. A massive copper bat hovers over the entrance, light fixtures shaped like bats are suspended from overhead beams, and specialty drinks include Bat Bite, a blood-colored frozen concoction fashioned with triple sec, rum, lemon juice, and grenadine. The bar help has been known to don cat outfits, while clientele lean toward fashionable nocturnal black. Celeb patrons include Brooke Shields, who was among those who showed up for a post-screening party for the movie (you guessed it), *Batman Returns*. This trendy restaurant/dance club, which once was a church and later a recording studio, has three floors. A limited (but interesting, and reasonably priced) menu features main-course salads such as Peking duck and fresh grilled tuna, and entrées such as grilled chicken served with spicy black-bean-and-corn salsa, grilled swordfish steak, and farfalle with black olives, tomato, and capers. There are eight-ounce burgers, turkey club, and marinated eggplant and mozzarella sandwiches, and sides of pommes frites. Starters include calamari, spring rolls, and warm goat-cheese salad.

Le Bat Bar, 311 W 57th St, New York, NY 10019, 212/307-7228. Restaurant Mon-Fri 11:30 am-midnight, Sat & Sun 5:30 pm-12:30 am. Disco Mon-Sun 10 pm-4 am.

Best Rock Club to See Local Bands

Kenny's Castaways

Regardless of the ebb and flow of musical fashions from rock to punk to disco to electronic to rap back to rock, New York has remained a prime spot for ground-breaking talent. Artists as diverse as Bob Dylan, Paul Simon, Lou Reed, Patti Smith, Blondie, the Talking Heads, the Beastie Boys, and They Might Be Giants either came from New York or got a significant career boost while headquartered here. Who'll be the Next Big Thing to come out of the Big Apple? It's hard to predict, but the chances are that if they're a local rock band, you can catch them first at this Village favorite. Kenny's has been pulling in big crowds for years for its mix of (mostly) rock and (some) folk acts, with the majority of its booking being local bands. Such recent success stories as Cyndi Lauper and the Smithereens played here before moving up the ladder of popularity—perhaps you can see a future critical or popular success or two before their following grows (not to mention their ticket prices!). Kenny's is definitely one of the top spots in the Village to see live rock; if no particular act on any given week's schedule appeals, try the Monday night open jam (at midnight) for an unstructured, rollicking musical party.

Kenny's Castaways, 157 Bleecker St, New York, NY 10012, 212/473-9870. Nightly; music begins around 9 pm.

Best Relocated Honky-Tonk

Lone Star Roadhouse

The old Lone Star Café, which was downtown on Fifth Avenue, is gone, which could have spelled disaster for the city's country-music fans and transplanted Texans. But, almost quicker than you could say "Remember the Alamo!," the owners of the old Café opened this bigger, slightly different incarnation of the Lone Star. The exterior of this club resembles one of those gaudy tour buses, decorated with pastel murals, seen tooling up and down the interstates, ferrying various country or rock musicians to their next gig. Inside, the Lone Star is full of people who have been wearing cowboy hats and dancing the two-step well before Garth Brooks and the recent country-music boom hit the big time. The decor features a variety of Texas-themed doo-dads, many of which made the trip uptown from the old spot. The music offered here is, of course, mostly country, but there is more than a little rock, folk, and blues mixed in for good measure. The bookings are certainly eclectic: the "Godfather of Soul," James Brown, and New Orleans' first musical family, the Neville Brothers, have played here, and they are definitely not your average 10-gallon-hat performers. The food is basic, but fairly authentic Tex-Mex fare (including great chili). This may also be about the only place in town to try the unofficial dish of Texas, chicken-fried steak.

Lone Star Roadhouse, 240 W 52nd St, New York, NY 10019, 212/245-2950. Music nightly at 9 pm.

Best Intimate Rock Club for Occasional Superstar Performances

The China Club

Head down the stairs into a smallish (capacity 250) basement room, decorated mostly in blue with Oriental touches, and you find yourself in "the living room of rock" (as the China Club likes to bill itself). Indeed, like a living room (or perhaps a rumpus room?), it plays intimate host to many drop-in rock stars (David Bowie, in particular, seems to have an affinity to playing surprise mini-sets here). The success—and classy cachet—of this club has spawned offshoots in other cities, but these other branches seem to skate along on the considerable reputation of the Big Apple version. In other locations, the semi-promised drop-ins are fewer and farther between—but this one is the real McCoy. It usually stays crowded late, especially if a big star is playing a big show at the Garden (or another large venue in or around town). But even if Eric Clapton or Stevie Wonder *don't* drop in, chances are that you'll be entertained by the young-and-hungry rock 'n' rollers who are booked nightly. The China Club likes to play it cool, but the atmosphere is fairly casual—you don't have to look like (or dress like) anything in particular to fit in.

The China Club, 2130 Broadway at 75th St, New York, NY 10023, 212/877-1166. Nightly 10 pm-4 am.

Best Classic Punk Club

CBGB

Its glory days of the late 1970s, when this club served as a launching pad for such punk/new wave luminaries as the Ramones, Blondie, and the Talking Heads, may have passed, but this grungy-but-comfortable spot is still a good place to hear various types of (usually loud) music. CBGB attracts its share of patrons in leather and spikes—as well as less-violently bedecked fans—for an everchanging lineup of hardcore, thrash, post-punk, and other rock bands. This club is narrow, dark, and rather cave-like, with exposed beams and walls covered with graffiti, but the sound system is great and its tiny stage has hosted dozens of hot bands on their way up (a recent example of which is the band Living Colour). You never know which of today's headliners will become tomorrow's superstars—and you can see them here first. The unusual name? It isn't code—just an abbreviation from the club's earlier, omnimusical days. It's short for CBGB OMFUG, which stands for "Country, Bluegrass, and Blues—and Other Music From the Underground."

CBGB, 315 Bowery, New York, NY 10003, 212/982-4052. Daily 8:30 pm-2:30 am.

Best Bet for Alternative Rock

The Marquee

Because of its size and influence, New York is a "must" stop for every touring rock band. But most bands that pass through town aren't popular enough to play to the stadium-sized crowds that see the big names (at the Garden or out at the Meadowlands). Many of these up-and-coming bands—the kind that get play on college or other "alternative" radio stations—instead perform at this club, where appreciative fans pack the place to catch their favorite groups. The Marquee has been holding down the alternative-rock fort on this somewhat desolate block near the West Side Highway for years, and is considered *the* main spot in town to hear the current darlings of college radio before they make it big and hit the mainstream or simply fade away. The bookings here always include lots of British bands—often in their U.S. debuts—making the Marquee a great place to see the next big "movement" or "scene" in British rock (after, for example, the Liverpool bands of the late 1980s and the pseudo-psychedelic Manchester groups of the early 1990s). The occasional blues act or smaller mainstream band also plays here....But, in general, if you're looking for a place to see such groups as the Stone Roses or the Judybats, the Marquee is for you. *Note of orientation:* The heavy concentration of British acts is understandable once you know that this is a sister club of sorts to the famous Marquee in London, which once showcased such then-new groups as the Rolling Stones, the Who, and the Kinks in the 1960s.

The Marquee, 547 W 21st St, New York, NY 10011, 212/929-3257.

Best Disco You *Might* Be Able to Get Into

Stringfellow's

Yes, the conditional "might" in the title of this listing does refer to the fact that this primarily singles club employs an admission policy that can be described charitably as "selective." Those who don't care what the fuss is about probably simply would call it inane. Those unswervably bent upon gaining entrance, tend to dress *way* up to pass muster with the fashion police who man the doors, affecting black clothing and a look that says, "I don't care if I get in, but I *do* belong here." Owned by the peripatetic Peter Stringfellow and a spin-off of his exclusive London club of the same name, this is a very 1970s-style disco, flashy and camp. Its slightly-over-the-top stylishness involves lots of mirrors, glittery decorations, a pink marble bar, and waitresses in revealing get-ups. Some nightclubbers don't like the attitude or atmosphere, but a stop here is *de rigueur* when Stringfellow himself is around, throwing his legendarily outrageous and bombastic parties. This nightspot is also a restaurant prior to 11 p.m., the bewitching hour when a separating wall ceremoniously rises, signaling a stampede to the dance floor.

Stringfellow's, 35 E 21st St, New York, NY 10010, 212/254-2444. Tue-Sat 8 pm-4 am.

Best Disco You Can Get Into

Palladium

Once a concert hall, the Palladium has been stylishly remodeled into a state-of-the-art dance club by famed Japanese architect Arata Isozaki. This is a logical successor to the pioneering Studio 54 (the Palladium was started by that club's founders), and is large and lively—a good representation of a "typical" Manhattan disco. The club's decor is highlighted by rotating selections of art (ranging from wall-covering murals to site-specific experimental installations) by hot and/or up-and-coming N.Y. artists. Video monitors are placed strategically throughout; spacious balconies overlook the dance floor. This huge club holds 3,500 and is usually packed with mixed crowds of straights and gays, yuppies and artsy types. The Palladium also hosts live-performance "dance parties," featuring MTV music acts. The sound is excellent and there are plenty of video screens—but sightlines during performances are only so-so once you get away from the very front of the room. Some haughtily categorize this club with the Limelight and look at it askance (since both clubs have liberal door admission policies). The crowd may not be diehard clubbers, but the Palladium, nonetheless, can offer a fun evening of dancing and nightlife. The club's separate (and harder-to-get-into) Michael Todd Room is a VIP-style enclave for more intimate—yet still high energy—dancing and partying: Friday nights are best here.

Palladium, 126 E 14th St, New York, NY 10003, 212/473-7171. Thu-Sat 8:30 pm-4 am; Michael Todd Room, Thu-Sat 9 pm-4 am.

Best Club for Dancing, Posing, and "Training"

The Tunnel

One almost expects the lights of a rumbling BMT express train to appear at the end of this tunnel, what with this Chelsea club's massive brick archways looming over abandoned railroad tracks. This unique mélange of exposed brick, crisscrossing steel beams, and other site-specific details makes the Tunnel an interesting nightclub to see, as well as to be seen at. It also offers a warren of smaller rooms and passages off a long, cavernous (and, at times, nearly deafeningly loud) main room, plus a somewhat more intimate basement for conversation or, at least, quieter dancing (the basement is often booked for private parties). The club attracts a good-looking, eclectic crowd (sharp Armani suits, well-worn leather get-ups), and has a reputation as being a good spot for a first look at the latest dances ("vogueing"—striking magazine-model-like poses on a crowded dance floor—was in style here long before Madonna released her smash hit about it). It can be occasionally dead here early—which, in the relative time of nightclubbing, can mean as "late" as 1 or 2 a.m.—as those in-the-know make this the last stop of a fashionably late evening.

The Tunnel, 220 Twelfth Ave (entrance on W 27th St), New York, NY 10001, 212/244-6444. Wed-Fri 9 pm-4 am, Sat 10 pm-4 am.

Best "Members-Only" Dance Club That Is Worth Joining

Sound Factory

This huge, hot, and happening dance club probably appeals to inveterate clubbers who absolutely love huge, hot, and happening dance clubs. Those who think they'd like to visit a few times (or even more), probably won't object to paying the membership fee ($15-$25, which is almost always demanded of first-timers or other non-regulars) to enter this haven of '90s club culture. This is one of the latest "big crowd" clubs, and, on any given weekend, it may attract a long line. The Sound Factory recently (as of this writing) celebrated its third anniversary. Of course, that isn't a long time compared to many of the city's jazz or other music clubs, but it's a veritable lifetime among popular dance clubs. This place has weathered the migration of those fickle club-hoppers who switch fealty with the opening of the each *next* new club—and is still highly regarded by most segments of the city's dance-club society. One of the reasons is that Sound Factory continues to offer a wild scene of hot, loud music (usually non-stop, beat-heavy House music) and is densely packed with whirling bodies in a big, open space. While this club isn't for everyone, no one group dominates—the crowd is a well-integrated mix of males and females, whites and blacks, and gays and straights. Those who want to experience "prime time" here, may wish to take a nap beforehand. Some nights, things don't really start jumping until around 4 a.m.!

Sound Factory, 535 W 27th St, New York, NY 10001, 212/643-0728. Fri & Sat midnight-7 am.

Best Bet for a Musical Visit to the Tropics

S.O.B.'s

The music mainly offered here is as easy as "ABC"—as in Africa, Brazil, and the Caribbean. (The initials that this club is casually known by stand for Sounds of Brazil.) The lively "World Music" played here is big with students, expatriates of more equatorial climes, and simply serious dancers. They all come to S.O.B.'s to boogie along to the sensual rhythms of samba, bossa nova, reggae, salsa, and other highly danceable music offered by both recordings and by live bands. (Another not-to-be-discounted draw is the popular Brazilian food; but, make no mistake, the beat is the thing here.) With the fake palm trees overhead and the dance-sweaty crowd on the floor, this high-energy spot can seem as dense and moist as a rain forest; if the polyrythmic pleasures of this club's pulsing music can't pull you out onto the (usually packed) dance floor, you should probably consider yourself an official wallflower. S.O.B.'s is a great place to spend Carnival if you can't make it to Rio.

S.O.B.'s (Sounds of Brazil), 204 Varick St at W Houston St, New York, NY 10014, 212/243-4940. Open Mon-Sat; music begins around 9:30 pm.

Best Bet for Ballroom Dancing

Roseland

Some people's response to hearing about the Roseland or about ballroom dancing in general is disbelief, as if it's amazing that this place is still around and that people still come here to dance. Dance, they do, to sprightly big-band swing music, and, on certain nights, to a spicy Latin-oriented band. This historic spot dates from the 1920s, and has been considerably spiffed up recently. It pulls in big crowds every Saturday night—but Thursday, Friday, and Sunday also have their own crowds of loyal supporters (many regulars never miss a week). Undoubtedly, many singles go in hopes of meeting that special someone with a shared passion for ballroom dancing and perhaps even of joining the list of 600-plus couples who met here and later married (the list covers the walls of the ballroom's lobby). A restaurant and bar are popular spots to take on refreshment and nourishment between periods of tripping the light fantastic. After midnight, the Roseland becomes a disco, attracting a different crowd of dancers; it also hosts occasional concerts and parties. Those who think that the Roseland is helplessly old-fashioned and out of it, might consider that hot funk-rocker Prince has used this old hall as a surprise tune-up spot before major concert tours.

Roseland, 239 W 52nd St, New York, NY 10019, 212/247-0200. Thu-Sun 2:30 pm-5 am.

Best Music Clubs Where the Audience Are the Performers

Speakeasy, Sun Mountain, and Lion's Den

For wannabes with a hankering to climb onstage and entertain an audience with their playing and singing—perhaps by even performing an original song—the traditional "Open-Mike" nights (usually on Mondays) at these clubs are a good place to start. The Speakeasy is the granddaddy of these clubs; it still carries on the torch of New York's 1960s folk scene, when Bob Dylan and Joan Baez (among others) were holding forth here and at the Bitter End. Located in the back of a Greek restaurant, the Speakeasy offers live folk music every night of the week (the only club in the city to do so), with the bookings fairly evenly split between the best modern acts and some of the oldies-but-goodies. Open-mike night is popular here because of the club's pedigree, and the varied performers can be as fun to watch as to join. A similar (if less storied) atmosphere can be found at Sun Mountain, a small, darkish downstairs room, where original compositions about lost love are often the order of the night. For those who would rather lead a band than perform solo, the Lion's Den is the place to go. This club provides a grizzled (but usually amiable) house band to back up any would-be balladeers; as you might guess, the sounds here can be a bit louder and more aggressive than the folkie offerings at the other clubs. Most open-mike performers are not likely to be "discovered" and offered a recording contract while strumming their acoustics at these clubs, but for the don't-quit-your-day-job level of musicians, it can be an enjoyable experience.

Speakeasy, 107 Macdougal St, New York, NY 10012, 212/598-9670. Sun Mountain, 82 W 3rd St, New York, NY 10012, 212/477-0622. Lion's Den, 214 Sullivan St, New York, NY 10012, 212/477-2782.

Best Dance Club That's No Horror

Nell's

Named after and co-owned by Nell Campbell, one of the co-stars of the cult movie *The Rocky Horror Picture Show*, Nell's has for years been considered one of the top clubs in New York. The main floor of this Village club pulls off the improbable feat of looking like an English gentlemen's club, with imposing chandeliers, overstuffed velvet couches, and huge oil paintings that look as if they have been hanging in the same spot since Queen Victoria's coronation. This room is where light suppers and decent Hard Rock Cafe-type fare is served. Below this faux-elegant dining, drinking, and mingling area is the club's always-jumping basement dance floor. Nell's is a good spot for stargazing, attracting such celebrities as Robert DeNiro, Sting, and Prince. Although Nell's no longer is cutting-edge chic, its doormen can be daunting (rumor has it that Cher, in a rare down-dressing day, was once refused admission), but, for an interesting and singular experience, many consider it worth getting decked out and giving it a try. Nell's tends to be *very* crowded on weekends.

Nell's, 246 W 14th St, New York, NY 10011, 212/675-1567. Daily 10 pm-4 am.

Best Harlem Music Mecca

Apollo Theater

It would have been a shame if the historic theater that (among *many* other entertainment triumphs) first offered the musical genius of such stars as Lena Horne and Ella Fitzgerald, and which helped launch the career of Michael Jackson had closed its doors forever out of neglect and apathy. For a time it looked as though the Apollo's days were numbered. But, after a rocky period in the late 1970s and early 1980s, the jewel of Harlem entertainment glitters brightly once more. This classic theater (built in 1913, when, ironically, it served white audiences only) has been spruced up and is once more showcasing the best of up-and-coming or already-there talent in—mostly, but not solely—black music and comedy. In addition to various scheduled concerts and variety showcases, a great time to visit the Apollo is Wednesday night for the traditional weekly Amateur Night competition. Not only are these usually entertaining for audiences, but they are also raucous trials-by-fire for the performers. Apollo fans are famous for their enthusiasm, for *or* against any given act. No vaudevillian hook is necessary here for faltering acts—the crowd will literally (and loudly) "boo" them off the Apollo's stage. *Note:* For a taste of the Wednesday night spectaculars, tune in to the weekly "Showtime at the Apollo" television show.

Apollo Theater, 253 W 125th St, New York, NY 10027, 212/749-5838. Show days and times vary; Amateur Night, Weds 7:30 pm.

Best Bet to (Occasionally) Spot "The Boss"

The Bottom Line

Many are the nights when this famous rock club presents shows that mean more to the musicians than the "fans" attending the show. This is because the Bottom Line has a reputation for hosting record-company sponsored showcases where ticket availability is limited because the company buys huge blocks of ducats to stack the crowd in favor of their artists. This, in turn, is supposed to pump up a positive review or help create a buzz among deejays and other industry folk. The good news is that these events usually only take place during the club's early shows; to cheer with the "real" fans, our suggestion is to hold out until the late shows. This large club usually features rock acts (with a smattering of folkies and country artists). It still offers an interesting line-up of (mostly) up-and-coming acts, but some say that its heyday of providing cutting-edge excitement (such as the days when Bruce "The Boss" Springsteen made this his NYC base of operations) is past. But those are probably the same people who missed Springsteen's unannounced performance here the week before his first-ever live television appearance (on "Saturday Night Live"). And if "The Boss" still likes to hang out here, it ought to be good enough for all those rock 'n' roll naysayers. The Bottom Line has also recently attracted attention for its intriguing occasional songwriter series, where notable rock, folk, or blues writers/performers explore and explain the art of songwriting. This club also offers basic burgers, pizza, and snacks.

The Bottom Line, 15 W 4th St, New York, NY 10012, 212/228-6300. Showtimes vary; often at 8 and 11 pm.

Best Avant-Garde Music and Performance Club

The Knitting Factory

We have a friend who says that this fairly unclassifiable place is both *so* New York, and, yet, at the same time, *not* New York. Her explanation: The music and other performances here are new, vital, and almost always challenging and exciting, just like the club's host city. However, she also thinks that The Knitting Factory is pretty much bereft of attitude, moderately priced, and a comfortable spot to be— somewhat *unlike* the Big Apple. (She's a native New Yorker, and is therefore allowed to think that way and *still* love the city.) The music and performance art offered here is sometimes wildly avant-garde, other times just outside the mainstream; it usually involves some form of rock (even if minimalist or experimental), but can also include jazz and classical. Nightly performances are presented upstairs, while the main floor area offers drinks, mingling, and conversation, as well as the occasional "small" performance (such as a monologuist or an acoustic duo). The Knitting Factory can definitely be considered "counterculture," but it is certainly not affected or elitist. From time to time, it also features poetry and fiction readings by local authors.

The Knitting Factory, 47 E Houston St, New York, NY 10012, 212/219-3055. Nightly 5:30 pm-4 am.

Best Historic Comedy Club (and More)

The Duplex

This club lives up to its name—it is split-level and has a somewhat split personality, too. Downstairs is a rollicking good-timey piano bar sort of place, where, between rounds, your waitress may make a sidetrip to the microphone to deliver a pleasant, clever rendition of a pop or show tune. And this entertainment may be followed by not-so-pleasant-nor-clever renditions of similar tunes, as the sing-along microphone gets passed around. The upstairs area is a more traditional cabaret, featuring musical or comedy performers nightly. The downstairs piano bar area also showcases young and/or new comedic talent every Saturday night, in keeping with the Duplex's tradition. This is, after all, the new location of a club that gave Woody Allen, Rodney Dangerfield, and Joan Rivers significant exposure early in their careers. (Allen's recent biography recounted how the then-25-year-old novice crafted his early stand-up act upstairs at the old Duplex doing two shows a night, six nights a week for several months for no money—playing to audiences that averaged less than a dozen each night.) The Duplex claims to be the city's oldest cabaret, having spent more than 40 years on Grove Street, around the corner from where it is located now. It still attracts a loyal crowd of regulars, and is very popular with gays and lesbians.

The Duplex, 61 Christopher St at Seventh Ave, New York, NY 10014, 212/255-5488. Shows nightly; times vary.

Best Comedy Club That *Does* Get Respect (Even If Its Owner Doesn't)
Dangerfield's

What are the guys to do when their spouses or women friends want to spend a harmless night gazing at the "entertainment" on display at the women-only Chippendales (see separate listing)? Well, they could wait out the ladies at this classic comedy club, just a few doors down from the famous house of beefcake. This club is practically prehistoric by modern comedy standards—the master of "no respect," Rodney Dangerfield, opened it more than 20 years ago, when his comedy career was stuck in a bit of a limbo between his original stand-up successes and his eventual movie hits. You're not likely to see Rodney here these days (although he does make occasional appearances), but his club is well known—and appreciated—for booking the sort of talented newcomers that Rodney likes to befriend and boost (which, in recent years, has included Andrew Dice Clay and the late Sam Kinison).

Dangerfield's, 1118 First Ave at 61st St, New York, NY 10021, 212/593-1650. Shows nightly; times vary.

Best Comedy Clubs with Choices
Caroline's and Caroline's at the Seaport

This pair of comedy clubs also gives patrons a couple of choices: near Midtown or near Wall Street? Up-and-coming jokesters or big-name comedians? These sister clubs have their differences, but both usually supply a solid evening of entertainment. The original Caroline's (on Eighth Avenue) is one of the many comedy clubs left over from the stand-up boom of the 1980s. It also launched a cable television comedy show that features many of the fine comics booked here. Today, it is complemented by the new, larger Caroline's located at the South Street Seaport.

The new location hosts the medium-to-big comedy names (from sitcoms, movies, and cable specials), while the original Caroline's mostly showcases less-heralded comics, usually in longer sets than the few minutes they can occasionally scrape together on the late-night talk shows. In fact, Caroline's is one of the pioneers of allowing comics—even unknown ones—to spend an entire hour or more at a time in front of an audience.

Caroline's, 333 Eighth Ave, New York, NY 10001, 212/924-3499. Wed-Sat 5 pm-3 am. Caroline's at the Seaport, 89 South St (Pier 17 at the South Street Seaport), New York, NY 10038, 212/233-4900. Open nightly; show times vary.

Best Comedy Club with a Descriptive Name

Catch a Rising Star

As its name implies, this is a good spot to "catch" new comics before they hit it big. (In fact, this club's name is usually shortened to simply "Catch"—as in "Who's at 'Catch' tonight?") It wasn't too many years ago that you could've seen Robin Williams or Billy Crystal performing on stage here—and, these days, such big-name performers as Eddie Murphy, Roseanne Arnold, and "Saturday Night Live" cast members, among others, have been known to make occasional drop-in appearances. This club offers a small, intimate atmosphere—which, as comedy-club veterans know, means don't sit in the front half of the audience unless you don't mind having your hairstyle, tie, or date being the target of the comic's zingers. Even with a mostly unknown crop of performers, this place is usually considered a good bet for a night of yucks. And you never know when tonight's headliner will become tomorrow's TV or movie star—and you can say you saw them way back when.

Catch a Rising Star, 1487 First Ave at E 77th St, New York, NY 10021, 212/794-1906. Shows nightly; times vary.

Best Comedy Club with a Non-Descriptive Name

The Improvisation

This club is more commonly referred to as "the Improv," yet its name is a bit of a misnomer. Rather than offering true improvisational comedy (à la

Chicago's famed Second City), the Improv features
the usual crew of stand-up comedians—with the
occasional magician thrown in. This is yet another
New York comedy original with a regular "Evening
At..." type of cable television show. This was the first
Improv; the hot one out in Lotusland is a successful
knockoff. The Improv has been knocking 'em dead
for about 25 years, and audiences in years past
caught heavy, heady doses of such now-legendary
comic geniuses as Richard Pryor and Robin Williams. The bookings here usually include a good
selection of medium-to-big names, without many
clunkers....Except for the occasional—and inevitably
bad—comedy magician (someone here seems to have
a soft-spot for jokey, hokey Mandrakes). But it usually is worth waiting until the magician disappears
for an appearance (especially late at night) by one
of the club's superstar alumni.

The Improvisation, 358 W 44th St, New York, NY
10036, 212/765-8268. Nightly; shows and times vary.

Best Revival Movie Houses
Theater 80 St. Marks and Film Forum 2

Although VCRs and movie cassettes are becoming
the rule rather than the exception, there remains a
niche for the revival movie house. Simply put, not
all movie fans want to see their favorite film classic
shrunk to TV size. Also, there is something
otherworldly and more than a little magical about
sitting in a large, dark theater with a crowd (or even
a smattering) of strangers to share the experience of
a fine film. Unfortunately, some of the city's best and
most beloved revival houses have closed or been
converted into first-run theaters. Recent years saw
the loss of the Thalia (which claimed to be the
country's first revival house) and the popular Regency. But a number of choices remain for fans who
want to see old movies (and even important films of
recent vintage) on a big screen. The Theatre 80 St.
Marks is small and has seen better days, but it
provides great double features, ranging from 1930s
screwball comedies to Hitchcock thrillers and noted
foreign films. The features change daily. The Film
Forum 2 is the middle theater of an unusual triplex.
Theaters 1 and 3 offer weeklong (or longer) bookings
of recent foreign, independent, or otherwise "small"
films. Film Forum 2 runs thematic double features
or single films followed by rare film or video clips of
a related nature. Some special showings can run for
several days or a week, but, usually, the films change

daily. The double-feature aspect can provide an interesting way to compare a director's or actor's work, or to contrast similar themes in different movies. Our all-time favorite revival-house pairing was *Casablanca* followed by Woody Allen's Bogart-inspired fantasy, *Play It Again, Sam*, especially since the Allen film begins with him sitting in a revival theater, watching the end of *Casablanca*. Special revival-type showings can also be found at some museums or art schools.

Theater 80 St. Marks, 80 St. Marks Pl, New York, NY 10003, 212/254-7400. Film Forum 2, 209 W Houston, New York, NY 10014, 212/727-8110.

Best Bet for a "Girls' Night Out"

Chippendales

This is the well-known spot for pecs, pecks, and peeks. Chippendales has become a nearly "must" for bachelorette soirees, birthday parties, and other "girls'" nights out (and, yes, it *is* for females only). The "dancers" ("prancers" might be more accurate) look like exhibitionist rejects from "American Gladiators"—all bulging biceps, shoulder-length (or longer) hair, and perfect orthodontia. They grin and bare it (or, at least, *nearly* all of it) for a usually boisterous and always appreciative crowd. Patrons wishing to reward the never-blushing dancers tuck dollar bills into their barely-there G-strings, usually garnering a thank-you kiss from the beefcake and an energetic whoop from the crowd. For patrons needing proof that they *really were* at risque Chippendales, there is a wide variety of souvenir clothing, calendars, and other assorted knickknacks (the nudie-boy playing cards seem to be a perennial favorite). *Note to men:* The singles action is said to be hot-hot-hot in the bars nearest this club after the show lets out...for those who can stand comparison to a hunk named Snake.

Chippendales, 1110 First Ave at 61st St, New York, NY 10021, 212/935-6060. Wed-Sun from 8:30 pm.

MUSEUMS, GALLERIES, THEATERS, & OTHER SITES

Best Collection of Museums on One Street (with Its Own Festival)

"Museum Mile" on Fifth Avenue

This is perhaps the greatest concentration of cultural sites in one place *anywhere* in the world. On a stretch of Fifth Avenue, from about 70th Street north to 106th Street, are some of New York's most glittering cultural jewels, including the Frick Collection, the Metropolitan Museum of Art, the Guggenheim Museum, the Museum of New York City, the Cooper-Hewitt Museum, El Museo del Barrio, the National Academy of Design, the International Center of Photography, and the Jewish Museum. Additionally, just off Fifth Avenue (or within a block of it) are the Museum of Modern Art, the Whitney Museum of American Art, and the Museum of Television and Radio. Each June—on the first or second Tuesday of the month)—a "Museum Mile Festival" is held, with participating museums offering special events and free admission. During the festival, Fifth Avenue is closed to traffic between 82nd and 104th streets, and is instead filled with musicians, dancers, artists, and other various street performers. (For more information on the festival,

153

call 212/397-8222.) *A note of advice:* If you're planning a museum stroll along this street, avoid Mondays, the day that most of the city's major museums are closed.

"Museum Mile," Fifth Ave (north of 70th St), New York, NY.

Best Little-Known Museum in Manhattan

National Academy of Design

This pleasant little find (underutilized, both by visitors and residents), was established in 1825 as a school of drawing; today, it traces America's homegrown artistic tradition. Modeled after London's Royal Academy, it is run by painters, sculptors, architects, and other artists, and offers an extensive collection of paintings, photographs, sculpture, and prints, mostly from the 19th and 20th centuries. The museum's permanent collection is full of works by the Academy's elected members; it also hosts some of the best visiting exhibitions to come to town. The Academy is associated with the nearby School of Fine Arts, where it offers classes in art *and* in art appreciation. The Academy also sponsors an Annual Exhibition, one of the last remaining open-museum competitions in this country. *Trivia note:* One of the Academy's founders was inventor Samuel F. B. Morse, who was also a portrait painter of note.

National Academy of Design, 1083 Fifth Ave (at 89th St), New York, NY 10128, 212/369-4880. Tue noon-8 pm, Wed-Sun noon-5 pm.

Best Museum That's Not a "Flash" in the Pan

International Center of Photography

Picture this: A little-known, but delightful museum and gallery of photography, housed in a pleasant landmark building on Fifth Avenue on the Upper East Side. While other museums have notable photography collections, this singular museum is devoted solely to photography. Its permanent collection displays works by most of the 20th century's most important photographers, including Henri Cartier-Bresson, Man Ray, and Yousuf Karsh. The ICP also offers the finest touring photographic exhibitions, good lecture series, and an exhaustive resource library. Recognizing the importance of video art in recent years, the ICP has added a screening gallery for video installations. The museum shop offers a vast selection of how-to photography books, top-level coffee-table-style art catalogs, and quality photography posters. A Midtown branch of the ICP (1133 Sixth Avenue; 212/768-4680) offers pieces from the museum's permanent collection as well as rotating visiting exhibitions; this satellite location actually has *more* exhibition space than the "main" museum on Fifth Avenue.

International Center of Photography, 1130 Fifth Ave (at 94th St), New York, NY 10128, 212/860-1777. Tue noon-8 pm, Wed-Fri noon-5 pm, Sat & Sun 11 am-6 pm.

Best Museum a Ferry Ride Away
Staten Island Institute of Arts and Sciences

Less than five minutes' walk from the ferry terminal in St. George (look back for spectacular views of Manhattan's skyline) are galleries featuring the work of Staten Island artists as well as important traveling shows. Changing exhibits interpret the Institute's vast holding of more than two million artifacts exploring the art, natural science, and cultural history of Staten Island. Exhibitions include such eclectic subjects as Staten Island's harbor herons, a traveling show about the Hopi Indians, vintage clothing and accessories, the Fine Art of Dining (with a silver and china collection), and Beetlemania (from the Institute's insect collection). The museum's art collection includes fine and decorative art dating from ancient to contemporary times. For a unique child's birthday celebration, ask about a Dinosaur Party, where youngsters "dig up" fossils, reassemble a dinosaur skeleton, create stick puppets and clay dinosaurs, and see the film *Dinosaurs*. The museum shop has a small, but nice, selection of gifts ranging from 75-cent rocks, to please children, to an $80 elegant hand-quilted vest from Peru. Included are prints and sketches of Staten Island, plates, figurines, hand-painted tiles, and hand-crafted wooden boxes.

Combine a visit to this museum with a ferry ride and a stop at Lil's Eatery (see separate listings).

Staten Island Institute of Arts & Sciences, 75 Stuyvesant Pl, NY 10301, 718/727-1135. Mon-Fri 9 am-5 pm, Sun 2-5 pm. Suggested donation $2.50, seniors and students $1.50.

Best Art a Ferry Ride Away

Snug Harbor Cultural Center

On summer evenings there are outdoor concerts in the meadow, perhaps the New York Philharmonic, the Tommy Dorsey Orchestra, or Chuck Mangione. In December, you can shop for choice merchandise assembled from the shops of different museums around the metropolitan area. Throughout the year, this wonderful showcase of performing arts offers changing art exhibits in two galleries; classes in fine arts, crafts, and photography; recitals; opera; silent-film festivals; and jazz, classical, and folk concerts. The setting for this cultural smorgasbord is a nationally landmarked historic district that includes some of the country's finest examples of Greek Revival architecture. Summer-long, an ongoing Sculpture Festival sprawls over 80 acres of landscaped lawns, meadows, and parkland. Now that a trolley service connects Snug Harbor with the ferry terminal, this flourishing arts center is accessible by public transportation. Founded in 1801 as a hospital and home for retired sailors, it was the first of its kind in the United States. It includes an award-winning children's museum (see separate listing) and a botanical garden with a Victorian rose garden, a greenhouse with seasonal displays, and annual sales of birdseed and bulbs.

Snug Harbor Cultural Center, 914 Richmond Terrace, Staten Island, NY 10301, 718/448-2500. Admission charges and times vary according to attraction or event.

Best Museum That's a Nice Place to Visit...but You Wouldn't Want to Live There

Lower East Side Tenement Museum

In the late 19th century the Lower East Side was packed with immigrants fleeing the pogroms of Russia. More than 300,000 people were crammed into a square mile of Lower Manhattan, working in sweatshops and struggling with pushcarts and crammed into threadbare, decaying tenements that lacked privacy, light, and ventilation. The harsh realities of this grim housing is recreated at this free historical museum, located in an actual abandoned tenement. It traces the bitter struggles of these immigrants who were to endure the most appalling living conditions in the effort to escape tyranny and build a new life. The museum offers changing exhibits, forums, theater presentations, and other programs on immigrant history. On Sundays there are wonderful living-history tours, such as a neighborhood walking tour, "Peddler's Pack," led by a guide costumed in immigrant garb, and "The Street Where We Lived," another historical walking tour led by a university professor.

Lower East Side Tenement Museum, 97 Orchard St, New York, NY 10002, 212/431-0233. Tue-Fri 11 am-4 pm, Sun 10 am-3 pm.

Good Place to Learn About New York *Before* You Explore It
Museum of the City of New York

New York past and present—and even some projections of New York of the future—mingle and delight at this informative and entertaining museum. This is a great place for visitors to orient themselves to the city and its fascinating history—but it is also a terrific (if somewhat overlooked) place for residents to learn more about their home. Photos, dioramas, and historical recreations explore the many faces and phases of the city, from the days of the Indians and Peter Minuet through its brief period as the U.S. capital through the "melting pot" years and ever-expanding periods of boom to today's megalopolis. The best of these include a recreation of the ornate Moorish-style bedroom of John D. Rockefeller's Fifth Avenue mansion and a presentation of furniture, paintings, and personal effects that belonged to Alexander Hamilton. Of special note is the Theater Collection, focusing on the city's longtime role as the unofficial theater capital of the world (only London comes close), and the exquisite Toy Collection, full of little trinkets of days past—and probably of more interest to nostalgic parents than to today's kids (not a Ghostbuster nor Ninja Turtle in sight!). Providing a good overview of the museum's collection and of the city's history is *The Big Apple,* a thorough multimedia blitz, which shows the times and places of New York through film, still photos, music, narration, and sound effects. For tourists who like their history on the hoof (as it were), the Museum of the City of New York offers a great series of informed neighborhood walks. *A bit of history:* This museum was originally housed in Gracie Mansion, before it became the mayor's official residence (see separate listing).

Museum of the City of New York, 1220 Fifth Ave (at 103rd St), New York, NY 10029, 212/534-1672. Tue-Sat 10 am-5 pm, Sun 1-5 pm.

Best Film Funhouse

American Museum of the Moving Image

Stare into the computerized "Magic Mirror" to see how you look clad in satin boxing trunks from the movie *Rocky* or the genie costume worn by Barbara Eden on the TV show "I Dream of Jeannie." Ponder movie and television collectibles galore, ranging from cowboy-star lunch boxes and a letter from Mary Pickford to Mickey Mouse Club souvenirs and an incredible collection of 3-D paraphernalia. Unquestionably, this is a fun place, with movie-fan magazines, photographs, and posters among the 70,000 or so objects in its collection. But it also is a classroom for serious students of film (and television) chronicling the industry's technological achievements (with an incredible collection of motion-picture hardware), and of the creative process, from make up and costumes to script-writing and set decoration. There are two theaters where movies, ranging from classics to experimental, are screened. The 195-seat Riklis Theater is one of the most sophisticated and versatile in the country. The wonderfully wacky Tut's Fever faux-Egyptian movie palace, populated by sculptures of movie luminaries, such as Orson Welles and Mae West, is the spot to head for adventure serials from the silent era. The museum is located at the site of the Astoria studios where W.C. Fields, the Marx Brothers, and Gloria Swanson made movies, and where Woody Allen and Sidney Lumet still do.

American Museum of the Moving Image, Thirty-Fifth Ave at 36th St, Astoria, NY 11106, 718/784-4777. Tue-Fri noon-4 pm, Sat & Sun noon-6 pm. Adults $5, seniors $4, children $2.50.

Best Museum in Which to Buy a Subway Car

New York City Transit Museum

Sometimes bewildering (even to longtime residents), often reviled, occasionally dangerous—and yet, so a part of New York as to make the city almost unimaginable without it. The subway is all of these things and more. For buffs who are interested in the subway's history—or even for everyday "straphangers" who just want to see how the whole system works—this museum is a delightful find. Located underground, in an abandoned subway station (it was a shuttle stop from 1936 to 1946), this museum displays old transit artifacts (posters, signs, maps, more than a dozen old trolley and subway cars) and information about the current operation of the subway. Of special interest is the intricate display board that shows where all the trains in the system are at any given time. Dedicated transit buffs will want to visit on the third Saturday in November, when the Transit Museum holds a special sale of original subway memorabilia, including uniforms, signage, fare boxes, and, when available, even old subway cars! This annual event also includes a tour of the closed and preserved City Hall subway station—note the ornate chandelier and the old theater posters. *A transportation note:* How to get here? Take the subway, of course! The museum is accessible from the Jay Street, Boro Hall, and Court Street stations (call for details and directions). The museum's entrance fee? One subway token.

New York City Transit Museum, Boerum Pl & Schermerhorn St (underground), Brooklyn, NY, 718/330-3060.

Best Museum Afloat

Intrepid Sea-Air-Space Museum

This floating museum is, itself, part of history. Housed onboard the 900-foot-long, 150,000-square-foot aircraft carrier (big, yes—but modern carriers, as an exhibit points out, are even larger), the museum displays more than 70 historic aircraft (*and* spacecraft) on its deck. Audio-visual and interactive exhibits trace the history and influence of the United States Navy, showcase the technology involved in sailing and flight, and follow the *Intrepid* from its WWII days through Vietnam to its involvement in NASA programs (as the primary chase ship during the splashdowns of Mercury and Gemini spaceships). Even among all these patriotic displays, one area stands out: the Hall of Honor, which celebrates the recipients of the country's highest recognition of valor and sacrifice, the Congressional Medal of Honor. Docked adjacent to the *Intrepid*, and also part of this museum, are a Vietnam-era destroyer and a guided-missile submarine. For visitors wanting to schedule an entire nautical-theme day, these exhibits are near the starting point for the Circle Line's around-Manhattan boat tours (see separate listing).

Intrepid Sea-Air-Space Museum, Pier 86, W 46th St at the Hudson River, New York, NY 10036, 212/245-0072. Wed-Sun 10 am-5 pm.

Best Hands-On Museum
New York Hall of Science

Live shows are a feature of the newest permanent exhibit at this hands-on museum of science and technology, originally built in Flushing Meadows for the 1964-65 World's Fair. "Actors" in these shows are microbes—the world's tiniest creatures—enlarged by as much as 1,000 times and viewed through an easy-to-use new microscope invented for the museum. It is part of the "Hidden Kingdoms—World of Microbes" exhibit that focuses on the millions of microorganisms around us and how they affect health and the environment. At this interactive museum, visitors are encouraged to pull a 400-pound pendulum with nothing but a string and miniature magnet, create a bubble big enough to swallow them, and pedal an airplane propeller as they investigate and experiment with science and technology. "Feedback" offers a look at the principles and workings of self-sensing machines, while "Structures" encourages visitors to swing on ropes and build with giant blocks (kids love this exhibit!) as they explore why things stand up. "Realm of the Atom" allows examination of the world's first three-dimensional, dynamic model of a hydrogen atom magnified a billion times. The largest exhibit, "Seeing the Light," is a journey into the world of color, light, and perception. On weekends are family workshops and an operating ham radio station. A gift shop has books, puzzles, and related projects and activities.

New York Hall of Science, 47-01 111th St, Corona, NY 11368, 718/699-0005. Wed-Sun 10 am-5 pm. Adults $3.50, seniors & children 3-18 $2.50.

Best Spot to Remember the Holocaust (and Thousands of Years of Cultural History)
Jewish Museum

There *are* sad moments of remembrance here—but, on the whole, this is a museum of preservation and celebration. The Jewish Museum's collection of religious artifacts and other culturally significant pieces comprises one of the country's largest collections of historical Judaica. The heart of this 14,000-item museum is the Treasured Heritage collection, which offers items from Jewish cultures throughout history and from around the world. Many of these pieces were saved by German (and other European) Jews who shipped their valuables and artifacts out of Europe before the Nazis clamped down on them.

These items are joined by photos, paintings, drawings, sculpture, and other pieces of art, all contained in a beautiful French Renaissance mansion. (This building is currently undergoing renovation and expansion; during this construction, exhibits may be temporarily found at the New-York Historical Society; see separate listing.) This museum offers lecture series, traveling art exhibits, readings, films and videos, and theatrical performances relating to the "Jewish experience"; it also regularly offers special children's theater and other learning programs for youngsters.

Jewish Museum, 1109 Fifth Ave (at 92nd St), New York, NY 10128, 212/399-3344. Mon-Thu noon-5 pm, Sun 11 am-6 pm.

Best Bit of the Smithsonian East of the Hudson

Cooper-Hewitt Museum

Not *all* of the Smithsonian's fine museums are in Washington, D.C. Housed in a 64-room mansion built by Andrew Carnegie, the Cooper-Hewitt Museum is the Smithsonian Institution's National Museum of Design. It specializes in decorative arts, including textiles and fabrics, clothing, architectural drawings (it houses the world's largest collection), ceramics, jewelry, prints, and so on. Including more than a quarter of a million pieces, spanning the history of design and decoration over more than 3,000 years, this is considered the best collection of its kind in the world. The Cooper-Hewitt includes an excellent library and research collection; during summer, free classical and jazz concerts are offered in the mansion's large (one-quarter of a block long) and lovely garden. The collection was mostly gathered by the Hewitt sisters (granddaughters of Peter Cooper, of Cooper Union fame) around the turn of the century; the Carnegie Foundation later made this a gift to the Smithsonian.

Cooper-Hewitt Museum, 2 E 91st St, New York, NY 10128, 212/860-6898. Tue 10 am-9 pm, Wed-Sat 10 am-5 pm, Sun noon-5 pm.

Brooklyn's Biggest Secret

The Brooklyn Museum

It's really too big to be a secret. Yet this immense, sprawling museum—one of the world's largest—frequently is overlooked by visitors, taking a back seat to its Manhattan counterparts. As a result, it often is uncrowded, sometimes downright empty. As big as it is, this neo-classical behemoth, in the heart of Brooklyn's Park Slope neighborhood, is about to get bigger. It is only one-fifth of its intended size, with megabuck expansion going on through the mid-1990s. Despite its low profile, the museum is a storehouse of treasures, containing about 1.5 million works of art housed in a beaux-arts, six-story, 450,000-square-foot structure designed in 1893. Here, are watercolors by Winslow Homer and John Singer Sargent; oils by Monet, Cézanne, Degas, and O'Keeffe; prints by Goya and Rembrandt; and sculptures by Frederick Remington. Its collections represent virtually the entire history of art, ranging from one of the world's foremost Egyptian collections to one of the country's most comprehensive holdings of American painting and sculpture. The acclaimed collection of decorative arts includes 28 rooms covering a historic span from a 17th-century Brooklyn Dutch house to an art deco study—all complemented with matching furnishings. The wealth even extends outdoors, with a graveyard of demolition—gargoyles, friezework, and other architectural ornaments from razed New York City buildings.

The Brooklyn Museum, 200 Eastern Pkwy, Brooklyn, NY 11238, 718/638-5000. Adults $4, students $2, seniors $1.50.

Best Bet for Dinosaurs and Diamonds, Totem Poles and Tigers

American Museum of Natural History

By the happenstance of geography, this is the only one of New York's big, important museums *not* located on (or just off of) the "Museum Mile" of Fifth Avenue (see separate listing). Of course, its incredible collection of natural artifacts is more than enough reason for some museum going on this side of the park. The American Museum is the largest natural history museum in the world, offering some 40 different halls of natural wonders. From ancient mummies through period costumes to space rocks—this museum exhaustively covers the sum total of human knowledge of our natural world. The exhibits are legion (it's hard to do the museum justice in less than a full day or two), but a number of them stand out. First and foremost may be the dinosaurs, for this museum offers the world's largest collection of dinosaur skeletons—including a five-story-tall Barosaurus, which is the largest single dinosaur exhibited in the world. This alone makes the American Museum a great spot for kids, but they will likely enjoy many of its other treasures. Adults may find more to their taste in the Hall of Minerals and Gems, a glittering collection of diamonds and other precious stones that makes the offerings at Cartier and Tiffany seem like small change. Also of special note is Naturemax, the city's largest movie screen (four stories tall, six stories wide), where exciting films on natural phenomena are shown. Attached to the museum, yet separate, is the Hayden Planetarium (see separate listing). A note for potentially frazzled adults: For a respite from the hoards of kids (many in school groups) who descend here, head for the museum's classy main gift shop; there is also a separate kids-oriented shop.

American Museum of Natural History, Central Park West at W 79th St, New York, NY 10024, 212/873-1300. Mon, Tue, Thu, & Sat 10 am-4:45 pm; Wed & Fri 10 am-9 pm; Sun 11 am-5 pm.

Best Museum Devoted to Original Americans

National Museum of the American Indian

The revitalization of this museum coincides with growing interest in Indian topics, spurred by realistic and sympathetic portrayals of Indian history in the popular media, including the Academy Award-winning film *Dances with Wolves*. For years, this museum was housed in Audubon Terrace (at Broadway and West 155th Street), and it almost closed for good or left town before it moved down to the shuttered (since 1971) U.S. Custom House, a massive beaux arts structure built in 1907. The result is a great pairing of collection and facility, keeping them both vital and accessible. This museum offers the world's largest collection pertaining to the indigenous peoples of the Americas—not only North American, but also Central and South American Indians, as well as Eskimos (or, more accurately, the Inuit). While the attention-grabbers probably are Crazy Horse's rifle and Sitting Bull's war bonnet, no less fascinating are collections of carvings, paintings, pottery, weavings, and other hand-crafted artifacts, including everyday utensils and tools, weapons, and spiritual items. The relocation of this museum to Lower Manhattan makes a thematic visit to here *and* the Ellis Island Immigration Museum (to see the before and after sides of immigration) easily possible.

National Museum of the American Indian, U.S. Custom House, Bowling Green, New York, NY 10004, 212/283-2420. Tue-Sat 10 am-5 pm, Sun 1-5 pm.

Best Museum Devoted to *Non-Original* Americans

Ellis Island Immigration Museum

From 1892 to 1954, some 17 million immigrants (mostly from Europe) entered this melting pot of a country through this fabled portal, giving meaning to Lady Liberty's "huddled masses, yearning to breathe free." The current brick-and-limestone building was constructed in 1898 (after an earlier structure burned down); it was restored in 1991 after a well-publicized fund-raising effort. Displays include a touching collection of artifacts that immigrants inadvertently left behind here (such as photos, clothing, toys, etc.), taped oral-history recollections of people who passed through this facility, photographs of Ellis Island as it appeared during the height of its use, historical text outlining the processing of the immigrants, and artwork depicting the immigrant experience. Outside, on the eastern side of the island, the American Immigrant Wall of Honor lists more than 200,000 immigrants who entered the U.S. through Ellis Island (and whose family's donations—$100 per plaque—helped foot a considerable part of the bill for the island's renovation). The boats that journey here from Battery Park also stop at Liberty Island (home of the Statue of Liberty), making a combined, coming-to-America sightseeing jaunt to both sites easy to accomplish. A perhaps-staggering numerical note: It is estimated that more than 40 percent of the United States population can be traced to immigrants who entered this country through Ellis Island.

Ellis Island Immigration Museum, Ellis Island, New York Harbor, New York, NY 10004, 212/269-5755. Boats depart for Ellis Island daily from 9:30 am-3 pm (every half-hour); last boat returns 5:15 pm.

Superior Snapshots of Turn-of-the-Century Life

Alice Austen House Museum & Garden

In a quiet Staten Island backwater freshened by bay breezes is a water's edge cottage that was the home of pioneer photographer Alice Austen (1866-1952). Austen took pictures with a passion, creating one of the finest photographic records of turn-of-the-century American life. With this remarkable photographic record as a guide, the home and garden have been restored to appear as they did in the 1890s. Birdhouses once again sit above the peaks of dormer windows, huge rustic gates and sweeping lawns dotted with shade trees and flowering bushes recreate a honeysuckle-scented Victorian landscape. Almost in the shadow of the Verrazano Narrows Bridge, this gabled home offers a spectacular view of the Manhattan skyline and of freighters plying the shipping lanes of The Narrows. Changing exhibits explore themes inspired by the photographer's work and times, using images from a collection of nearly 3,000 negatives. Full of spontaneous vitality, Austen's pictures document the Staten Island social scene and colorful street life in Manhattan. She photographed socialites enjoying tennis, bicycling, and motoring, as well as immigrant peddlers, shoeshine boys, and newsgirls. The museum has a gift shop of Victoriana and shows a video about the photographer's life, *Alice's World*, narrated by Helen Hayes.

Alice Austen House & Museum, 2 Hylan Blvd, Staten Island, NY 10305, 718/816-4506. Daily noon-5 pm. Suggested donation $2.

George Washington Supped Here

Fraunces Tavern Museum

George did *lots* of things here—he ate, slept, drank, and held meetings here; in fact, this is the very spot where Washington gave his farewell address to his Revolutionary War officers in 1783. Originally constructed in 1719 (and rebuilt and restored—to original plans, with original materials—in 1907), Fraunces Tavern displays a fine collection of Colonial and Revolutionary artifacts, including some authentic Washington memorabilia. The tavern part of this museum is still open, offering visitors some of Washington's supposed favorite dishes, such as its Yankee pot roast and a dish dubbed "Chicken à la Washington." Dining here is average; frankly, the restaurant's strengths are mostly in its history. But this can be a pleasant combined eating and exhibit-browsing site. Fraunces Tavern also hosts occasional special presentations (such as lectures and seminars), which address and assess the myth, image, and reality of our country's first president. This building, part restoration, part original, was one of the first projects to renew historic structures undertaken in the U.S.; the restoration was so successful, that John D. Rockefeller came here for ideas when planning Colonial Williamsburg.

Fraunces Tavern Museum, 54 Pearl St, New York, NY 10004, 212/425-1778. Museum, Mon-Fri 10 am-4 pm; restaurant, Mon-Fri 7:30 am-9:30 pm.

Best Museum in a Structure Built for a President's Daughter

Abigail Adams Smith Museum

Washington *didn't* sleep here, but he is remembered in this museum's artifacts; even its eponymous Mrs. Smith, daughter of President John Adams, didn't sleep here—but her horses did (while she slept in a house nearby). In the late 1700s, this East Side area was way out in the boonies, and Abigail settled here with her husband, Col. William Stephens Smith. All that remains from their farm and 23-acre estate is this nine-room Federal-style stone building (which was built in 1799 and served as a stable), another of the few 18th-century structures left in Manhattan. The structure (which served as a hotel and private residence between its stable and museum days) houses a well-displayed collection of period furnishings and decorations, as well as mementoes of the Adams and Smith families, including letters from George Washington, clothing, and other personal effects. The museum offers special presentations focusing on the Smiths and their contemporaries and on Colonial-era life in general. A lovely backyard is landscaped with flowers, plants, and rocks, mostly presented in an authentic period fashion and tended by a colonial preservation group. This is a joyously blooming sight each spring.

Abigail Adams Smith Museum, 421 E 61st St, New York, NY 10021, 212/838-6878. Mon-Fri 10 am-4 pm.

Best Spot to See All of New York at Once...If You're Afraid of Heights

The Queens Museum of Art

The Empire State Building soars over Manhattan— just 15 inches tall. A ride on the Staten Island Ferry carries you only 22 feet. The Bronx Zoo sprawls over 1,500 square inches. Gullivers can explore the Lilliputian world of New York at The Panorama, built for the 1964-65 World's Fair. It is the world's largest architectural scale model, occupying 9,335 square feet. Built to a scale of 1" to 100', it shows all five boroughs of New York in exacting detail. Tourists orient themselves to the great maze that is the city, while residents search for their homes and places of employment. More than 865,000 buildings, made of plastic and wood, are represented on The Panorama. There are parks and playgrounds, wharves and warehouses, and bridges made of brass. During the night cycle, 3,172 colored lights blink on, just as they do when dusk cloaks the real city. And just as the city changes, so does The Panorama. Architects and others constantly donate models of new buildings, while a complete update is expected to be ready by 1993. In addition to this fascinating model, the museum features changing fine art exhibitions and education programs throughout the year.

The Queens Museum of Art, New York City Building, Flushing Meadows Corona Park, Queens, NY 11368, 718/592-5555. Tue-Fri 10 am-5 pm, Sat & Sun noon-5 pm. Adults $2, seniors & students $1.

Best Art Collection to Take a Spin Through

The Guggenheim Museum

This famous museum offers a top selection of contemporary art—not the least of which is the controversial building itself (Frank Lloyd Wright's only public building in New York). What *does* this strange spiral building most resemble? A washing machine? A snail? A corkscrew? What *is* definite is that the Guggenheim is an interesting spot to see some of the best art of the last 100 years. Opened in 1959, just after Wright's death, the museum offers works ranging from Van Gogh, Pissaro, Cézanne, and Manet to Kandinsky, Klee, Mondrian, and Ernst. A new addition to the Guggenheim has just opened, after years of planning and debate—and two years of construction during which the museum was closed. This 10-story tower, based loosely on designs that Wright had made for a possible addition, rises behind the existing building, setting an unobtrusive backdrop for its still-surprising countenance. Some say this new structure isolates the original building from its surroundings and takes away some of the impact of its contrast with "regular" city buildings. But, the fact is, this new tower adds 20,000 square feet of new exhibition space (bringing more of the museum's permanent collection into frequent view) and has allowed the restoration of parts of Wright's original structure that had been hidden away as storage or office space. Revel in the architectural rebirth of this classic by taking the elevator to the top of the museum's original building, and "take a spin" down through the museum's ramp of amazing art.

The Guggenheim Museum, 1071 Fifth Ave, New York, NY 10128, 212/360-3500. Wed-Sun 11 am-5 pm.

Best Collection of Purely American Art

The Whitney Museum of American Art

The Gertrude Whitney that this museum is named for was a member of the Vanderbilt family who established this fine collection of contemporary American art, starting it in her studio-home in one of the old converted stables off Washington Square Park in Greenwich Village. (Since then, the Whitney has moved a number of times, finally into this attractive 1966 structure.) This museum boasts an impressive, nearly 10,000-piece collection of modern American art—including works by O'Keeffe, Calder, Hopper, Johns, and Pollock. In fact, were MOMA not in New York, this would probably be the city's modern art standard-bearer...albeit of only American works. The Whitney also presents some of the best shows of modern American art—*and* spreads its collection around the city to other sites. There is a Whitney branch at the Equitable Center (787 Seventh Avenue at W. 51st Street; 212/554-1000), which features a permanent collection of eight modern American artists, depicting facets of their native regions (this pleasant peaceful exhibition space is adjacent to an auditorium where free music, dance, and theater performances are presented); there is also a branch at the Philip Morris Building (120 Park Ave; 212/878-2550), which is best known for its outstanding Sculpture Court (which includes works by Calder, Oldenberg, and Lichtenstein).

The Whitney Museum of American Art, 945 Madison Ave, New York, NY 10021, 212/570-3676. Tue-Sat 11 am-6 pm, Sun noon-6 pm.

Top Spot for Tibetan Treasures

Jacques Marchais Center of Tibetan Art

Clinging to a hillside are two stone monastery-like buildings and terraced gardens, serene with a meditation arbor and a lotus pond with goldfish. Designed in Tibetan architectural style, with thick walls, tiny windows, and overhanging cedar rafters, the buildings resemble a Buddhist mountain temple. Inside is one of the largest collections of Tibetan art in North America. Displays include Tibetan bronze images, paintings, and ritual artifacts as well as representative forms of art from Japan, Nepal, China, India, and Southeast Asia. Separate showcases focus on the geography and people of Tibet, deities, ceremonial masks and statues, monks and monasteries, and clothing, dolls, and children. A sacred three-tier Buddhist altar, with its prayer wheels and offering urns, is occasionally used by some of the estimated 200 Tibetans living in the metropolitan area. Rich in brass, bronze, and copper figurines of deities and Buddhas, the collection also includes notable examples of jewel-encrusted Nepalese metalwork, silver ceremonials, Tibetan miniature paintings and jewelry, dance masks, and decorative Chinese cloisonné. A gift shop carries Nepalese jackets, Tibetan shirts, Oriental jewelry, and incense.

The Jacques Marchais Center of Tibetan Art, 338 Lighthouse Ave, Staten Island, NY 10306, 718/987-3500. Open Apr-Nov, Wed-Sun 1-5 pm. Adults $3, seniors $2.50, children $1.

Best Art Gallery Founded by the Son of a Famous Impressionist Painter

Pierre Matisse Gallery

One of the first questions from first-time visitors to this fine art gallery is, "Is the Pierre in this gallery's name related to Henri?" And the answer is indeed "Yes"—this gallery's late owner (he died in 1989) and namesake was the son of famed French Impressionist painter Henri Matisse. The Matisse Gallery has long been an important conduit of modern European art to America. Consider this: When Pierre Matisse was first showing works by such artists as Miro and Chagall in New York in the 1930s, they were virtually unknown, even among museum-going art lovers. Today, of course, these and many other artists supported by this gallery have become important figures in modern art. This gallery is one of many located on 57th Street (see separate listing); in fact, the building housing the Matisse Gallery, the Fuller Building, is home to several other fine art galleries. (P.S. This art deco tower is the building the Fuller Company moved to when they left the famous Flatiron—née the Fuller—Building.)

Pierre Matisse Gallery, 41 E 57th St, New York, NY 10022, 212/355-6269. Tue-Sat 10 am-5 pm. Closed July & August.

Best Bet for Art from Picasso to Pollock

The Museum of Modern Art

What started with a donation of eight prints and a drawing is today a collection of more than 100,000 pieces representing the finest art from 1880 to the present. Opened in 1929, MOMA (as it is commonly referred to) is considered one of the world's top collections of contemporary art—if not *the* top. All of the big names of modern art are represented, with notable multiple holdings in works by Picasso (more than 60), Matisse (more than 30), and Jackson Pollock (nearly 20). MOMA also has a great collection of architecture and design, which includes fascinating displays of drawings, models, and actual items that are deemed to have artistic value (such as automobiles, furniture, and electronic equipment). This museum was also one of the very first to treat fine films as art, and, therefore, worth preserving, celebrating, and exhibiting in a museum setting; watch for special presentations of films from the museum's extensive collection (there are up to six screenings here every day; info from 212/708-9490). There is a lovely garden, dominated by a huge weeping willow, and offering some sculpture (including a Picasso and a Rodin); on summer weekends, concerts are held here. MOMA recently doubled its exhibition space and opened two new restaurants that overlook the sculpture garden (a nice, romantic spot for a meal or drinks). MOMA has an outstanding museum store, offering modern-art books, prints, and other *objets d'art*.

Museum of Modern Art, 11 W 53rd St, New York, NY 10019, 212/708-9850. Fri-Tue 11 am-6 pm, Thu 11am-9 pm.

Best Most Art

Metropolitan Museum of Art

Confronting the largest art museum in the *entire* Western Hemisphere—as well as one of the finest museums in the world—the guide writer's dilemma parallels that of the museum visitor: Where to start? This is such an immense museum—its permanent collection includes more than *three million pieces* of art, one million of which are usually on display at any given time; it is probably best to selectively sample areas of key personal interest (or schedule a couple of days to do the Met more fully). Some things here cannot be ignored, such as the incredible collection of paintings from all eras and areas; this collection includes works by Rembrandt, Titian, Raphael, Rubens, Van Dyck, El Greco, Gainsborough, Reynolds, Rousseau, Manet, Monet, Cézanne, Gauguin, Renoir, Degas, Van Gogh, Seurat, Toulouse-Lautrec, and Picasso. Additionally, the Met's collection of Roman, Greek, Egyptian, and Islamic art and artifacts are among the top of any museum, *anywhere*. Another highlight is a terrific group of meticulously recreated period rooms, ranging from 18th-century French and American homes through a reconstructed pre-World War I Frank Lloyd

Wright living room. The Met also offers a rooftop sculpture garden, which is a nice warm-weather spot. This huge building (started in 1895, and added to on and off since then) can get massively crowded, especially when hosting a limited-time special exhibition. Overwhelmed visitors can escape to several great gift shops (the Met's catalogs are also striking reading) and a restaurant and bar that are stylish places to meet.

The Metropolitan Museum of Art, Fifth Ave at E 82nd St, New York, NY 10028, 212/879-5000. Sun, Tue-Thu 9:30 am-5:15 pm; Fri & Sat 9:30 am-8:45 pm.

Perhaps *the* World's Top Gallery for Contemporary Art

Leo Castelli Gallery

This is both one of the top galleries anywhere for modern art and the site of a bit of art history. The Castelli Gallery was the first place where the late Andy Warhol exhibited his controversial and ground-breaking Campbell Soup cans and Brillo boxes. Today, it is still the place for the best in modern paintings, sculptures, and drawings, and is thought of in many international art circles as perhaps the single most important U.S. gallery. Besides Castelli's long-standing relationship with Warhol and his art, this gallery also presents the works of such artistic luminaries as Jasper Johns, Robert Rauschenberg, and Claes Oldenburg. This is a must-see spot for people who want to know what the Next Big Thing in art will likely be, since the Castelli Gallery is usually at the leading edge of modern art. (The respected Sonnabend Gallery and a handful of other galleries are also in the 420 West Broadway building where this gallery is located.) Another branch of the Castelli Gallery, at 578 Broadway (212/431-6279), also acts as a publisher of limited-edition prints, photographs, and posters created by noted artists and photographers.

Leo Castelli Gallery, 420 W Broadway, New York, NY 10012, 212/431-5160. Tue-Sat 10 am-6 pm.

Best Collection of Classic Hispanic Art

Hispanic Society of America

Founded in 1894, this stately museum traces the history—through art—of Spanish- and Portuguese-speaking people, from their European homelands, to settling in North, Central, and South America. On

display are paintings (including murals and frescoes), sculpture, a variety of decorative arts, and
special exhibits, such as a recreation of Spanish
monastic tombs. The museum's permanent collection includes works by Goya, El Greco, and
Velazquez; also noteworthy are works by some lesser-
known artists—for example, the stunning room full
of typical Spanish murals by Joaquin Sorolla y
Bastida. The Hispanic Society of America hosts
excellent traveling exhibitions of Spanish and Mexican works and good series of lectures within its
exquisite terra-cotta walls; the museum offers one
of the country's best reference libraries on its subject. For a top-notch collection of contemporary
Hispanic art, visit El Museo del Barrio, in a predomi-
nantly Hispanic Upper East Side neighborhood (see
separate listing).

Hispanic Society of America, Broadway at W 155th
St, New York, NY 10032, 212/926-2234. Tue-Sat 10
am-4:30 pm, Sun 1-4 pm. Closed August.

Best "Gallery Row"

57th Street

Part of what makes New York a world-class fine arts
capital is its large number and wide variety of art
galleries. There are gallery-clustered neighborhoods
such as SoHo and Madison Avenue on the Upper
East Side, but the big-name and big-money art is
usually found in the galleries of 57th Street, in the
blocks just east and west of Fifth Avenue. Most of
these are not storefront galleries; they are usually
located on the upper floors of the buildings they
occupy. Some addresses house a number of different
galleries, making browsing convenient. The art here
is expensive—but browsing costs nothing, although
it probably is best to affect an air of someone ac-
customed to paying $500,000 for a piece of art. A
sampling of the best in "Gallery Row" includes Blum/
Helman (20 W. 57th Street; 212/245-2888), offering
a large selection both of older, established artists,
and younger, up-and-comers; Terry Dintenfass (50
W. 57th Street; 212/581-2268), which generally
presents the works of established 20th-century artists; Andre Emmerich (41 E. 57th Street; 212/752-
0124), known for contemporary European and
American artists—including David Hockney—and
also some nice museum-quality antiquities; Sidney
Janis Gallery (110 W. 57th Street; 212/586-0110),
which has a longstanding commitment to modern
art and is museum-like in its presentation and
attention to detail (Janis's exquisite private collection is now exhibited at the Museum of Modern Art);

Kennedy Galleries (40 W. 57th Street; 212/541-9600), which shows only American art (of all eras); Marlborough (40 W. 57th Street; 212/541-4900), for a top-level collection of painters, sculptors, and photographers in a huge gallery; and Pace (32 E. 57th Street; 212/421-3292), one of the best in the city, exhibiting such artists as Louise Nevelson, Jean Dubuffet, Isamu Noguchi, Mark Rothko, and the current leading light of the modern art world, Julian Schnabel (Pace Editions, also at this location, publishes fine art prints).

Best Art Collection in a Lived-In Mansion

The Frick Collection

Once upon a time, Fifth Avenue was filled with grandiose mansions built by the city's wealthy families. Today, most of those buildings are gone, but this one (on the corner of Fifth Avenue and 70th Street) remains, not only representing the structural achievements of a bygone era, but also presenting an impressive collection of art. Built in 1914 for Carnegie Steel Chairman Henry Clay Frick, this was one of the last of the great Fifth Avenue mansions. It offers a wonderful private collection of European paintings from the 14th to the 19th centuries, with a particularly heavy representation of excellent 18th and 19th century artworks. Works displayed here include those by such artists as Renoir, Rembrandt, Vermeer, Velazquez, and Whistler. What sets the fine art of the Frick Collection apart from other museums is its preserved mansion setting, full of exquisite Italian and French furnishings and decorated in an ornate, artistic style. This gives visitors a full idea of how some wealthy art patrons of the late 19th and early 20th centuries lived. (Amazingly, the Frick family still uses part of this incredible repository of art as a residence!) The Frick also presents lecture series and chamber music concerts.

The Frick Collection, 1 E 70th St, New York, NY 10021, 212/288-0700. Tue-Sat 10 am-6 pm, Sun 1-6 pm.

Best Collection of Contemporary Hispanic Art (and More)

El Museo del Barrio

Established in 1969, and now the cultural center of the Hispanic "El Barrio" neighborhood on the Upper East Side, this museum presents the art and culture of people of Puerto Rican, Spanish, Mexican, and

Latin American background. Mostly made up of contemporary paintings, drawings, sculpture, and other art, this collection makes a good counterpoint to the more classic collection of the long-established Hispanic Society of America (see separate listing). This museum offers not only art and artifacts, but also presents music, theater, dance, and film/video by Hispanics, many from in and around this diverse neighborhood. Part of its charm is its nice local feel—El Museo del Barrio is definitely part of its neighborhood (in fact, *barrio* means neighborhood). Also offered is an interesting "Writers at El Museo" program, which provides a workshop for local aspiring writers and also presents readings by prominent Hispanic authors and journalists.

El Museo del Barrio, 1230 Fifth Ave (at E 105th St), New York, NY 10029, 212/831-7272. Wed-Sun 11 am-5 pm.

Best Medieval Art in a Recreated Medieval Setting

The Cloisters

This Upper Manhattan museum is not only a great place to see medieval artifacts—it is also one of the most peaceful, contemplative spots in a city not known for its calm. The Cloisters consist of monastic rooms shipped from throughout Europe, and reassembled here. Opened in 1938 (and run by the Metropolitan Museum of Art), it was stitched together out of pieces of five European cloisters, plus some churches, chapels, and other medieval structures. Displayed within these historic walls are a wide selection of medieval art and artifacts—including the historically significant Unicorn Tapestries from 16th-century France, illustrated manuscripts, wood carvings, glasswork, and other religious and decorative items. Perhaps the nicest spot here—and one of the least Manhattan-like spots in all of Manhattan—is the Cloisters garden. This tranquil place offers fragrant beds of flowers and herbs (most transplanted from their native Europe); it is perfect for a few peaceful moments before hurrying off to the next stop. Special events include a daily concert of Gregorian chants held in the garden and, every Saturday, special workshops for children, exploring some facet of medieval life, such as cooking, craft making, and music. The Cloisters is perched on a hill overlooking the Hudson, and it owes its nice view to the west to the foresight of its primary sponsor:

John D. Rockefeller, Jr. bought the area of the Palisades just across from the Cloisters to prevent it from being adversely developed; today, it still offers a scene of unspoiled natural beauty.

The Cloisters, Fort Tryon Park, New York, NY 10040, 212/923-3700. Tue-Sat 10 am-4:45 pm, Sun noon-4:45 pm.

Best Site of a Failed Peace Conference

The Conference House

It could have turned out differently. But for a peace conference that failed, America today might have been part of the British Commonwealth! At the southern tip of Staten Island, this handsome stone manor house built about 1680 was the site of a peace conference held on September 11, 1776. It was hosted by Admiral Lord Howe, in command of His Majesty's Atlantic Squadron and attended by Benjamin Franklin, John Adams, and Edward Rutledge. It was the last time America would be treated as a colony, and it was a prelude to war—a bitter, eight-year struggle. The house has been restored and furnished to the style of the mid-1770s, interpreting the life of Col. Christopher Billup, who remained loyal to the British crown during the Revolutionary War and fled to Canada at its end. Masonry used to build the house was made of local, unusually small, stones and mortar, mixed with ground sea shells gathered at the island shore. There are periodic demonstrations by costumed interpreters of such crafts as chair caning and rushing and spinning and weaving. A full annual calendar includes such events as a crafts show and fair, sing-along concerts, boat cruises, and Independence Day celebrations.

The Conference House, 7455 Hylan Blvd, Staten Island, NY 10307, 718/984-2086. Mar-Dec Wed-Sun 1-4 pm. Adults $2, seniors & children 6-12 $1.

Best Collection of One Man's Toys

Forbes Gallery

Successful publisher, unabashed capitalist, motorcycle and ballooning fanatic, and friend to Elizabeth Taylor—the late, larger-than-life Malcolm Forbes certainly had a zest for life. The acquisitions that can go along with such a zest (*and* a not-inconsiderable fortune) can be found in this public display, which

is located in the lobby of the Greenwich Village
headquarters of *Forbes* magazine. This mini-mu-
seum is pretty much a collection of Forbes's collections, centered around his most famous possessions,
the fabulous Fabergé jeweled eggs, created for the
Russian czars. This is believed to be the largest
collection of these intricate and delicate ornaments
in the world. This maze-like gallery also displays
collections pertaining to other of Forbes's passions,
such as toys (especially soldiers—some *12,000* toy
soldiers—and model boats), trophies from various
events, historical manuscripts, rare books, a rotating collection of paintings and photographs, and
Lincoln memorabilia (including an authentic "Hon-
est Abe" stovepipe hat). All in all, this is a delightful
little present to the public from the departed Mr.
Forbes.

Forbes Gallery, Forbes Building, 62 Fifth Ave (at
12th St), New York, NY 10011, 212/206-5548. Tue-Sat
10 am-4 pm.

Best Place to Read Between the Lions

The New York Public Library

With more than six million books (and 12 million
periodicals), this library rivals the Library of Congress for the title of the country's largest. The greatest percentage of books in this pan-city system are
housed in the "main" library (officially known as the
Central Research Branch), contained in a solid beaux
arts structure that sprawls over two city blocks
smack in the middle of Midtown. This building has
undergone some recent spiffing up—its ornate
Gottesman Exhibition Hall has been restored (and
now hosts occasional receptions and recitals) and
the DeWitt Wallace Periodical room now sports more
than a dozen new *trompe l'oeil* murals. Whether
visitors are looking for a particular book or just
looking to check out the building's classic architecture, the Central Research Branch is worth a browse.
The bad pun (is that redundant?) about "reading
between the lions" refers to the library's famous
"guard lions," Patience and Fortitude, who stonily sit
book-ending the library's steps. The library's lions
got their names from none other than New York
Mayor Fiorello La Guardia.

The New York Public Library, Central Research
Branch, Fifth Ave & W 42nd St, New York, NY
10018, 212/930-0800. Mon, Thu-Sat 10 am-6 pm;
Tues & Wed 11 am-7:30 pm.

Best Bet for Historic Books

The Pierpont Morgan Library

This is not only a fine library, but is also a great *museum,* giving the public a glimpse of personal wealth, circa turn-of-the-century New York. Built as a home in 1906 by financier J. Pierpont Morgan, it was reopened by his son in 1924 as a library/ museum. It looks like what it was—an old-money, ornately decorated mansion, with such touches as antique furnishings, wrought-iron railings and steps, and plenty of Morgan-family artifacts. But the high-light and main thrust is the priceless collection of rare and antiquarian books. The incredible collec-tion includes a Gutenberg Bible (one of less than a dozen in the world), an autographed Shakespeare First Folio, illustrated manuscripts dating back to medieval and Renaissance times, and other rare books and original manuscripts, many autographed by their authors—all in all, just a few typical items from the personal library of one of the country's richest men of the late 19th and early 20th centu-ries. Recently, the library added more exhibit space with the acquisition of J. Pierpont, Jr.'s adjacent brownstone (itself no slouch in the mansion depart-ment, with 45 rooms!) and constructed an elegant and delightful glass-enclosed garden to connect both buildings. A fine book shop offers a variety of quality art books, research tomes, classical sheet-music manuscripts, and a series of beautiful prize-winning note cards. (P.S. Don't bother bringing your NYC library card to check books out—use of the collection is restricted to qualified scholars doing research.)

The Pierpont Morgan Library, 29 E 36th St, New York, NY 10016, 212/685-0008. Tue-Sat 10:30 am-5 pm.

Second-Oldest Historical Society in America

New-York Historical Society

While the Museum of the City of New York (see separate listing) orients visitors to the Big Apple by showing off vistas and airing opinions of the city, this historic-in-itself museum continues with its mission of saving and preserving old New York (which can mean the 18th century or even last week). Its col-lection of artworks (including an excellent selection of American portraits and perhaps the largest col-lection extant of longtime Harlem resident John

James Audubon's bird watercolors), photos, and artifacts tell today's visitors what the city's past was like—and will tell future visitors what today's New York was like. Housed in a 19th-century granite mansion across the street from Central Park, the Historical Society also offers the city's best research library and an extensive New York City newspaper morgue (quite a collection in itself when you realize that New York once had more than a dozen daily papers!), making it a valuable resource for scholars and the curious alike. (Until completion of the restoration of the Jewish Museum—see separate listing—portions of its collection will be housed here.) *Punctuation note:* The hyphen in this museum's name is not a typographical error, but, rather, a popular way of spelling the city's name back when this museum was founded, in 1804; it's a bit quirky today, but it has stuck.

New-York Historical Society, 170 Central Park West at W 77th St, New York, NY 10024, 212/873-3400. Tue-Fri 11 am-5 pm, Sat 10 am-5 pm, Sun 1-5 pm.

Best Bet for Verbalized Verse

Academy of American Poets

New York has always been a breeding ground as well as a subject for American poets—from Manhattan native Walt Whitman's celebrations of self and city to Hart Crane's symbolic musings about the Brooklyn Bridge and Langston Hughes chronicling bits of Harlem's "Golden Age." For nearly 60 years, the Academy of American Poets (today located on the Upper East Side) has been the city's—and, indeed, the country's—little-known headquarters for poetic art. Such classic poets as Robert Frost and Ezra Pound, and radical, capital-eschewing poet and playwright e.e. cummings have given readings here, drawing enthusiastic crowds of poetry fans. Modern poets still read (or, in the case of the more "dramatic" readers, *perform*) at this location and at special readings sponsored by the Academy at various locations around the city. The Academy offers a yearly $10,000 prize for poetry, which can keep a struggling writer in plenty of pencils and pads. Other spots in the city for occasional poetry readings include the Knitting Factory, La Mama E.T.C., the Kitchen, and P.S. 122 (see separate listings), as well as neighborhood library branches and a variety of "avant-garde" bars and clubs. For many years, poets have congregated for readings in the main sanctuary of St. Mark's-in-the-Bowery Church (Second Avenue at East 10th Street), home of the well-known "Poetry Project."

Academy of American Poets, 177 E 87th St, New York, NY 10128, 212/427-5665.

Best Coins to Fit the Bill

American Numismatic Society

This is an educational, enjoyable place for dedicated coin collectors, curious novices, or even history buffs without any particular interest in coins. It is enjoyable because the atmosphere of the American Numismatic Society is far from the stuffy feeling one might assume would go along with currency collecting. The Society presents the world's largest collection of historic and contemporary currency—with a strong emphasis on both historic coinage (from ancient Rome, Greece, Byzantium, and other classical cultures) and U.S coins and currency (from 1793 copper pennies to the present). Exhibits cover the history of coins, from ancient times to today's currency; methods of preventing counterfeiting; and coin-related art, such as commemorative medals by famous designers. This is the home of what may be the best numismatic-related research library in the world.

American Numismatic Society, W 155th St & Broadway, New York, NY 10032, 212/234-3130. Tue-Sat 9 am-4:30 pm, Sun 1-4 pm.

Best Place East of Hollywood to See Stars

Hayden Planetarium

Movie buffs may remember the Hayden from a romantic scene in *Manhattan*, in which Woody Allen and Diane Keaton flee here to escape a rainstorm. The highlight of the Hayden is a film of a different sort: the stunning "Sky Show" (in the Sky Theater), where the wonders of space are projected on a 75-foot domed ceiling by a special computerized Zeiss Star Projector (which, itself, looks like some sort of deep space probe). From your seat in this theater, you can travel nearly anywhere in the universe, watching the birth of black holes, the death of stars, or the visitation of comets (call 212/769-5900 for a schedule of sky shows). The Hayden also presents exhibits on astronomy and navigation (including a selection of historic telescopes, compasses, sextants, and other pieces of equipment), space exploration, and meteorites—including a sample that weighs 68,000 pounds. On weekends, the Hayden offers a popular series of laser-light shows set to rock music

(212/769-5921 for information). *Money-saving note:*
Enter the Hayden first, and your entrance fee will
also cover the adjacent American Museum of Natural
History (however, it doesn't work the other way
around).

Hayden Planetarium, Central Park West at W 81st
St, New York, NY 10024, 212/769-5920. Mon-Fri
12:30-5 pm, Sat & Sun noon-5 pm.

Best Bit of the Sea by the Sea
New York Aquarium

While you wouldn't expect to find dolphins and
whales just off the shore of Brooklyn, you can find
them (and many more marine creatures) just *in* from
the shore, at this aquarium on Brooklyn's boardwalk. The New York Aquarium opened in 1896 in
Manhattan and moved to this site in 1957. Overseen
by the New York Zoological Society, which also runs
the Bronx Zoo (see separate listing), the aquarium
exhibits more than 20,000 aquatic creatures, most
notably including penguins, seals, sharks (in a
90,000-gallon tank), walruses, turtles, and, of
course, the popular dolphins. Way back in 1897,
this was the first aquarium to exhibit beluga whales;
today, the aquarium features two performing belu-
gas who delight crowds with their aquatic ballet.
These performances and the aquarium's other
trained-animal shows (such as those featuring dolphins and seals) are presented only when the weather
is good. But even on inclement days, the shows'
stars can be observed during their feeding times
(these times are posted daily). Other popular attractions include an exhibit that encourages young
explorers to touch starfish, shells, and other sea
dwellers, and—a recent addition—the Native Sea Life
exhibit, which depicts a variety of marine creatures
in recreations of their natural habitats. For waterfront fun of a different kind, Coney Island is adjacent
to the aquarium (see separate listing).

New York Aquarium, Boardwalk & W 8th St,
Brooklyn, NY 11224, 718/265-3474. Daily 10 am-
4:45 pm.

Best Site for "Old Salts" of All Sorts
South Street Seaport

It is somewhat ironic that the restaurants and entertainment centers of this popular tourist area are
better known than its *original* mission. That goal was
to create a museum and historic recreation depicting

New York's old days as a bustling seaport. The shops, ships, and slips all have the recreated look of 18th- and 19th-century New York. The "museum" actually is spread out over numerous buildings, ships, and other sites. Some highlights: The old multiple-masted sailing ships open to inspection (above all else, be sure to check out these); the preserved solid buildings of Schermerhorn Row (bounded by Fulton, South, John, and Front streets), once warehouses and now housing retail shops; the authentic and colorful Fulton Street Fishmarket, which still operates here, selling fresh seafood to restaurateurs and retailers; and a multi-media presentation that orients visitors to the historic nature of this area and New York's role as perhaps the busiest port of the 19th century. Additionally, there are plenty of restaurants, cafés, and other vendors here (some of which are covered elsewhere in this book). Perhaps this site's problem is that it *isn't quite* a historical recreation, à la Richmondtown Restoration, nor a "festival marketplace," like Baltimore's Harborplace. Still, as a sometimes wobbly hybrid, South Street Seaport remains as a solid destination, *both* as a historical site and a modern playground. (As to its "playground" reputation, on many weeknights—and *especially* on Friday evenings—this area absorbs hoards of Wall Streeters looking for after-work diversions; unless you enjoy being awash in crowds wearing silk blouses and "power" ties, it is perhaps best to clear out of here on Fridays by 3:30 p.m.)

South Street Seaport, 207 Water St, New York, NY 10038, 212/669-9400. Daily 10 am-5 pm (shops and restaurants open later).

Best Experimental Theater
La Mama E.T.C.

First, a few notes about names: The "La Mama" of this theater's name is founder/director Ellen Stewart, the godmother of New York's avant-garde theater scene; the "E.T.C." stands for "Experimental Theater Club;" and it is commonly referred to by actors, writers, and regulars who hang out there as Café La Mama, the original name it opened under (as more café than theater). Stewart's East Village institution has been around for 30 years, offering the best and brightest of experimental theater (playwrights Sam Shepard and Lanford Wilson—among many other writers and actors—got important early boosts here). Its long, sometimes strange run almost ended recently, when money problems threatened to close the multi-theater complex; these problems have not entirely ceased, but public awareness of the situation (garnered by sympathetic press coverage) has helped attract funds and other support, allowing the theater to continue offering its unique brand of spectacle. A *New Yorker* writer once said admiringly that La Mama is a place to go "to see actors dance and dancers act," an apt description of the sometimes physical, sometimes poetic, almost always interesting art that is presented here. For culture vultures who prize a bit of risk taking in their theater art, La Mama is a treasure that deserves continued support.

La Mama E.T.C., 74A E 4th St, New York, NY 10003, 212/475-7710.

Best Jazz in Church
St. Peter's Church

They strike an incongruous note positioned alongside the altar at this Lutheran church—the drum set, piano, bass, and sound-recording equipment. But listed for the service along with a scripture reading, psalm, meditation, and benediction is a "refreshment of music"—specifically, jazz. This is when a trio of musicians slips up front and a vocalist renders a lively jazz version of "There Will Never Be Another You" and "I Didn't Know What Time It Was." Jazz vespers are held on Sundays at 5 p.m., usually followed by a jazz concert at 7 p.m. Adjoining the Citicorp Building, the church looks as progressive as its music, with a mottled granite floor, blonde cubist pews, cushions in bright geometric designs, sleek bleacher seating, and a huge painting of an angel and a deer chased by dogs. The church has stark white walls with sharp angles, wood-encased organ pipes that resemble a modernistic artwork, and a ladder of glass windows that look out onto the concrete-and-glass slab of a Midtown office building. Since the church initiated Jazz Vespers in 1965, it has featured many top performers.

St. Peter's Church, 619 Lexington Ave, New York, NY 10022, 212/935-2200.

Best Concerts in a 19th-Century Tavern
Richmondtown Restoration

From winter candlelight tours to spring antiques markets, summer concerts, and fall crafts fairs, this historic village offers fun things to do, year-round. Occupying 96 acres of Staten Island greenbelt, it provides a realistic slice of early Americana, show-casing three centuries of history and culture. Songs are sung and tales are told in a recreated 19th-century tavern during a popular weekend concert series (Jan-Apr). Visitors sip mugs of beer or cider by a wood stove and listen to folk and traditional music. Included are Scottish and Irish airs and ballads, 1920s tunes played on ukulele and banjo, English Music Hall ditties, bawdy British ballads, sea chanteys, a zany jug band, and old-time country fiddle music. Another program on selected summer weekends features 19th-century outdoor dinners accompanied by special entertainment. Richmondtown offers workshops in quilting, needlepoint, 19th-century contra dancing, and (as a parent-child project) creating Victorian valentines. Lectures focus on early settlers, colonial cooking, and historic architecture. More than half of the 25 historic buildings are open to the public, with interpreters reenacting tasks of period householders, farmers, merchants, and tradesmen (July-Aug and on special-event days).

Richmondtown Restoration, Staten Island Historical Society, 441 Clarke Ave, Staten Island, NY 10306, 718/351-1617. Wed-Fri 10 am-5 pm Sat-Sun 1-5 pm. Adults $4, students, seniors, youths 6-18 $2.50.

Liveliest Stage in the Park

SummerStage

This is where the fat lady *also* sings! On summer evenings at the Rumsey Playfield in Central Park you are likely to find fully staged productions by the New York Grand Opera company of such classics as Mozart's "The Marriage of Figaro" and Verdi's "Stiffelio." But there is much more—because the SummerStage is where you also will find toe-tapping jazz and soulful blues, plus rock, folk, gospel, and country music, and a wide range of other entertainment. The further good news is that it all is free! Since the mid-1980s, this event has been presenting the best in music, dance, and the spoken word. Included are performances of modern dance as well as readings and performances by novelists, poets, and lyricists—the likes of John Cage and Joyce Carol Oates. On Sunday afternoons, there is musical adventure as the festival celebrates the many colors of world music, from Jamaican reggae and Haitian chants and dancebeats to South American mambo, hot sounds from Trinidad, and the music of Cameroon, Zimbabwe, and other African countries. SummerStage runs from mid-June to early August

with events usually held Wednesday through Friday.
In addition to the wide-ranging free events are special fund-raising concerts (tickets usually under $20)
by such well-known performers as the Neville Brothers and Simply Red.

Central Park SummerStage, Rumsey Playfield, mid-
park at 72nd St, New York, NY 10021, 212/360-2756.

Best Bard in the Park

New York Shakespeare Festival

Bard buffs will find Shakespeare's works performed
in Central Park during this annual festival—as they
like it, and sometimes as they never have seen them
before. Traditional productions of such favorites as
A Comedy of Errors and *As You Like It* are scheduled
during July and August along with such experimental works as a Brazilian version of *A Midsummer
Night's Dream*, set in the Amazon rain forest and
performed in Portuguese (with an English synopsis
provided). Although admission is free, tickets are
required. These are available at the Delacorte Theater at 6:15 p.m. (for an 8 p.m. curtain) on the day
of the performance, one per person. These productions feature such well-known actors as Elizabeth
McGovern and Donald Moffat. A nice adjunct to a
festival performance is a visit to the Shakespeare
Garden, just south of the theater and planted with
flowers, trees, and shrubs mentioned in the author's
works. With rustic fencing and benches, it is a
contemplative spot for reading, people-watching, or
simply relaxing.

New York Shakespeare Festival, Delacorte Theater,
Central Park, mid-park at 79th St, New York, NY
10024, 212/861-7277.

Best Art Deco Theater (Perhaps in the Entire World)

Radio City Music Hall

People who grew up in American medium-to-small
towns in the middle decades of this century probably
have fond memories of ornate art deco movie palaces
(that perhaps also served as vaudeville houses and/
or "legitimate" theaters), invariably called something
like "The Bijou." All but a few of these are gone,
supplanted by box-like multiplex cinemas. New Yorkers (and, of course, visitors) can still pay their re-
spects at the initial shrine of detailed art deco
theaters, Rockefeller Center's (see separate listing)
classic Radio City Music Hall. Built in 1932, during
the early years of the Great Depression, this huge

theater offered a seating capacity of 6,000 as well as the world's largest chandelier *and* pipe organ. Although movies are shown occasionally—the likes of restored films and silent movies with an orchestra—the principal attractions now are theatrical and musical performances. Even those unable to (or uninterested in) taking in a show, may wish to opt for the hour-long guided tour, which shows off all parts of the historic theater. For holiday visitors, from November through early January Radio City Music Hall offers its famed Christmas Spectacular, an excellent family-oriented holiday show that includes the world-famous, high-stepping Rockettes dancing troupe. *Trivia note:* This hall's huge stage is the length of an entire city block!

Radio City Music Hall, Sixth Ave at W 50th St, New York, NY 10020, 212/757-3100.

Best Bets for Performance Art
The Kitchen & P.S. 122

As it is in other artforms, New York is the country's leading spot for performance art, that quirky hybrid of monologue, exhibitionism, improvisation, philosophy, song-and-dance, and deadpan stand-up comedy. The Kitchen was the city's original presenter of performance art, and is also the place where such performance artists/actors as Eric Bogosian (*Talk Radio, Sex, Drugs, and Rock 'n' Roll*) and Ann Magnuson (*Making Mr. Right,* TV's "Anything But Love") got important early exposure. The Kitchen is also a leading center for video art, showing a variety of original pieces that seem to have more in common with Andy Warhol or Monty Python than with MTV. For years, the Kitchen was headquartered in SoHo (in a space that had once been a hotel kitchen—hence its name); its newer Chelsea digs, in a long, skinny building that was once an icehouse, offers even more theater, video viewing, and gallery space. Another top presenter of performance art is P.S. 122, a nicely surviving East Village bastion of the avant-garde. Once a New York Public School, the "P.S." in its name now stands for "Performance Space." It is run by the artists who perform or exhibit there, and also offers a varied selection of film, video, painting, photography, music, and dance. Performance art of varying stripes and types can also be found (among other performances) at the Knitting Factory and La Mama E.T.C. (see separate listings).

The Kitchen, 512 W 19th St, New York, NY 10011, 212/255-5793. Hours and days vary. P.S. 122, 150 First Ave at E 9th St, New York, NY 10009, 212/228-4249. Hours and days vary.

Best Bet for Close-Together Off-Broadway Theater

"Theater Row"

As its non-specific name implies, "Off-Broadway" isn't confined to any one area of the city, with theaters popping up all over the place. Traditionally, there have been a clutch of Off-Broadway theaters in Greenwich Village, but, in the last 15 years, a concentrated collection of these theaters and repertory companies has become established on West 42nd Street, west of Ninth Avenue. This so-called Theater Row offers a challenging variety of entertainments at prices below the big shows found in the theaters a few blocks to the east. There are about a dozen fine theaters here, including the Samuel Beckett, the Houseman, Playwrights Horizons, the Theater Row, and the Douglass Fairbanks. The influence of these have led to the creation of a revitalized theater-oriented neighborhood; the Theatre Arts Bookstore, a popular place for scripts and how-to acting books, is nearby, as are a few pleasant bistros and cabarets. Not part of this scene, but a *definite* off-Broadway must-mention is *The Fantasticks*, which is playing at the Sullivan Street Playhouse, down in the Village, as it has been continuously since *1960*!

Best Bet For Yuletide Ballet (and More)

New York City Ballet

For many New Yorkers, it just wouldn't be the holiday season without the city's three popular year-end totems: the character balloons of Macy's Thanksgiving Day Parade, the bright and ornately decorated tree at Lincoln Center, and the New York City Ballet's annual presentation of *The Nutcracker.* Offered throughout December, this version of the Tchaikovsky classic delights children and adults alike, and has truly become a city tradition. Accordingly, tickets for these performances disappear quickly (although standing-room tickets are often available), dictating some judicious planning for holiday-season visitors. The rest of the season at this company, which was founded by Lincoln Kirstein and famed choreographer George Balanchine, also offers fine dance. (City Ballet vies for the city's crown as top ballet troupe with the mercurial American Ballet Theater; see separate listing.) It is currently run, to continued acclaim, by noted dancemeisters Jerome Robbins and Peter Martins (who both apprenticed under Balanchine), and presents new dances each season, as well as rotating classics from the Balanchine catalog. This company is housed in Lincoln Center's New York State Theater (see separate listing), which is one of the best—if not *the* best—places around to see fine dance, since it was specifically designed to be the home of the New York City Ballet. This is the only major dance company in the country that runs its own dance school, the Julliard School of American Ballet.

New York City Ballet, New York State Theater, Lincoln Center, W 64th St & Broadway, New York, NY 10023, 212/870-5570. Seasons run from November-February and April-June.

Best Place for a Variety of Top Ballet Companies (and a Nutcracker!)

City Center Theater

For ballet beyond ABT and City Ballet (see separate listings), head to this theater, a bit south of Central Park, near the theater district. Built in 1924, this Moorish-flavored landmark building, which was once a Masonic Temple, plays host to a number of excellent ballet troupes, including the Joffrey Ballet (which winters on the West Coast after its fall season here); the respected, black-oriented Dance Theater of Harlem; the Martha Graham Dance Company; the Alvin Ailey American Dance Theater; and such smaller local troupes of renown as the mostly experimental Trisha Brown Company, the Merce Cunningham Company, and the Paul Taylor Company (the last two are both led by former students of the great Martha Graham). This theater also regularly hosts visits from innovative dance troupes from across the country or from abroad. The "seasons" of these various troupes last anywhere from a few weeks to a few months, making the calendar of events eclectic, to say the least. The City Center Theater was originally the home of the New York City Ballet and New York City Opera (see separate listings) before they moved to the New York State Theater in Lincoln Center. For those unable to get tickets to City Ballet's *Nutcracker* (or who just want a bit of a change for their holiday-season dance), the Joffrey concludes its season here by presenting its own adaptation of *The Nutcracker* each December.

City Center Theater, 130 W 55th St, New York, NY 10019, 212/581-7907.

Perhaps America's Best Ballet Troupe

American Ballet Theatre

Founded in 1940, this is the country's most-respected and oldest major ballet company. It has presented some of the finest, most challenging dance and produced some of the country's best dancers of the last few decades. Until recently, this high-powered troupe was under the direction of world-famous dancer-choreographer-actor Mikhail Baryshnikov; his departure several years ago left things in a bit of an uproar, but the ABT has continued to maintain its reputation by presenting some of the finest dance in the city, and, in fact, in the entire country. Headquartered in the Metropolitan Opera House (during the summer, when the Opera is dark), the ABT presents both classic dances and new works by such choreographers as Twyla Tharp (who has long been associated with the company) and Natalia Makarova. Tickets for the ABT aren't inexpensive and are popular; however, standing-room tickets are usually available the day of any given performance (rabid fans have been known to line up at dawn for these). The ABT shares the Metropolitan Opera House with various traveling ballet troupes, such as the Bolshoi and the Royal Ballet.

American Ballet Theatre, Metropolitan Opera House, Lincoln Center, W 64th St & Broadway, New York, NY 10023, 212/799-3100. Season runs from May-July.

Greatest Conglomeration of Professional Theater in the World

"The Theater District"

Here it is—for many, the pinnacle of what New York has to offer: a scope and variety of professional theater that is unmatched anywhere in the world (topping even London's stellar theater scene). The majority of this dramatic, comedic, and musical theater is presented in an area roughly bounded by 41st and 53rd streets, and Sixth and Eighth avenues. This district, located just north of the seedy neon of Times Square, is home to more than 35 theaters. This is "Broadway," whether the theaters are on the "Great White Way" (most of them are not) or on the surrounding streets. Some of the theaters are old and a bit run-down; none are really architecturally notable; but their looks are not what attracts audiences. Instead, crowds flock to see big-name stars in lavish productions—and, make no mistake, New York theater *does* bring out the big-name stars. As this is being written, actors appearing in plays in the Theater District include Alec Baldwin, Jessica Lange, Gene Hackman, Glenn Close, Richard Dreyfuss, Gregory Hines, Alan Alda, Eli Wallach, and Al Pacino—and this is far from an atypical week! Among the most notable theaters in the district are the Martin Beck, the Shubert, the Royale, the Booth, the Majestic, the Barrymore, the Richard Rogers, and the Neil Simon (the last two are *both* offering Neil Simon plays currently—it is unusual for "Doc" Simon to not have at least one play running at any given time). Additionally, there are three theaters that are home to Broadway's current "Big Three" of long-running musicals (the odds are strong that *all* of these three will still be running by the time you read this): the Imperial with *Les Miserables*, the Winter Garden with *Cats*, and the Broadway with *Miss Saigon*. Reduced-price tickets are often available (for all but the hottest shows) from the nearly 20-year-old Tkts booth near Times Square or its newer branches at the World Trade Center (see separate listing) and in Brooklyn Heights.

Best Theater Ticket Bargains

Tkts

Although you won't find tickets to such hot shows as *Miss Saigon* and *Phantom*, and your credit cards won't work, this ticket agency in the heart of the theater district offers a good selection of half-price, day-of-performance tickets. The line can look daunting, stretching from the George M. Cohan statue that looks south onto Times Square. But it moves fast—with an average wait of 30 minutes or so, depending upon weather, time of day, and time of year. Pass the time listening to steel bands and other street musicians, checking which shows are available (usually at least a couple of dozen are posted), and discussing with line mates the relative merits of available shows as you prepare your short-list of preferences. Another diversion is watching who buys tickets from scalpers hawking ducats to tough shows. There usually are takers, despite signs warning about illegally obtained tickets. Tkts has a service charge of $1.50 per ticket for these cash-only (traveler's checks OK), half-price transactions. Matinee tickets available one day in advance. Other branches at 2 World Trade Center and in Brooklyn.

Tkts, Duffy Sq at Broadway & W 47th St, New York, NY 10036, 212/354-5800. Matinees from 10 am, evening performances from 3 pm.

Best News You Can Use About Free Movies, Concerts, and Theater

Free Time

Invest a buck on this tabloid that provides a calendar of free and low-budget cultural events in Manhattan. You don't need to spend a fortune to enjoy films, theater, and concerts in New York. Every month about 200 free and low-cost cultural events are scheduled. This paper steers you to the most stimulating freebies. A typical issue lists such events as open rehearsals of the New York Philharmonic, performances by the Dance Theater of Harlem, pianist Andre Watts performing with the New York Youth Symphony, readings of a series of new plays at the American Globe Theatre, and a jazz concert by a Latin quintet. A sampling of free movies in one issue included such classics as *A Streetcar Named Desire*, *The Yellow Submarine*, the *Star Wars* triology, the Oscar-winning foreign film *Journey of Hope*, and a three-day film retrospective celebrating the career of actress Claudette Colbert. Included are lectures and museums with free admissions and a listing of wintergardens in Manhattan. The paper is produced by Russian emigré Natella Vaidman, who worked as a physics teacher in Moscow and as a computer programmer in New York (and delivered chicken while searching for a job in the United States).

Free Time, 20 Waterside Plaza, Suite 6, New York, NY 10010. One dollar at newsstands; $12.90 for 12 monthly issues.

SPORTS (SPECTATOR)

Best Big-Time (and Smaller-Time) Tennis
U.S. Open and Tournament of Champions

Each late August, the New York sporting focus shifts from the dog days of the baseball season and football training camp and focuses on that genteel sport of gentlemen who vociferously argue line calls and ladies who grunt when returning baseline backhands. The U.S. Open is the American national title and one of tennis's four Grand Slam events (along with Wimbledon, the French Open, and the Australian Open). This tournament regularly draws the sport's biggest names (Boris, Andre, Ivan, John, and Jimmy; Martina, Steffi, Gabriela, and Monica) and provides some premium thrills. The only downside is the difficulty in obtaining tickets—but, for those willing to spend the better part of a day waiting in line (or willing to *pay* someone who has waited in line), it is a possibility. And for tennis buffs who would like to play on the National Tennis Center's storied courts, it is possible to reserve playing time when the tournament is not in full swing. For smaller names, easier-to-get tickets, and a touch of history, try the Tournament of Champions at the West Side Tennis Club in Forest Hills. This tourney is offered each May at the one-time home of the U.S. Open (before it outgrew this facility).

U.S. Open, National Tennis Center, Flushing
Meadow Park, Queens, NY 11368, 718/592-8000.
U.S. Open ticket orders (place by May), 718/271-
5100. Tournament of Champions, West Side Tennis
Club, 1 Tennis Pl, Forest Hills, Queens, NY 11368,
718/268-2300.

Best New York Sports Soap Opera
New York Rangers and New York Islanders

Since hockey is measurably less popular than the
other three major American sports, the fates of the
two New York hockey teams seem to be inextricably
intertwined in the minds of their rabid fans. First,
the good news—the Rangers are back! Perhaps not
all the way, but...they've made considerable progress
over the last few years. Although they were one of
the NHL's Original Six teams, the Rangers have not
won a Stanley Cup since 1940. (Long-time Ranger
goalie "Gump" Worsley once, when asked which team
gave him the most trouble, responded, "the Rangers.") But, now led by superstar Mark Messier, the
team is once again among the top half-dozen teams
in the league. Tickets to Rangers' home games at
Madison Square Garden are a tough find—but prac-
tices are sometimes open to the public (info available
at 914/967-2040). As for the Islanders—for years,
while the Rangers slumbered, this suburban team
(based out on—as their name suggests—Long Island, at the Nassau Coliseum) had the market to
itself, winning four consecutive Stanley Cups in the
early 1980s. Today, this team has fallen from its
former perch of dominance—seeming to prove the
axiom that New York can't have two winning, competitive hockey teams at the same time. However, the
Islanders still have their fans (and easier-to-get tickets)—*and* their hopes for a better team anytime soon.
Until then, the world continues to turn for New York
hockey.

New York Rangers, Madison Square Garden, W
33rd St & Seventh Ave, New York, NY 10001, 212/
564-4400. New York Islanders, Nassau Coliseum,
Uniondale, Long Island, NY 11553, 516/587-9222.
Season runs from approximately October through
April.

Best Bet for Pro Football, No Matter Which "New York" Team You Root For

Giants Stadium

New York, New York? More like "New Jersey, New Jersey." The two pro football teams that bear the Big Apple's moniker play across the Hudson in Jersey. Although, from time-to-time, there have been calls for these two teams to take the name of their adopted state, they both remain New York's teams (*especially* the Giants, while they are winning). This 77,000-seat football stadium is part of the Meadowlands Sports Complex, and has seen some victorious seasons lately (from *one* of its teams, anyway). Whatever the respective won-loss records, this stadium jumps all season, hosting one team one week and the other the next (there are some back-to-back weeks for each team, depending upon the schedule). Tickets for both of these teams are tough to come by (again, especially the successful Giants), but single seats are sometimes available. The football equivalent of a "subway series," the rare Giants-Jets game, turns New York into a football madhouse for a week. Giants Stadium also hosts the occasional mega-sized rock concerts (Bruce Springsteen, the Grateful Dead, etc.) during the summer. Transportation is available on airport-style buses, departing from the Port Authority Bus Terminal in Manhattan (212/564-8484).

New York Giants, Giants Stadium, Meadowlands Sports Complex, East Rutherford, NJ 07073, 201/935-8222. New York Jets, Giants Stadium, Meadowlands Sports Complex, East Rutherford, NJ 07073, 201/421-6600. Season runs from September through December.

Best Pro Basketball Team Whose Former Greats Include a U.S. Senator

New York Knicks

From the hardwood floors of the Knicks' home court at Madison Square Garden to the hallowed halls of the U.S. Senate—it's more than a short jumpshot, but it *is* a possible trip to make. Current New Jersey Senator Bill Bradley was a mainstay (along with Willis Reed and Dave DeBusschere) on the Knicks' championship teams of the early 1970s. Today, former Lakers coach Pat Riley has elevated the Knicks back to the upper reaches of the NBA, making a Knicks game one of the hottest tickets in town (dedicated celebrity fans include Woody Allen and Spike Lee). But, do not despair if you can't get tickets, because this is *not* the only game around town. Across the Hudson, in the Meadowland's Brendan Byrne Arena, the New Jersey Nets toil in considerably less limelight. Now led by Chuck Daly— the flashy, hard-working coach who won two championships with the Detroit Pistons and led the superstar-filled 1992 U.S. Olympic team to gold— the Nets hope to throw off their lowly status and compete once more.

New York Knicks, Madison Square Garden, W 33rd St & Seventh Ave, New York, NY 10001, 212/564-4400. New Jersey Nets, Brendan Byrne Arena, Meadowlands Sports Complex, East Rutherford, NJ 07073, 201/935-8888. Season runs from approximately November through April.

Best Post-Season College Basketball Tourney for Teams That Don't Get into the N.C.A.A. Championship Tournament

The National Invitational Tournament

Actually, as most college basketball fans probably know, there are *two* NITs held each year at Madison Square Garden—the first is a season-opening tourney in November, featuring a small, by-invitation field, usually including a number of the country's top teams. The more famous tournament is the one held in March as an adjunct to *the* national championship tournament sponsored by the NCAA (the latter is held at different sites each year). The NIT invites the best teams in the country after the NCAA picks its top 64, meaning that more small, little-heard-of, yet still competitive schools play in the NIT than in the big-time, big-budget NCAA. This always-in-New York tournament was once considered *the* championship to strive for in college basketball— until it was overtaken in popularity and prestige by the NCAA tourney—and it still showcases some exciting post-season action. The later rounds of the NIT can be a tough—but definitely worthwhile—ticket to obtain.

The National Invitational Tournament, Madison Square Garden, W 33rd St & Seventh Ave, New York, NY 10001, 212/563-8300. Held each November (season-opening) and March (championship).

Best Place to Watch "the Doc" Operate

Shea Stadium

Back in the mid-1960s, the Beatles played a number of celebrated concerts here—and, it must be noted, they played *much* better than the Mets team that played here in those same years! Then, the inept expansion team of 1962 (of whom manager Casey Stengel famously asked, "Can't anybody here play this game?") became the "Miracle Mets," the surprise World Series winner of 1969. Since then, the team has had its ups and downs, but soared back to win the 1986 World Series, and has been in contention on and off ever since. The team recently added slugger Bobby Bonilla to complement Dwight "Doc" Gooden, perhaps the National League's best pitcher through most of the '80s, so fans have some reason to expect great things from their Metropolitans. The 55,000-seat Shea is a noisy, breezy place—planes still roar overhead on their way to and from La Guardia and winds swirl, especially in the early spring and fall (so dress warmly, especially for night games). It is accessible by public transportation; a subway stop is within safe walking distance of the stadium. *A historical/sartorial note:* The Mets' seemingly-strange uniform colors (orange and blue) were chosen to symbolize a connection to New York's departed National League teams—blue for the Dodgers and orange for the Giants.

New York Mets, Shea Stadium, 126th St at Roosevelt Ave, Flushing, Queens, NY 11368, 718/507-8499. Season runs from April through October.

Best "House That Ruth Built"

Yankee Stadium

This is one of the most storied stadiums in all of sport, home to the legendary "Bronx Bombers" of Ruth, Gehrig, DiMaggio, Mantle, Maris, Jackson, and Mattingly. To be sure, the Yanks have had some rocky times of late, but hope springs eternal that the fabled pinstripers will return to their place of prominence in baseball's pantheon. This 57,000-seat stadium was built in the 1920s, during the heyday of the Ruth-Gehrig era (the 1927 team is still held up as perhaps the finest ever in baseball); it was remodeled—gutted, really, and rebuilt inside its shell—in 1976. It is still a marvelous place to watch a game, whether the Yankees win or lose. Be sure to check out the monuments to the team's greatest players.

A safety note: Yankee Stadium's Bronx neighborhood can be a little daunting; it's best to leave the park promptly at night, and, if taking the subway back, stick with the crowd as they head for the station.

New York Yankees, Yankee Stadium, 161st St & River Ave, Bronx, NY, 212/293-6000. Season runs from April through October.

Best Pro—and Amateur—Boxing

Madison Square Garden

Heavyweight championship bouts in pro boxing have mostly followed the lure of cash out of major cities such as New York and Chicago into the gambling meccas of Las Vegas and Atlantic City. But, there are still matches to be seen in New York. And if they don't rival the Muhammad Ali championship victories of the mid-1970s which were held here, they can still offer thrills to boxing fans. Regular bouts are scheduled into the Garden at least twice a month, with the occasional lower-weight championship fights drawing huge crowds. Showcasing (generally) younger and hungrier boxers, is the January-through-March Golden Glove series, which sees the area's best amateurs duking it out in the Garden's Felt Forum (a smaller sports arena inside MSG). Boxing fans interested in seeing the local up-and-comers—and those who may wish to lace up the gloves themselves to try a speed bag or a sparring partner—should head for Gleason's Gym in Brooklyn (75 Front Street; 718/797-2872), a longtime boxing hangout with a real *Rocky* sort of feel.

Madison Square Garden, W 33rd St & Seventh Ave, New York, NY 10001, 212/465-6741.

Best Bet to See the Titans of Pro Wrestling

Madison Square Garden

Still going strong after nearly a decade since the beginning of the Hulk Hogan era, professional wrestling continues to pack in the crowds for its unique spectacle. By now, even the children who delight most in the matches (and who make up a good portion of the audience) know that "good" will prevail over "evil," even if the script takes a short detour through chair-throwing and fighting-outside-the-ring territory. They know, too, that the cartoonish heroes and villians will continue to change allegiances and even sides (it helps to keep up on who's who by watching the cable television wrestling shows each week). No matter—this remains an entertaining event for its devotees, and the Garden presents at least one big-name night or weekend of wrestling every month. Of special note are the various "Wrestlemania" or other "World Championship" bouts, which are held here usually once a year. (And, if you can't tell the good guys from the bad guys, ask any pint-sized spectator, who will likely be able to tell you far more than you'd ever want to know about each of the wrestlers.)

Madison Square Garden, W 33rd St & Seventh Ave, New York, NY 10001, 212/563-8300.

Best Bet for Bets and Breakfast

Belmont Park

For the best of American horse racing (or, at the very least, for *one-third* of the best of American horse racing), head out to Belmont Park on Long Island on a Saturday in mid-June. From May through July and from September through mid-October, this track presents a schedule of racing by top thoroughbreds. The highlight of the year, not only here, but for horse-racing fans throughout the entire Northeast, occurs when Belmont Park hosts the prestigious Belmont Stakes, the final jewel in U.S. racing's triple crown (after the Kentucky Derby and the Preakness). As you might expect, this can be a tough ticket to obtain, but it is considered worth it by racing afi-cionados. Even if you don't attend the Belmont Stakes, there is plenty of fine racing to be found here. For a special treat, try the "Breakfast at Belmont," a family-style outing available on week-ends and holidays during the racing season. It in-cludes a trackside breakfast, a tour of the facilities, a chance to watch the horses being put through their morning paces, and some perhaps-valuable handi-capping tips. Belmont Park is conveniently acces-sible from Penn Station via the Long Island Railroad.

Belmont Park, Hempstead Turnpike & Plainfield Ave, Elmont, NY 11003, 718/641-4700.

Best Close-In Horse Racing

Aqueduct Racetrack and Meadowlands Racetrack

It wasn't until the Mets finally put it all together and won the World Series in 1986 that baseball overtook horse racing as New York's favorite spectator sport. If you find that hard to believe, check out the crowds of rabid bettors (and, presumedly, a few non-betting racing fans) that flock to these tracks each season. Aqueduct, in Queens, offers a schedule of thoroughbreds each October through May; and Meadowlands, at the Meadowlands Sports Complex in East Rutherford, presents thoroughbreds from September through December and trotters from December through August (it also simulcasts important races from other tracks—and takes bets on these races—year-round). Of the two, the Meadowlands is newer, with more restaurant facilities and a less grungy atmosphere, and Aqueduct is easier to reach (via the subway). The area's biggest racing day is to be found at Belmont Park, out on Long Island (see separate listing), home of the Belmont Stakes.

Aqueduct Racetrack, Rockaway Blvd at 108th St, Jamaica, Queens, NY, 718/641-4700. Meadowlands Racetrack, Meadowlands Sports Complex, East Rutherford, NJ 07073, 201/935-8500.

Best Spot to Yawn at a Cricket Match
Van Cortlandt Park (and Other Venues)

Sticky wickets in the Big Apple? Expatriated Brits, former British Commonwealth types—from Australia, India, New Zealand, Pakistan, and the West Indies—and curious New Yorkers head for various cricket pitches around the boroughs to witness this most British of sports, which comes complete with tea breaks and players dressed in immaculate whites. In England, where the rules of the game were developed in the 1740s, an innings can last all day and a game may stretch to five days. Cricket elevens that compete in the New York area manage to fit the game into a single summer's day. League matches are played on Saturdays and Sundays in Van Cortlandt Park in the Bronx, where there are 10 pitches. Other cricket venues around the boroughs include Walker Park on Staten Island (where the Staten Island Cricket Club was formed before the turn of the century), Marine Park in Brooklyn, and Flushing Meadows Corona Park in Queens. Spectators are welcome and there is no admission fee. With fielding positions such as silly mid-off and square leg, and with a pair of batters performing at the same time, the game may be confusing to Mets and Yankee fans. But it *is* a pleasant way to spend an afternoon. Tea, anyone?

Van Cortlandt Park, W 242nd St & Broadway, Bronx, NY, 212/430-1890.

SPORTS (PARTICIPANT)

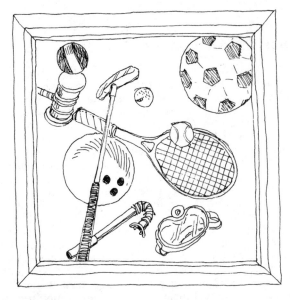

Best Spot for Sports of All Sorts

Central Park

Whether it is the rough-and-tumble of a pick-up game of touch football, a genteel game of croquet, or the casual pitching of a horseshoe, Central Park is the spot for sports of all sorts. Seasonal activities include swimming at Lasker Pool at 106th Street and mid-park (daily Jul-Aug 11 a.m.-7 p.m.), tennis on more than two dozen clay courts and four all-weather courts at West 93rd Street and West Drive (season permits available at the Arsenal; reservations for permit-holders 212/280-0205), and roller skating and miniature golf at the refurbished Wollman Rink at 62nd Street and mid-park (212/517-4800). In winter, the Wollman Rink, with the city skyline as a fetching backdrop, is a popular spot for ice skating, offering snack-bar facilities, lockers, skate rentals, lessons, and covered seating. Oblivious to the hustle and bustle of surrounding Manhattan, lawn bowlers and croquet players, clad in traditional, immaculate whites, pursue their refined games on well-kept greens (and in a clubhouse) north of Sheep Meadow in Central Park (permits, 212/360-8133). For games of a more cerebral sort, the Chess and Checkers House at 64th Street and mid-park has indoor and outdoor tables available for play on weekends (11:30 a.m.-4:30 p.m.). The expansive, versatile park also

provides an outlet for runners, joggers, boaters, bi-
cyclists, and equestrians (see separate listings).
Central Park Conservancy, 830 Fifth Ave, New York,
NY 10021, 212/988-8826.

Best Shop for Sports of All Sorts
Paragon

Whether it's throwing a softball or a punch, tossing
a football or a dart, or just getting in the swim of
things, this mammoth sporting goods store seems to
have something for anyone who ever broke a sweat
or attempted to coordinate hand and eye. From
baseball, basketball, football, and soccer, to bowling,
golf, tennis, and roller-blading, this multi-level
warehouse, located near Union Square, has the
sporting world covered for clothing, footwear, and
equipment, including more esoteric pastimes such
as lacrosse and horse-shoe pitching. In addition to
sporting goods, Paragon also has a well-stocked
outdoor department, with tents, backpacks, sleeping
bags, hiking boots, climbing gear, camp stoves, de-
hydrated food, books, and compasses, as well as a
large stock of fishing gear. A large section devoted
to exercise and fitness has weights, stationary bicycles, treadmills, and stair-climbing machines. For
winter-sports enthusiasts, there is a good selection
of downhill and cross-country ski equipment, ice
skates, and sleds, as well as handsome down-filled
parkas. Not only is the selection awesome, but prices
are good, too.
Paragon, 867 Broadway, New York, NY 10003, 212/
255-8036. Mon-Fri 10 am-8 pm, Sat 10 am-7 pm,
Sun 11 am-6 pm.

Best Bet for Baths
Tenth Street Baths

In an era of sleek health clubs and computerized
fitness machines, this East Village bathhouse is an
anachronism. As the last surviving home of Russian
and Turkish baths in Manhattan, it is a throwback
to the era when immigrants, crowded into tenements
on the teeming Lower East Side, looked to steam
heat and a vigorous rubdown to relieve the tensions
of surviving the mean streets of turn-of-the-century
New York. There also are traditional Swedish baths.
Guaranteed to get circulation percolating with a jump
start, is the *platzka* rub—a brisk, tingling scrub with
a brush fashioned from softened oak branches.
Rabbis include a visit here as part of their strict life-
styles; entertainment celebrities sometimes are seen

purifying themselves of excesses. Options range from penetrating steam created by water on heated rocks, to ice-cold soakings and tough, deep massages; facilities include pool, exercise room, rest area, lockers, sun deck, restaurant, and bar. Robes, slippers, and towels are included in the admission price. Thursdays and Sundays are men only. Wednesdays are reserved for women.

Tenth Street Baths, 268 E 10th St, New York, NY 10009, 212/473-8806. Daily 9 am-10 pm.

Best Bet for Central Park Bicycle Rentals

Loeb Boathouse

Bicycling on the streets of Manhattan generally is for kamikaze delivery riders or others with suicidal tendencies. Nonetheless, there are almost 100 miles of bikeways around the boroughs, with Central Park the choice for many New York recreational bicyclists. For fume-free pedaling, urban bicyclists head for the park on weekends, when its routes are closed to vehicular traffic. Those needing to rent bicycles head for the parking lot of Loeb Boathouse, tucked away on the northeast corner (Fifth Avenue side) of the lake. Pick up a map from the Visitor Information Center at the Dairy (see separate listing) and orient yourself by referring to numbers on lampposts—the first two digits correspond with the nearest numbered east-west street. Bicyclists must ride with the flow of traffic or risk a summons. Check with the boathouse for occasional free bike clinics. Other bicycle rental shops in Manhattan include Metro Bicycles (1311 Lexington Ave; 212/427-4450) and Bicycles Plus (204 E 85th St; 212/794-2201).

Loeb Boathouse parking lot, Central Park (at 75th St), New York, NY 10023, 212/861-4137. Apr-Oct Mon-Fri 10 am-dusk, Sat-Sun 9am-dusk. $6-$12/hour (I.D. required).

Top Shop for Pedal Pushers

Stuyvesant Bicycle

Sports bicyclists tend to be purists, fussy about weights and sizes of frames and wheels, gear ratios, and aerodynamics. This big bicycling emporium on the south edge of Gramercy Park carries a wide range of lightweight frames and bicycles built for racing, but it also is a virtual bicycling supermarket. Kids can select their first two-wheelers here (the same shop where their parents may have bought their tricycles). The shop carries a wide range of touring bicycles, plus mountain, triathlon, and dirt bikes, tandems, and unicycles. There are folding bicycles to fit into that high-rise closet, and sleek Italian imports light enough to be lifted and balanced on one finger. Accessories include handlebar, saddle, and pannier bags, helmets, shoes, toe clips, gloves, water bottles, mirrors, locks, car racks, and colorful, body-hugging clothing. This bike shop also does repairs and has a vast inventory that includes all manner of spare parts as well as repair kits and other essentials. New York has close to 100 miles of bikeways, and on weekends, Central Park closes its roads to vehicular traffic, making it an ideal venue for urban bicyclists (see separate listing).

Stuyvesant Bicycle, 349 W 14th St, New York, NY 10014, 212/254-5200. Mon-Sat 9:30 am-6 pm, Sun noon-5 pm.

Best Track to Race a Bike

Siegfried Stern Kissena Velodrome

Would-be Olympians—and other serious bicycle racers—push their machines at a fast clip around this track. Originally built for racing trials for the 1964 Olympic Games in Tokyo, this velodrome is one of only two such tracks remaining in the Northeast. Renovated and resurfaced (with new lineage designed to racing specifications), the track was reopened in the summer of 1991. Since the 1964 trials, weekly bicycle races, which spectators are welcome to attend, have been held at the track. The track also is used extensively by bicycle racers who compete in programs sanctioned by the U.S. Cycling Federation. During the season, serious racers train here most evenings. But the velodrome also is a place for Walter Mittys. No rentals are available, but anyone showing up with wheels—preferably a racing-style bicycle— may use the track at no charge. Those who show up for a short spin—or merely to watch—will find other diversions in this pleasant park. There is a nature center and tours operated by the Urban Park Rangers, tennis courts, playgrounds, trails that swing through brush populated by many pheasants, and a pond with a resident snapping turtle.

Siefried Stern Kissena Velodrome, Kissena Park, Booth Memorial Ave & Parson Blvd, Queens, NY 11415, 718/520-5936.

Best Place to Row, Row, Row Your Boat

Central Park Lake

Rowing a boat on the lake in Central Park has one of those another-place-another-time feelings—like being on the Serpentine in London or Bois de Boulogne on the edge of Paris. Rentals of aluminum rowboats are obtainable from Loeb Boathouse (subject to season and weather conditions). The placid, meandering lake is spanned at its narrow waist by the cast-iron, Vaux-designed Bow Bridge, said to be one of the most beautiful bridges in the park. Movie buffs may remember the lake from the chilling political drama, *The Manchurian Candidate*, when brainwashed Lawrence Harvey literally jumped into it on command. To equip yourself with a picnic lunch to take boating, stop at the romantic Boathouse Café (see separate listing)—or settle at one of its water's-edge tables. For the ultimate romantic excursion, hire a Venetian-style gondola along with an authentically garbed gondolier to propel you and a Significant Other gently around the Lake (see separate listing). Boat rentals in other boroughs are available at Clove Lake, Staten Island (718/442-7451); Meadow Lake, Queens (718/699-9596); and Prospect Park Lake, Brooklyn (718/287-9824).

Loeb Boathouse, Central Park (at 75th St), New York, NY 10023, 212/517-2233. May-Oct Mon-Fri 10 am-5:30 pm, Sat-Sun 10 am-6:30 pm. $8/hour ($20 refundable deposit).

Toughest Scrums

Rugby Football

It was during a soccer game at England's Rugby School in 1823 that a schoolboy disregarded the "no hands" rule, scooped up the ball, and sprinted toward goal. This breech led to the game of rugby football, forerunner of American football. British-style rugby is popular in New York, with about 40 clubs in the metropolitan area. League games are played in spring and fall, usually on Saturdays, with tournaments throughout the year. Locations around New York include Van Cortlandt Park in the Bronx (home of the highly competitive Old Blue Rugby Club) and at Randalls Island close to the ramp off the Triborough Bridge. Columbia College and the New York Athletic Club also field teams. Rugby is a contact sport, played 15-to-a-side, in which kicking, tackling, and lateral and backward passing are allowed. Blocking and forward passing are prohibited. Play begins from a "scrummage"—a huddle in which players of both teams attempt to kick the ball to a teammate. A touchdown, called a "try," is worth three points, five if converted by a placekick. A dropkick scores four points, a placekick earns three. A game comprises two 40-minute halves (although, during summer, these often are shortened to seven minutes with teams using only 7 players a side instead of the regulation 15). Most clubs welcome potential new players who, along with spectators, also may join in the rugby postgame tradition of repairing to a local watering hole for suds and songs. Rugby hangouts include the Red Lion, popular with Irish expatriates and that also fields the Village Lions rugby team (151 Bleeker St; 212/473-9560), and Drake's Drum, owned by rugby players and offering rugby games on big-screen TV (1744 Second Ave, 212/289-7510). Information about rugby in the United States is contained in *Rugby* (212/787-1160).

Metropolitan New York Rugby Union, P.O. Box 5212, Grand Union Station, New York, NY 10163.

Best (and *Only*) Spare Place in Manhattan

Bowlmor Lanes

Manhattan has no more bowling alleys to spare. While fans of this popular pastime of middle America will find a number of bowling lanes around the outer boroughs, in Manhattan, unless they patronize this old-time bowling alley, they will strike out. While Manhattan's bowling alleys have closed down, one-by-one, this Greenwich Village institution thrives— perhaps because it has been around so long (more than half a century), because it has a reputation as a celebrity hang-out, and because it also functions as a bar and grill. This two-level bowling alley offers a pro shop with shoe rentals, and 44 brightly illuminated lanes (that contrast with a dark, moody bar). While waiting for the early evening leagues to clear out (just as in Milwaukee and Omaha), bowlers sip a brew or two, munch on a sandwiches from the grill, and pump quarters into a lively jukebox. Serious bowlers, looking for shoes, shirts, bags, customized bowling balls, and other accessories head for V. Loria & Sons (at 178 Bowery; 212/925-0300).

Bowlmor Lanes, 110 University Pl, New York, NY 10003, 212/255-8188. Sun-Thu 10 am-1 am, Fri & Sat 10 am-3 am.

Best Bet to Saddle Up and Ride Off

Claremont Riding Academy

In an era long before roller blades and lightweight, stripped-down bicycles, Manhattan was studded with riding academies. The lone, flourishing survivor is the Claremont Academy, which was established before the turn of the century. Conveniently located on the Upper West Side (at Columbus and Amsterdam), not more than a horseshoe's toss from Central Park, it makes good use of the park's 4.4 miles of bridle paths. For adults and children wishing to develop a good "seat" and mastery of the slender English saddle, this multi-story stable complex offers group and individual lessons at an indoor ring. It also provides streetwise rental mounts to experienced riders who wish to canter along Central Park's trails from sunrise to dusk. Those seeking horseback riding in the boroughs have a number of options. In the Bronx, Pelham Bit Riding Stables (212/885-0551) supervises riding in Pelham Bay Park and Van Cortlandt Riding Stables (212/543-4333) provide mounts for the trails of Van Cortlandt Park. In Queens, Forest Park's Lynne's Riding School (718/261-7679) and Dixie Dew Stables (718/263-3500) offer horseback-riding lessons and rentals.

Claremont Riding Academy, 175 W 89th St, New York, NY 10024, 212/724-5100.

Top Spots for "Tennis, Anyone?"

USTA National Tennis Center

Tennis in and around New York isn't all Forest Hills and Flushing Meadows, nor Steffi, Martina, and Boris. In gritty neighborhoods around the boroughs, tennis buffs battle it out on tennis courts maintained by the New York City Department of Parks and Recreation. Among the more scenic settings in Manhattan are the clay and hard courts overlooking the Hudson River at two locations in Riverside Park (at W 96th and W 119th streets) and the outdoor clay and hard courts surrounded by trees in Central Park (mid-park near 94th Street). You can sign up for lessons at the Tennis House in Central Park. Season permits are required for play on municipal courts—with modestly priced single-play tickets also available at various locations. The park season runs April-November. For those with the ambition to play on the hallowed ground of the USTA National Center at Flushing Meadows-Corona Park, home of the U.S. Open, there are fast Deco Turf II courts available for public play. Although there are 29 outdoor and 9

indoor courts at USTA, they are much in demand;
call several days ahead for reservations.

USTA National Tennis Center, Flushing Meadows-
Corona Park, Flushing, NY 11368, 718/592-8000;
New York City Department of Parks and
Recreation, 212/360-8133.

Prime Paths for Running and Jogging

Central Park

More than a century ago, when Olmstead and Vaux
created Central Park, they laid out 58 miles of paths.
Today, many of these paths are the preserve of
dedicated joggers, runners, and speed walkers who
use them as a venue for training and daily exercise
(although the prudent stay away from remote areas
such as the thickly wooded Ramble and avoid the
park after dark). One spot where you're sure to have
the company of other exercisers—perhaps too many
of them!—is the busy 1.58-mile soft-surface track
that encircles the Reservoir, close to the geographic
center of the park. Celebrities such as Madonna are
among those who run laps around the Reservoir.
Those who run on traveled roads are advised to use
the lane closest to the curb and run against the flow
of traffic. Serious runners may wish to contact the
New York Road Runners Club, said to be the world's
largest club for runners. It provides a clubhouse,
clinics, and maps and sponsors weekly races (it
holds more than 150 annually) and group runs in
the park. The club also sponsors the New York City
Marathon (see separate listing), the world's largest
marathon, which now attracts in excess of 20,000
competitors. It had its genesis in Central Park in
1970 when little more than 100 runners showed up
to pound out four laps around the park.

New York Road Runners Club, 9 East 89th St, New
York, NY 10128, 212/860-4455.

Most Grueling Guided Tour of New York

New York City Marathon

This may be the swiftest way to beat New York's
infamous traffic gridlocks and visit all five boroughs.
This annual 26.2-mile guided tour of New York is
taken by more than 20,000 sweaty people, usually
on the first Sunday of November. The world's largest
marathon, it is viewed by an additional 2.5 million
people. The swiftest complete the tour in a little more
than two hours. Attracting elite runners from around

the globe, this marathon is a good spectator event as well as one for *fit* participants (preferably with at least six months' training). You can watch the start on Staten Island alongside the Verazano Narrows Bridge and catch the finish in Central Park at the Tavern on the Green at West 67th Street—and of course view this moving mass of humanity at many points along the way. The sponsor of the race, the New York Road Runners Club, provides a map of the course and handles registration (limited to 25,000). Spectators will find some music and entertainment along the route. Setting the men's course record in 1989 was Juma Ikangaa of Tanzania who completed the course in 2:08:01. On the women's side, Allison Roe of New Zealand established a new mark for the course in 1981 with a time of 2:25:29. Prize money for first to fifth places for both men and women is $20,000, $15,000, $10,000, $5,000, and $2,500.

New York City Marathon, New York Road Runners Club, 9 E 89th St, New York, NY, 212/860-4455.

Best Spots to Get in the Swim

The obvious advice to visitors to New York who enjoy swimming is simply to choose a hotel that has a swimming pool (which, of course, is not always possible). The choices are numerous, including the Vista Hilton International Hotel and Le Parker Meridien (see separate listing), which have sleek indoor heated pools) and the Ramada Inn (790 Eighth Avenue), which offers a rooftop outdoor pool. There are, however, other options for visitors (or residents) who are not staying at a hotel with a pool. The Sheraton Manhattan Hotel (formerly the Sheraton City Squire, 790 Seventh Avenue; 212/621-8591) offers non-guest privileges at its fifth-floor, glass-enclosed swimming pool for a day-use fee of around $20. In addition to use of the heated, 24' x 50' pool, this price includes use of gym, sauna, sun deck, and lockers for men and women. Towels are provided. Popular municipal pools include the Carmine Street Recreation Center (7th Avenue South and Clarkson Street; 212/397-3107), and the West 59th Street Recreation Center (between West End and Amsterdam Avenues; 212/397-3159), both of which have indoor and outdoor pools.

Best Beaches in the Boroughs

Rockaway Beach and Riis Park

In the 19th century, these beaches in Queens were an exclusive playground of New York's movers and shakers. Today, they remain the best beaches in the boroughs, with excellent surf and accessibility by subway. Poking a bony finger into the Atlantic, the Rockaway Peninsula helps protect the entrance to New York harbor. It is fronted by a strand of sandy beach more than seven miles long that stretches alongside pounding ocean surf. The beach is paralleled most of its length by a boardwalk (replete with food stands). Popular here are traditional seaside activities, such as surf fishing, beachcombing, outdoor art fairs and concerts, and amusement-park rides. Riis Park (named for a crusading journalist who fought for better recreational facilities around the turn of the century), offers a mile-long stretch of ocean beach, a boardwalk, fitness trail, kiddie playgrounds, and facilities for shuffleboard, handball, and paddle tennis. Because Rockaway is part of the Gateway National Recreation Area, there are various nature tours and photo safaris led by National Park Service rangers.

Gateway National Recreation Area, Breezy Point District, Rockaway, NY 11691, 718/474-4600.

Best Nearby Beach Beyond the City Limits

Jones Beach State Park

This barrier-island beach—a strand of white sand fronting the ocean for about 6.5 miles—is New York's playground, accessible via the Long Island Railroad (and connecting buses), by special buses from Manhattan, and by auto across a causeway. With 10 million visitors a year, the park, which opened in 1929, unquestionably gets a lot of wear and tear. But New Yorkers and out-of-town visitors seem to delight in the series of eight Atlantic Ocean swimming areas at Jones Beach (with a special beach for surfing), the additional beach at Zach's Bay, and an Olympic-size swimming pool. It is all contained within a state park that offers more than 2,400 acres of recreation that includes a 1.5-mile boardwalk with games and entertainment, roller skating, pitch-and-putt and miniature golf, and softball and baseball diamonds. There are snack stands throughout the park plus a sit-down restaurant offering ocean views. Along with the ocean beaches, a major attraction is the Jones Beach Theater, its stage on a man-made island that sits in Zach's Bay. With 10,000 seats, this outdoor theater stages concerts with such name entertainers as Neil Diamond, Elton John, and the Beach Boys.

Jones Beach State Park, Ocean Dr, Wantagh, Long Island, NY 11793, 516/785-1600.

Spiffiest Urban Spa

The Peninsula Spa

Tone your body; pamper your hair and skin; dine on delicious, healthful meals; enroll in a special program to bounce back from jet lag—and while you're at it, enjoy sweeping views of the Manhattan skyline. This luxurious urban spa, perched atop the elegantly refurbished Peninsula Hotel, offers personalized one-on-one training, fitness evaluations, and nutrition counseling. The glass-enclosed, 35,000-square-foot, tri-level club features a glass-enclosed swimming pool with whirlpool, and a wraparound sundeck overlooking Fifth Avenue. You can sign up for aerobic conditioning classes (including aqua aerobics), yoga, and body sculpting. Two strength-training rooms have a complete line of Cybex systems, free weights, and state-of-the-art cardiovascular fitness equipment including Stairmasters, Lifecycles, treadmills, ski machines, and the Gravitron system designed to equalize body weight while training. Spa options include full-service hair salon, facials and body treatments, and Swedish, Shiatsu, and a range of other massages. Luxurious lounges and dressing rooms feature mahogany lockers, all-marble bathrooms, and steam and sauna rooms. Weekend packages are available in conjunction with the Peninsula Hotel (see separate listing).

The Peninsula Spa, 700 Fifth Ave, New York, NY 10019, 212/903-3910.

Best Spot for All-Season Ice Skating

Sky Rink

When summer's heat and humidity blanket Manhattan like a damp cloth, and New Yorkers are hastening to swimming pools and beaches, this ice rink is a good place to cool off. While the pretty outdoor rinks in Central Park and at Rockefeller Center may be tops for atmospheric skating when there's a nip of frost in the air, the Sky Rink offers the advantage of staying open year around. Because of this, it is the choice of serious athletes as well as recreational skaters. This Olympic-size rink is the training choice of Olympian world-class skaters. Figure-skating champions such as Dorothy Hamill have used this well-kept ice to nail down compulsories and practice routines. Private lessons are available, as well as equipment rentals. There is a well-stocked skate shop and a coffee shop. Appropriately named, this rink may be the highest in Manhattan. It is on the 16th floor of a Midtown skyscraper between Ninth and Tenth Avenues.

Sky Rink, 450 W 33rd St, New York, NY 10001, 212/
695-6556. Hours vary for public skating.

Best Spot for Holiday Season Ice Skating

Rockefeller Center Ice Rink

This sunken outdoor rink is Manhattan's best-known
ice-skating venue—thanks to movies such as *Splash*,
which had Tom Hanks wobbling around it. In summer, this spot is occupied by an outdoor café; during
winter, you can sit inside, enjoying a drink or meal,
and watch the skaters through a restaurant window.
Usually, there are some first-class performers skim-
ming effortless around the rink, knowing they have
a captive audience. During the holidays, this is an
especially charming spot, dominated by a giant
Christmas tree with its lights twinkling in the gray
December dusk. There is a fee for skating—pricier
at this high-visibility location than elsewhere. You
can rent skates and on some days skate until midnight. And when ankles begin to feel the strain, this
19-building complex is a maze of diversions, with
restaurants, shops, television studio tours, lobby art
and outdoor sculptures (including, alongside the ice
rink, the bronze-and-gold-leaf statue of the Greek
god Prometheus).

Rockefeller Center Ice Rink, 1 Rockefeller Plaza (at
Fifth Ave), New York, NY 10020, 757-5731. Oct-Apr,
Sun-Thu 9 am-10 pm, Fri & Sat 9 am-midnight.

Most Scenic Spot for Ice Skating, Roller Skating, and Miniature Golf

Wollman Memorial Rink

This open-air rink in Central Park is the place to be
on crisp winter evenings, as the frost begins to coat
the stark, leafless trees that surround it, and etches
the breaths of skaters gliding effortlessly around the
perimeter or carving exacting figure eights. At night,
the glinting lights of the Manhattan skyline provide
a romantic backdrop. The rink was built in the early
1950s and rebuilt some 30 years later when entrepreneur Donald Trump shunted aside the bureau-
cratic bumbling that had long stalled rebuilding the
deteriorated facility (which had been closed for seven
years) and quickly got the job done. It offers a terrace
for spectators, skate rentals, lockers, lessons, and
a snack bar. The enormous rink (33,000 square feet)
often becomes extremely crowded, drawing around

10,000 skaters each season. There is ice skating from November to early April. For the remainder of the year the rink is open for roller skating and miniature golf.

Wollman Memorial Rink, Central Park at 63rd St and East Dr, New York, NY 10021, 212/517-4800. Mon 10 am-5 pm, Tue-Thu 10 am-9:30 pm, Fri & Sat 10 am-11 pm, Sun 10 am-9:30 pm.

KIDS

Best Dining Spot for Breakfast with Kids

Royal Canadian Pancake House

Were they allowed, some kids would choose chocolate for breakfast (and some adults would, too, come to think of it). Here's a breakfast spot where kids (of all ages) could satisfy this craving. Included among more than 50 different kinds of pancakes—with fillings ranging from corn to cranberries—is a selection richly imbedded with chocolate chips. There also are white-chocolate pancakes and versions featuring a variety of nuts and berries. A popular choice are oven-baked apple pancakes, light and fluffy and full of flavor. Be sure to bring a hearty appetite; pancakes are so humongous that they threaten to spill off the plate. The bill of fare also includes a dozen different kinds of French toast, 18 varieties of waffles, and a selection of crepes. For breakfast traditionalists there are omelettes and other egg dishes. It is rumored that JFK, Jr. slips in here from his job in the DA's office. Because there often are long waits on weekends, parents are advised to be prepared to amuse hungry, fidgety kids (or try a late-late brunch—or early dinner).

Royal Canadian Pancake House, 145 Hudson St, New York, NY 10013, 212/219-3038. Daily 7 am-midnight.

Best Dining Spot for Lunch with Kids

Ed Debevic's

For kids, it's a trip back in a time machine, just like in the movies. For adults, it is pure nostalgia. For everyone, Ed's can be great fun, recreating with three separate theme areas a '50s-era diner, '60s-era coffee shop, and '40s-era night club. There are wise-cracking, gum-popping wait staff, Beatles records on the jukebox, and such diner staples as meatloaf sandwiches, wet fries (with gravy), chili dogs, banana cream pie, and thick milk shakes. A selection of comfort food includes chicken fried steak, chicken pot pie, roast turkey, and fried chicken, with mashed potatoes, gravy, creamed corn, fresh vegetable, and biscuits (although '90s kids might prefer the thin-crust pizza and hamburgers). Fountain creations include old-fashioned malts, ice-cream sodas, phosphates, sundaes, and a root-beer concoction called a Black Cow. Turquoise is the theme color of the '50s dining room, while the '40s space includes a black-and-white art deco bar. The '60s room has fake brick walls decorated with memorabilia of that decade. This faux-greasy spoon is ultimate kitsch with signs requesting that if service doesn't live up to Ed's promise—don't tell anyone.

Ed Debevic's, 661 Broadway, New York, NY 10012, 212/982-6000. Sun-Tue noon-midnight, Wed & Thu noon-1 am, Fri & Sat noon-2 am.

Best Dining Spot for Dinner with Kids

Mickey Mantle's

Although the current generation of young baseball fans have their own crop of idols, none yet can match the accomplishments of Mickey Mantle, home-run slugger of the 1950s, who is among major-league baseball's Top Ten all-time home-run leaders. This restaurant is a shrine to Mick's accomplishments, and a fun place to take young baseball fans to dinner. It is crammed with baseball memorabilia, including uniforms, gloves, caps, photographs, trophies, and autographed bats and balls. Although the food is far from haute cuisine, the menu offers plenty of kid-pleasers. Of course, in a baseball-themed restaurant, hot dogs are popular fare, along with massive hamburgers, ribs, chicken, fries, salads, sandwiches, and other standard offerings, with shakes and hot-fudge sundaes in demand with younger baseball fans. Watch the fortunes of the present-day Yankees (along with videos of historic games) on giant-screen televisions. Watch, too, for an appearance by the eponymous slugger-turned-restaurateur, who usually is willing to autograph postcards and baseball cards. (This also is a late-night spot for a drink and a sandwich.)

Mickey Mantle's, 42 Central Pk S, New York, NY 10019, 212/688-7777. Mon-Sat noon-1 am, Sun noon-midnight.

Best Dining Spot for Dessert with Kids

Rumpelmayer's

Populated by kids, parents, grandparents, and a virtual zoo of enormous stuffed animals, this classic ice-cream parlor off the hotel lobby of the St. Moritz on the Park features soft tones of pink, multiple mirrors, and lots of faux-marble. Favorites include a pot of hot chocolate with whipped cream, ice-cream sodas, thick milk and malted shakes, and that New York creation, the egg cream. There is a selection of ice cream, sorbets, and frozen yogurt (try the mango or banana fudge), and such traditional fountain fare as banana split, frozen eclair with whipped cream and chocolate sauce, and peach melba. Adult favorites include strawberries Romanoff (in orange liqueur), a version of pear Hélène (with crème de cassis and vanilla ice cream), and various liqueur-flavored coffees. A small-but-varied menu includes appetizers (such as potstickers, crab cakes, and escargot) soups (including gazpacho and black bean), salads, hot and cold sandwiches, burgers, pizza, omelettes, a few pasta selections, and entrées such as chicken pot pie, lamb chops, prime rib, and grilled swordfish. Service is at a soda-fountain counter or tables.

Rumpelmayer's, 50 Central Park S, New York, NY 10019, 212/755-5800. Daily 7 am-midnight.

Best Dining Spot for Dessert with Kids (and Toy Shopping)

Serendipity 3

Should there be a wait for a table at this restaurant and ice-cream parlor, there are plenty of diversions. That is because this East Side favorite doubles as a gift boutique. An eclectic selection includes postcards, jewelry, mugs, glasses, hand-painted T-shirts and other clothing, toys, and novelties. Desserts include a range of fountain creations, such as ambrosial hot-fudge sundaes, banana splits, and high-quality ice cream with a variety of delicious toppings. Its famous signature dessert is frozen hot chocolate—although frozen espresso also is worth a try. For those who prefer a course or two *before* dessert, there are chili, sandwiches, burgers, foot-long hot dogs, miniature pizzas, and casseroles. Although its general Victorian ambience and marble-and-wire soda-fountain furnishings make this a good spot for an afternoon outing with children, Serendipity stays open late enough to make it a popular post-theater or -club venue for late-night decadence (Andy Warhol had a weakness for this spot, as do Brooke Shields and other celebs).

Serendipity 3, 225 E 60th St, New York, NY 10022, 212/838-3531. Mon-Thu 11:30 am-12:30 am, Fri & Sat 11 am-2 am, Sun 11:30 am-midnight.

Super Spot for Clark Kents and Lois Lanes

Staten Island Children's Museum

Interactive exhibits at this award-winning children's museum introduce youngsters to contemporary issues and current affairs. At the "It's News to Me" exhibit, youngsters can try their skills at reporting and TV newscasting at a simulated studio as they learn how the print and electronic media function. They also learn about the history of journalism and about the media's potential to influence and shape attitudes and opinions. There is an abbreviated version of the famous "War of the Worlds" broadcast made by Orson Welles in 1938 that spread panic among listeners who believed the realistic account of the invasion of New Jersey by Martians. Special exhibits, programs, and workshops focus on science, architecture, the arts, biology, and other topics. Free programs include mime, dance, storytelling, puppet shows, and other performances suitable for children ages 5-12. Now that a half-hourly trolley shuttle service runs between the Staten Island ferry dock and Snug Harbor Cultural Center, this museum is accessible from Manhattan by public transportation. The ferry ride (see separate description) is itself a wonderful adventure for children.

Staten Island Children's Museum, (at Snug Harbor Cultural Center), 914 Richmond Terrace, Staten Island, NY 10301, 718/273-2060. Wed-Fri 1-5 pm, Sat-Sun 11 am-5 pm.

Best Museum for a Hot Time

New York City Fire Museum

Fans of the movie *Ghostbusters* may recall that the wise-cracking poltergeist-fighters were headquartered in an old city firehouse. Visitors won't see Bill Murray sliding down a pole at this museum, but it does make good use of another abandoned NYC fire station. Housed in an attractive and restored beaux-arts-style station built in 1904, this museum traces the development of this city's fire department and honors those who have served in it. Firefighting artifacts, such as tools, uniforms, pictures, and even old firetrucks (ranging from horse- and man-drawn to early motorized versions) are interestingly and informatively presented. A special exhibit covers the notorious 1911 Triangle Shirtwaist Company fire (where 146 young female workers were trapped in an unsafe factory fire), which shocked the city and led to the institution of stricter fire codes. A series of lectures and presentations at the museum involve fire prevention, safety, and other firefighting topics. This is the largest firefighting museum in the country, and, even without a dalmatian out front, is very popular with kids.

New York City Fire Museum, 278 Spring St, New York, NY 10013, 212/691-1303. Tue-Sat 10 am-4 pm.

Best Medieval Castle That's Not Make-Believe or Sand

Belvedere Castle

It's a whimsical landmark slap in the middle of Manhattan. This mock medieval castle delights youngsters who enjoy scrambling over its ramparts. It also offers a varied program of family activities. In Italian, the word *belvedere* means "fine view," and that precisely is what Belvedere Castle delivers, perched as it is upon Vista Rock, the highest rocky outcropping in Central Park. Visitors climb stone steps to terraces overlooking the park, the nearby city, and adjacent Turtle Pond (an important habitat for park insects and reptiles). Recently renovated, this castle serves as the Central Park Learning Center, where visitors may attend a variety of workshops and view exhibits on geology, botany, and other subjects, including meteorology—the castle houses a National Weather Service Station. At the Discovery Chamber, children learn about the park through activities and games. Weekend family workshops revolve around such subjects as Japanese fish printing, making pop-up books, and surrounding a favorite picture with a frame made from natural objects gathered in the park. A gift shop carries books and nature-related items.

Belvedere Castle, 79th St, south of the Great Lawn, Central Park, NY 10024, 212/772-0210. Tue-Sun 11 am-5 pm (until 4 pm mid-Oct–mid-Feb).

Merriest Amusement Ride in the Middle of the City
Carousel Ride

For a nostalgic (and inexpensive) ride on a turn-of-the-century merry-go-round, head along the 65th Street Transverse west of the Central Park Children's Zoo. Built in 1903 by eminent woodcarvers Stein and Goldstein, the carousel was moved to Central Park in 1951 and features 58 large hand-carved horses and chariots and ornate decorative cherubs and clowns. A four-minute ride with a background of traditional organ music costs 90 cents. The carousel is adjacent to the Heckscher Playground. Children also love to watch the animal figures on the bronze Delacorte Musical Clock located east of the carousel (between the children's and main zoo). The fascinating musical clock was completed in 1965. Its animated animals perform on the hour and half hour.

Carousel, Central Park, mid-park at 64th St, New York, NY 10024, 212/879-0244. Daily 10:30 am-4:30 pm (weather permitting).

Best Bet for Beady Eyes
Staten Island Zoo

A small boy of my acquaintance not only prefers this compact, 8-1/2-acre zoo to its larger and more famous counterparts, but he even enjoys its logo. The first "o" in "Zoo" is represented by a coiled serpent. It is appropriate. The zoo's noted reptile exhibit includes the world's most complete collection of North American rattlesnakes. Youngsters especially enjoy visiting on Saturday mornings to join the popular "Breakfast with the Beasts" program, which allows them to help feed animals as they learn about animal diets. Many kids head for the animal hospital that has a nursery viewing area, or to a state-of-the-art aquarium. Recent modernization created another exhibit popular with youngsters that helps them understand a crucial environmental problem—a South American tropical rain forest. Other kid-pleasers include a children's zoo and a miniature farm. A breezy (and inexpensive!) ride on the Staten Island Ferry (see separate listing) combined with a visit to see the vaunted collection of rattlesnakes—there are close to three dozen varieties, found only in the Western Hemisphere—make a nice outing.

Staten Island Zoological Society, Inc, 614 Broadway, Staten Island, NY 10310, 718/442-3100. Daily 10 am-4:45 pm. Adults $3, children 3-11 $2.

Best Spots for Telling Tales

Central Park Conservatory Water and Playgrounds

There is magic in a children's story and, as if by magic, a storyteller shows up in Central Park at 11 a.m. on Saturday mornings during the warm-weather months (and on some Wednesdays at the same time) to spin tales to please youngsters. In actuality, the magic is courtesy of the New York Public Library (212/340-0906), which sponsors the talented storytellers. Appropriately, the meeting site for these sessions for children ages five and older is beneath a statue of that master teller of tales, Hans Christian Andersen. The statue is located at Conservatory Water (a pond near the easterly perimeter of the park at 74th Street), also the site of bronze statues of Alice in Wonderland and the Mad Hatter, over which kids love to scramble. Another program, "Sandbox Stories," sponsored by the Central Park Conservancy (212/360-2766) rotates on different days of the week at close to a dozen playgrounds. At these free, 45-minute sessions, children ages three to eight years accompanied by an adult can listen to stories from around the world told by professional storytellers.

Storytelling, Central Park, beside Hans Christian Andersen statue, 74th St at Conservatory Water, New York, NY 10023, 212/340-0906.

Best Spot to See the Greatest Globe

Daily News Building

Kids, who may not be especially receptive to geography lessons and the lobbies of office buildings, may change their minds during a visit to this Midtown landmark. This brown-brick, 37-story, art deco tower, home of the tabloid *Daily News*, was designed in 1930 by Howells and Hood (a firm that five years earlier had won an international competition to design Chicago's famous newspaper building, the Gothic Tribune Tower). As the centerpiece of its lobby, it has a huge, rotating globe that, at 12 feet in diameter, is said to be the world's largest. Related geographical gizmos include time clocks, maps, solar charts, wind-direction signs, and, etched into the lobby floor, a huge compass with bronze lines indicating relative distances to major U.S. cities. There's a history lesson for kids, too, in the form of enlarged reproductions of notable front-page *Daily News* stories. A little gallery has changing exhibits of news photos.

Daily News Building, 220 E 42nd St, New York, NY 10017, 212/949-1234. Mon-Sat 9 am-5 pm.

Best Playground For *All* Children

Playground for All Children

What is special about this playground is that "special" children—those with disabilities—mingle and play with non-disabled children. This prototype playground in Flushing Meadows Corona Park offers creative programs year-around in arts and crafts, sports, garden/nature crafts, storytelling, and puppetry. Playground facilities are handicapped-accessible—swings and see saws, for example, may be operated by hands and feet. This fun park includes a 12-foot-long rocking suspension bridge and a brightly colored tubular climbing unit, both of which are wheelchair accessible. At a "soft play" area with protective padding, children can climb and hang from ropes and roll and tumble without injuring themselves. There is a curved track where kids can run, skate, wheel, or walk, and an arena for basketball and other team sports. In a large meadow, children can spread out picnics and frolic on a grassy rolling hill. Youngsters plant and tend flower and vegetable gardens and, on hot summer days, cool off under the spray of the park's water wheel. Workshops introduce children to small animals such as rabbits, gerbils, hamsters, and various birds, and teach how to care for them.

Playground for All Children, 111-01 Corona Ave, Corona, NY 11368, 718/699-8283. Mon-Fri 1:30-5 pm, Sat & Sun 10 am-5 pm.

Best Underground Discoveries

Brooklyn Children's Museum

Although it dates back to 1899, this pioneering children's museum remains cutting-edge contemporary. Located in high-tech quarters that are mostly underground, it constantly updates exhibits. "Night

Journeys," for example, explores sleep from a child's perspective. Youngsters can try out a folding cot, Egyptian bed, and other types of beds, examine nighttime fears, compare human and animal sleep needs, and view an interactive video about dreams. At "Animals Eat," youngsters engage in fun-filled games to learn the eating habits of animals, how animals get energy from the sun, and how they adapt to their surroundings to obtain food. At the Boneyard, they compare the size and functions of bones. Young children make leaf rubbings and bag puppets; older kids engage in hands-on science experiments and workshops as they explore the laws of chemistry and physics. Youngsters become super sleuths at "The Mystery of Things," using their senses to solve puzzles—identifying mystery smells inside squeeze bottles, sounds made by a tea kettle, type-writer, and telephone, the feel of objects they must match with their hands instead of their eyes. Objects from everyday American life are incorporated into the museum's design. A turn-of-the-century subway kiosk serves as an entrance, a massive drainage pipe is neon-lighted to provide a "people tube" connecting display areas, an oil tank houses an auditorium.

Brooklyn Children's Museum, 145 Brooklyn Ave, Brooklyn, NY 11213, 718/735-4400. Mon-Fri 2-5 pm, Sat-Sun & school holidays 10 am-5 pm. Admission $2.

Biggest Kids' Parties

Brooklyn Children's Museum

Brooklyn's great hands-on museum—the first in the world designed expressly for children—knows how to throw a party. A big one! In June, a festival for children and parents attracts more than 30,000 visitors, the museum's single largest event. Called "Balloooon," it includes dance, workshops, and a parade led by costumed stilt-walkers, as the museum's signature balloon wafts 30 feet overhead. Another enormously popular event is the annual Halloween Monster Mash. There are such activities as face painting, potato carving, and storytelling with a macabre musical serenade by a trio of witches. Providing a suitably eerie setting for these frightful goings on is the massive neon-lighted drainage pipe which serves as a "people tube" connecting the museums various exhibit areas. Check the museum calendar for a full program of special events that are scheduled year-round—magic shows, African ballet, the Motown Sound and other '60s music, ice cream socials, and thoughtful shows such as "Discover Dance" (showing how dances are created from everyday gestures, sports movements, words, and feelings) and "Laugh Out Loud" (with stories, pranks, and sing-along designed to produce big belly laughs).

Brooklyn Children's Museum, 145 Brooklyn Ave, Brooklyn, NY 11213, 718/735-4400. Mon-Fri 2-5 pm, Sat-Sun & school holidays 10 am-5 pm. Admission $2.

Best Matinee That May Be an Illusion
Mostly Magic

As its name suggests, this Greenwich Village nightclub-theater-restaurant dedicates itself to the art of prestidigitation, and on Saturday afternoons offers a magic show for children. These hour-long performances usually involve two magicians and are geared to kids ages 4 to 10 years. Audience participation is encouraged, and, given the natural inhibitions of youngsters, there usually is no shortage of volunteers. Magic and comedy shows for adult audiences are scheduled nightly. For youngsters interested in performing magic of their own, a pair of Manhattan shops offer a mixed bag of tricks, ranging in price from a buck or two to thousands of dollars. Flosso-Hornmann Magic Company (45 W 34th Street, 212/279-6079) offers tricks and a magic museum; Tannen's Magic (6 W 32nd Street, 212/239-8383) will sell you a trick simple enough for a pre-schooler to manage—or the trappings of a grand illusion.

Mostly Magic, 55 Carmine St, New York, NY 10014, 212/924-1472. Children's matinees, Sat 2 pm.

Best Children's Theater with Strings
Swedish Cottage Marionette Theater

Back in 1876 when America was celebrating its centennial with a huge exposition in Philadelphia, an old schoolhouse was brought over from Sweden. A year later it was purchased by New York's city council for $1,500 and placed in Central Park. After being put to various uses, in 1947 the building became the home of a workshop for a marionette theater and in 1972 part of the venerable building was converted to a marionette theater. Although the troupe has suffered budget cuts that have curtailed its touring and shortened its season, the charming 75-seat theater survives and stages shows with hand-crafted puppets, sets, and costumes. In fact, the entire production, from scripts to lighting, is the work of the theater's small staff. Performances include such perennial favorites as *Cinderella*, *Rumpelstiltskin*, and *Alice in Wonderland*, plus such experimental works as a rock version of *Peter Pan* with the music written by the staff, and *The Magic Flute*, adapted from the Mozart opera.

Swedish Cottage Marionette Theater, Central Park at W 79th St, New York, NY 10024, 212/988-9093. Mid-Oct–mid-Jun, Tue-Fri 10:30 am & noon (groups of 10 or more); Sat (gen'l public) noon & 3 pm. Adults $5, children $4 (reductions during group performances).

Best Adaptations of Children's Theater Classics

Little People's Theater Company

In an age of Ninja Turtles and brash Bart Simpson, such classics as *Cinderella*, *Goldilocks*, *Sleeping Beauty*, and *The Three Little Pigs* are still pleasing youngsters—especially when these stories are given a comedic spin. Since 1968, this talented theatrical company has been entertaining children with humorous adaptations of classic tales—for example, *Humpty Dumpty Falls in Love*. Each season, beginning right after Labor Day and continuing until late June, the company stages about eight productions at the Courtyard Playhouse, with two performances each Saturday and Sunday afternoon. The shows are designed for children between ages 2 and 9 years; audience participation is encouraged. Over the holidays there are shows such as *Wilbur the Christmas Mouse* and *Santa Claus and the Christmas Bell*. Performances by this long-running Greenwich Village theatrical group are extremely popular and reservations are essential.

Little People's Theater Company, Courtyard Playhouse, 39 Grove St, New York, NY 10014, 212/765-9540. Sat & Sun (early September-late June) 1:30 pm & 3 pm.

Best Contemporary Children's Theater

Theatreworks/USA and The Paper Bag Players

Original musicals with a topical theme are the forte of Theatreworks/USA. Its productions, at the Promenade Theatre, include the likes of *Class Clown*, an upbeat musical focusing on the question of illiteracy; a musical retrospective of Dr. Martin Luther King, Jr.; and works dealing with environmental protection and other social issues. Some shows are free.

Farther north on the Upper West Side, the well-known Paper Bag Players perform for children on weekends at the Symphony Space Theatre, a vast hall, dating back to the early 1900s, that was an ice rink and movie house in former lives. Today, it hosts a variety of performing arts, from jazz to classical concerts. True to its name, The Paper Bag Players is a children's theatrical company that makes adaptive use of brown-paper grocery bags and cardboard boxes, as well as assorted household implements for its costumes, props, and sets. These musical productions are recommended for children ages 4 to 9 years.

Theatreworks/USA, Promenade Theatre, 2162 Broadway, New York, NY 10024, 212/420-8202. The Paper Bag Players, Symphony Space Theatre, 2537 Broadway, New York, NY 10025, 212/864-5400.

Best Bet for Broadcasting Memories
The Museum of Television and Radio

There are large quotas of fun and history at this museum, which helps preserve America's radio and television heritage. Until its founding in 1975 (as the Museum of Broadcasting), this record of America's broadcasting history was being saved only by private enthusiasts and collectors. Here is where Kermit the Frog is on display, along with other Muppets and characters from "Sesame Street" and "Fraggle Rock." This is also where visitors can hear the voice of Franklin D. Roosevelt leading America out of the Great Depression and witness key moments in the civil rights movement. They can also study performances of Helen Hayes, Orson Welles, and Laurence Olivier, and laugh with Lucille Ball and Ernie Kovacs. Visitors access a collection of more than 40,000 programs chosen for their artistic, cultural, and historical significance and view or listen to them in private console rooms. There also are daily screenings and radio presentations at five locations, including the 200-seat Principal Theater and the more intimate 90-seat Mark Goodson Theater—plus a full calendar of exhibitions, seminars, and other special events. For children ages 8 to 14 years, there are special weekend programs and workshops. In 1991, the museum moved to this brand-new site (next door to the legendary "21" Club—visited by many legendary broadcasters of the past).

The Museum of Television and Radio, 25 W 52nd St, New York, NY 10019, 212/621-6800. Tue, Wed, Fri & Sat noon-6 pm, Thu noon-8 pm.

Best British Kids' Game to Go Nuts About

Conkers

To botanists it is *Aesculus hippocastanum;* to Ohioans it is the buckeye; to the English it is the horsechestnut tree. Since the late 19th century, the tree has provided the means to a simple game that has entertained generations of English schoolboys. The game, called "conkers," uses the fruit of the horsechestnut tree, the *nonedible* nuts that, in fall, ripen and burst from their spiky green cases (the same buckeyes that many Americans use for craft projects). The game is simple. A hole, about the diameter of a meat skewer, is punched through the buckeye—or conker—and threaded with about 15 to 18 inches of twine, multiply knotted at one end to prevent the conker from slipping through. The string with the dangling horsechestnut is held at arm's length while an opponent is permitted to swing at it with his conker. Each player takes turns trying to smash the other's conker until one emerges victorious. The winning conker then is credited with a victory and accumulates "kills"—on the honor system—until it, too, inevitably is smashed. The victorious conker assumes the victory tally of any conker it vanquishes. British schoolboys, coveting conkers with prodigious victory tallies, employ various dubious means of toughening their warrior-horsechestnuts, such as soaking in vinegar and baking in an oven. Part of the fun of the game is harvesting horsechestnuts. In New York, this can be accomplished in Central Park in Strawberry Fields (see separate listing), dedicated to John Lennon, who undoubtedly played conkers as a schoolboy.

Strawberry Fields, Central Park, Central Park West at W 72nd St, New York, NY 10029, 212/397-3156, 8 am-dusk.

Top Docs for Dollies

New York Doll Hospital

Whether for major or cosmetic surgery, children have been taking their cloth, rubber, and plastic playmates to this second-story East Side doll hospital since shortly after the turn of the century. Mothers, as well as their children, enjoy visiting, curious to see if they might spot dolls similar to ones they had as children. Much of the fascination is in seeing the array of spare doll parts and watching a skilled "surgeon" at work. In addition to repairing torn teddies and bruised Barbies, the New York Doll Hospital also appraises, restores, and buys antique dolls. And, of course, it sells vintage dolls. Collectors head here in search of rare 19th-century European dolls, venerable teddy bears, and such collectibles as Shirley Temple and other celebrity dolls. This family-owned business started out as an adjunct to a hairdressing salon, where children accompanying their mothers were encouraged to bring their dolls for a hairdo.

New York Doll Hospital, 787 Lexington Ave, New York, NY 10021, 212/838-7527. Mon-Sat 9:30 am-6 pm.

Nicest Nannies for a Night

The Baby Sitters' Guild, Inc.

New York can be a great city for kids, with lots of fun museums, puppet shows and other entertainment, and outdoor activities, such as boating, bicycling, and kite flying. But there are times when parents need an adults-only outing, perhaps to dinner and a concert or the theater and a spot of late-night club hopping. This is when Mary Poppins (or a reasonable facsimile thereof) would be a blessing. The next best thing might be a sitter from this baby-sitting service that is licensed, bonded, and has been in the business of taking care of youngsters since 1940. Its well-trained sitters are multilingual, with varied and interesting backgrounds. It is relatively easy to find a sitter suited to individual needs. Sitters will travel to a home or a hotel, with a four-hour minimum for each assignment. With this and other New York baby-sitting services, expect to pay around $10 an hour (for one or two children in the same family), with add-ons for infants under 1 year old, additional children, traveling time (higher after midnight), and foreign languages.

The Baby Sitters' Guild, Inc., 60 E 42nd St, New York, NY 10165, 212/682-0227, -0352.

SHOPPING

Best New Kid from Brooklyn

Century 21

A friend, whose reverence for shopping is exceeded only by that of her mother, treats visits to outlying discount malls as pilgrimages, planned and executed with the religious fervor that must have accompanied the Crusades. When she discovered this larger version of the Brooklyn discount department store, tucked away in the canyons of Wall Street, it was as if she had found the Holy Grail. Three busy floors are packed with designer clothing for men, women, and children, as well as other top-name merchandise at deeply discounted prices. Find Ralph Lauren shoes and LA Gear tennies priced around $30, and an array of casual, informal, and intimate women's apparel bearing such desirable labels as Liz Claiborne, Bill Blass, Adrienne Vittadini, and Victoria's Secret. For men, there are 100 percent silk ties by Christian Dior and Mario Valentino for $9.97, famous makers' shirts from $9.97 to $27.97, and Italian silk suits by Ferre, valued at $1,360, priced at $359-$499. Stylish Wall Street brokers jostle for elbow room at counters loaded with imported sweaters and at racks of leather and suede jackets. There is a large white-goods department; bargain-priced cosmetics, toiletries, and drugs; cassettes and CDs;

dishes and fine crystal; and an entire wall lined with
Seiko clocks. My friend likens the store, opened in
1990, "to finding T.J. Maxx as a department store."
She cautions women to wear body suits to try on
clothing, since there are no dressing rooms.

Century 21, 22 Cortlandt St, New York, NY 10007,
212/227-9092. Mon-Fri 7:45 am-7 pm, Sat 10 am-
6:30 pm. (Also at 472 86 St, Brooklyn, NY 11209,
718/748-3266. Mon-Wed 10 am-7:30 pm, Thu 10
am-9 pm, Fri 10 am-7:30 pm, Sat 10 am-9 pm, Sun
10 am-6 pm.)

Best Store for Those Who *Do* Look at Price Tags

Dollar Bill's

Don't be fooled by the name. This is *not* one of those
"everything-for-a-dollar" stores. Instead, this is a terrific find for bargain shopping for men's and women's
clothing. (Confusion over the name is understandable—this store's Grand Central Terminal location
was once a Rexall drugstore and then *was* a one-
price store...when that pre-inflation price was only
69¢!) Dollar Bill's offers deeply discounted clothing
by such renowned designers as Armani, Ungaro,
Versace, and many others. And these bargains are
definitely not "seconds" or otherwise damaged goods.
Some are last year's styles, while others are over-
stocked merchandise or items seized by U.S. Customs from unauthorized importers. Originally, Dollar
Bill's carried only women's fashions, but now it
stocks men's suits, slacks, overcoats, sports jackets,
coats, shirts, and underwear; these join voluminous
stocks of clothing for women, including dresses,
skirts, suits, sweaters, blouses, accessories, and
underwear. The quantity and quality of items can
vary from week-to-week (or even from day-to-day),
which means that frequent browsing can be the
most rewarding approach. There is a somewhat less
hectic Dollar Bill's further north in Midtown at 880
Third Avenue (212/888-6666).

Dollar Bill's, 99 E 42nd St (in Grand Central
Terminal), New York, NY 10017, 212/867-0212. Mon-
Fri 8 am-7 pm, Sat 10 am-6 pm.

Most Exclusive Shopping "Street" Under One Roof

Henri Bendel

This avant garde department store of high-fashion
women's clothing, shoes, accessories, and cosmetics

began life in 1896 as a tiny hat shop. Now affiliated
with The Limited, it sprawls over three graystones
just around the corner from the elegant Peninsula
Hotel (see separate listing) and draws some of its
upscale clientele from among the moneyed guests
who stay there. Within the store are a series of
salons—more like individual boutiques—that are
outlets for many of the world's eminent couturiers.
The center building has an atrium with a grand
winding staircase accessing a mezzanine full of glitzy
hot designer sweaters. Each of the three buildings
has stunning window displays and awnings in the
store's signature colors of brown-and-white stripes.
This color scheme is perpetuated on the store's distinctive bags that customers carry as a cachet of
exclusivity. This is a spot where shoppers may need
high credit-card limits (even with the reductions
produced by excellent sales), as they rub elbows with
the rich and famous—perhaps Bendel customers
Cher or Streisand—and browse to a background of
contemporary rock music. Many of the store's well-
heeled clients show up in June and October when
it features its renowned custom-created cashmere-
sweater extravaganza.

Henri Bendel, 10 W 57th St, New York, NY 10019,
212/247-1100. Mon-Wed, Fri & Sat 10 am-6 pm, Thu
10 am-8 pm, Sun noon-5 pm.

Best Suburban Mall in the Heart of Manhattan

A & S Plaza

With nine levels and around 60 stores, this atrium-
style mall, gleaming with high-tech glass and
chrome, would seem more in place in the burbs than
in the heart of Manhattan. Suburban-mall shoppers
will recognize such familiar names as Compagnie
Internationale Express, Chess King, Ann Taylor, Sam
Goody, County Seat, The Body Shop, This End Up,
and Lady Foot Locker. Specialty shops offer hand-
knit sweaters, suede and leather clothing, batteries
and small electronics, cartoon-character clothing,
watches, and accessories, sunglasses, hand-tooled
leather goods from Greece, Indian pottery, jewelry,
and rugs, Irish imports, luggage, and New York
souvenirs. Anchoring it all is the multi-level A & S
Department Store, sleek with lots of glass and mirrors, tall ficus trees, and American flags. Serving the
soaring atrium are glass elevators studded with
Hollywood-style lights. Entertainment is scheduled
regularly on two stages. A food court on level seven
has a branch of Sbarro and Häagen-Daz, plus

counters with deli food, burgers, salads, steak sandwiches and fries, Chinese food, and Middle Eastern
specialties.

A & S Plaza, Sixth Ave & 33rd St, New York, NY
10001, 212/465-0500. Mon, Thu, Fri 9:45 am-8:30 pm;
Tue-Wed 9:45 am-6:45 pm; Sat 10 am-6:45 pm; Sun
11 am-6 pm.

Best Street of Bargains...and Dross
Orchard Street

Fortify yourself with a deli breakfast or lunch at
Katz's (see separate listing) and head for this bargain
mecca on the Lower East Side. The seedy stretch of
Orchard Street from Houston (just steps away from
the famous deli) to Rivington once was jammed with
the pushcarts of Jewish immigrants. Today, the carts
are gone and the shops, festooned inside and out
with cut-rate designer clothing, handbags, shoes,
and other goods, seem to be owned increasing by
Asians and other new-wave immigrants. Kordol
Fabrics has its walls lined with bolts of cloth—wor-
sted and flannel suiting, linen, and imported crepe
and tissue faille. Rita's Leather Fair is a small boutique with unisex jackets where you might get a good
price on a black or white leather bolero jacket and
skirt. Fleischer's men's shop has Adolfo and
Courrèges shirts from France and suits for $150-
$300 (with a tailor around the corner ready to make
them fit). Vogue has luggage, soft leather handbags,
and glitzy jewel-studded purses, with labels from
Ann Klein and Coach. Veetal has furs, sequinned
dresses, and a back room full of women's sportswear. As you work your way up a street crammed
with merchandise ranging from pure junk to high
quality, you'll find shop owners vocal and insistent
as they entice customers in off the street. On Sundays, this teeming street is New York's version of
London's Petticoat Lane.

Orchard Street, New York, NY 10002.

Best Budget Shopping (Ain't It a Bitch?)
Syms

How basic can you get? Outside, this store is painted
white. Inside, the decor is mostly black. Service is
no-frills. Prices are bare bones. With its prominent
motto, "An educated consumer is our best customer,"
the store highlights off-season buys with duplicate
pricing. Raincoats, for example, might show a September price of $199 and a July price of $165.

Labeling also compares Sym's discounted merchandise—up to 50 percent—with nationally advertised prices. Women not overly concerned about wearing last season's fashions are happy enough to snap up dated—but deeply discounted—designer clothing. Men head to the second floor to browse acres of shirts—Bill Blass, Gant, Hathaway, John Weitz, Christian Dior, and Liberty of London, with silk shirts selling for $24.95 instead of the $45.00 nationally advertised asking price. The range of merchandise includes clothing and shoes for men, women, and children (outsizes, too), plus linens and accessories. A third floor is stocked with luggage and briefcases, while the basement offers discount prices on suits, tuxedos, and overcoats. Unlike some cut-price stores, Syms mostly leaves intact the well-known labels on its merchandise—although, sometimes, there are super bargains, such as cotton polo shirts with the label cut off selling for $5.00.

Syms, 42 Trinity Pl, New York, NY, 212/797-1199. Mon-Wed 8 am-6:30 pm, Thu & Fri 8 am-8 pm, Sat 10 am-6:30 pm.

Best Store for Those Who *Don't* Need to Look at Price Tags

Gucci

What started as Guccio Gucci's saddle shop in Florence, Italy, has blossomed into the world-famous Gucci chain, offering the finest in leather goods, clothing, shoes, and accessories. There are two side-by-side outposts of that fashionable retailing empire on Fifth Avenue. The leathers (luggage, wallets, purses, and cases for keys, glasses, and checkbooks, etc.) that sprung from Italian saddle making are still prominently displayed, but shoppers at these exclusive and pricey shops are as likely to be looking for fashionable clothes as they are for rich leather goods. The featured clothing ranges from suits and dresses to more informal (yet still crisply stylish) weekend wear, such as sweaters, slacks, skirts, and suede and leather jackets. Head-to-toe Gucci fans can top off their wardrobes with hats and/or scarves and a selection of fine dressy and casual shoes. All of these goods—not to mention their browsers and buyers—are fussed over by an attentive and informed staff. Detractors deride the conspicuous consumers who insist on clothing and accessories bearing the intertwined Gucci "G"s, but die-hard customers swear by the style and quality of the chain's goods. There probably is little argument that the cost of this stylish consumption is high—be sure to be packing plenty of cash (or plastic) when shopping at Gucci.

Gucci, 683-685 Fifth Avenue, New York, NY 10022, 212/826-2600. Mon-Wed, Fri & Sat 9:30 am-6 pm; Thu 9:30 am-7 pm.

Leggiest Leather Look
North Beach Leather

It's name screams "California" and, sure enough, this high-fashion store does have a West Coast counterpart—and a visiting West Coast clientele. Entertainment celebrities shop here for minuscule minis, stylish leather jackets and coats, swaggery bolero jackets, and soft, supple leather pants designed to fit like an extra skin. In addition to soft leather clothing and accessories, this sleek East Side boutique carries a selection of suedes in high styles and hot colors. It carries men's and women's clothing in trendy and contemporary styles, including jeans, blazers, shirts, skirts, and blouses in neutral shades of brown, basic black, and a rainbow of bold colors. Some items are beaded, bejeweled, and otherwise studded with glittery ornamentation. This high-style designer clothing carries expectedly hefty—but not necessarily out of sight—price tags.

North Beach Leather, 772 Madison Ave, New York, NY 10021, 212/772-0707. Mon-Fri 10 am-7 pm, Sat 10 am-6 pm, Sun 1-6 pm.

Best Bet for Button Gluttons
Tender Buttons

For anyone who enjoys sewing, or knows anyone who likes to sew, this is a great shop to stock up on unusual buttons or to find an uncommon gift. A stock of thousands of buttons includes buttons made of brass, cloth, shell, ivory, steel, mother of pearl, rhinestone, wood, glass, papier-mâché, china, silver, plastic, and horn. Some are intricately embroidered; others are hand-painted. They come in an awesome range of shapes—square, round, triangular, and so on, along with buttons shaped like animals, flowers, birds, cartoon characters, and sports paraphernalia. There is a large selection of military buttons as well as an interesting selection of antique buttons and sets of buttons to spiff up an old outfit or replace an incomplete set on a blazer. Also in stock are unique cuff links, studs, stick pins, and antique buckles. Prices range from less than one dollar to several hundred dollars for rare collector's items. This bright, museum-like store is where you might find prized 18th-century Wedgwood buttons, an art deco buckle, or, perhaps, a pair of gold cuff links with a golf theme.

Tender Buttons, 143 E 62nd St, New York, NY 10021, 212/758-7004. Mon-Fri 11 am-6 pm, Sat 11 am-5 pm.

Best Bet for Non-Traditional Women's Fashions

Gallery of Wearable Art

Non-traditional is definitely the operative word. While outfits from this store aren't typically as outrageous as, for example, those that Madonna wears, neither are they anything that a woman would want to wear to a corporate meeting or even to a day at the office. Instead, shoppers will find brightly and shockingly painted clothing (the expected denim, but also more formal gowns, jackets, blouses, and skirts), hand-made amalgams of under- and outerwear (maybe Madonna *does* shop here), and dozens of interesting or just plain puzzling accessories, jewelry, and head-gear. It has been said that the clothing here makes a statement, although the exact wording of that statement may remain unclear. An unexpected part of this store's stock is the fascinating array of ar-tistically created and decorated wedding dresses, perhaps providing the answer to the question "What does an East Village *artiste* wear to her wedding?" Currently entrenched on the East Side, this is a curious bit of SoHo (where it was formerly located) that has wandered uptown. A few blocks away is another spot for "wearable art" as women's clothing, Julie: Artisan's Gallery (687 Madison Avenue, 212/688-2345).

Gallery of Wearable Art, 43 E 63rd St, New York, NY 10021, 212/GALLERY. Mon-Fri 10:30 am-6 pm, Sat 11 am-5 pm.

Best Shop to Spin a Yarn

The Yarn Company

Look for a painted redbrick building with fire es-capes in front, across the street, and just a little north of Zabar's fantastic food emporium (see sepa-rate listing). On street level is the Marvin Gardens restaurant with its small sidewalk café. Upstairs is a wonderful repository of more than 300 yarns in a rainbow of colors. Made from all-natural fibers, selections include silk, mohair, chenille, and, of course, wool (including alpaca lamb's wool). The shop carries yarns from such well-known suppliers as Rowan, Missoni, Anny Blatz, and English-based Kaffe Fassett. If you don't know how to knit but would like to, you'll not only find all the supplies you'll need, but also expert instruction at classes that are held 7-10 p.m. after the store is closed. Ditto for needlepoint. This is a good shopping spot for one-of-a-kind sweaters, especially at end-of-the-season sample sales held in January and June. Specialties include creating custom-made sweaters and installing silk linings in knitted sweaters, in coats, and in jackets.

The Yarn Company, 2274 Broadway, New York, NY 10024, 212/787-7878. Tue-Sat 11 am-6 pm, Sun noon-5 pm.

Best Waist-High Views of Shoes
Shoofly

This is a shop for tiny feet and fat wallets. All of the children's shoes sold here are imported—from Italy, France, Spain, England—and are priced from $30 up to $140. The selection ranges from classic patent leather to thick crepe-sole creepers in gaudy colors. With furnishings that look as if they might have come from the enchanted forest, animal footprints on the floor, and a tiny handle on the door at kid-height, this is a spot where children probably won't get bored with shopping. Accessories include rows of tiny socks on clothes pegs; suspenders that feature polka dots, vegetables, and cartoon characters; miniature bow ties; and some tote bags. Owner Roz Viemeister also has assembled an intriguing stock of children's hats, including a plaid deerstalker, floppy hats bedecked with daisies and ribbons, straw hats, cloth caps, a felt bowler, and a whimsical Elmer Fudd number. A side room carries a selection of larger sizes, teens through adults.

Shoofly, 506 Amsterdam Ave, New York, NY 10024, 212/580-0045. Mon-Sat 11 am-7 pm, Sun noon-6 pm.

Best Upscale Children's Clothing
Cerutti

When well-heeled Manhattan mothers want to outfit their little girls in velvet-and-lace party dresses or their little boys in their very own navy blue blazers, the chances are good that they visit this East Side children's store. Cerutti is well known, well admired, and well shopped for its useful range of classic kids' styles from America and Europe, including a good mix of casual and formal outfits. There are always plenty of frilly party dresses and little suit-and-tie ensembles—but there are also scaled-down leather bomber jackets, sequinned jeans jackets, hand-knit sweaters from Italy and Ireland, and a variety of other baby clothes and growing kids' jeans, jumpers, sweatpants and sweatshirts, pajamas, and other clothes. And, for those special-occasion or one-of-a-kind outfits, Cerutti offers a custom-order clothes service (not cheap, but many consider the results worth the cost). Prices vary and are generally on the high side—although there are occasional relative bargains to be found in all age groups. Sizes available run from newborns to size 14 for girls and to size 16 for boys.

Cerutti, 807 Madison Ave, New York, NY 10021, 212/737-7540. Mon-Sat 9 am-5:30 pm.

Best Bet for Babying Baby

Au Chat Botté

When cost is no object to outfitting a baby (or a child), this classy Madison Avenue boutique is the place to shop. Much of its specially made children's wear is imported from (or made of materials from) France, Italy, and England. Some are frilly, others are just cute—all are on the pricey side. The stock includes lacy christening outfits, silky party dresses, crisp little sailor suits, and many outfits reminiscent of those seen in Victorian baby pictures. Not everything available here is special-occasion clothing, but even everyday clothing—sweaters, overalls, sleep-wear—is of high quality and is generally stylish (although, quite frankly, not really suited for a rough-and-tumble day in the park or trip to the sandbox). Sizes run from newborns for both sexes up to boys' size 6 and girls' size 12; an entire special room of gorgeous tiny outfits is devoted to clothes for newborns. Au Chat Botté also offers a line of fine children's furnishings, including bassinets, cribs, dressers, changing tables, and beds.

Au Chat Botté, 903 Madison Ave, New York, NY 10021, 212/772-7402. Mon-Sat 10 am-6 pm.

Next Best Thing to Harrod's Food Hall

Zabar's

Harrod's it ain't! But this West Side food emporium gives the famous London food hall a run for its money. Despite its marvelous array of international foodstuffs, Zabar's retains an essential New York earthiness. Behind five adjoining storefronts, this sprawling store, with worn tile floors and ceilings festooned with colanders, pots, and Zabar mugs, has departments for major food categories. Displaying huge wheels of cheese, a well-stocked cheese department (Zabar's began as a neighborhood cheese shop) offers such specialties as Amish raw-milk cheddar and Spanish manchego. Showcases tempt with tenderloin of pork in phyllo pastry, Belgium mushroom pâté, veal roulade, turkey sausage, black-pepper salami, and a variety of pasta salads such as tortellini with sundried tomatoes. Containers of soup include lobster bisque and cream of asparagus. To a background of classical music, shoppers ponder an array of smoked fish and caviar, shelves packed with jars of hazelnut butter and pistachio butter, colorful containers of olive oil, and imported chocolates, mustards, chutneys, and vinegars, racks of tea, and barrels of coffee. Nine different bakeries provide such specialty breads as raisin five-grain, European dark rye, and sourdough cheddar cheese rolls, and a mélange of baguettes, bialys, and so on. There are bargains, too. One day I noted gouda going for $2.49 a pound and a 20-piece fine china dinner set reduced from $50.00 to $17.98. The mezzanine is crammed with housewares and gadgets.

Zabar's, 2245 Broadway, New York, NY 10024, 212/787-2000. Mon-Fri 8 am-7:30 pm, Sat 8 am-midnight, Sun 9 am-6 pm.

Next Best Thing to Fortnum & Mason

Balducci's

If Zabar's is reminiscent of Harrod's, there certainly are shades of Fortnum & Mason about this family owned Village grocery. It operates with style and offers the same kind of quality, variety, color, and sheer overwhelming volume of wonderful foodstuffs. Below green awnings, windows stretching half a block foretell of the goodies that await—stacks of fresh fish and crustaceans, piles of earthy loaves, tempting pastries and candies, slabs of prime aged beef, and thick wheels of aged cheese. Inside are cases full of prepared foods—stuffed veal, duck leg in porchetta, and chicken rollatini—and counters hanging with whole hams and brimming with marvelous pâté and tempting sausages, such as chicken and apple, duck, and andouille. Staff, immaculate in white coats and hats and bow ties, will help you select from Balducci's house-label packages of tortillas and pasta—perhaps a wild-mushroom or ricotta-spinach ravioli. A vast meat department offers thick prime loin of lamb chops, slabs of ribs, and boneless center cut loin of pork, while a colorful array of produce includes zucchini flowers, radicchio, and peppers of every hue. There are sacks and gleaming brass-and-glass containers of coffee, and a fish market with arctic char, New Zealand cockles, turbot, marlin steaks, fresh Portuguese sardines, and sweet-water prawns—all in ice-packed cases above tanks filled with live lobsters and crabs. If you can't find it here, you maybe won't find it in New York.

Balducci's, 424 Sixth Ave, New York, NY 10011, 212/ 673-2600. Daily 7 am-8:30 pm.

Most Ravishing Ravioli
Raffetto's Corporation

Cooks who use their noodles head for this Greenwich Village pasta-maker, which has been around since 1906. This fourth-generation storefront family business (which has a large production area in back) produces an incredible variety of egg and spinach noodles—fresh pasta that includes gnocchi, manicotti, fettucine, vermicelli, and wonderfully light chicken-filled tortellini. Ravioli fanciers head here for those wonderful little pasta pockets. Multicolored round- or square-shaped raviolis are filled with various combinations of meat, seafood, cheese, spinach, vegetables, fresh and porcini mushrooms, pesto, and even (in season) pumpkin. Fresh pasta noodles in various widths are flavored with saffron, mushrooms, black-squid ink, parsley-basil, tomato, and special custom-created flavors. Those for whom rissotto is a specialty, shop here for arborio rice. Celebrity customers include Bernadette Peters, Isabella Rosellini, and Willem Dafoe. In fact, so good is this pasta that many of New York's favorite gourmet shops rely on it, as do restaurants such as the romantic and popular Lincoln Center area Café des Artistes and the hip Village diner, Aggie's.

Raffetto's Corporation, 144 W Houston St, New York, NY 10012, 212/777-1261. Tue-Sat 8 am-6 pm.

Prime Pick for Paprika (and Other Spices)
Paprikas Weiss Importer

More than a century ago, a Hungarian immigrant began selling imported paprika. Today, this family-run business still offers paprika—in three styles: hot, half-sweet, and sweet—as well as a wide range of imported herbs, spices, and other foodstuffs and a good selection of cookware, cookbooks, and gift items. This revamped shop in the old Yorkville European neighborhood is the spot to shop for Spanish saffron; snowy-white aged Czechoslovakian and Austrian monastery cheeses; Hungarian hunter, winter, and peppercorn-flavored sausage; Trappist cheese; double-smoked bacon; and satiny, mild and sweet salami. There is ham from Hungary and Westphalia; imported Hungarian goulash paste and paprika paste; and a world of peppers—16 different kinds. Also imported from Hungary are a wide range of preserves—including apricot, black currant, red currant, peach, plum, and raspberry, and such condiments as pickled cucumbers, red pepper salad, and yellow peppers stuffed with white cabbage. For the sweet tooth, there are Croatian coffee- and hazelnut-flavored wafers and biscuits, cordial-filled chocolates and candies, chocolate-covered orange peel, and Swiss truffles. There is a wide variety of European baking supplies and kitchen gadgetry that includes all manner of graters, grinders, sausage-makers, and pasta machines.

Paprikas Weiss Importer, 1572 Second Ave, New York, NY 10028, 212/288-6117. Mon-Sat 9 am-6 pm.

Prime Pick for Peking Duck

Kam Man Foods

With long hours and a huge inventory, this vast Chinatown supermarket is the place to stock up on herbs, teas, condiments and spices, dried seafood, and a wide range of Oriental delicacies. Kam Man, which is noted for its crisp, roasted duck and delectable barbecued pork and chicken, also creates delicious meat-and-vegetable-filled pancakes called *joong*. As one of New York's largest and most authentic Chinese markets, Kam Man carries fresh meat, vegetables, and other perishables, along with noodles, mushrooms, ginseng and other roots, and all manner of wondrous Chinese remedies, as well as kitchenware, housewares, and even some furniture. On an expedition into Chinatown, which is home to about 150,000 of New York's huge Chinese population, this exotic market is the place to absorb local color and also is an excellent spot for gift shopping, with a good selection of jade, ivory, and imported dishes and cooking utensils.

Kam Man Foods, 200 Canal St, New York, NY 10013, 212/571-0330. Daily 9 am-9 pm.

Best Baker's Dozen of Bagels

H & H Bagels

This bustling, battered shop is known for product rather than ambience. Yellow-painted walls are adorned with framed Norman Rockwell prints (including the famous "Homecoming" from May 26, 1945), while three brass chandeliers strike an incongruous note in this time-worn establishment. Refrigerator cabinets are packed with kosher and non-kosher products, including lox, smoked sable, and containers of spread, including cream cheese flavored with vegetables, scallions, and lox, salads of tuna, shrimp, and salmon, and chopped herring. They also stock juices and premium ice creams. But bagels are this bakery's bread and butter! They can be bought by the baker's dozen (13 for the price of 12) and varieties include plain, sourdough, salt, wholewheat, raisin-cinnamon (one of the most popular), pumpernickel, oat bran, garlic, sesame, poppyseed, and onion. H & H makes up to 70,000 bagels a day and ships them across the country and to such foreign destinations as Holland, Japan, and France (where specialty mini-bagels are popular). They also make bialys. With a minimum order of two dozen, they will ship bagels anywhere in the country.

H & H Bagels, 2239 Broadway, New York, NY 10024, 212/595-8000, 800/NYBAGEL. Daily 24 hours.

Best Bread in Little Italy

D & G Bakery

Don't hurry too quickly along Spring Street, or you might miss this narrow-fronted bakery. Look for an old-fashioned door with a huge window and brass handle and latchplate, and you'll have found what arguably is the best Neapolitan bakery in Little Italy. Arrive early enough, and the shelves behind its old wooden counter still may be crammed with fresh-baked loaves and it may not yet have run out of prosciutto bread, thick and chewy and studded with slivers of meat, one of the bakery's most popular items. Other specialty loaves incorporate ham, salami, provolone cheese, and olive oil. Dense whole wheat round loaves, coarse-grained and properly moist, also are well worth an early visit. Bread is baked daily by hand in the basement of a tenement around the corner, in a coal-fired brick oven that has been in continuous use for more than 100 years. Its traditional recipe was handed down by master-baker Guido Pradella, who founded the bakery nearly three decades ago. It involves kneading dough by hand and waiting patiently through several risings.

D & G Bakery, 45 Spring St, New York, NY 10012, 212/226-6688. Daily 8 am-2 pm.

Best Bet for French Bread

JP's French Bakery

Behind the counter are racks of golden-crusted, white-dusted loaves that cry out to have a hunk twisted off them. You'll find buttery croissants and brioche, crusty baguettes, and loaves of every conceivable shape, all baked on the premises every morning. Besides the scrumptious breads, there are fresh-baked Danish—raisin, prune, apricot, blueberry cream cheese, and pecan-honey-cin- namon—plus apple and raspberry turnovers and apple-cinnamon twists. This busy storefront offers a showcase filled with rich cakes (sponge cake with a trio of different chocolates is a best seller), another packed with tarts and pastries (try bread pudding with peaches or mocha almond meringue), and a third brimming with salads such as niçoise, chicken curry, and roasted chicken fettucine. There is limited seating at three tiny tables and at counter stools. Steaming black caldrons of soup might include potato leek, tomato basil, and French onion with cheese. There's an extensive sandwich menu, plus sandwiches made to order. With fresh-looking white- tile walls and an array of tempting food, this is a good spot for soup, salad, and sandwich—and bread, cake, and pastries to go.

JP's French Bakery, 54 W 55th St, New York, NY 10019, 212/765-7575. Mon-Fri 7 am-7:30 pm, Sat 8 am-6 pm, Sun 9 am-5 pm.

Best Bet for Fresh Produce

Union Square Greenmarket

Farmers' markets not only bring a variety of fresh produce direct from grower to consumer, but also provide good therapy. When browsing vendor-to- vendor, stopping to buy and chat, it is easy to forget big-city pressures. This is where New Yorkers shop for organically grown vegetables—examining glisten- ing greens and hydrophonic tomatoes, pinching plums for ripeness, and searching out hard-to-find ingredients. Scattered across the boroughs, 18 city- sponsored greenmarkets operate on varying days, some seasonally, others year-round. Perhaps the largest and most popular is the Greenmarket at Union Square. This was a grim slum frequented by drug dealers until massive revitalization brought flowers, concerts, fancy restaurants, and expensive apartments. On market days, farmers from the surrounding countryside truck in fresh produce, ranging from massive leeks to delicate shallots. The variety includes herbs, garlic, berries, nectarines, peaches, honey, mushrooms, grape juice, maple syrup, corn, house plants, and flowers. In addition, there are eggs, poultry, cheeses, fresh and smoked game, pond-raised fish, homemade sausage, and baked goods. A greenmarket is the perfect spot to provision a picnic.

Union Square Greenmarket, E 17th St and Broadway, New York, NY 10003, 212/566-0990. Year-round, Wed, Fri, Sat.

Best from Scoop to Nuts
Economy Candy

This penny candy store has been around for more than 50 years and has sort of turned gourmet— without losing sight of its original mandate of low-priced confectionery. From bulk bins you can scoop up jelly beans, candy corn, and gum and spice drops—or pistachios, cashews, and raisin nut mix. But you'll also find gourmet coffees ground to order, a wide selection of teas, and imported chocolates. The selection of dried fruits is extensive—apples, apricots, dates, figs, nectarines, peaches, pears, and a variety of mixed fruit. Try tart dried cranberries, one of the newer items. There is an equally large selection of nuts, plus crunches, mixes, and snacks (hot Cajun mix and green peak snacks are popular items), as well as dietetic candies and low-calorie confection, such as three-calorie mint candies. The eclectic stock includes Irish whiskey cake; jalapeño caviar; mustard, oils and vinegars from Spain, France, and Italy; Lindt chocolate bars; and Dröste and Ghirardelli cocoa. A wide range of imported preserves includes Tiptree from England (James Bond's favorite breakfast jam) and Chamborg from France. There are various kinds of exotic honey and a whole range of fillings and fruits for baking.

Economy Candy, 108 Rivington St, New York, NY 10002, 212/254-1832, 800/352-4544. Sun-Fri 8 am-5:30 pm, Sat 10 am-5 pm.

Savviest Sausage Shopping
Faicco's Pork Store

When you're looking for authentic Neapolitan sausages, head for this butcher shop in the heart of

Greenwich Village, where Italian pork sausage is a specialty. You'll find display cabinets filled with sausage wheels, homemade dry sausage (hot or sweet), plus spicy pepperoni and Messina Sicilian salami. Sopressata sausage also is available in hot and sweet versions. With white-tiled walls and white-painted ceiling, this meat market is festively decorated with red, white, and blue streamers. Shop here, too, for pork cutlets, chops, roasts, back ribs and country-style ribs, liver, and prime boneless tenderloin. Complementing the Italian sausage are a variety of cold cuts and Italian cheeses that include extra sharp and semi-sharp provolone and smoked mozzarella that is made daily. Bakery products include a fine rendition of prosciutto bread. Shelves are stacked with colorful cans of olive oil. The store has another branch in Brooklyn (6511 11th Ave; 718/236-0119).

Faicco's Pork Store, 260 Bleecker St, New York, NY, 212/243-1974. Tue-Sat 8 am-6 pm, Sun 9 am-2 pm.

Best Shop to Say Cheese

Cheese of All Nations

For me, a highly subjective test of a cheese shop is to ask if it carries oka. Made in a Quebec monastery, it is a cheese I came to enjoy in Canada. This shop has it—not surprisingly, since it lists more than 1,000 varieties of cheese. These range from Albanian valsic, a sharp, crumbly cow's milk cheese, to Sir Posny, a delicate, firm cheese made from sheep's milk in mountainous Montenegro (formerly part of Yugoslavia). The shop, on a somewhat seedy street, isn't very fancy, with a refrigerated case of goat's cheese; wheels of Cheshire, Italian, and Dutch cheeses; half-wheels of Italian asiago sharp cheese; and common varieties such as Danish tilsit and havarti, plus almost 50 cheese spreads made on the premises and shelves packed with crackers and Swedish crispbread. It is its catalog that holds the fascination, filled with such exotica as tourag, made by the Berber tribes of Africa; eishel, a low-fat creamy cheese from Israel; and mellow, nutty manchego from Spain. In addition to the retail shop, there is a cheese-fanciers' organization, a cheese-of-the-month club, and various related enterprises.

Cheese of All Nations, 153 Chambers St, New York, NY 10007, 212/732-0752. Mon-Fri 8 am-5:30 pm, Sat 8 am-5 pm.

Best Shop That Has It Down to a Tea
McNulty's Tea & Coffee Co., Inc.

Walking into this store is an olfactory experience. Visitors are assailed with the rich aroma of coffee and tea garnered from around the world, from Jamaica to Java, from Costa Rica to China. This is a fascinating place to browse. Wooden shelves are lined with colorful boxes and cans; sacks of coffee and chests of tea with obscure markings from around the world are visible everywhere. The bins, chests, and scales—such as a vintage red-and-brass weigh scale on the counter—date back to the last century. Established in 1895, this merchant is a virtuoso of teas, ranging from the traditional black, green, and Oolong teas, to flavored, herbal, and blended teas. Its stock includes black teas from India, Sri Lanka, China, and Russia, Oolong teas from China and Taiwan, and green teas from China and Japan. It also offers its own blends, teas from such famous purveyors as Fortnum & Mason, Jacksons of Piccadilly, and McGrath's of Ireland, and 32 flavored teas, from apple pie to wild cherry. There's also a range of decaffeinated and herbal teas. Topping the price list of rare teas is Golden Darjeeling from India at $24 a pound. Prized coffees include famous Jamaican Blue Mountain at $18 a pound (although Jamaican High Mountain, a full-bodied aromatic coffee can be purchased for about half that price). A score of flavored coffees include chocolate-raspberry, orange, and pecan. While you're visiting, pick up a brochure with tips on brewing the perfect cup of coffee.

McNulty's Tea & Coffee Co., Inc., 109 Christopher St, New York, NY 10014, 212/242-5351, 800/356-5200. Mon-Sat 11 am-11 pm, Sun 1-7:30 pm.

Best Vintage Spot for Vintage Wines
Acker Merrall & Condit

The fine vintage wines at this West Side shop aren't the only things that are well aged. This store traces its heritage to a wine merchant established in Manhattan in 1820. Spacious, but not huge, and often crowded, but never noisy, AM & C is the spot many oenophiles head to browse and buy their favorite potables. It offers a good assortment of American wines (with an especially heavy concentration of California product), and also features good German, French, and Italian selections (the wines are grouped by region). AM & C is well known for its wide selection of fine burgundies, which is among the best in the city. The store's extremely helpful staffers really know their regions, vintages, and vintners, and are willing to take time with non-expert customers. This store is open later than most Manhattan liquor stores—until 11:30 p.m.—making this a good spot for last-minute gifts or for provisioning late-night gatherings. (Another AM & C strong point is the number of half-bottles available of a variety of wines—far more than can be found in other stores in the city.) Other top spots in Manhattan for wines include Morrell & Company (535 Madison Avenue, 212/688-9370), run by wine expert Peter Morrell; Sokolin (178 Madison Avenue; 212/532-5893), which attracts discerning shoppers; and Sherry-Lehmann (679 Madison Avenue; 212/838-7500), well stocked and classy—but with service that can be a bit snooty.

Acker Merrall & Condit, 160 W 72nd St, New York, NY 10023, 212/787-1700. Mon-Sat 11 am-11:30 pm.

Biggest Bottle Business in the Big Apple
Astor Wine & Spirits

Imbibers or gift-givers looking for anything from an aged single-malt Scotch to a Chardonnay to serve with dinner head to this lively, sprawling Greenwich Village/East Village liquor store extraordinaire. (In fact, this spirit supermarket claims to be the largest liquor store in the entire state.) The dozens of brands of spirits, wine, and assorted sundries can be truly intoxicating—for example, nearly two dozen brands of vodka (including Russian, Polish, and Finnish varieties). It is this depth of selections—plus competitive-to-cut-rate prices—that have built Astor's solid reputation. Less discerning types rely on Astor's house-brand liquors and wines, which, while not top-shelf, are fairly well regarded for their price range. The one complaint about Astor is hit-or-miss levels of service—sometimes helpful, other times less so (perhaps to be expected in a store that is so large and has such a diverse inventory). Another good spot for spirits is Garnet Liquors (929 Lexington Avenue; 212/772-3211), known for its large selection and good prices—watch for its occasional sales to save even more. (*Note:* Because of New York's liquor laws, beer drinkers have to be satisfied with the selection available at supermarkets or other approved retailers; liquor stores carry only wine and spirits.)

Astor Wine & Spirits, 12 Astor Pl, New York, NY 10003, 212/674-7500. Mon-Sat 9 am-9 pm.

Best Tobacconist No One Can Hold a Match To

Nat Sherman

Cigars, naturally cured and meticulously rolled in the Cuban-Spanish tradition, are handsomely packaged in cedar and in individual humidor jars. Party cigarettes, 6-1/2" long, come in assorted colors, from red and green to lilac and orange. A French-made briar pipe trimmed with diamonds and gold is priced at $3,000. An antique-coin pocket cigar cutter sells for $350. For $5,000 you can order a Swiss mahogany humidor with a built-in humidity system. Find these items at a tobacconist, established in 1930, which numbers among its clients such celebrities as Milton Berle, Sylvester Stallone, George Segal, Alan King, and David Letterman. Customers' cigars, imported from the Canaries, Honduras, and Jamaica, are held until needed in a huge cedar-lined vaulted cold humidor, where they mature while they wait for their owners to claim them. Custom-made cigarettes are chemical-free and contain only pure tobacco. Smoking accessories and other gifts include smoke-trapper ashtrays, lizard-skin cigar cases, gold-plated cigar cutters, lighters, fountain pens, shaving brushes and stands, and ornaments such as a crystal tennis ball.

Nat Sherman, 500 Fifth Ave, New York, NY 10110, 212/246-5500. Mon-Sat 10 am-5 pm.

Top Spot for Pet Pipes

Pipeworks & Wilke

Petting a Wilke pipe—polishing it with the hand while smoking it—improves its appearance. So counsels this shop that has been making pipes of seasoned, unpainted briar root since 1872. "The open pores allow the moisture to come to the surface," it tells customers, "and when spread and rubbed will cause a beautiful permanent luster." This advice has been directed to Eddie Fisher, Bing Crosby, Basil Rathbone, and other notables, many of whom have signed photographs on display. Originally, two sisters—the "Wilke girls"—ran the shop. Today, most pipes are made by owner Elliott Nachwalter, with prices ranging from $55 to $1,000—(for a straight-grain, handmade Grecian briar). On display is the owner's collection of old tobacco tins, plus a changing assortment of vintage pipes, some as much as 200 years old, mostly gathered at estate sales and all of which are for sale. Wilke blends tobaccos and offers an array of accessories—lighters, pouches, knives, walnut pipe stands, rests, ashtrays, and humidors. Because no paint, stain, varnish, or chemicals are used on these pipes, they need no breaking in. "Breaking in," Wilke points out haughtily, "is only another way of saying 'burning off the paint.'"

Pipeworks & Wilke, 16 W 55th St, New York, NY 10019, 212/956-4820. Mon-Fri 10 am-6 pm, Sat 10 am-5 pm.

Best Place to Go Back in Time
Time Will Tell

For people who would rather sport a classic wristwatch or a pocket railroad timepiece than a flashing, beeping digital watch, this cozy and friendly shop is an idea whose time has come (or, indeed, whose time never. passed). More than 1,000 watches are on display, attracting both serious collectors looking to add a rare piece to their collections and fashionable sorts looking for a unique accessory with a touch of history. The variety ranges from 19th-century pocket watches through the earliest modern wristwatches from around the turn of the century through the sleek, art deco-ish timepieces of the periods just before and after World War II; unabashed nostalgics may even find an early Mickey Mouse or Lone Ranger model in stock. Brands include the expected top names in watches (such as Patek Philippe, Rolex, Cartier, and Bulova) as well as special handmade pieces by long-forgotten artisans. Time Will Tell also has a selection of lizard, alligator, leather, and other types of watchbands, and deftly handles repairs on all types of vintage and contemporary watches. Another good spot for antique watches—as well as full-size clocks of all types—is Fanelli Antique Timepieces (1131 Madison Avenue; 212/517-2300).

Time Will Tell, 962 Madison Ave, New York, NY 10021, 212/861-2663. Mon-Sat 10 am-6 pm.

Top Togs for British Secret Agents
Alfred Dunhill of London

If James Bond lived in New York, he undoubtedly would shop here. The fastidious 007's lighter of choice was a Dunhill, and he also had a predilection for shirts fashioned from silk-like Sea Island cotton. This New York outpost of the famous London tobacconist and haberdasher carries both. For those who admire (and can afford) that very British Savile Row look, it also does fine custom tailoring of suits, blazers, and shirts, and carries a range of high-priced, conservative ready-made clothing. A top-quality selection of leather goods includes hand-tooled luggage, bench-made shoes, belts, and wallets. Bond also would find here militarily striped silk ties, gold cuff links, money clips, and an array of other luxurious accessories, including watches, jewelry, writing equipment, and toiletries. For smokers, the shop carries a wide range of pipes, pouches, stands, tools, and related accoutrements, as well as cigars, humidors, and the coveted Dunhill lighters. It also custom blends tobaccos.

Alfred Dunhill of London, 450 Park Ave, New York, NY 10022, 212/753-9292. Mon-Wed Fri & Sat 9:30 am-6 pm, Thu 9:30 am-8 pm.

Best Bet for Brollies and City Slickers

Uncle Sam

When it rains in Manhattan, taxicabs are difficult to find. Umbrellas are much easier. With the onset of raindrops, vendors selling cheap umbrellas appear on street corners as suddenly and plentifully as mushrooms after a storm. Trouble is, the brolly that you buy on the quick and on the cheap may not outlast the shower. Better head for this Midtown shop that has been selling and repairing umbrellas since 1866. It stocks close to 50,000 umbrellas and parasols and about 1,000 canes. The selection is bewildering, with canes and umbrellas of every size, shape, and color hooked onto retaining bars. The stock includes giant beach and garden umbrellas. The window display is eye catching and owner Sandra Schwartz will tell you that the store has been at the present location for more than 25 years, originally part of a mini-chain of four shops. The surviving shop also sells slickers and has a back-of-the-store repair room where umbrellas are recovered and repaired.

Uncle Sam, 161 W 57th St, New York, NY 10019, 212/582-1977. Mon-Fri 9:30 am-6 pm, Sat 10 am-5 pm.

Best Shop That Makes Scents

Aphrodisia

Look for the porcelain cat—and sometimes a live cat—in the window...then follow your nose. It's apparent what this shop is all about as soon as you enter and are greeted by the tantalizing fragrances of herbs, spices, flowers, and oils. With more than 1,000 jars of herbs and spices and nuts and dried fruit, plus herbal cosmetics, an herbal apothecary, a large culinary department, and a bodycare shop, this store offers fascinating browsing (and a fat mail-order catalog). The cook will find seasonings ranging from agar-agar to zebrovka, including such exotica as galangal, as well as the familiar rosemary, parsley, and sage, and a variety of salsa and Tex-Mex blends. For the pastry chef are Tahitian vanilla beans and bourbon vanilla extract. Filling the fragrance shop is the heady perfume of gardenia and jasmine and the warming scents of sandalwood and cedar. The shop carries an assortment of potpourri, herbal teas, and books, plus preparations for bath, hair, face, and skin. The herbal apothecary, popular with "folklore herbalists," includes a recently added selection of Chinese and ayurvedic botanicals.

Aphrodisia, 264 Bleecker St, New York, NY 10014. Mon-Sat 11 am-7 pm, Sun (except July-Aug) noon-5 pm.

Sweetest Smelling Sidewalks

Bath Island

This shop not only sells products to make you smell good when you scrub in the tub, but it also makes the sidewalk in front smell good. "We wash the sidewalk daily, and two or three times a week we use scent," says Sebastian Rafala, co-owner with Janet Loeffler. "It lasts a couple of days." The attractive storefront has hardwood floors, an old enamel claw-footed bath tub filled with plastic bubbles in the window, and another inside brimming with natural sponges. All products are biodegradable and include shampoos, rinses, and conditioners for the hair, bath oils and body shampoos, lotions, shaving soaps, creams, lip balms, cleansers, and colognes. Scented glycerin soaps are available in two dozen fragrances ranging from apricot and black rose to lavender and sea aloe. Perfume oils come in more than 70 fragrances, from bayberry and black poppy to violet and white ginger. The shop does custom scenting and also has a mail-order business. Custom gift baskets, with potpourri as filler, begin at $15. Kimonos, made of 100 percent cotton by a local seamstress, make unusual gifts at $80, as do distinctive T-shirts with fish designs ($16).

Bath Island, 469 Amsterdam Ave, New York, NY 10024, 212/787-9415. Daily noon-8 pm.

Best Spot to Smell Presidential (by 1789 Standards)

Caswell-Massey

The Old World look and genteel attitudes found at this shop are more in character with a true British "chemist's" than an American drugstore. In fact, it is *the original* American drugstore—the country's oldest, established in 1752. The store's atmosphere is dark and timeless, heightened by wooden walls and shelves full of glass jars and metal bins that have been holding remedies and notions for scores of years. Among the specialties that Caswell-Massey has long been known for are a large selection of special handmade scented soaps (such as almond, coconut, and a grove of fruit scents), as well as a variety of bath oils, powders, large natural sponges, rich hand and face creams, and house colognes for which the recipes pre-date George Washington. (And, you can actually buy the cologne Washington himself favored—or wife Martha's perfume—when the first First Family were Caswell-Massey customers). They get less and less call for it these days, but you can even find several varieties of snuff here! Caswell-Massey also has branches at South Street Seaport (21 Fulton Street; 212/608-5401) and the 2 World Financial Center building (225 Liberty Street; 212/945-2630).

Caswell-Massey, 518 Lexington Ave, New York, NY 10017, 212/755-2254. Mon-Fri 10 am-7 pm, Sat 10 am-8 pm, Sun noon-5 pm.

Best Bet to Cure That 3 A.M. Nagging Ache

Kaufman Pharmacy

Relief can be only a phone call (and a cab ride) away with the assistance of this trusty, 24-hour-a-day, seven-day-a-week pharmacy. Although there are pharmacies on many New York street corners, Kaufman is the only around-the-clock drugstore in the city, and will even deliver orders to any address in Manhattan (at any hour) for only the additional cost of the cab fare. Kaufman offers a full pharmacy department (with pharmacists always on duty), as well as a wide variety of over-the-counter medications, notions, cosmetics, medical/surgical supplies, toiletries, magazines and books, and other goods you would expect to find in a modern drugstore. This store also has a food counter offering snacks, sandwiches, and full meals (although no one ever mistook

Kaufman's food for Le Cirque's); however, you won't be able to get a pastrami at 3 a.m. to go along with your aspirin, bandages, and vitamins—the food counter portion of the store closes at 10 p.m.

Kaufman Pharmacy, 557 Lexington Ave, New York, NY 10022, 212/755-2266. Daily, 24 hours.

Savviest Shop for Safe Sex
Condomania

Even during its most blatantly bohemian and care-free hippy days, Greenwich Village never saw the likes of this shop. Its *raison d'etre* is the latex pro-phylactic. With the latest Top 10 tunes playing in the background, shoppers make their selections from more than 200 varieties of condoms. According to a sales assistant, the most popular kind are those that glow in the dark! Rounding out the inventory are a variety of condom-related novelty items including cards, T-shirts, books, and such whimsical articles as a take-off on the erstwhile pet-rock phenom-enon—a "Pet Rubber" complete with a care-and-training booklet. This small shop in the middle of a block on busy Bleecker Street has, of course, in the enlightened '90s, a serious purpose underlying its caprice. It has locations in six other cities.

Condomania, 351 Bleecker St, New York, NY 10014, 212/691-9442. Sun-Wed 11 am-11 pm, Thu-Sat 11 am-midnight.

Best Bet for the Record
J & R Music World

If you are interested in buying a piece of recorded music at a discounted price, head for this huge warehouse across from the bubbling fountain in City Hall Park. With stairway walls plastered with music posters, J & R is a rambling entertainment depart-ment store where you can shop for compact and laser discs, tape cassettes, videos, and even LP records (which seem to have been rendered an endangered species by advancing technology). The huge discount outlet offers more than 25,000 selec-tions of CDs, cassettes, and LPs, covering the usual range of pop, rock, jazz, classical, gospel, show tunes, movie soundtracks, and country & western. You'll also find a wide assortment of electronic equipment and accessories—mini TV sets, Walkman units, camcorders, cassette decks, CD players/changers, and DAT decks plus a wide array of headphones, and such electronic gadgetry as monster cable, anten-nas, audiophile accessories, and universal remotes.

Next door is sister store Computer World, with an enormous range of discounted hardware and software.

J & R Music World, 23 Park Row, New York, NY 10038, Mon-Sat 9 am-6:30 pm, Sun 11 am-6 pm, 212/732-8600 (for a free catalog: 800/221-8180).

Best Bet for Hard-to-Find 45s and Albums

Bleecker Bob's

It's not on Bleecker Street (it's about a block away, on West 3rd), but it *is* run by a Bob—"Bleecker Bob" Plotnik, a crusty, unreconstructed fan of rock music from Elvis Presley through Elvis Costello and beyond. This Village landmark is the best spot in the city to find old rock, R&B, reggae, punk, and various independent-label and import albums and 45s. The selections can be a bit hard to zero in on without help, since the albums are lumped together by genre, rather than alphabetically by artist. However, the knowledgeable and helpful staff seem to know where every last record is in the shop's maze of racks (and, besides, the mass grouping makes browsing more of an adventure for the shopper who likes to be surprised). I have a young out-of-town associate who was thrilled to finally find the long-out-of-print first Lou Reed solo record here after years of searching; regular customers would not be shocked to find Reed *himself* (a longtime New Yorker) picking out some obscure oldies in the racks at Bob's. Another good oldie record store that *is* on Bleecker is The Golden Disc (239 Bleecker Street, 212/255-7899). Its rock selection isn't as voluminous as Bob's, but it does offer good selections of jazz, blues, and folk music, and also has a large CD section.

Bleecker Bob's Golden Oldies, 118 W 3rd St, New York, NY 10012, 212/475-9677. Sun-Thu noon-1 am, Fri & Sat noon-3 am.

Best Store for Sound Advice

Harvey Electronics

For just any stereo-CD-cassette setup, consumers can shop any of the discounters or "superstores" that offer electronics. But for top-of-the-line electronics—sold by experts who know their systems—in-the-know audiophiles head to this Midtown shop. All of the big-name components are offered here—Yamaha, Panasonic, Mitsubishi, Bang & Olufsen, Nakamichi, Sony, Denon, and so on. Shop for a complete ensemble, or for individual peripheral pieces to enhance an existing stereo system. All of the systems and components are prominently displayed and set up for test listening, meaning that you can browse and compare performance, rather than just rely on names on a sealed carton. Harvey also features a helpful, knowledgeable staff and a service department that helps customers maintain the equipment they buy. In general, the prices reflect the quality of the merchandise and the level of service....But occasional sales on some items can bring the prices more in line with those charged by chain retailers. (Harvey also offers a selection of top-notch video equipment.)

Harvey Electronics, 2 W 45th St, New York, NY 10036, 212/575-5000. Mon-Fri 9:30 am-6 pm, Sat 10 am-6 pm.

Best Bet for All Kinds of Music (and Even Some Musicians)

Tower Records

Somewhat amazingly, this very large music store—which quite believably claims to offer more CDs, tapes, and records under one roof than any other New York store—isn't a bland music "supermarket," but manages to project more personality than most smaller, quirkier shops. A big reason for this is the interaction between the passing parade of all types of music fans who shop here (from old classical "longhairs" to shaved-head punks) and the often artistically inclined (or just bizarrely dressed) employees. And, beyond the entertaining spectacle of watching a gray-haired grandmother ask a purple-haired girl with an earring in her nose where the Barbra Streisand records are, Tower also offers more conventional entertainment, such as special promotional record-signings or mini-concerts by a variety of rock, rap, jazz, and classical artists. (These are usually announced ahead of time on an in-store roster, but from time-to-time, there are also impromptu appearances or performances by big-name artists.) But, distractions aside, a large music store lives or dies on the depth of its selections—and Tower delivers the goods in that respect, offering nearly every record by nearly every major-label artist (and plenty of import and minor-label selections as well). There is also a Tower Records on the West Side (1965 Broadway; 212/799-2500), where the selection is almost as good as the main outlet down in the Village (including a large videocassette annex next door), but the atmosphere is decidedly less eclectic and electric.

Tower Records, 692 Broadway, at 4th St, New York,
NY 10012, 212/505-1500. Daily 9 am-midnight.

Best Jewel of a Neighborhood
Diamond District

Diamonds are forever along this bustling block of
Midtown Manhattan. It is America's center for trade
in precious gemstones, with links to Amsterdam and
South Africa. On both sides of the street an array
of dealers, large and small, occupy jewelry shops and
tiny booths in multi-merchant diamond exchanges.
Historically, the diamond trade has been dominated
by Hasidic Jews, who wear beards and curled
sidelocks, dress somberly in severe dark suits, black
hats, and shoes, and inevitably tote bulging briefcases and satchels. These ultra-Orthodox Hasids
can be seen on the sidewalks and in the delis of this
bazaar-like neighborhood, where Yiddish is the principal language of business, and deals worth hundreds of thousands of dollars are closed on a
handshake. This is a colorful spot for browsing—and
even for bargaining and buying for anyone who has
a reliable notion of values. However, much of the
trade is wholesale, between dealers and brokers.
Originally, the diamond district was located on the
Lower East Side around the Bowery and Canal
Street, and later followed the carriage trade uptown.

Diamond District, W 47th St between Fifth and Sixth
Avenues, New York, NY 10036.

Best Furnishings Designed by a Knight
Conran's

Fashionable Londoners know about trendy Biben-
dum restaurant, designed by Sir Terence Conran
and housed in the remarkable refurbished Michelin
Tyre Company headquarters that also bears Sir
Terence's imprimatur (see *London's Best-Kept Secrets*). Conran's British chain of home-furnishings
emporia now has expanded internationally. This
American flagship store, with its line of contemporary furnishings designed with clean, simple lines,
blends nicely into the modern-looking Citicorp Center in Midtown Manhattan. These smart, affordable
furnishings include chairs, couches, convertible sofa
beds, coffee tables, bed frames, bureaus, children's
furniture, and utility carts, much of it imported from
England. In addition to stylish modular furniture,
there is a variety of glassware, china, pottery, lighting, window shades, kitchen equipment, linens,
fabrics, wallpapers, toys, tote bags, planters, desk

accessories—much of it high-tech and on the cutting edge of fashion. There are two other Manhattan branches (2248 Broadway; 212/873-9250 and 2-8 Astor Place; 212/505-1515).

Conran's, Citicorp Center, 160 E 54th St, New York, NY 10022, 212/371-2225. Mon-Fri 10 am-8 pm, Sat 10 am-7 pm, Sun 11 am-6 pm.

Best Bet for Birds and House Calls

Bird Jungle

It is by no means unique in the annals of entrepreneurship for a hobby to grow into a business. Here is a hobby that has grown into a menagerie! Ford Fernandez was an insurance broker who enjoyed keeping exotic birds as pets. Almost a dozen years ago he decided to open a shop, and the result is the Bird Jungle, offering the largest variety of birds in Manhattan. Occupying a busy corner in the Village (at W 11th Street), this shop attracts more than 100 visitors a week, including such celebrity bird fanciers as Yoko Ono, Jessica Lange, Whoopi Goldberg, and Lauren Hutton. They come to admire the colorful plumage of a variety of parrots, budgerigars, parakeets, myrnah birds, and other exotic varieties. "This shop is the most popular petting zoo in Greenwich Village," says Fernandez. Of course, visitors also come to buy, at prices that range from $10 to $12,000 (the latter for a hyacinth macaw). The shop dispatches birds to destinations as distant as Morocco and Saudi Arabia and also supplies birds for photo shoots and for TV shows. For those who already have birds as pets, the shop will make house calls to clip nails and trim beaks. However, visitors to the owner's home no longer will find feathered pets there. "After a day at the shop," says Fernandez, "I don't want to go home to any squawks."

Bird Jungle, 401 Bleecker St, New York, NY 10014, 212/242-1757. Mon-Fri 12:30-6:30 pm, Sat 11 am-6:30 pm, Sun 11 am-5:30 pm.

Most Cerebral Pawn Shop (at Which to Spend a Knight)

Village Chess Shop

On sandlots and neighborhood basketball courts around the boroughs, would-be sports superstars hone the skills that will carry a talented, lucky few to fat pro contracts. Given the astronomical purses that Bobby Fischer is playing for these days, they might also be well advised to head for this Greenwich

Village chess emporium. It's a shop, and it's entertainment. Open from noon to midnight, this comfortable meeting room is the spot to find a chess partner and play a match for a nominal $1.50 an hour—or shop for a chess set. An incredible inventory of chess sets includes hand-carved and -painted pieces imported from around the world. They come in a wide range of sizes and are fashioned in a variety of materials, including ivory, wood, onyx, pewter, brass, silver, and ceramics. These sets are priced to suit every pocket. Here's where you also can pick up a book on chess strategy or shop for a number of other games, including cribbage and backgammon.

Village Chess Shop, 230 Thompson St, New York, NY 10012, 212/475-9580. Daily noon-midnight.

Best Selection of Gifts from Around the World

United Nations Gift Center

The perfect spot to seek out an unusual gift, this basement shop carries merchandise that is as colorful, varied, and interesting as the delegates to the United Nations who conduct their business in the General Assembly upstairs. It is crammed with imports from member countries around the world—paintings and folk crafts, toys and dolls, jewelry and clothing, masks and sculpture, leatherwork and beadwork. There are silks from India, carvings from Africa, lacquered wood from Russia, and puzzles from Germany, along with Eskimo soapstone, Indonesian batik, and basketry from Central America. There are items bearing the United Nations symbol and a series of dolls dressed in the native costumes of member nations. Of interest to budget-conscious shoppers, much of the merchandise sold here is inexpensive, and all of it is exempt from sales tax. *Dining suggestion:* The Delegates Dining Room is open to the public on weekdays and offers pleasing views of the East River.

United Nations Gift Center, UN General Assembly Building, First Avenue at E 46th St, New York, NY 10017, 212/963-7700. Daily 9 am-5 pm.

Merriest Music Makers

Rita Ford Music Boxes

Avid collectors tend to be single-minded about their particular passion, ever searching for new acquisitions. Collectors with an eye for music boxes of every conceivable kind head for this delightful specialty shop. In effect, it is more like a museum, with many rare and valuable antiques and knowledgeable salespersons ready to demonstrate any particular box. With a dozen or so music boxes tinkling their merry way with tunes ranging from nursery rhymes to Mozart, this shop is a pleasant oasis in this busy East Side neighborhood. Among one of the world's finest collections of working music boxes, are pieces dating from the early 19th century. Many are heavily ornamented with dazzling gemstones, silver scrollwork, and gold trim, with intricate movements created in Switzerland, France, and Germany. As classical music plays, ballerinas pirouette, animals cavort, birds fly, children play, and carousels spin. Although prices can range up to tens of thousand of dollars for exceptional European music boxes and uncommon early-American pieces, there are also hand-crafted contemporary models that are moderately priced, and inexpensive mass-produced music boxes imported from Japan. The shop also does restoration and repairs.

Rita Ford Music Boxes, 19 E 65th St, New York, NY 10021, 212/535-6717. Mon-Sat 9 am-5 pm.

Best Boxes to Puzzle Over

An American Craftsman

For a unique, irresistible gift, choose a puzzle box hand-crafted by Richard Rothbard, owner of this unusual shop. Created from exotic woods such as zebrawood, cocobolo, padauk, and bubinga (but also more familiar varieties such as maple, walnut, and buckeye) these boxes fit together as intricately as a jigsaw puzzle—except that they are infinitely more creative and complex. None of the woods are stained, and the pieces—which are real conversation pieces!—are finished with natural oil and a lacquer sealer and need only an occasional dusting. Prices range from $25 to $2,500. Also on display are a variety of wood-related works of 600 other craftspersons. Included are hand-carved pen-and-pencil sets, letter openers, sculptures, mobils, hand mirrors, picture frames, wine racks, ladles, and candelabra. An alluring window display makes browsing virtually mandatory. There is a second location in Morristown, N.J. (163 South St at Elm; 201/538-6720), while gallery-owner Rothbard, who dubs his work "boxology," exhibits at various juried craft fairs.

An American Craftsman, 317-321 Bleecker St, New York, NY 10014, 212/727-0841. Sun-Thu noon-8pm, Fri & Sat 11 am-11 pm.

Best Museum to Shop for Artful Gifts

Guggenheim Museum Store

Where to shop for ties silk-screened from original Russian textile designs from the 1920s? Or how about a child's coloring book featuring the vibrant colors and forms of modern art? Just as the quirky Frank Lloyd Wright-designed Solomon R. Guggenheim Museum (see separate listing) should be a crucial stop on any New York City museum tour, so its shop should be a "must" on a Manhattan shopping binge. Located at both the Uptown museum and the new SoHo branch, the Guggenheim Museum Store offers an attractive range of artful gifts, including exhibition catalogues, art and architecture publications, and artist-designed gift items including jewelry, textiles, toys, notebooks and note cubes, wall and pocket calendars, the exclusively designed Guggenheim Museum watch, gold-plated alphabet pins using the alphabet designed by Frank Lloyd Wright for the facade of the museum, and chocolate bars molded in the shape of the controversial Wright building. Additional shopping suggestions include hand-painted ceramics designed exclusively for the museum, jigsaw puzzles featuring favorite works from its collection, and umbrellas, T-shirts, baseball caps, and tote bags featuring either a fantasy design or a geometric design. (For a food stop, the museum's cafeteria offers above-average fare.)

Guggenheim Museum Store, 1071 Fifth Ave, New York, NY 10128, 212/423-3870. Tue 11 am-7:45 pm, Wed-Sun 11 am-4:45 pm.

Best Department Store to Shop for Byzantine Art

Metropolitan Museum Shop in Macy's

Should conventional departments at Macy's stump you when shopping for an unusual gift, head for the 34th Street balcony housing this satellite gift shop. Stocked with many objects produced for or by the museum, it offers art books, prints, and wonderful copies of sculpture, jewelry, and other decorative-arts objects in silver, glass, stone, and textiles. The high-quality copies make excellent gifts. You can spend as little as $30 on a pair of panther-head earrings created during the Egyptian XII Dynasty around 1786 B.C., or as much as $1,000 on a Chinese 18th-century porcelain ginger jar. For $6.95 you might take home a Chinese late-18th century gold-plated bookmark, or spend $17.50 on a silk necktie of 16th-century Iranian design or of a pattern adapted from a motif on a box of the Byzantine period. Other ideas: Greek stone plaques, a 19th-century sterling silver kiddush cup, a marble Roman relief, Napoleonic pins, and 17th-century Indian bracelets. The adjacent Café L'Étoile, with cane chairs and lace café curtains, is an elegant spot for lunch or tea. Enjoy a bowl of onion soup, shrimp, roast chicken, niçoise salad, or eggs Benedict. Or stop by for an ice-cream creation—perhaps a chocolate ice-cream float in espresso topped with whipped cream.

Metropolitan Museum Shop, Macy's, 151 W 34th St, New York, NY 10001, 212/695-4400. Mon, Thu, Fri 10 am-8:30 pm; Tue, Wed, Sat 10 am-7 pm; Sun 11 am-6 pm.

Best Bet for Things You Didn't Even Know You Needed

The Sharper Image

When the stress of shopping in Manhattan gets the better of you, step into this upscale emporium of gadgetry for a 700-year-old Chinese antidote. A pair of smooth metal balls, ornamented with enameled dragons, are designed to be rolled in the palm, à la Captain Queeg. Each rings with an inner chime (one high, one low) and the pair come in a wooden box covered with silk brocade. Or for those tired feet, there are Mephisto shoes made by a small company in France and claimed to be "like walking on a bed of feathers." Such is the stock of this South Street Seaport outlet of the chain of stores that are fun to browse. There are cushioned auto seats, aviator sun glasses, soccer balls bearing the flags of 24 nations, a computerized chess board that provides coaching, a full-size, fold-down mountain bicycle, underwater watches, ultrasound bug shield, a sports radar gun, stylish leather luggage, and an electronic organizer with 256K of memory. Or how about a table-tennis robot that launches ping-pong balls at you for non-stop practice? Sometimes it's possible to run into a sale—such as silk shirts that were marked down $15 on one visit. Other Manhattan locations at 4 W 57th Street and Madison Avenue at 73rd Street.

The Sharper Image, South Street Seaport, Pier 17, New York, NY 10038, 212/693-0477. Mon-Sat 10 am-9 pm, Sun 11 am-7 pm.

Best Bet for Things You Didn't Even Know Existed

Hammacher Schlemmer

Until you walk into this store, it never may have occurred to you that you might like to own an automatic potato-chip maker, a baseball cap with a built-in AM/FM radio, or a terry bathrobe in a colorful Incan design. Or how about a Charles Lindbergh commemorative flight jacket, an illuminated pen, or a red-and-gold 1890s popcorn cart (priced to go at $1,300!)? This is the ultimate store for entertaining browsing, full of gadgets that you know you'd love to own (such as a lighted electric revolving tie rack) but which you also know you can live perfectly well without. The emphasis is on high-tech merchandise, electronic gadgetry, and sports- and fitness-related items. The shop (with branches in Beverly Hills and Chicago and a mail-order business) offers top-of-the-line merchandise (for top dollar) with an unconditional guarantee. You'll find articles that are strictly functional, such as a wide-mouth toaster, perfect for bagels, muffins, and doorstep-sized toast slices; an electric jar opener, ideal for stubborn air-sealed lids; and a space-saving shoe cabinet. And you'll enjoy such whimsical items as a coin bank in which a dog jumps through a hoop and deposits a coin from its mouth to a barrel (1888 original antique, $2,500; reproduction $39.95).

Hammacher Schlemmer, 147 E 57th St, New York, NY 10022. Mon-Sat 10 am-6 pm.

Best Shopping Spot Before Halloween (or a Wild Party)

Gordon Novelty Co.

As you might guess, October is this shop's busiest season, when the big kids (with a few actual kids in tow) flock to pick out or accessorize their latest Halloween party costumes. And whether those selections are traditional vampires, clowns, pirates, or pop-culture figures such as Madonna or the latest scandalized politician, the chances are good that this long-established shop (more than 65 years old) will be able to supply the wherewithal to transform its customers—at least for a night—into their favorite fantasy figures. Gordon claims to offer the largest selection of masks and full costumes in the entire city, and supplements these with a staggering array of hats (more than 500, ranging from palace guard to cowboy to futuristic space traveler), wigs, makeup, and various accessories (such as fake weapons, costume jewelry, and the like). Of course, the stock is the same year-round—and is definitely less picked-over in other months—meaning it doesn't have to be Halloween to find a good costume-party getup. Gordon also stocks a variety of tacky novelties (of the "X-ray Spex" type that were advertised in the backs of comic books) and magic tricks. Another spot for silly or scary masks and costumes is Forbidden Planet, a comic book and science fiction/fantasy store (see separate listing).

Gordon Novelty Co., 933 Broadway, New York, NY 10010, 212/254-8616. Mon-Fri 9 am-4:30 pm.

Best Shop Promising That "Shoplifters Will Be Disintegrated"

Forbidden Planet

While the staff of Forbidden Planet may not actually have laser blasters behind the counter to discourage shoplifters, the offbeat humor of the above-mentioned prominently posted sign gives shoppers an idea of what's up. With comic books (as well as science fiction and fantasy-themed items) no longer being strictly kid stuff, this large, well-stocked store has become popular with collectors of all ages. In addition to the typical *Batman* and *Spiderman* titles, this whimsical shop offers a wide variety of harder-to-find comic books from all the major publishers, as well as plenty of rarer titles (including racy and violent, adult-oriented comics from Japan and France, and "graphic novels," the darker and more complex book-length comics that have become popular in recent years). In addition to comic books, Forbidden Planet offers "regular" books, videocassettes, toys and action figures, games, posters, trading cards, masks and costumes, and a wide selection of magazines about comics and science fiction, fantasy, and horror movies and television shows. Downstairs is the spot for serious collectors, with ranks of plastic-wrapped vintage comics selling for many times their original cover prices. There is also a Forbidden Planet outlet at 227 E. 59th Street (212/751-4386).

Forbidden Planet, 821 Broadway, New York, NY 10003, 212/473-1576. Mon-Thu & Sat 10 am-7 pm, Fri 10 am-8 pm, Sun noon-6 pm.

Best Shop That's on Target

Darts Unlimited

If you ever find yourself in a neighborhood pub casually tossing darts into a board, beware of challenges to a "friendly" game by anyone carrying his or her own set of darts. Chances are you'll lose—perhaps to someone equipped by this Gramercy Park shop that has been catering to the needs of dart players for more than 20 years. Its specialized stock, much of it imported from England, includes hundreds of different types of darts, ranging from tournament-quality to inexpensive sets for beginners. A knowledgeable staff will help you select the weight that feels most comfortable. The range of flights is even more comprehensive, with a variety of colors, shapes, and designs, in plastic, laminated paper, foil, and traditional feathers. For dart playing at home, there are the finest imported boars'-bristle boards and an array of accessories that include point sharpeners, fancy carrying cases, cabinets, scoreboards, backboards, books about technique and different games, copies of the official dart-player's rules and regulations, and, for math deadheads, a cheat-sheet called an "out card" that computes the throws required to finish a game.

Darts Unlimited, 30 E 20th St, New York, NY 10003, 212/533-8684. Tue-Fri noon-5:30 pm, Sat 11 am-4 pm.

Best Place to Buy Before You Fly

Big City Kite Company

On the first bright weekend in spring, kite-flyers head for Central Park. But before they do, many first stop at Manhattan's biggest kite store. This East Side shop carries more than 200 varieties of kites, along with all manner of accessories, such as cord, winders, and tails. Although the shop is a kaleidoscope of colors guaranteed to delight children, not everything here is child's play. Serious kite flyers visit to discuss aerodynamics and such worrisome subjects as fractured spars, and to shop for expensive acrobatic stunt kites. But this also is a fine place to shop for a child's first kite, an inexpensive plastic model that will enable a youngster to soar like an eagle. There are mass-produced kites, skillfully wrought handmade models, and kites imported from China, Japan, and Britain. There are simple flat kites with streamer tails, and complex triangular, square, and hexagonal box kites. An incredibly colorful array includes kites made of nylon, silk, paper, and plastic, and those shaped like birds, fish, animals, and superheroes. Each spring, the store sponsors a kite-flying extravaganza in Central Park.

Big City Kite Company, 1201 Lexington Ave, New York, NY 10028, 212/472-2623. Mon-Wed & Sat 10 am-6 pm, Thu 10 am-7 pm.

Best Toy Store That Parents Can't Resist

F.A.O. Schwarz

This state-of-the-art emporium of fantasy is more a happening than a toy store. There are dollhouses to walk into, drivable kiddy cars, and a menagerie of giant stuffed animals. Mechanical robots do your bidding, an animated, singing 28-foot-tall clock tower is encircled with costumed characters and moving mechanical toys, and a huge keyboard on the floor invites willing feet to tap out tunes (as Tom Hanks did in the movie, *Big*, in a sequence filmed at this mega-toy store). Kids and not-too-reluctant-parents head for a huge department of the latest electronic games, computers, video toys, and other high-tech divertissements. A world of dolls that move and talk (or simply are passive and cuddly), includes not only Barbie, Ken, and friends, but a lot of blue-blooded cousins. Long-time favorites include electric trains, building blocks, magic tricks, kites, toy soldiers, planes, and scale-model cars. This flagship store of the chain that started pleasing youngsters in the mid-19th century may be the closest thing to Disneyland in New York. A greeter in toy-soldier costume, complete with black bearskin hat, ushers shoppers into a store cleverly divided into interest-grabbing departments—literally stores within a store. It's the kind of place, though, where parents might be tempted (or cajoled) into giving their credit cards a workout.

F.A.O. Schwarz, 767 Fifth Ave, New York, NY 10153, 212/644-9400. Mon-Wed, Fri & Sat 10 am-6 pm, Thu 10 am-8 pm, Sun noon-5 pm.

Most Enchanting Toy Store

Enchanted Forest

It's a zoo in here—or, at least, a menagerie of furry stuffed animals (and a virtual gallery of exquisite hand-crafted toys and collectible folk crafts). This delightful SoHo toy store is worth a visit just to browse, with a setting reminiscent of a scene from

Beauty and the Beast. Its make-believe enchanted forest, where eminently adoptable denizens peek out at visitors, is complete with a waterfall and rustic bridge. This land of fantasy is home to a variety of whimsical animals—plush bears, wolves, lions, giraffes, cats, apes, and birds, as well as trolls and not-so-scary beasts that can range in price from a few dollars to several hundred dollars. The kid- and adult-pleasing inventory tucked away within this mock forest includes a selection of story and coloring books, puzzles, masks, simple musical instruments, puppets, yo-yos, tops, kaleidoscopes, and other lovingly wrought toys that do not rely on computer chips to give pleasure to young recipients.

Enchanted Forest, 85 Mercer St, New York, NY 10012, 212/925-6677. Mon-Fri 11 am-7 pm, Sun noon-6 pm.

Best Supermarket of Toys

Toy Park

This large, bustling store may not have the storied cachet of F.A.O. Schwarz (see separate listing), but neither does it have that famed retailer's esoteric selection and accompanying (often high) prices. True, shoppers may not find anything more challenging here than the usual coterie of toys advertised on Saturday morning television, but—let's face it—those are usually the things kids really want, anyway. This cavernous Upper East Side store offers all of the old and new favorites, from Barbie and Ken to the Teenage Mutant Ninja Turtles, in addition to such standards as dolls, stuffed animals, board and electronic games, action figures, puzzles, blocks (and other building toys), arts and crafts supplies, wagons, and bicycles. The store's size allows it to have a large stock of each item—a big plus when that "must have" item is suddenly all the rage and harder to find (à la Cabbage Patch Dolls several years ago). There is a smaller Toy Park location on the Upper West Side, at 624 Columbus Avenue (212/769-3880). For another large selection of toys—usually at good prices—the mega-chain Toys "R" Us has an outlet in Manhattan (1293 Broadway; 212/594-8697), plus several stores in the outer boroughs and the surrounding suburbs.

Toy Park, 112 E 86th St, New York, NY 10028, 212/427-6611. Mon 10 am-6 pm; Tue, Wed, Fri, Sat 10 am-7 pm; Thu 10 am-8 pm; Sun noon-5 pm.

Best Bet to Do Your Bidding

Sotheby's and Christie's

In New York, as in many other cities around the world, these two venerable London-based firms are *the* places to find auctions offering collectibles that run the gamut from multi-million-dollar pieces of Impressionist art to celebrity mementos. Sotheby's is usually the house that gets the big headlines for the blockbuster artwork it auctions from time to time, but collectors and buyers also know to keep an eye on the listings available at the house's regular category auctions, which include furniture, jewelry, rugs, clocks, glass, books, and other items. Christie's is perhaps a bit less staid than its famous competitor, and is known for a willingness to auction almost anything. This means that in addition to the expected art, jewelry, and furniture, buyers are likely to find spirited auctions of toys, wines, stamp and coin collections, and, in an ever-growing trend, memorabilia from the worlds of movies, television, and popular music. (Both of these auction houses also have subsidiaries that hold more frequent auctions of generally less-expensive pieces; these are Sotheby's Arcade, 1334 York Avenue; 212/606-7147 and Christie's East, 219 E. 67th Street; 212/606-0400.) Even if the various and sundry items offered at these houses (and their assorted offshoots) are not within the bounds of your budget, observing a fast-paced and high-powered auction can be an entertaining way to spend an afternoon. However, be sure not to tug your ear or wave at an acquaintance across the room, unless you don't mind becoming the accidental owner of a Van Gogh painting or an Elvis Presley guitar!

Sotheby's 1334 York Ave (at 72nd St), New York, NY 10021, 212/606-7000. Mon-Sat 10 am-5 pm, Sun 1-5 pm. Christie's, 502 Park Ave at 59th St, New York, NY 10022, 212/546-1000. Mon-Sat 10 am-5 pm, Sun 1-5 pm.

Best Flea Markets

Annex Antiques Market and Greenflea's/P.S. 44 Market on Columbus

With many of the smaller specialty antique and collectible shops being forced out of business (or, at least, into itinerancy) by the high cost of real estate and rents throughout New York, these two year-round, weekly flea markets represent somewhat of a final frontier of affordable and interesting goods. In general, the quality of the items offered usually falls well below that of goods offered in the city's top antique shops, but prices are usually fair and some treasures can be found among the eclectic and fascinating array of wares. The Annex market is an outdoors, weekend, in-almost-any-weather affair located in a parking lot in the heart of the Flower District on the eastern edge of Chelsea. Anywhere from several dozen to several hundred dealers congregate here weekly, offering recent and vintage clothing, jewelry, books, records, glass, paintings and drawings, and a variety of furnishings, ranging from true antiques to restorers' specials. (As with the crowds, the weather dictates the number of dealers on any given weekend.) The West Side's Greenflea's/ P.S. 44 Market is the Annex's chief rival, and is only open on Sundays. Its name varies by describer—P.S. 44 refers to the school at the address and is the older name; Greenflea's is a more upscale name being offered by the people who currently run this conglomeration. This indoor/outdoor market is especially big on clothes and jewelry, but also often offers a good selection of antique furniture. Either of these markets are good bets for bargains and for a taste of rubbing shoulders with "true" Manhattan shopping mavens.

Annex Antiques Market, W 26th St & Sixth Ave, New York, NY 10010, 212/243-5343. Sat & Sun 9 am-6 pm. Admission $1.00; free parking. Greenflea's/ P.S. 44 Market on Columbus, Columbus Ave & W 76th St, New York, NY 10023, 212/316-1088. Sun 10 am-6 pm. Free admission.

Best Antique Mart
The Manhattan Art & Antiques Center

Even though shopping malls are not very good places for finding unique antique stores, some of the best antique shopping in New York *can* be found in a mall—a specialized antique dealers' mall, that is. Spread out over three large floors and including more than 100 different dealers, this market is a great place to shop or even just browse. Under one roof, collectors can find furniture, rugs and quilts, glass, silver, gold, watches and clocks, pottery, clothing, paintings and drawings, books, and dozens of other items that range from "affordable" to museum quality. Of special note is the quantity of shops and/ or stalls offering a variety of foreign goods, with heavy concentrations of English furniture, Oriental rugs and decorative items, and Eastern European and Russian artworks and handicrafts. The juxta-positioning of these varied items can be illustrated by the fact that you could walk out of the center with a $5 baseball card—or with a $50,000 piece of antique art. Although the bargains waiting to be discovered can certainly be relative, the prices are generally lower than those on comparable items found in individual shops. Admission to the center is free and nearby parking is available.

Manhattan Art & Antiques Center, 1050 Second Ave, at 55th St, New York, NY 10022, 212/355-4400. Mon-Sat 10:30 am-6 pm, Sun noon-6 pm.

Best Bet for English Antiques Without Crossing the Atlantic

Arthur Ackerman & Son, Inc.

It has become ironically axiomatic that even when you cannot find particular English antiques (especially furniture and decorative items) in England, you may well find them at this upper Midtown shop. This well-established dealer has long been considered the North American leader in 18th-century English furnishings, meaning that if it doesn't stock a specific item, its staff will likely be able to obtain the piece or steer you to a direct British source. Collectors will find a large selection of (among others) high- and lowboys, dining room sets (and/or individual pieces), desks, writing tables, and beds. This is also a top spot for English equestrian decorations (a particular passion of the Ackermans), offering dozens of prints, oils, and porcelains and other figurines with riding and/or hunting themes. Between the solid furnishings and warm, tweedy decor, this comfortable and friendly shop will likely remind you of an English private club or country estate. Other leading purveyors of English antiques include Florian Papp, Inc. (962 Madison Avenue; 212/288-6770), which is also very strong in 18th-century furniture; and the two Amdur Antiques shops (950 Lexington Avenue; 212/472-2691 and 1193 Lexington Avenue; 212/472-2691), whose specialties are accessories and decorative items, such as candlesticks, vases, glassware, and clocks. *Neighborhood note:* The stretch of 57th Street that is home to Ackerman & Son also offers a heavy concentration of fine-art and antique galleries and dealers.

Arthur Ackerman & Son, Inc., 50 E 57th St, New York, NY 10022, 212/753-5292. Mon-Fri 9 am-5 pm, Sat 9 am-4 pm.

Best Combination Store and Museum

Urban Archaeology

Whether you're looking for a single snarling stone gargoyle from a demolished New York office building or the entire furnishings of an old soda shop, try Urban Archaeology. The recovered treasures at this store can help satisfy cravings to own a little piece of the city. Housed in a huge warehouse-type multi-level space, Urban Archaeology both preserves and gives new life to salvaged detritus from (mostly) New York buildings and sites. Dedicated rehabbers could use material found here to re-create an 1890s pub in their basement or a 1920s banker's office in their den. Meanwhile, ardent accessorists will find bits of stained glass, art deco mirrors, wrought iron, and terra cotta to decorate their homes or offices. Other treasures include roomy claw-foot bathtubs, vintage pinball and slot machines, ornately carved pool tables, glittering chandeliers, chairs (including the inevitable dentist and barber chairs), and stone and iron garden and park benches. There are doors and doorknobs, as well as cabinets, lamps, brass bathroom fixtures, and columns of various heights (which make perfect table bases or plant stands). All in all, this is a delightful source that is fun to browse. Two other similar outlets offering bits and pieces of New York's past are Irreplaceable Artifacts (14 Second Avenue; 212/777-2900), offering a mix of interior and exterior decorations and ornamentations; and Lost City Arts (275 Lafayette Street; 212/941-8025), which specializes in commercial and civic signage and advertising, such as subway signs and neon-lit logos and clocks.

Urban Archaeology, 285 Lafayette St, New York, NY 10012, 212/431-6969. Mon-Fri 8 am-6 pm, Sat 10 am-4 pm.

ROMANTIC

Most Romantic Restaurant for Dinner

One If By Land, Two If By Sea

This is so much the quintessential romantic restaurant, that one wonders if Central Casting didn't take a hand here. There are red-velvet banq-uettes, flickering candlelight, four working fireplaces, fresh flowers at every table, comple-mentary artwork, and a view of a pretty courtyard and garden. A pianist plays love songs at a grand piano as wait staff in tuxedos provide discreet service. The setting for this charming Greenwich Village restaurant is a land-mark converted carriage house, making this the pluperfect spot to go with someone special. The sig-nature dish is a first-rate rendition of beef Wellington. Also recommended are rack of lamb, veal chops, and various grilled meats. Good fish selections include such innovative preparations as mahi mahi with shallots and honey sauce. This restored two-level 18th-century carriage house once belonged to Jefferson's controversial vice-president, Aaron Burr. This is a pricey restaurant where it is not uncommon to spot a famous face or two (for those who have eyes for anyone but their dining companions).

One If By Land, Two If By Sea, 17 Barrow St, New York, NY 10014. Sun-Thu 5:30-11 pm, Fri & Sat 5:30 pm-midnight.

Most Romantic Spot for *the* Dinner

Café des Artistes

For a special-occasion splurge, this West Side restaurant, with leaded-glass windows, abundant flowers, and sensuous murals of nude nymphs frolicking
in the woods, is one of Manhattan's most romantic
(and among its most expensive). A location near
Lincoln Center also makes it a choice for after-
concert suppers (for performers as well as concertgoers). The restaurant is off the lobby of the elegant
Hotel des Artistes apartment building, built in 1918
to provide studios for artists such as Norman
Rockwell and Howard Chandler Christy, who painted
the striking murals. Other famous tenants were Nöel
Coward, Isadora Duncan, and Rudolph Valentino.
(The movie *My Dinner with André* was filmed on
location here.) French cuisine features, terrines,
pâtés, duck confit, sausage *en croute*, salmon served
four ways, steak tartare, sautéed crabs, scallops
Provençale, smoked leg of lamb, roast baby chicken,
and steak au poivre. Exquisite desserts include a
notable flourless chocolate torte, lemon torte, and
key lime pie. The asparagus season in late spring
brings out the chef's creativity. Weekend brunch is
extremely popular.

Café des Artistes, 1 W 57th St, New York, NY 10019,
212/877-3500. Mon-Sat noon-12:30 am, Sun 10 am-
11 pm.

Most Romantic Dinner by the Lake

Boathouse Café

Whether you are seated at an umbrella table at
water's edge or on the dock under a gay yellow-and-
white-striped awning, this pretty café at the Loeb
Boathouse at the lake in Central Park provides you
with a pleasant spot to watch the world drift by.
Couples in rowboats move languidly across the still
waters. On cue, it seems, the inevitable flotilla of
ducks parades by. And—shades of Venice—a gondola poled by a traditionally clad gondolier trans-
ports a twosome on a romantic ride on the placid
lake. As a fanciful waterside spot for lunch, dinner,
or just a cocktail, this water's-edge café has no equal
in Manhattan. The Boathouse, with its redbrick
facade, green copper roof, and classical dormer
windows, is tucked away at the northeast tip of the
lake. Decent northern Italian fare ranges from salads
and pastas to a number of fish selections—although
the setting is the prime attraction. There is jazz in
the evening and a convenient trolley pick-up for

dinner guests at Fifth Avenue and 72nd Street. Combine dinner with a romantic gondola ride (see separate listing). During inclement weather, inside seating also offers a good view (and, perhaps, a more moody, dramatic outlook) of the water.

Boathouse Café, Loeb Boathouse, Central Park (at 75th St), New York, NY 10023, 212/517-3623. Late-Mar–early–Nov Sun-Thu 11:30 am-9 pm, Fri & Sat 11:30 am-11 pm.

Most Romantic Dinner on a Barge
River Café

Occupying a former barge on the East River at the foot of the Brooklyn Bridge, this utterly elegant restaurant is a romantic spot to sip champagne and nibble on caviar at a table for two that offers a nonpareil view of the Manhattan skyline. Picture windows capture an ever-changing view of the river traffic, an alfresco dining area is decked with enormous bouquets of flowers. There's a cocktail lounge with a piano bar that does justice to Gershwin and Berlin as the cocktail crowd enjoys spectacular sunsets and lights twinkling on to illuminate New York's spectacular skyscrapers. Presiding over this romantic waterfront café, French-trained chef David Burke offers innovative American cuisine, dishes featuring buffalo, smoked salmon, quail, fresh oysters, and smoked chicken sausage. Try such specialties as sweetbreads sautéed in white wine and basil, red lentil soup rich with chorizo, pheasant breast with wild-mushroom sauce, rack of lamb with onion tart and marinated artichoke, and grilled squab with smoked bacon and a pepper salad. Desserts feature many rich chocolate concoctions as well as banana parfait, cinnamon pudding, and a superb crème brulée.

River Café, 1 Water St, Brooklyn, New York 11201, 718/522-5200. Mon-Thu noon-2:30 pm, 6-11 pm; Fri & Sat noon-2:30 pm, 6-11:30 pm; Sun noon-3 pm, 6:30-11 pm.

Most Romantic Dinner Under the Stars
Tavern on the Green

Certainly this restaurant, with its sylvan setting in the heart of Central Park, attracts more than its share of tourists. But it remains popular, too, with New Yorkers in search of a locale for a romantic dinner. Its attractions include dining on a terrace in a storybook setting surrounded by leafy parkland

and enhanced by Japanese lanterns and thousands of twinkling lights, dancing under the stars to the music of an orchestra, and horse-drawn carriages waiting to provide a post-dinner ride. In fact, what is one of Manhattan's most spectacularly romantic restaurants began life in the late 19th century as a sheepfold for a flock that grazed on nearby meadows. Food may seem incidental to the setting, but it is generally well prepared and expensive (although *prix-fixe* pre-theater dinners are a bargain). Selections range from formal French cuisine, such as roast duckling, to more casual fare of pasta and salads, sandwiches and mixed grills. Creative appetizers and velvety desserts—try the chocolate truffle cake—round out the menu. Romance, of course, knows no season, and nor is this just a summer place. The glitzy Crystal Room, with its chandeliers, murals, stained glass, and plaster-relief ceiling, is the ultimate in elegance and offers woodsy views that are splendid when winter spreads its clean, white mantle on the park.

Tavern on the Green, Central Park West at W 67th St, New York, NY 10023, 212/873-3200. Mon-Fri 10:30 am-11 pm, Sat 5:30-11 pm, Sun 11:30 am-11 pm.

Most Romantic Dinner Party

Cellar in the Sky

It is *très romantique*, this intimate room tucked away in a raised, windowless alcove—actually, a working wine cellar—in the center of the celebrated Windows of the World restaurant on the 107th floor of the World Trade Center. With only 10 oak tables matched with comfortable leather director's chairs, reservations are essential. So is punctuality, because, with only one seating, after a short grace period the doors close and the party begins. And what a party it is, the array of wine glasses at each place setting foretelling the treats to come. Five outstanding wines accompany a seven-course dinner, with a menu that changes every other week. With everyone keeping pace, dining here is like attending a private dinner party (in fact, people sometimes book the entire room for just such a purpose). A tuxedo-clad classical guitarist entertains unobtrusively from one corner, and there are glimpses of the city through the doorway and gaps in the glass wine racks. A typical menu: chef's canapes, chilled tomato mousse with freshly smoked salmon, glazed wild mushroom cannelloni, medallions of monkfish over glazed endive, roasted loin of lamb, a selection of cheeses, peach tart, Colombian coffee, and petits fours.

Cellar in the Sky, 1 World Trade Ctr, New York, NY 10048, 212/938-1111. Mon-Sat at 7:30 pm.

Most Romantic Dinner Cruise

The World Yacht Club

For a romantic night out on the waters surrounding Manhattan, board one of the yachts of this mini-cruise line for a dinner cruise. The twilight-skyline scenery can't be beat as you head down the Hudson River and out to the harbor on one of five yachts. The food is pretty much what you'd expect—a continental menu of such entrées as prime rib, roasted chicken, and beef Wellington, accompanied by selections from a surprisingly good wine list. But dining is only part of the attraction. The entire package of food, scenery, atmosphere (that romantic feeling of escape even a short cruise can provide), and dancing under the stars to live music is what makes the World Yacht Club popular. (These cruises are also favored places for marriage proposals and for wedding receptions.) The ships include both open and enclosed areas, making this a year-round outing. There are also lunch and Sunday brunch cruises (which, with buffet-style food, are a bit less romantic, but can be a nice, if touristy, change of midday pace—especially for showing off sights to visitors). For the dinner cruises, you can board an hour beforehand for cocktails while the yacht is docked (drinks, however, are not including in the cost of the dinner cruise). Taxis are the best way to get to the boarding pier—not because its western Chelsea neighborhood is necessarily unsafe, but because it is a little desolate and not easily accessible by bus or subway. (Circle Line Cruise offers daylight sightseeing cruises around the island of Manhattan, without meals—see separate listing.)

The World Yacht Club, Pier 62 at W 23rd St, New York, NY 10011, 212/929-7090. Apr-Dec: Mon-Sat, lunch & dinner cruises; Sun, brunch cruises; Jan-Mar: Sat, lunch & dinner cruises; Sun, brunch cruises.

Most Romantic Spot for Sunday Brunch

Peacock Alley

This is a legendary spot. Cole Porter tunes are played on Cole Porter's piano—a Steinway (scarred with marks from martini glasses) that the composer, who lived in the Waldorf-Astoria Towers, bequeathed to the hotel. The name derives from when the hotel was divided in two, located on the current site of the Empire State Building, and New York's elite, dressed in their finery, would strut through a connecting corridor on their way to society balls and dinners. Sunday brunch is served buffet style, around the distinctive art deco clock in the main lobby. The menu varies week to week and includes such dishes as curried lamb with raisins and coconut, grilled marinated chicken on vegetable coulis, grilled plum tomatoes, beef Wellington with Madeira sauce, roast loin of lamb farci with mint sauce, freshly smoked venison with black currant dressing, smoked salmon, country pâté, and sliced York ham. Salads include the famous Waldorf salad, smoked chicken with red grapes and hazelnuts, confit of duck and shiitake mushrooms, and artichoke à la Greque. Providing the grand finale is a spread of more than a dozen desserts, including Grand Marnier soufflé, raspberry mousse, and Russian *bobka* coffee cake, a blend of apples, chocolate, and nuts.

Peacock Alley, The Waldorf-Astoria, 301 Park Ave, New York, NY 10022, 212/355-3000. Sunday brunch 11:30 am-2:30 pm.

Most Secluded Garden Restaurant
Courtyard Café & Bar

This secluded garden restaurant is a lovely surprise, tucked away within the Doral Court Hotel on the fringe of Midtown near Murray Hill. The courtyard has white-latticed umbrella tables with classical Greek statues and a fountain. Well-prepared Italian-American specialties are another good reason for visiting. Grilled entrées such as swordfish with black beans and brook trout with fried leek and eggplant salad vie with innovative pastas—as penne with smoked salmon, beurre blanc, and chive, and linguine with vegetables and jumbo shrimp. Pizza selections include a five-cheese version and pizza with andouille, marinara, and smoked mozzarella. Large salads serve as a satisfying luncheon entrée; choices include niçoise, cobb, grilled pineapple chicken with greens and macadamias, and grilled sirloin with greens and sherry shallot vinaigrette. Appetizers include gazpacho, steamed clams and mussels, and fresh spinach with raspberry vinaigrette and crumbled goat cheese. For those preferring indoor seating, the pretty dining room is decorated with oil paintings and a divider brimming with flowering plants. Napery is a pretty pale blue.

Courtyard Café & Bar, Doral Court Hotel, 130 E 39th St, New York, NY 10016, 212/685-1100. Daily 6:30 am-11 pm.

Most Romantic Café with a Garden Terrace

Café La Fortuna

Within easy reach of Lincoln Center and the Metropolitan Opera House, this West Side café attracts many concertgoers. In summertime, a garden terrace is a pleasant retreat from Manhattan's steamy city streets. Located just west of Central Park, this café is a long-time neighborhood favorite that attracts strollers who stop by for a revivifying cup of tea, glass of chocolate-flavored iced cappuccino, or dish of homemade gelato. During winter, this is the spot for exquisitely rich hot chocolate. There is a good selection of teas and, of course, espresso and frothy cappuccino are served to perfection. The Italian pastries and cookies are difficult to resist—the smooth, creamy cheesecake is superb. Pleasing opera buffs who stop here after attending a performance at the Met is a collection of memorabilia that includes photographs of opera's brightest stars and old 78-rpm records. A one-time patron was John Lennon, whose photograph has pride of place.

Café La Fortuna, 69 W 71st St, New York, NY 10023, 212/724-5846. Mon-Thu 1 pm-1 am, Fri 1 pm-2 am, Sat noon-2 am, Sun noon-1 am.

Most Romantic Village Coffee Houses

Caffè Dante/Caffè Reggio

Somehow, the streets of Greenwich Village seem perfect for unhurried street cafés where espresso and pastries can be taken at leisure and where lingering and people watching seem to go with the territory. Caffè Reggio, with tiny tables, soft lighting, and fine art, is one of the neighborhood's oldest coffee houses, dating back to the 1920s. More recently, its moody interior has provided a locale for movies about New York's crime families. The espresso and frothy cappuccino are superb (as are iced summertime versions), and there are delicious pastries and sandwiches made with high-quality imported Italian ingredients. Another long-time Village favorite, Caffè Dante has similar appeals and is a sometimes hangout of N.Y.U. students. Salads and sandwiches are good here, too, and the pastries are scrumptious, with cheesecake a particular favorite. Both of these friendly Macdougal Street coffee houses have sidewalk tables.

Caffè Dante, 79 Macdougal, New York, NY 10012, 212/982-5275. Sun-Thu 10 am-2 am, Fri & Sat 10 am-3 am; Caffè Reggio, 119 Macdougal, New York, NY 10012, 212/475-9557. Sun-Thu 9 am-3 am, Fri & Sat 10 am-4 am.

Choicest Spot for Italian Ice

Bleecker Street Pastry

Get your Italian ice to go—choosing from about half a dozen flavors including original lemon, peach, strawberry, and blueberry. Or take a seat at one of 15 marble-topped tables to sip an espresso or cappuccino (hot or iced), an aranciata, limonata, mocaccino, mineral water, or even a prosaic Coca-Cola or 7-Up. This Greenwich Village café has a European feeling, with dark wood paneled walls decorated art deco style and cases filled with tempting pastries, including many Neopolitan selections. Italian pastries include cannoli, sfogliatelle, tiramisu, Italian cheesecake, and tartufo. Other baked goods range from croissants and Danish to apple strudel and apple turnovers. This is a nice spot for conversation—or to enjoy quiet companionship, perhaps while sharing newspaper sections and lingering over an iced mocha.

Bleecker Street Pastry, 245 Bleeker St, New York, NY 10014, 212/242-4959. Daily 7 am-10 pm.

Most Romantic Spot for After-Theater Champagne and Caviar

Petrossian

Of course, the name tells you that this is the spot to go for Russian caviars—beluga, osetra, and sevruga are the royal names, with regal prices to match. They are served with toast and butter. Pressed caviar is served with blini and crème fraîche. A perfect accompaniment is chilled vodka, served in a slim tall glass, and available in such flavors as lemon, honey, and pepper. Or you may opt for an elegant flute of champagne. The handsome marble bar is flanked by mirrors with etched art deco nudes. The dining room is dark, with tables dressed with fresh lilies, starchy white napery, and flickering triangular candles. There are bronze figurines in the window and even the retail counter in the foyer, stacked with jars of precious comestibles, is somehow elegant with sheared apricot drapes. North Atlantic smoked salmon, a delicacy introduced by the Petrossian family in Paris in the 1920s, is a worthy late supper item, as is Petrossian's renowned foie gras. Other tempting selections include smoked trout omelettes and smoked *cod roe* Napoleon with fresh tarragon.

Petrossian, 182 W 58th St, New York, NY 10019, 212/245-2217. Mon-Sat 11:30 am-1 am.

Most Romantic Spot to Be Seen Having Champagne and Caviar

The Russian Tea Room

Splurge on a leisurely luncheon at this famous restaurant where entertainment celebs and other movers and shakers occupy assigned booths. While you're in the mood to impress, point out that it was the center booth where Dustin Hoffman and Sidney Pollack played out that hilarious scene in the movie *Tootsie.* Outside, look for a landmark red silk banner and red awning. Inside, the decor is done in garish red and green with marble-topped counters, red leather banquettes, and gleaming samovars. Russian caviar—sevruga, osetra, beluga, and pressed—runs from about $40 to $65 an ounce and is served with blinis. Other appetizers include Nova Scotia and Irish smoked salmon, herring, and a medley of Russian hors d'oeuvres. Russian specialties include eggplant casserole au gratin baked in sour cream, Georgian lamb sausage, and Caucasian *shashlik*—marinated leg of spring lamb, broiled on a skewer with tomatoes, green pepper, and onion. If you're up for an egg dish, try a red caviar omelette with sour cream or scrambled eggs with smoked salmon. There's hot or cold borscht with sour cream and *pirojok* (meat-filled pastry)—peasant fare at Manhattan prices.

The Russian Tea Room, 150 W 57th St, New York, NY 10019, 212/265-0947. Mon-Fri 11:30 am-11:30 pm, Sat & Sun 11 am-11:30 pm.

Most Romantic Setting for Grandma's Recipe

Adrienne

Although executive chef Adam Odegard has studied and cooked around the world, it is his Dutch-Norwegian grandmother's recipe for hot banana walnut tart that is a dessert highlight at this signature restaurant in the grand Peninsula hotel. The elegant dining room, accented by Belle Époque sconces, exudes a romantic art nouveau ambience with soft-hued salmon-pink walls and thick, sculpted carpeting. The menu offers primarily contemporary European and American fare, with Asian and Middle Eastern influences. Applewood-smoked salmon with honey-mustard mascarpone is a Bavarian specialty from Munich, while ginger chicken with spicy mango relish owes its origins to Hong Kong. Roasted lamb chops with eggplant compote, parsley jus, and tabouleh salad are influenced by the chef's tenure in Jerusalem. Other dishes reflect Odegard's classical training in Paris and the cuisine of his Dutch homeland. The menu also features items that are particularly low in calories, sodium, and saturated fat.

Adrienne, The Peninsula, 700 Fifth Ave, New York, NY 10019, 212/247-2200. Daily noon-10 pm.

Best Spot for a Spot of Tea and Star Spotting

Mark's

Madonna has been known to take afternoon tea at this dining room in the beautifully refurbished art deco Mark hotel. So have other pop stars and a goodly number of art dealers and CEOs. Certainly, the tiered dining room is a tranquil, romantic spot, with a faux skylight illuminating richly paneled walls decorated with classical prints and gold-framed mirrors. Darjeeling or Earl Grey in a china cup is at the heart of this multicultural ritual: teas from the Orient, style from the British, and the comfortable ease of American manners (tea-takers dress in blue jeans as well as designer outfits and business attire). A selection of international teas are served with homemade raisin scones with mascarpone and fruit preserves, delicate tea sandwiches, and miniature pastries. Teas are served on butler trays with silver tea strainers and Villeroy & Boch china. Mark's also stocks herbal teas and increasingly popular fruit teas—mango, passion fruit, blackcurrant, peach, and vanilla.

Mark's, The Mark, 25 E 77th St, New York, NY 10021, 212/879-1864. Daily 2:30-5:30 pm.

Proudest Spot for Afternoon Tea (or Vodka)

Waldorf-Astoria Lobby/Peacock Alley

Afternoon tea has been a tradition at The Waldorf-Astoria since the 1890s, when The Waldorf, then at the present site of the Empire State Building, set aside an entire room solely to tea service. Today, the tradition continues in Peacock Alley, the hotel's stylish restaurant that extends into the famous lobby, one of New York's most fashionable people-watching spots. Between 2:30 p.m. and 5:30 p.m. a classical harpist provides background music as delicate china is set out and patrons ponder a selection of teas that include traditional favorites such

as Earl Grey, Darjeeling, and Keemun English breakfast tea, as well as specialty blends such as black
currant, peppermint, and cinnamon-orange spiced
tea. A tempting selection of finger sandwiches is
served on three-tiered plates, along with an assortment of miniature pastries, napoleons, cream puffs,
fruit tarts, and the kitchen's memorable macaroons.
Traditionalists enjoy scones served with Devonshire
cream and preserves. A newer tradition in Peacock
Alley is the serving of Petrossian caviar (with blinis
or toast points and crème fraîche) accompanied by
champagne or chilled vodka, plain or flavored.

Lobby/Peacock Alley, The Waldorf-Astoria, 301 Park
Ave, New York, NY 10022, 212/355-3000. Tea daily
2:30-5:30 pm.

Most Romantic Spot for a Spot of Tea After Shopping

Rotunda at The Pierre

For couples who enjoy shopping together, or for
assignations after solo shopping expeditions, this
choice for afternoon tea is conveniently close to the
shops of Fifth Avenue. The Pierre, an elegant landmark hotel that dates back to 1930, celebrates traditional afternoon tea daily between 3:00 p.m. and
5:30 p.m. It is served in the classic Rotunda, where
love-seats, tables, and chairs are arranged in small,
private clusters. Providing an old-world setting for
this European custom, the Rotunda has a white
marble staircase, domed ceiling, floor-to-ceiling
murals, and ornate light fixtures. Afternoon tea
includes the choice from a variety of fine teas, finger
sandwiches, scones, and assorted pastries, all presented on delicate three-tier trays and fine china.

The Pierre, Fifth Ave at 61 St, New York, NY 10021,
212/838-8000.

Most Romantic Carriage Rides

Horse-and-Carriage Rides

Although those so inclined now can take a romantic
ride in a hansom cab in many of America's major
cities, there is something especially romantic about
an evening jaunt through Central Park. With a top-
hatted livery at the reins on his or her elevated seat,
the well-trained horse clip-clops through the quiet
thoroughfares of the park. The greenery is cloaked
in mysterious dark shadows and the illuminated
Manhattan skyline provides a romantic backdrop,
sometimes with stars twinkling overhead. Pick up a

carriage at Grand Army Plaza in front of the Plaza Hotel (at West 59th Street and Fifth Avenue) and adjacent to the southeast corner of the park—or arrange to have one pick you up after a romantic dinner at Tavern on the Green (see separate listing). Costs runs to around $15 to $20 for the first 20 minutes, $5 for every additional 15 minutes—plus tip. Carriages are available both in open and glass-enclosed versions, depending on the season—although, even in winter (and depending upon one's companion), it can be fun to snuggle close under a blanket.

Carriage Rides, Grand Army Plaza (W 59th St and Fifth Ave), New York, NY 10019.

Most Romantic Stroll

The Promenade, Brooklyn Heights

Poised atop a bluff that slopes down to the water's edge, the Promenade is one of the most romantic spots for strolling. There are iron lamps, stretches of greenery, and benches where you'll find people with brown bags of croissants, bagels, and coffee leisurely reading the Sunday *Times* or simply enjoying the cityscape. This dramatic vista of the spidery latticework and Gothic towers of the Brooklyn bridge and the lower Manhattan skyline across the river attracts crews filming television commercials and such movies as *Annie Hall* and the romantic *Moonstruck*. Built in the 1950s above the Brooklyn-Queens Expressway, this scenic lookout offers an impeccable view of the Statue of Liberty. On a clear day, it is possible to see as far as the distant Verrazano Narrows Bridge (the longest suspension bridge in the country). At occasional craft festivals held on the Promenade, you can buy art and pottery and watch chairs being caned at a booth beside a stone marking George Washington's headquarters. In 1776 during the Continental Army's long retreat, Washington led his men under the cover of fog and darkness to safety in Manhattan, a Dunkirk-like evacuation that spared the Army. For a romantic drink, dinner or perhaps Sunday brunch, head for the elegant River Café (see separate listing), offering superb (and pricey) cuisine on a former barge anchored at the foot of Brooklyn Bridge.

Information from: The Fund For The Borough of Brooklyn, Inc, 16 Court St, Brooklyn, NY 11201, 718/643-3480.

Best Gondola Ride West of Venice
Central Park Boathouse

"This is the most romantic thing you can do in Manhattan," said the young man at the Central Park Boathouse making arrangements for a gondola ride around the park's 22-acre lake. One had to believe he knew of what he spoke. He was planning to use the occasion to propose marriage. The authentic Venetian gondola, imported from Italy, holds up to six persons and is propelled around the lake by a gondolier clad in traditional Venetian garb. To complete the occasion, arrangements can be made for food and beverages to be served during the outing, from box lunches to a three-course meal accompanied by champagne. As might be expected, using a gondola ride as the setting for a marriage proposal is not an original idea—albeit a romantic one. "A lot of our business comes from guys planning to propose marriage," said the gondolier, who gets plenty of practice at being discreet. The gondola may be rented by private parties outside of normal operating hours at the rate of $150 an hour. The Boathouse Café is a pleasant spot with an outdoor terrace and soothing views of the lake.

Central Park Boathouse, 74th St at East Dr, New York, NY 10021, 212/517-4723. Jun 1-Sep 30 (depending upon weather), daily 6-10 pm, $35/half hour.

Best Roses and Posies
Twigs

When love is in bloom, head for this old-world florist to find every blooming thing. Whether it is a simple bouquet of long-stemmed roses, a posy of delicate wildflowers, exotic orchids, or a special centerpiece for a candlelight dinner, this shop rises to the occasion. With a mélange of colors and perfumed air, this Greenwich Village florist is reminiscent of an English country garden (and, indeed, some of its stock is imported from England and elsewhere in Europe). Choose from more than a score of different varieties of roses, as well as violets, daisies, and popular seasonal blooms, such as tulips, daffodils, and gladiolus—all awaiting the creative talents of florists who fashion them into imaginative bouquets and arrangements. Along with this array of cut flowers, are potted plants, pretty hanging baskets, miniature topiary, and innovative container plantings. Twigs specializes in creating artistic custom arrangements for parties and other occasions. Uptown from this pretty shop, in neighboring Chelsea, a whole world of flowers awaits early risers interested in wandering the wholesale flower district (see separate listing).

Twigs, 381 Bleecker St, New York, NY 10014, 212/620-8188. Mon-Fri 9 am-6 pm, Sat 10 am-5 pm.

Most Roses and Poses
Flower District

Head at first light for a four-block area of Chelsea and you not only can buy the freshest flowers in the city, but you also might see your florist there buying fresh flowers. Although the dozens of dealers head-quartered here are primarily interested in the whole-sale trade, they will sell to individual customers who usually can expect lower prices than they will find at retail florists. Shop, too, for plants to brighten window boxes, a wide variety of house plants, and other greenery, as well as seeds, shrubs, and dried flowers. In addition to being an excellent spot to select fresh cut flowers and potted plants for some-one special, this area off Sixth Avenue (between West 26th and 29th streets) also is a bright, colorful spot, with water glistening on blooms and leaves like morning dew—set amid a drab, weary neighbor-hood—for an early morning stroll with someone special, perhaps before breakfast for two in a Village café. *Historical note:* The stretch of West 28th Street between Broadway and Fifth Avenue once was Tin Pan Alley, the world-famous center of the music-publishing industry.

Flower District, Sixth Ave between W 26th and 29th sts, New York, New York, NY 10001.

Best Place to Shop to Your Heart's Content
Only Hearts

This is a shop where it is always Valentine's Day. It calls itself "the shop for the shameless romantic" and, in keeping with its name, stocks only heart-shaped merchandise, items decorated with hearts, and books about hearts. Its cupid-inspired inventory includes everything from cards, party favors, and heart-shaped collectibles, to diaphanous lingerie, hand-painted underwear, sportswear, and even fly swatters shaped like you know what. The inventory of this West Side specialty shop also includes heart-shaped laundry baskets, picnic hampers, hole punches, waffle irons, ice-cube trays, and bird cages.

Prices range from 25 cents for a heart-shaped balloon to more than $1,000 for a piece of heart-themed jewelry. There is, not unexpectedly, a California branch (in Santa Monica), although this West Side store, which has been on Columbus Avenue for more than 15 years, attracts a large following of celebrity customers. These include Dustin Hoffman, Cher, Madonna, Robert DeNiro, Sean Penn, Olivia Newton-John, and Bruce Springsteen.

Only Hearts, 386 Columbus Ave, New York, NY 10024, 212/724-5608. Mon-Sat 11 am-8 pm, Sun noon-7 pm.

Top Shop for Tantalizing Trousseaus

La Lingerie

For that sexy-but-sophisticated look, this shop carries the finest intimate apparel, much of it imported from Europe, some of it hand-embroidered, and most of it high-priced. Dried flowers and baskets of potpourri help create a boudoir setting at this discreet lingerie store. From captivating peignoirs and slinky teddies, to comfortable cotton nightdresses and silky pajamas, La Lingerie offers an array of nightclothes and underthings created from the finest silk, satin, lace, cotton, and chiffon. Brides-to-be can register here for a whole trousseau of tantalizing lingerie and nightwear. The inventory of this indulgent shop also includes lacy bras and bodices, sheer silk slips, gowns, robes, silk stockings, and garter belts, plus a small selection of fleecy slippers, glamorous mules, lovely lingerie cases, silk-covered hangers, and other accessories, as well as bright bikinis, cover-ups, and other beachwear.

La Lingerie, 792 Madison Ave, New York, NY 10021, 212/772-9797. Mon-Sat 11 am-7 pm.

PARKS & GARDENS

Last Native Forest (and Best Wild Berries)

Inwood Hill Park

At the northern tip of Manhattan are the borough's last native forests. In a city crushed for living and working space, this park offers more than 100 acres of lush woodlands and forest. Among 100-year-old native trees are red oaks and enormous tulip trees measuring 25 feet around and towering 90 feet above the forest floor. Carpeting the woods and meadows of this 197-acre park are such wildflowers as day lilies, butterfly weed, and Jack-in-the-pulpit; lining paths at the park's high northwestern sector are blackberry, raspberry, and black currant bushes. In spring and fall the woods are alive with warblers migrating along the Atlantic flyway; September is the month to spot broadwing hawks circling the Hudson. A high ridge along the park's western perimeter provides spectacular views of the Hudson—west to the Palisades, south to the George Washington bridge, and north as far as the Tappan Zee bridge. At a saltwater marsh, refuge for a rich variety of waterfowl, it is possible to spot a great blue heron standing motionless as it fishes, and a snowy egret ruffling its elegant plumage against a warm spring breeze. Adjoining this rugged park is historic Fort Tryon Park and the art and architecture of the Cloisters (see separate listings).

Inwood Hill Park, Upper Manhattan Heights, Manhattan Department of Parks, 16 W 61st St, New York, NY 10023, 212/408-0100.

Best (and Most Convenient) Wilderness Area

Palisades Interstate Park System

In the Hudson Highlands, just 45 miles from New York City, bobcats prowl and hawks soar overhead. Wildlife is plentiful and more than 240 species of birds inhabit the wilderness trails that stretch atop the towering Palisades, north of the George Washington Bridge. These trails are part of a park system that encompasses 80,000 acres and includes a pair of state parks, Bear Mountain and Harriman. Hikers and campers choose the latter, for its wilder country, still lakes, the campsites around Lake Welch, and rustic cabins for rent at Sebago Beach. Bear Mountain State Park is more developed, offering a large playing field, picnic groves, rowboat and pedal-boat rentals, a swimming pool, bathhouse with lockers, and nature trails. It is the site of many annual festivals, including Festa Italiana (spring), Country Music Festival (summer), and Oktoberfest. Open year-round, the park has an active winter program of ski jumping, sledding, ice skating, Christmas festivals, craft shows, and winter carnivals. Stay overnight at picturesque Bear Mountain Inn, a stone-and-timber lodge built in 1914, set among the woods beside Hessian Lake. It is a perfect getaway spot with cheery fireplaces and dining on basic American fare (don't miss the apple cobbler!). Accommodations are in the main inn and in secluded stone lodges across the lake.

Palisades Interstate Park Commission, Bear Mountain, NY 10911, 914/786-2701. Bear Mountain Inn, 914/786-2731.

Best Bet for Birding

Jamaica Bay Wildlife Refuge

Osprey and hawks circle over a wilderness rich with flora—wildflowers and brambles, yucca, bayberry, and cattails. A flourishing wildlife population includes muscrats, salamanders, rabbits, squirrels, snakes, chipmunks, turtles, frogs, bats, bees, and butterflies. They inhabit more than 9,000 acres of a pristine preserve that includes upland fields and woods, saltwater marshes, several ponds, and an open expanse of bay and islands. The surprise is that this wilderness all is contained within the city limits of New York, barely a dozen miles from the stone-and-steel canyons of Manhattan. Administered by the National Park Service, it is one of the country's notable urban wildlife refuges and part of the Gateway National Recreation Area, which includes other areas of Brooklyn and nearby New Jersey. In spring and fall, thousands of birds migrating along the Atlantic Flyway stop here. Among more than 325 species that have been recorded are herons, egrets, and ibises. There are self-guided nature trails and ranger-led hikes, as well as programs such as craft and photography workshops, astronomy lectures, and "moon prowls."

Jamaica Bay Wildlife Refuge, Gateway National Recreation Area, Floyd Bennett Field, Brooklyn, NY 11234, 718/474-0613.

Best Plantings for All Seasons

Planting Fields Arboretum

In the dead of winter, greenhouses are filled with sweet-scented orchids, cactus, bougainvillaea, poinsettias, and a noted camellia collection. In spring, they're abloom with perennials and Easter lilies, followed by summer annuals and fall chrysanthemums. When the outdoor gardens awaken from their winter slumber, the 409-acre arboretum offers a spectacular display of trees and shrubs, with sweeping lawns planted with beech, linden, cedar, fir, elm, tulip, oak, and maple. There are showy beds of daffodils, and one of the finest rhododendron and azalea collections in the East. Mature groupings of hollies and recent extensive planting of magnolias help round out the collection. Enter this beautiful preserve through the magnificent Carshalton Gates, fashioned from hand-wrought iron and dating from 1712, and include a stop at Coe Hall. This 65-room, Tudor-Revival mansion, completed in 1921, is an integral part of this Gold Coast-era estate. It is exquisitely furnished and features outstanding craftsmanship in its hand-carved chimneys, dressed stonework, and symbolic carvings. The Hay Barn has been converted to a multi-purpose, air-conditioned function hall for concerts, theater, arts and crafts exhibits, and flower shows. This truly is a wonderful destination for an outing on Long Island.

Planting Fields Arboretum, P.O. Box 58, Oyster Bay, NY 11771, 516/922-9201. Mid-Apr–Oct 10 am-5 pm, Nov–mid-Apr 10 am-4:30 pm. Adults $1.50 (separate admission to Coe Hall).

Best Blooming Things
Steinhardt Conservatory

This $25-million, state-of-the art conservatory is a recent addition to the venerable Brooklyn Botanic Garden, which has been providing a rich natural oasis for Brooklynites since 1910. Three major pavilions re-create the environments of three different climate zones. In the arid climate pavilion, visitors are transported to the Sonoran Desert with its giant saguaros and other cacti and succulents. The tropics pavilion is organized according to fragrances and the use of tropical flora as food and medicine, and in industry. The pavilion focusing on the warm temperate regions has a fern grotto and a limestone cave. A bonsai museum with exhibits drawn from the garden's renowned large collection showcases the lilliputian world of bonsai gardening, and an aquatic house features two pools and an exquisite orchid collection. The Trail of Evolution shuttles visitors back 200 million years as it traces the history of plants from the Precambrian era to the present. It focuses on their adaptability to harsh environments where they are baked by sun, blown by winds, soaked by rains, and submerged in water.

Steinhardt Conservatory, 1000 Washington Ave, Brooklyn, NY 11225, 718/622-4443. Apr-Sept, Tue-Sun 10 am-5 pm; Oct-Mar, Tue-Sun 10 am-4 pm. Adults $2, seniors & children 3-12 $1.

Most Bully Garden
Wave Hill

Teddy Roosevelt once was a resident of the well-preserved Georgian mansion that sits on an expansive Hudson River estate, providing the Bronx with a splendid oasis of scenery and culture. Other former illustrious occupants of the house, built in 1843, once owned by financier George W. Perkins, and presented to the city in 1965, included Mark Twain and Arturo Toscanini. Today, with woodland nature trails, sweeping lawns, well-tended formal gardens, and greenhouses, the 28-acre estate provides nature lovers with a wonderful treat. A wide range of labeled flora includes hemlock, beeches, elms, and maples, overhanging wisteria, a rose garden, an herb garden, and collections of cacti and tropical and aquatic plants. Wave Hill offers a varied program of chamber-music concerts, traveling art exhibits, workshops, lectures, nature programs, and a chance to listen to rare recordings of Toscanini. This delightful botanical gardens hosts many events that are ideal for family outings, such as demonstrations of tapping maple trees to collect syrup.

Wave Hill, 675 W 252nd St, Bronx, NY 10471, 212/549-2005. Wed-Sun 10 am-4:30 pm. Adults $4, seniors & students $2.

Palms, Concerts, and All That Jazz
Winter Garden/World Financial Center

As its name suggests, this garden offers *indoor* greenery—principally provided by 16 tall palm trees with sea-foam green metal benches at their bases. Part of the World Financial Center, this atrium has a barrel-vaulted ceiling and sleek marble floors, walls, and stairs, creating a European-style piazza furnished with wooden café tables and bamboo chairs. Four galleries of shops and restaurants angle off the main piazza. In the courtyard, The Winter Garden Café is a nice spot for brunch, with vegetable and seafood antipasti bars set out on red-checkered table cloths. A small, but balanced Italian menu includes Tuscan white bean soup, thin-crust pizza, frittatas, pasta, and creative sandwiches, such as chicken pesto club with smoked bacon and basil mayonnaise. Outside, an immaculately landscaped park fronts the Hudson River, providing boat slips and a plaza that is the site of events such as SummerFair, with sidewalk sales and entertainment by jugglers, magicians, mimes, a Dixieland band, and a barbershop quartet. Free concerts (including appearances by such notables as the Preservation Hall Jazz Band) are held year-round (see separate listing). A suprawide corridor connects with the World Trade Center complex and the New York Vista hotel (see separate listing).

Winter Garden/World Financial Center, 200 Liberty St, New York, NY 10281, 212/945-0505.

Best Spot to Start Exploring Greenwich Village
Washington Square Park

The history of this park is almost as intricate and interesting as that of its surrounding neighborhood. This was originally worthless swampland, was made into a "potter's field" (a cemetery of unmarked graves for the poor or unknown), and even served as the site of public hangings until it became a park in 1828. It really began booming in 1889, when a wooden arch was dedicated to mark the centennial of George Washington's inauguration. This temporary structure proved so popular that it was rebuilt in marble a few years later. Today this American "Arc de Triomphe" is the center of this pleasant—if, at times, a little funky—park. Here you'll find joggers, dog-walkers, skateboarders, mimes, musicians, artists and artisans, peddlers, bored-looking punkers just loafing around, and, unfortunately, the occasional shady figure. However, this last situation has been improving (a young friend recalls a not-too-distant time when he couldn't go 10 yards at a time here without being offered some sort of illegal substance), and the park is definitely considered safe—it often attracts sizable crowds very late on hot summer nights. *Note:* Be sure to check out Macdougal Alley and Washington Mews (the same small street, east and west, respectively, off Fifth Avenue), a half-block north of the park; these narrow streets offer charming little houses and workshops that were converted from stables, outbuildings, and garages of the swanky town homes on and around the park.

Washington Square Park, Fifth Ave at Waverly Pl/ Washington Square N, New York, NY 10012.

Best Park at the Top of Manhattan

Fort Tryon Park

Not quite at the northern tip of Manhattan, this 62-acre park was landscaped by Frederick Law Olmsted on land donated to the city by the Rockefeller family. Well known as the home of the Cloisters (see separate listing), a branch of the Metropolitan Museum of Art that blends medieval architecture and art and provides an appropriate background of medieval music, the park is a destination in its own right. Its attractions include a splendid flower garden, an herb garden with species dating back to the Middle Ages, and rolling wooded hills overlooking the Hudson. Enjoy strolling the park's terraces and climbing to its hilltop for nonpareil views of the wooded bluffs of the New Jersey Palisades. Atop the hill, visitors can inspect the remains of Fort Washington, dating back to the Revolutionary War. The fort was captured by the British toward the end of 1776. These steep, leafy hills provide a challenge for joggers. Adjoining this park is Inwood Hill Park (see separate listing), with dense, rugged woods and a put-in place paddlers launch kayaks for trips down the Hudson alongside natural rock outcropping. This also is a spot to experience a stretch of primitive shoreline, with marsh and woodland vegetation that is surprisingly close to the heart of the city.

Fort Tryon Park, Upper Manhattan Heights, Manhattan Department of Parks, 16 W 61st St, New York, NY 10023, 212/408-0100.

Best Park at the Bottom of Manhattan

Battery Park

These days, this breezy oasis of greenery along the Hudson at the foot of Manhattan lies in the shadow of the towering high-rise office buildings and condos that are part of a major development spurt. Named after the battery of cannons originally placed along the shoreline, the 22-acre, water's-edge park offers lawns, sculpture, cherry trees that blossom in spring, and the chance to view Castle Clinton, one of five remaining harbor fortifications. Built of red sandstone in 1812 to defend New York from attack by the British, the castle later served as a concert hall (where "Swedish Nightingale" Jenny Lind sang) and then as a depot through which eight million immigrants entered America (as the forerunner to Ellis Island). Another landmark adjacent to the park is one of the original subway-station entrances, built in 1904. Today, souvenir, T-shirt, and snack vendors and street musicians ply tourists journeying to Ellis Island, the Statue of Liberty, and on the Staten Island ferry. The park's tree-shaded esplanade offers good views of these famous harbor sights. In summer, the park is the venue for lunchtime concerts, folk dancing, and occasional festivals.

Battery Park, Lower Manhattan, Manhattan Department of Parks, 16 W 61st St, New York, NY 10023, 212/408-0100.

Largest Park

The Greenbelt

New York City's largest park is *not* Central Park— it is this 2,500-acre nature preserve in the center of Staten Island. With its freshwater and tidal wetlands, upland woods, and open fields, it provides a setting to enjoy and learn about nature without traveling far from the city. Special programs include hiking, cross-country skiing, bird watching, and environmental science. Among the areas linked by The Greenbelt are High Rock Park, with glacial ponds, freshwater swamp, deciduous hardwood forest, three gardens, and six walking trails; William T. Davis

Wildlife Refuge, an ideal spot to observe migrating birds; and Reed's Basket Willow Swamp (named for the purple willow trees once raised by the Reed family for weaving baskets), threaded by streams and abundant with flowering shrubs and wildflowers. In spring, enjoy carpets of wildflowers—yellow-flowering spicebush, white-flowering shadbush, and fragrant pinxter and swamp white azalea. In summer, shaded woodlands, their floors blanketed with ferns, offer cool respite from the heat. Fall paints the hardwoods with showy autumnal hues and brings a bounty of fruit and nuts that attracts migrating birds. In winter, hikers and cross-country skiers watch for tracks in the snow and for woodpeckers and chickadees. Maps and brochures are available.

The Greenbelt, 200 Nevada Ave, Staten Island, NY 10306, 718/667-2165.

Best Long, Skinny Park

Riverside Park

Paralleling three miles of Hudson River shoreline, stretching north from West 72nd Street toward the George Washington Bridge, this long, skinny park offers fine views of river traffic and of the distant Palisades bluffs in New Jersey. Its esplanade is a popular spot for strolling and also a favored route of joggers—remember *Marathon Man* with Dustin Hoffman and Laurence Olivier?—popular year-round, even in winter when bone-chilling winds whip off the Hudson. Vaux and Olmsted, architects of Central Park, also had a hand in creating this Upper West Side sliver of greensward. It offers public tennis courts (10 clay and 10 hard courts), baseball diamonds, and a number of statues, including the turn-of-the-century Soldiers' and Sailors' Monument at 89th Street, which replicates an original in Athens. There is a marina and yacht basin (at West 79th Street) where sailboats can tie up while their crews visit an art fair in the park or enjoy a free play (including performances of Shakespeare) or concert at the rotunda.

Riverside Park, Upper West Side, Manhattan Department of Parks, 16 W 61st St, New York, NY 10023, 212/408-0100.

Manhattan's Top Park

Central Park

Central Park, created in 1858 out of swampland by landscaper Frederick Law Olmsted and architect

Calvert Vaux, is a wonderful swathe of urban green-sward to use and enjoy. This miracle in the middle of Manhattan comprises 843 acres of open mead-ows, rolling woodlands, picturesque lakes and streams, and formal gardens, with 25 ballfields, 22 playgrounds, 30 tennis courts, and a wealth of sculpture and architecture. Anyone who has not recently ventured into the park and remembers its ragged, neglected appearance, may be surprised at the results of numerous restoration projects. In recent years, the Central Park Conservancy and the Parks Department have made a concerted effort to spruce up the old park. It remains a wonderful resource in which to enjoy a variety of activities ranging from running, skating, and boating, to chess, horseshoe pitching, kite flying, and simply strolling among the greenery on 58 miles of paths. (It also is prudent to heed warnings to avoid becoming a crime target by vacating the park before sundown and staying away from remote areas.) The park provides a wide range of family programs, offers specialized summer camps, and has zoos, playgrounds, a pup-pet theater, and a wonderful antique carousel to delight children. Free entertainment ranges from performances by the New York Philharmonic and Metropolitan Opera company to concerts featuring reggae and Brazilian jazz. There also is a delightful annual Shakespeare festival. For a nice overview, hop a trolley for an hour-and-a-half guided tour of the park and surrounding city that also allows riders to disembark to explore some of the park's major features, including Strawberry Fields (weekdays from Grand Army Plaza, Fifth Avenue at 60th Street, at 10:30 a.m., 1 p.m., 3 p.m.; 212/360-2727). (Refer to the index for numerous separate listings relating to events and activities in Central Park.)

Central Park Conservancy, 830 Fifth Ave, New York, NY 10021, 212/988-8826.

Best *Other* Park by Olmsted and Vaux

Prospect Park

About two-thirds the size of Central Park, this 526-acre Brooklyn park is endowed with many of the same characteristics: woodlands, meadows, hills, a large lake with a boathouse, brooks, streams, ter-races, landscaped pathways, playing fields, tennis courts, a skating rink, carousel, zoo, and a wide range of interpretive programs, participant sports, and concerts. It also was designed by Olmsted and Vaux, architects of the famous Manhattan park and now is undergoing long-term renewal. Within the park is a relocated 18th-century Dutch farmhouse that is a museum containing period furnishings, and a Quaker cemetery (in which actor Montgomery Clift is buried), tours of which are conducted by the Urban Park Rangers (see separate listing). The rangers, extremely active in this park, also offer fun seasonal events such as "April Fool's Nature Trivia" and—displaying a penchant for alliteration—tours dubbed "Woodland Warbler Watch" and "Ponder a Prospect Pond." On a more serious note is a series of workshops called P.O.W.E.R. (Protecting Our Woodlands and Environmental Resources). In the picnic house, ongoing activities include ballroom dancing, early-morning aerobics, yoga, and t'ai chi. At the entrance to the park is Grand Army Plaza, memorializing the Union Civil War victory and now incorporating a memorial to John F. Kennedy. Adjacent to the park are two other wonderful Brooklyn attractions: the Brooklyn Museum and the Brooklyn Botanic Garden (see separate listings).

Prospect Park, Brooklyn, NY 11215, 718/965-8900.

Best Little-Known Gem in Central Park

Conservatory Garden

Contrasting with the somewhat rugged landscape of Central Park, and not far from the noise and chaos of the city, is an island of well-ordered beauty and tranquility. Tucked away near the northeast boundary of the park are the exquisite formal gardens of the Conservatory, replete with bubbling fountains, flowering trees, and yew hedgerows. While each season brings its particular beauty, spring is the time when the crabapple allées flanking the center lawn are crowned with clouds of pink and white blossoms, as narcissus peek through the ivy, and songbirds seem to be in full throat. Highlights of this six-acre garden include half-century-old wisteria clinging to the delicate ironwork of a pergola; the Secret Garden with its reflecting pool with the bronze statues of two children, Mary and Dickon, from *The Secret Garden*, a children's classic by Frances Hodgson Burnett; the classical French-style North Garden, with its bronze fountain—a garden that puts on a dazzling springtime display of 20,000 colorful tulips, and a fall show of 5,000 chrysanthemums; and the Woodland Slope, planted with more than 500 ferns and 1,500 wildflowers, including bluebells, forget-me-nots, May apples, and geraniums. Separating the garden from the rest of the park are wrought-iron fences with stylized gates made in Paris in 1894 for the former Vanderbilt mansion. The garden, which opened in 1937, takes its name from a complex of huge greenhouses built on this site in 1899.

Conservatory Garden, Central Park, Fifth Ave at E 105 St, New York, NY 10029, 212/397-3156. 8 am-dusk.

Best Place to Give Peace a Chance

Strawberry Fields

When transplanted Liverpudlian, the late John Lennon, lived in New York, he and wife Yoko Ono enjoyed a quiet oasis in Central Park. Now restored and maintained through a gift and endowment in the name of international peace from Yoko Ono Lennon, this lovely 2.5-acre, tear-shaped garden is named after the Beatle's song, *Strawberry Fields Forever.* It provides a quiet refuge among clusters of trees, rock outcroppings, and gently sloping meadows. Flora on display include graceful American elm; ginkgo, a tree saved from extinction by Chinese monks; leathery-leaved turkey oak; distinctive white birch with its papery bark; and mulberry, larch, horsechestnut, black cherry, and dogwood. In springtime, rhododendron present their spectacular pale-pink floral display; during summer there are clusters of fragrant white blooms of the sweet pepper bush; in fall, birds are attracted to the crop of yellow berries of the Russian olive tree; winter brings the berries of holly bushes to brighten the landscape. To learn more about this garden's many outstanding specimen trees, shrubs, and herbaceous plants, pick up a brochure, "A Walk in Strawberry Fields," for a self-guided tour that begins and ends near Central Park's Women's Gate at Central Park West and West 72nd Street. (Also near this location is a starburst marble mosaic impressed with the single word, *Imagine*, also a title of a John Lennon song.)

Strawberry Fields, Central Park, Central Park West at W 72nd St, New York, NY 10029, 212/397-3156. 8 am-dusk.

Dandiest Former Dairy in the Park

The Dairy

This restored Gothic building, circa 1870, decorated with excesses of Victorian gingerbread, once was a working dairy, complete with cows and milkmaids. It was designed to introduce city folk to the basics of dairy farming and to provide fresh milk for nursing mothers. The animals and their keepers have

long since gone and the building, restored and
spruced up with paint, serves as the Central Park
Visitor Center. This is where you can pick up brochures and a map and obtain park information via
a touch-screen computer featuring seven videotaped
tours of the park. Permanent exhibits include a 12-
foot-long scale model of the park and an interactive
exhibit about the park's history and design. On
Saturday afternoons there are fun family programs,
such as a workshop where participants use paper,
springs, electrical parts, and a 9-volt battery to create
a sculpture that lights up. Many of the tours led by
the Urban Park Rangers (see separate listing) start
here. The Dairy has a small gift shop.

The Dairy, Central Park, 65th St at mid-park, New
York, NY 10024, 212/794-6564. Tue-Thu, Sat & Sun 11
am-5 pm, Fri l-5 pm.

Best Urban Hiking
Urban Park Rangers

Take a hike, make a kite, watch a hawk, tour on a
bike. To help New Yorkers and visitors get the most
from the many splendid parks in metropolitan New
York, the Urban Park Rangers offer free interpretive
tours and workshops. This uniformed force of park
educators, created in 1979, also patrol parks, providing information, first aid, and a measure of safety.
Knowledgeable guides introduce the public to such
simple pleasures as the serene beauty of a landscape
blanketed in snow and a mother duck guiding her
eager young across a lake—and they relate the weird
and wonderful legends surrounding New York's
parks. Year-round weekend programs cover a wide
range of topics, including astronomy, park and
neighborhood history, urban wildlife, bird-watching,
and nature photography. Participants learn to make
naturalist gifts, discover edible fruit, and join such
specialized tours as a Halloween walk and a tour of
Columbus Park in Chinatown with a commentary in
Chinese. Youngsters ages 8 to 13 learn to identify
trees and plants, use maps and compasses, and
explore and maintain nature trails when they join
the Junior Ranger Naturalist Program (and earn T-
shirt, cap, and ID card).

Urban Rangers (Department of Parks and
Recreation): Manhattan 212/397-3080 (Central
Park), 212/304-3629 (Inwood Hill Park); Bronx 212/
548-7070 (Van Cortlandt Park); Brooklyn 718/287-
3400 (Prospect Park); Queens 718/699-4204
(Flushing Meadows Corona Park); Staten Island
718/816-5456 (Cromwell Recreation Center).

Best Walk to Pine Over

Arthur Ross Pinetum, Central Park

When all of the leaves have fallen and the hardwoods are stark and bare, Central Park's Pinetum provides a pleasant oasis of greenery. This large collection of pine trees from across the world includes such varieties as Austrian, Himalayan, white, mugo, and umbrella pines. A walk through this area is a fun—and educational—outing for parents to take with children. A nicely illustrated booklet that describes a children's walking tour is obtainable from the Central Park Conservancy. It explains how pine trees date back to the time of the dinosaurs and discusses the function of pine needles; the use of pine pitch to make turpentine, floor wax, and a Greek wine; how the tallest and straightest white pines were reserved for masts of Royal Navy ships; and how to judge the age of a pine tree by counting layers of branches, among other things. Enter the park at 81st and Central Park West and begin your walk just north of the Stone Building, near lamppost No. 8033 (refer to booklet for maps and directions). Appropriately, the tour starts near Belvedere Castle (see separate listing), reminiscent of a European castle that typically might be surrounded by dense, dark forests of Austrian pine.

Arthur Ross Pinetum, Central Park, 81st St and Central Park W, New York, NY 10024, 212/794-6564.

Best State-of-the-Art Small Zoo

Central Park Zoo

With an equatorial rain forest (with indigenous primates, free-flying birds, and slithering snakes) and a polar ice cap populated by waddling penguins, this 5-1/2-acre zoo has been revitalized in the style of the new-breed zoos that emphasize environment and natural habitat and eliminate confining cages. With three separate climate zones (temperate, tropical, and polar circle), the zoo houses polar bears in a glass-enclosed pool and penguins in an arctic habitat with underwater viewing windows. There is a bat cave, an alligator swamp, and a simulated African jungle. Reopened in the late 1980s, this remodeled zoo—it is America's oldest, with some buildings that were Depression-era WPA projects—exhibits close to 450 animals of more than 100 species. But a tiny fraction of the size of the massive Bronx Zoo, it doesn't attempt to be an all-things-to-all-people zoo with obligatory lions, tigers, and elephants. Instead, it houses specialized collections that include seals, puffins, arctic foxes, tropical birds, Asian red pandas, Japanese snow monkeys, river otters, pythons, and a variety of other birds, reptiles, fish, and insects. The zoo, operated by the New York Zoological Society, has a gift gallery and cafeteria. (The society also maintains the nearby Central Park Children's Zoo, which is closed for major remodeling.)

Central Park Zoo, 64th St & Fifth Ave, New York, NY 10024, 212/861-6030. Mon-Fri 10 am-5 pm, weekends & holidays 11 am-5:30 pm. Adults $2.50, seniors $1.25, children 3-12 years $.50.

Last Private Park in New York City

Gramercy Park

This beautiful little park and surrounding historic neighborhood is the result of a 19th-century attempt at land development. In the 1830s, Samuel Ruggles laid out this area, setting aside a block for private parkland around the homes that he was constructing. (He also laid out and named both Lexington Avenue—for the Revolutionary battle—and Irving Place—for his friend, writer Washington Irving.) Ruggles was attempting to re-create the feel of a London neighborhood, and succeeded nicely. Only the residents of the surrounding streets have keys to the wrought-iron gates that guard this attractive park—but the historic, pleasant streets around the park are worth a stroll...and perhaps you can charm a keyholder into letting you inside the park. (A little-known way in is to stay in the Gramercy Park Hotel—see separate listing—on Lexington just across from the park; guests have key privileges.) *Trivia note:* If you *do* get into the park, you'll see the statue at the center of the park of 19th-century actor Edwin Booth (depicted performing his most famous role, Hamlet), who once lived in one of the town houses around the park; he was one of the finest American actors of his day, but, sadly, is better known as the brother of Abraham Lincoln's assassin.

Gramercy Park, Lexington Ave between E 21st & E 22nd sts, New York, NY 10010.

Best Park for Reading

Bryant Park

To the immediate west of the magnificent beaux arts building of the New York Public Library is a rectangle of formalized greenery that is a pleasant (and convenient) spot to relax outdoors with a book or ponder a chessboard. This is especially true now that a long-needed restoration program is installing new landscaping, lighting, and benches and, coincidentally, driving out drug dealers who had plagued this Midtown park. At noontime during the week, the park is a colorful mélange of flower, food, and book vendors as workers come to eat lunch, read, study, listen to concerts, and browse the occasional art fair. Historically, this was the site of a potter's field, of America's first World's Fair with its voguish Crystal Palace (built in 1853 and destroyed by fire five years later), and of a Civil War parade ground. The revitalized park was first redesigned during the Depression as the result of a competition for out-of-work architects. Within the park is a booth that sells half-price, same-day tickets for performances of music and dance throughout the city and outer boroughs (for availability call 212/382-2323). The park was named for newsman and poet, William Cullen Bryant, whose impetus led to the creation of Central Park.

Bryant Park, W 42nd St at Avenue of the Americas, Manhattan Department of Parks, 16 W 61st St, New York, NY 10023, 212/408-0100.

Most Varied Entertainment in the Park

Central Park Programs

To perhaps the majority of visitors (and a goodly number of residents), Central Park simply is urban parkland mostly used for walking, jogging, running—and (to some minds) mugging. This does not take into account the vast and varied programs (either free or low-cost) obtainable in the park, ranging from a chess camp where youngsters receive lessons and participate in supervised play to a family workshop that compares live park turtles to the celluloid ninja variety. Other family workshops, usually held at Belvedere Castle or the Dairy (see separate listings), involve such activities as building and launching toy boats, learning from a landscape architect how to design a park, and exploring light and shapes with the resident park "bubble master." There also are one-week specialty camps in swimming, tennis, adventure science and nature, and wall climbing. Folk-dancing enthusiasts meet on weekends (2 p.m.-dusk) at the King Jagiello statue, east of Turtle Pond at 79th Street. For pure entertainment, there are the free performances of SummerStage at the Rumsey Playfield and the New York Shakespeare Festival at the Delacort Theater (see separate listings), while the Great Lawn, close to the geographic center of the park, is the site of philharmonic concerts and performances by the Metropolitan Opera. There are exhibits about the park at the Dairy and exhibits of art and photography at the Arsenal Gallery. A wide-ranging program of walks and talks is conducted by the Urban Park Rangers (see separate listing).

Central Park Conservancy, 830 Fifth Ave, New York, NY 10021, 212/988-8826.

Best Trees That Grow in Brooklyn

Brooklyn Botanic Garden

No matter what the season, this 52-acre preserve that began in 1910 on city wasteland, provides an oasis of natural beauty. In spring, avenues of Japanese cherry trees explode with dazzling pink blossoms, while magnolias show off their massive fragrant blooms. Summer brings the red, white, yellow, pink, and orange blooms of numerous bushes in the Cranford Rose Garden. More than 6,000 species are represented, splashing color alongside walkways and climbing over arbors and trellises. In autumn, there are splendid, multicolored displays of chrysanthemums, while winter heralds snowdrops and witchhazels and crocuses nudging through the snow. Then come vast carpets of bright yellow daffodils as the seasonal cycle repeats itself. A Japanese garden is a tranquil spot with a shrine, pavilion, pines, stone lanterns, and a lake with graceful bridges reflecting in the water and stepping stones simulating wild geese in flight. Specialty displays include an herb garden, fragrance garden (also labeled in Braille), and a garden showcasing more than 100 plants mentioned by Shakespeare. There's a celebrity path with stones inscribed with the names of famous Brooklynites, such as Eli Wallach, Danny Kaye, and Mary Tyler Moore; a well-stocked gift shop; the attractive Terrace Café; the Discovery Center for children (see separate listing); and the new Steinhardt Conservatory (see separate listing).

Brooklyn Botanic Garden, 1000 Washington Ave, Brooklyn, NY 11225, 718/622-4433. Apr-Sep, Tue-Fri 8 am-6 pm; Sat & Sun 10 am-6 pm. Oct-Mar, Tue-Fri 8 am-4:30 pm; Sat & Sun 10 am-4:30 pm.

Best Autumn in New York

Central Park "Autumn Leaf Tour"

Not all of the spectacular fall foliage is in New England. In the heart of Manhattan you can find maples, beeches, oaks, and other dramatically colored trees on a self-guided "Autumn Leaf Tour" of Central Park. Pick up a brochure for a three-mile walk that introduces eight species that showcase the work of autumn's paintbox. Included are a pair of maples—the Schwedler maple, with dense maroon foliage, and the largest red maple in the park, sporting yellow, orange, and red leaves. The sweetgum, one of the park's least-seen varieties, has brilliant red-and-gold leaves as well as rarer hues—a delicate rose red and a bronze-like purple—and attracts 12 varieties of birds to feed on its winged seeds. Near the Great Lawn, a pair of silver lindens distinctive enough to have appeared on posters show off their fall yellows, while the pin oak, the park's most common tree, spreads a red, airy canopy. In a small meadow, a magnificent four-trunked tupelo dresses up with scarlet leaves and dark-blue fruit that is eaten by many birds (the tough wood of this tree was used in colonial times to make salt-water-carrying pipeline). The common bald cypress has a yellow-tapered crown, while a specimen of cutleaf beech (on Cherry Hill between the Daniel Webster statue and Bethesda Terrace) is part of the park's original planting and has changed color more than 125 times.

Central Park Conservancy, 830 Fifth Ave, New York, NY 10021, 212/988-8826.

SIGHTSEEING

Best Stroll with Literary Giants

Brooklyn Heights

Preserved since 1965 as the Brooklyn Heights Historical District, this stylish neighborhood of brownstones and tranquil, tree-lined streets has provided sanctuary for many of America's literary giants. Herman Melville, Walt Whitman, Arthur Miller, Thomas Wolfe, and Truman Capote all once lived and worked here. Novelist Norman Mailer still does. Hundreds of pre-Civil War buildings are preserved in what once was a bucolic area of orchards and pastures known as Clover Hill. Abraham Lincoln, Mark Twain, and Charles Dickens all attended the redbrick Plymouth Church that was a station in the Underground Railway. A wrought iron fence surrounds a pretty garden with a statue of abolitionist preacher Henry Ward Beecher who "sold" a slave in protest at the church. Included in the 30-block historic district is an 1824 clapboard house and St. Ann and the Holy Trinity church, which has the first stained glass windows made in the United States. The church offers an excellent performing arts program of theater, dance, and music. While in Brooklyn Heights, take a stroll along the Promenade for a stunning view of Manhattan across the river and stop for a drink or a meal at the River Café, housed on an old barge (see separate listings). There's a

303

clutch of boutiques and bistros along fashionable
Montague Street (try the Leaf & Bean or the
Montague Street Saloon).

Information: The Fund for the Borough of Brooklyn,
Inc, 16 Court St, Brooklyn, NY 11201, 718/643-3480.

Best Spot to Watch the River Go By
Pier 17

Take the newspaper, a good book, perhaps something to snack on, and head for the end of Pier 17
at the South Street Seaport complex. Here, tucked
at the rear of the pier's upper-level food hall, are two
rows of wooden chaises lounges on a pair of decks
overlooking the Brooklyn Bridge and Brooklyn
Heights. It's a relaxing, breezy spot, reminiscent of
the aft deck of a cruise ship, where you can watch
tacking sailboats, roaring power boats, and the
commercial and tourist traffic on the East River.
Arrive early to be sure of a seat. A thermos of a hot
or cold beverage, according to the season, is a good
idea, as are binoculars. If you should tire of the
passing river scene, there's an interesting diversion
at the raw bar of the food hall. You can get a cold
beer and some oysters and study an aquarium of
colorful tropical fish and an adjacent tank containing lemon and leopard sharks. Feeding (with shrimp)
is a daily event at 6:30 p.m.

Pier 17, South Street Seaport, Fulton & South sts,
New York, NY 10038, 212/SEA-PORT.

Best Ride That Runs Like a Swiss Tram
Roosevelt Island Tramway

Take a ride on the Swiss-built aerial tramway that
connects Manhattan with Roosevelt Island in the
middle of the East River. A journey in the slick, red
car, powered by overhead cables, takes little more
than three minutes. But, for the price of a subway
token, it provides splendid views of Manhattan's
East Side (the island parallels Manhattan roughly
between East 48th and East 82nd streets; the tramway station is on Second Avenue at East 60th Street).
The ride also offers a bird's-eye view of the steel
latticework of the Queensborough Bridge, about
which F. Scott Fitzgerald waxed poetic in *The Great
Gatsby*, describing it as "the great bridge, with the
sunlight through the girders." The island is a mix
of luxury high rises (and some more modest ones)
and the eerie remains of some of the buildings that,

before the high-rolling developers moved in, were the reason the island was earlier known as Welfare Island. The island once housed a lunatic asylum, jail, almshouse, workhouse, smallpox hospital, and other somber institutions. In today's grand scheme, a park is being developed for use by the island's affluent new tenants and anyone else with the price of a subway ride. Diversions on the island—noticeably quiet with the absence of vehicular traffic—include visiting the restored Blackwell Farmhouse, which dates to the late 18th century, and strolling Roosevelt Island's breezy riverfront esplanades. The return journey to Manhattan may be accomplished via tramway or by subway (which has connected the island with Manhattan since 1989).

Roosevelt Island Tramway, Second Ave & 60th St, New York, NY 10021, 212/753-6626. Daily 6 am-2 am.

Best Cruise Bargain
Staten Island Ferry

At 50 cents, the 30-minute trip on the Staten Island Ferry is one of New York's great travel bargains. Combined with island sightseeing within easy reach of the ferry dock, it makes an entertaining and economical outing. Claim a place at the bow to watch the commerce of the busy harbor as Coast Guard cutters skim across the water and tour boats shuttle tourists to the Statue of Liberty. Strident horns clamor for attention as the ferry passes grimy wharves bristling with derricks. They conjure scenes from *On the Waterfront*—you half expect to see work-hungry longshoremen confronting union boss Johnny Friendly. Soon, the ferry has left behind Battery Park and the steel latticework of the Brooklyn Bridge. The Manhattan skyline shrinks to postcard size, and you pass Lady Liberty, her torch bright even in strong sunlight. A freshening breeze brushes away the cobwebs of the city as the Verrazano Narrows Bridge slips out of the haze and you can pick out autos crawling across it like ants on a fence rail. Nearing shore, you pass green-painted buoy No. 27, its chiming bell a welcoming carillon. Then, with a barely discernible bump, the ferry noses into her berth and you're ready to explore Staten Island (see separate listings for Staten Island attractions and eateries).

Staten Island Ferry, Battery Park, New York, NY 10013. Daily sailings every half hour.

Best Building Resembling a Monopoly Piece

Flatiron Building

From the east, it looks as if it's the skinniest building ever constructed, with its narrow, curved front seeming to define the entire building's width. From the north, it looks like the prow of a ship, cutting through a curtain of city buildings, slowly sailing up Broadway. Taken all at once, the triangular shape of the building struck its turn-of-the-century beholders as, well, a flatiron, and that's what they took to calling it. Built in 1902 (and, yet another brief New York holder of the title of "World's Tallest Building") by famous Chicago architect Daniel Burnham, this was one of the city's first steel-skeleton buildings—the definition of a "true" skyscraper—and has become one of New York's most scenic and best-loved buildings. The odd shape came about from Burnham's inventive use of the narrow, triangular lot on which it is built, where Broadway meets Fifth Avenue and 23rd Street. The Flatiron is 23 stories tall, and at the "prow" of its ship-like countenance, only six feet wide. (Its delicate looks did not go unnoticed by skyscraper-naysayers of this century's first decade; a sizable number of skeptical onlookers expected this structure to tumble down during the first few weeks after completion.) *Nomenclature note:* This was originally called the Fuller Building, after its primary tenant, but once the descriptive nickname took hold, the company joined the crowd and called it the Flatiron.

Flatiron Building, 175 Fifth Ave (at Broadway & E 23rd St), New York, NY 10010.

Best Building as Art Deco Monument

Chrysler Building

It's not as tall as the Empire State Building, not as new as the World Trade Center, not as imposing as the United Nations Building—still, for many native New Yorkers (*and* for many visitors), their most beloved building is the beautiful Chrysler Building. Why this popularity? Because this 1929 structure isn't just a building—it's a smartly adorned monument to the crisp angles and sharp lines that typified the (alas, short-lived) art deco movement in American architecture and design. The entire building is noteworthy, but these spots deserve extra attention: the detailed, ornate lobby (with original, recently restored elevator doors); the Sistine-style ceiling mural that sprawls across more than 100 square feet; and the automobile-inspired touches—hints of hubcaps, radiator grilles, and hood ornaments in the gargoyles, arches, and other decorations. Be sure to try to catch a glimpse of the Chrysler at sunset—its top arches take on an attractive mix of shine and shadow in the light of the setting sun. *Trivia note:* For about a year—until the Empire State Building was completed—this was the world's tallest building.

Chrysler Building, 405 Lexington Ave (between E 42nd & E 43rd sts), New York, NY 10174, 212/682-3070.

Narrowest House in New York

75-1/2 Bedford Street

The often-small size of New York houses and apartments is legendary. (We know a Chicago rental agent who, when showing apartments there, refers to walk-in closets as "New York studio apartments.") But this may be taking that truism to an extreme! At only 9-1/2 feet wide (and two stories high), this is thought to be the narrowest building in the entire city. This tiny wonder was built in 1873 (before then, it served as a narrow carriageway), and was a cobbler's shop and then a candy store before it became a residence. As a residence, it earned some notoriety for its famous tenants, most notably Edna St. Vincent Millay, Pulitzer-Prize-winning poet and playwright, and actor John Barrymore (at different times, of course). This is a simple (some have said "ugly") brick house without much to recommend it except its skinniness; it is a private residence and not open to the public, but it does make quite a hard-to-believe sight. Combine gawking at this house with a look at another historic Village house: the clapboard house next door at number 77. This is the Isaacs-Hendricks House, built in 1800, and believed to be the *oldest* house in Greenwich Village.

75-1/2 Bedford St, New York, NY 10014.

Manhattan's Last 18th-Century Farmhouse

The Dyckman House

Time, "progress," and monetary concerns have so surely worked their erosive processes against so many historic New York structures that it's no wonder that this house (way up in Inwood) remains as the only 18th-century farmhouse that Manhattan has to offer. Located on land that Jon Dyckman, an immigrant from Westphalia (now a region in Germany), settled in 1661, the present house was built (by his grandson, William) in 1783, although parts of it are believed to date to a 1725 structure on the Dyckman property. During the Revolutionary War it was occupied by both sides (at different times, of course). It was donated to the city in the early 1900s and has been turned into a model Dutch-English home of post-Revolutionary times, featuring (mostly) authentic furnishings. Perhaps the most pleasant part of the house is its re-created Colonial garden, which is perfect for strolls any time of the year (*something* is usually blooming). There is also a restored smokehouse and a re-created Revolutionary soldiers' hut in the backyard.

The Dyckman House, 4881 Broadway (at W 204th St), New York, NY 10034, 212/304-9422. Tue-Sat 11 am-5 pm.

Best Time Capsule of 19th-Century New York

Old Merchant's House

This East Village landmark, built in the early 1800s, isn't well known and isn't easily accessible (it's open only on Sundays), but it is quite special, even among the wealth of historic landmarks to be found in New York. Unlike many in the city, this historic home isn't a replica—it's an original four-story, Greek Revival house full of authentic furnishings, decorations, and personal belongings of the Tredwell family who lived here for more than 100 years. It is believed that more than 90 percent of the contents are authentic; most remain as they were in 1933, when Gertrude, then 93 years old and the last of the Tredwells, passed away (some say she haunts the third floor of this historic site). Named after the occupation of family patriarch, Seabury Tredwell, who was a hardware merchant, the Old Merchant's House is an exquisite time capsule of Old New York, capable of transporting visitors to its long-ago halcyon days. Holiday-season visitors will find a 19th-century Christmas celebration.

Old Merchant's House, 29 E 4th St, New York, NY 10003, 212/777-1089. Sun 1-4 pm.

Best House to Remember a Classic American Writer

Edgar Allan Poe Cottage

It was in this small clapboard cottage (built in 1812) that Poe and his young, sickly wife, Virginia (*and* her mother) lived from 1846 to 1849. Back then, this part of the Bronx was the distant country—Poe had moved here believing the fresh air would help his wife's health. Poe paid $100 per year for his rent, and is believed to have written a number of his classic works here (including his famous poem of lament, "Annabel Lee"). However, as was typical in Poe's life, when things went bad, they did so all at once—he couldn't make any money on his writing, Virginia's condition worsened, and then she died. Shortly thereafter, Poe left here (for what ended up being the last time) for a visit to Baltimore to try to consummate a deal to run his own magazine, but he was found mysteriously ill in the street there and died days later. Today, this historic site is maintained by the Bronx Historical Society, which has restored the cottage to what it would have looked like in Poe's days; it is furnished somewhat sparsely with period pieces and some Poe mementos. For Bronx visitors, the Poe Cottage is near other major sites, including the Bronx Zoo and New York Botanical Gardens.

Poe Cottage, Grand Concourse at E Kingsbridge Rd, the Bronx, NY 10467, 212/881-8900. Wed-Fri 9 am-5 pm, Sat 10 am-4 pm, Sun 1-5 pm.

Handsomest Church That Cares

St. Bartholomew's Church and Chapel

It's a sign of the times and the sign of a church that cares to find beds for the homeless in the vestibule and spread out beside grand pillars and beneath glittering gold mosaic ceilings. This Episcopal church also cooks meals for the hungry and distributes food packages and clothing to the needy. Built in 1918 in Romanesque style to replace an earlier structure, this richly detailed church is of interest architecturally as well as socially. The triple portal with three sets of magnificent bronze doors, was designed by Stanford White after a church in Gard, France. On the mullions of the west window, look for statues of Martin Luther, St. Paul, St. Francis of Assisi, and Phillips Brooks. The interior of the church, with great square piers supporting tower and dome, has a barrel vaulted ceiling, stone and marble veneer, a

pulpit built of yellow Siena marble, and many sur-
faces covered with warm, coffee-colored, rough-tex-
tured Guastavino acoustic tile. Note the four
stained-glass windows which flank doors in the north
transept. The chapel, accessed by steps from Park
Avenue, has a pair of handsomely sculpted bronze
doors, one showing the figure of St. John the Baptist
as a young boy, the other the figure of Jesus at a
similar age. A 32-page booklet enabling a self-guided
tour is available for $2.

St. Bartholomew's Church and Chapel, 109 E 50th
St, New York, NY 10022, 212/751-1616.

Best "Unfinished" Cathedral

Cathedral of St. John the Divine

Talk about cost and time overruns—work was started
on this Episcopalian church 100 years ago, and it's
still not completed! Admittedly, work did stop between World War II and the late 1970s, but it's
moving ahead again—although no one will venture
a definite guess as to when it will be done; the best
estimate is some time in the first decade of the next
century. When completed (whenever that is), this 14-
story-high, two-football-fields-long church will be the
largest Gothic cathedral in the world (and second
only to Rome's St. Peter's among the world's
churches). While the painstaking, medieval-style
construction (by hand-cut stones) continues, this
cathedral is open for business. The church is a
stunning (and sometimes overwhelming) mix of
styles—not hard to believe when you consider the
many different periods construction has spanned.
Scenic highlights include exquisite stained glass and,
curiously, a couple of doors and lampposts rescued
from the old Pennsylvania Station when it was torn
down in 1966. A special and unusual treat is the
Biblical Garden, a quarter-acre garden that hosts
only plants that are mentioned in the Bible. The
church also hosts a full calendar of concerts, art
shows, lectures, and theatrical events.

Cathedral of St. John the Divine, Amsterdam Ave
at W 112 St, New York, NY 10025, 212/316-7540.
Mon-Sat 11 am-5 pm, Sun 12:45-5 pm; inquire for
times of services.

Best Finished Cathedral

St. Patrick's Cathedral

This soaring, twin-spired cathedral took 21 years
(from 1858-1879) to complete—a mere eyelash compared to the 100-years-and-counting it's taking to

finish the Cathedral of St. John the Divine (see separate listing). This grand cathedral (across the street from Rockefeller Center) is the seat of New York's Roman Catholic Archdiocese, the preserve of influential (and sometimes controversial) John Cardinal O'Connor. Of note is the large, intricately constructed stained-glass "Rose" window, which is more than 25 feet across, and the massive pipe organ, which includes nearly 7,400 separate pipes. This cathedral replaced the smaller Old St. Patrick's down in Little Italy, which was built in 1815, but damaged in a fire in 1866; it was rebuilt two years later, but merely as a parish church (the cemetery at Old St. Patrick's is particularly historic, with graves dating to the early 1800s, even predating the completion of this one-time cathedral). *Architectural note:* The architect of the "new" St. Patrick's was James Renwick, whose other most notable work is the headquarters of the Smithsonian Institution in Washington, D.C.

St. Patrick's Cathedral, Fifth Ave & E 50th St, New York, NY 10022, 212/753-2261. Daily 7 am-9 pm; inquire for times of masses.

Best Church to Say "Washington Schlept Here"

St. Paul's Chapel

With rosy, pink-tinted walls, turquoise ceiling, and boxlike wooden black-and-white pews, this church might be more at home in George Washington's Virginia than in the heart of New York's financial district. Thus, it is not surprising to find the pew where George Washington worshiped over a period of almost two years during the time that New York City was capital of the United States. Built in 1776, this Georgian chapel is the oldest public building in continuous use in Manhattan. It is built of native stone with hand-crafted woodwork and carvings. The pulpit, an example of 18th-century craftsmanship, is surmounted by a coronet and six feathers, thought to be the only emblem of British nobility in New York surviving in its original place. Original cut-glass chandeliers, handmade in Waterford, Ireland, hang in the nave and galleries. Other notables who worshiped at St. Paul's include Prince William, later King William IV of England; Lord Cornwallis, famous for his surrender at Yorktown; and presidents Grover Cleveland and Benjamin Harrison. Shaded by tall trees and enclosed by gray railings, the churchyard's wooden benches are a cool place for quiet reflection when the sun beats down through the granite canyons of the financial district. During summer, on

Wednesdays at 5 p.m., there are concerts of traditional and contemporary jazz.

St. Paul's Chapel, Broadway & Fulton St, New York,
NY 10007, 212/602-0800.

Best Church for Noontime Concerts

Trinity Church

The severe spire of Trinity Church, reaching toward
the sky above Wall Street, was famous as the tallest
structure in 19th-century New York. Today, it is
dwarfed by the unimaginative slabs of the surrounding office buildings housing 20th-century commerce.
During warm weather, its shaded churchyard provides a cool, grassy haven for workers who tumble
out of nearby offices with their sandwiches and
salads, soft drinks, and bottled water. On Thursdays, a noontime concert series offers 45-minute
programs that range from Brahms, Beethoven,
Debussy, and Liszt, to traditional folk music from
around the world. The Neo-Gothic church, built in
1846, is the third on the site, serving a parish that
dates back to 1697. Recent restoration efforts have
scrubbed clean the building's time-blackened sandstone, returning the once-somber building to its
original reddish hue. Note the exquisitely carved
biblical scenes on each of the church's heavy bronze
doors; admire the beautiful stained glass behind the
altar. The original church, built in 1698, was lost in
the Great Fire of 1776. The second church on this
site was demolished in 1839. Markers indicate the
graves of Alexander Hamilton, Robert Fulton, William Bradford, and other notables buried in the
cemetery. A small, free museum chronicles the history of the church and its role in New York's history.

Trinity Church, Broadway at Wall St, New York, NY
10006, 212/602-0800.

Best Spot to Suit George Washington

Federal Hall National Memorial

Preservationists who decried the destruction of the
original Pennsylvania Station in the 1960s (which
ironically led to a heightened awareness of the city's
historic structures) should be glad they weren't
around in the early 1800s to helplessly watch the
abandonment and tearing down for scrap of the
original building on *this* site. The original Federal
Hall was built in 1699 and served as both New York's
first town hall and, in 1788, the United States's first
capitol. The following year, George Washington took
the oath of office and officially became this country's

first president at Federal Hall. But, alas, a mere 23 years later, with the federal government long moved out of town (to Philadelphia, and, later, of course, to the District of Columbia), Federal Hall was torn down. Another 30 years after that (in 1842), this replica was constructed, serving as first a customs house and later as a U.S. Subtreasury. Today, the rebuilt Federal Hall is a National Historic Site that displays artifacts of early New York, most notably the suit Washington wore when he became the country's first president, as well as a variety of personal items that belonged to Washington and his wife, Martha. Also located here is a museum dedicated to the study and the history of the American Constitution. Classical music concerts are offered at the hall weekly on Wednesday afternoons. Although this National Monument is closed on most federal holidays, it remains open on the two holidays that relate most to its history—Washington's Birthday and Independence Day.

Federal Hall National Monument, 26 Wall St, New York, NY 10005, 212/264-8711. Mon-Fri 9 am-5 pm.

Right Place for Rights
Bowne House and Friends Meeting House

As world events continue to demonstrate how freedom often must be hard-won, two buildings in Queens remind us that it was always thus. The Bowne House, built in 1661 in vernacular Dutch-English "saltbox" style, has a kitchen with a large fireplace and beehive oven. It was here that John Bowne, an English merchant and landowner held clandestine services when the Quaker faith was outlawed by governor Peter Stuyvesant. The house, which remained in the family until 1946, is furnished 17th- and 18th-century style, with a Chippendale secretary, kitchen implements, and items such as foot warmers and hot-water bottles. For his defiance, Bowne was imprisoned and exiled, but later allow to return. Free to worship, the Quakers built the Friends Meeting House in 1694. Just a few blocks from the Bowne House, it is the oldest religious building in New York in continuous use. An excellent example of Colonial architecture, it has simple plastered walls, heavy wooden beams, and plain wooden benches. Visitors are invited to attend Sunday meetings at 11 a.m. On thirty-seventh Avenue, near the Boone House, is a weeping beech with a spread of 85 feet. It is said that every weeping beech in America is descended from this tree, which grew from a shoot purchased in Belgium in 1847 by Samuel Parsons, a Quaker and nurseryman.

Bowne House Historical Society, 37-01 Bowne St, Flushing, NY 11354, 718/359-0528. Tue, Sat, Sun 2:30-4:30 pm. Adults $1, children 25 cents. Friends Meeting House, 137-16 Northern Blvd, Flushing, NY 11354, 718/358-9636. Tours first Sun afternoon of month and by aptmt.

Only Mayor's Mansion in the United States

Gracie Mansion

New York *is* the only major city in the country which has an official residence for its mayor. The irony is that the city anointed this mansion with that purpose during the term of one of the *least* imperial, most people-oriented mayors the city has ever had, the "Little Flower" himself, Fiorello La Guardia. However, when you consider the circumstances involved, the choice makes a little more sense: The city was set on choosing an official mayor's home and was leaning toward the grand Schwab mansion on Riverside Drive (which, alas, has since been torn down). La Guardia vetoed that pick on the grounds of its ostentatiousness. He consented to this alternative, which was older (built in 1799), more historic (it is believed to be one of the island's oldest continuously occupied homes), and, in his eyes, less of an aristocratic put-on. It is set on a pleasant, somewhat pastoral lot (this area *was* the wild, wild country when merchant Archibald Gracie had this house built) with a fabulous view of the East River. Inside, it is stocked with tasteful art and furnishings, much of which is on semi-permanent loan from some of the city's finest museums. A tour of this landmark is quite informative and enjoyable—mainly because tours are led by guides who really know their city and Gracie Mansion history and obviously enjoy relating it to visitors.

Gracie Mansion, East End Ave at E 88th St, New York, NY 10128, 212/570-4751. Tours available March through November; reservations required.

Bully of a Birthplace

Theodore Roosevelt House

Of the many places identified with Teddy Roosevelt—the American West, San Juan Hill, and, of course, Washington, D.C.—it is perhaps ironic that New York City does not readily spring to mind, since Teddy was the only U.S. president born here. Unfortunately, his Gramercy Park birthplace was torn down in 1916, 58 years after his birth. But, today, a replica of the three-story townhouse (built in 1923, several years after his death) is open to the public, offering artifacts of and views on Teddy and the Roosevelt family. This site offers a good collection of memorabilia, including many original Roosevelt furnishings, especially in the re-creation of TR's boyhood bedroom. And, yes, there are plenty of Teddy bears (which, of course, got their name from the wildlife-loving president) and big-game trophies on display here. The Roosevelt House offers free chamber music concerts every Saturday afternoon. In an effort to replicate the original home as closely as possible, the construction and furnishing of this hybrid of a site was overseen by Teddy's sisters.

Theodore Roosevelt House, 28 E 20th St, New York, NY 10003, 212/280-1616. Wed-Sun 9 am-5 pm.

Most Roundabout Way to See Manhattan

Circle Line Cruise Tour

A cruise around Manhattan may seem the ultimate touristy excursion, but it *is* an excellent way to get a great feel for the geography and the sights of the city. The cruise heads down the Hudson, past Ellis and Liberty Islands, up the East River, under the major bridges, past Roosevelt Island, up the Harlem River, through Spuyten Duyvil (and past the old railroad bridge there), and back down the Hudson. The narration that accompanies this tour is mostly entertaining and informative. (However, I was on a cruise when the guide related that one of the most-asked questions was "Can the Dakota building be seen from the tour?"—the answer was "No"—which she assumed was a popular question "because of what happened to Jack Lemmon there...." Of course, she meant *John Lennon*, who was shot outside of the Dakota.) Scenic highlights from the tour include: Grant's Tomb (see separate listing), the cliffs and old factory signs on the Jersey side of the Hudson, the Statue of Liberty on a sunny day (it practically *glows* in the water-reflected sunlight), and the interesting water-oriented side of Manhattan (especially the docks and bridges). This tour isn't cheap—$16 for adults, $8 for children—but, for the time (three hours) and the distance (35 miles), not to mention the sights, it is *definitely* worth it. A perhaps-obvious tip (but worth remembering): The earlier you get in line, the better your chance for a seat on the port (left) side of the boat (as you face front), so that you are on the Manhattan side (rather than the Jersey-and-boroughs side) throughout the tour.

Circle Line, Pier 83, W 42nd St at the Hudson River, New York, NY 10036, 212/563-3200. March-December; schedule varies by season.

Best New England Fishing Village in New York City

City Island

This small (230 acres; four blocks wide at its widest part) island in the Bronx seems to masquerade as a New England village—salty bungalows and Victorians (yes, some even with widow's walks), and plenty of boats, marinas, and seafood restaurants. Part of City Island's sense of isolation comes from the fact that it is surrounded by Long Island Sound and Eastchester Bay and is attached to the mainland by only one bridge. Highlights of this close-knit enclave (which attracts plenty of mainlanders each summer) include the New York Sailing School (212/885-3103), offering boat rentals and sailing instruction (it has been estimated that there are more boats in the marina here than there are full-time residents); the City Island Nautical and Historical Museum (212/885-1616), which traces the history of the island and of man on and under the sea (the latter represented by a mini-sub and scuba-diving equipment); and seafood restaurants, especially the Lobster Box, where lobster is prepared more than 20 different ways, and Johnny's Reef Restaurant (see separate listings).

City Island, the Bronx, NY 10464.

Best Old-Time Boardwalk Fun

Coney Island

At its height earlier this century as a sort of working-class resort, hundreds of thousands of people a day would visit Coney Island for fun and sun. The passing years have taken their toll and this old place ain't what it used to be. Even the famous baths, where earlier generations sweated off unwanted pounds, seem as worn and time weary as their elderly patrons. But Coney Island is still worth a visit for some amusement-park and beach fun—and for a Nathan's Famous hot dog at its original location (see separate listing). The Cyclone roller coaster, a wooden, bone-rattling ride that has been providing thrills and chills for more than 60 years, still pulls in crowds of kids (of all ages)—as does Astroland, the city's last major amusement park, which offers dozens of rides, games, and other sundry amusements (these are open daily during the summer, and on weekends in the warmer parts of spring and fall). Quieter, more relaxing fun can be found on Coney Island's beach, which has survived fairly well. It is clean and safe, and still attracts legions of sunbathers seeking escape from New York's legendary "tar beaches" (rooftops of buildings, where most New Yorkers work on their tans close to home). *An etymological note:* This "island's" unusual name comes from *konijn*, the Dutch word for rabbit (which were at one time this area's primary inhabitants).

Coney Island, Brooklyn, NY 11224.

Best Spot to Find Out the *Complete* Answer to the Long-Standing Question of "Who Is Buried in Grant's Tomb?"

Ulysses S. Grant National Memorial

Rising 150 feet and consisting of more than 8,000 tons of granite, this classic-style temple in Riverside Park, overlooking the Hudson River from a leafy hill, memorializes Grant, the victorious Civil War general and, subsequently, the country's 18th president (1869-1877). (A good view of this is available from the Circle Line tour boat—see separate listing.) The 1897 structure is decorated with carved scenes from Grant's life and busts of other Civil War figures; a couple of rooms of photographs also trace Grant's life and place in history. His words of amnesty and healing following the Civil War—"Let us have peace"—are carved above the entrance to the mausoleum. A special celebration is held here on the anniversary of Grant's birth, each April 27th. And, as to the famous question posed above: Both the former president *and* his wife Julia are entombed—*above* ground—in side-by-side black marble sarcophagi inside this mausoleum. Which means, technically, at least, *nobody* is actually "buried" here.

Ulysses S. Grant National Memorial, Riverside Dr (between W 120th & W 124th sts), New York, NY 10027, 212/666-1640. Wed-Sun 9 am-4:30 pm.

Best Place to See "Saturday Night Live," the Rockettes, David Letterman, and the New York City Christmas Tree

Rockefeller Center

Some have called this the country's first urban mall, but that limiting description does a great disservice to this sprawling shopping, entertainment, and office complex. Covering 22 acres, Rockefeller Center is the largest privately owned complex of its type in the world. Here is the GE (*née* RCA) Building, home to NBC and where such shows as "Late Night with David Letterman" and "Saturday Night Live" originate (advance tickets can be had for some shows; send a postcard to: NBC Tickets, {name of show desired}, 30 Rockefeller Plaza, New York, NY 10112). Also here is Radio City Music Hall, host to ice shows, concerts, and, of course, the world-famous high-kicking Rockettes (see separate listing). Tours of this theater are offered; info is available at 212/246-4600. This is a great place to visit any time of the year, but it becomes a must-see spot during the holiday season, when the famous sunken ice-skating rink is in full, glorious use, and the city's huge Christmas tree blazes brightly like a beacon of good cheer. (The lighting of the tree is quite an event—it takes place on the first Monday in December around twilight and attracts a large, joyous crowd.) Overall, Rockefeller Center is a nice place to visit, to stroll through (the landscaping is beautiful), or even to stop just to people-watch.

Rockefeller Center, W 47th to W 51st sts and Fifth to Sixth aves, New York, NY 10020. 212/698-8900.

ENVIRONS

Best Music Festival Held at an Historic Mansion

Caramoor Music Festival

The pastoral setting for this series of summer concerts is pluperfect—a meandering creek, leafy glen, woodlands populated by deer, formal gardens, and even an apple orchard in which pre-concert picnics are encouraged (and can even be catered, for those who call in advance). An Italianate mansion filled with priceless artwork offers tours (during the December holiday season, special twilight tours include a concert, strolling Renaissance musicians, decorations, refreshments, and seasonal items in the gift shop). But it is the summer music festival for which Caramoor is best known. It features an eclectic mix, from chamber music and piano concerts to jazz and ragtime. A pretty setting for small, intimate concerts is the Spanish Courtyard, flanked by the red-tiled roofs of the mansion, with a fountain, floral displays, and statues of lions cast in Siena, Italy from a 15th-century mold. Larger concerts—the likes of the Count Basie Orchestra and the Canadian Brass—are held at the Venetian Theatre, where all seats are covered, and where concert-goers enter through imposing iron-and-gilt gates with gateposts surmounted with sculptured Pegasus heads. Special children's programs range from clogging and Irish step dancing to English hornpipes and African boot dancing. A fall concert series is held in the music room of the mansion.

Caramoor Music Festival, Caramoor Center for the Music and the Arts, Girdle Ridge Rd, Katonah, NY 10536, 914/232-5035. Late June-late Aug.

Best Living History for All Seasons
Old Bethpage Village Restoration

No matter what the season, there is always plenty going on at this living-history museum that offers a taste of life in a typical rural Long Island village of a generation before the Civil War. Costumed interpreters walk the dusty roads, off to tend to their chores and pursue their pleasures. You'll find them selling penny candy and root beer in the shops, teaching at the one-room schoolhouse, cleaning their homes, and feeding livestock. The village offers a full calendar of special events. There are summer socials, 1860-rules baseball, an 1860 wedding, concerts of 19th-century music, and the Labor Day Harvest Home Festival, with dancing, music, and clambakes. In early fall, the bustling Long Island Fair has a flower show, livestock exhibitions, crafts, a farmers' market, and a marching band in Union blue. November brings Thanksgiving feasts and political campaigning for a 19th-century election. During winter, whale-oil lamps, flickering candles, and magic-lantern shows brighten gloomy afternoons, along with seasonal music, decorations, and mulled cider. In February, visitors help fashion valentines and celebrate Washington's birthday, while March brings a quilting bee and demonstrations of embroidery and rug hooking by bonneted village ladies. In spring, visitors encounter gardening, town meetings, outdoor games, and festivities surrounding the shearing of the village sheep. There is a Civil War encampment and a horticultural exhibition. The village has more than 45 historic buildings, most of them relocated from elsewhere.

Old Bethpage Village Restoration, Round Swamp Rd, Old Bethpage, NY 11804, 516/420-5280. Mar-Nov, Sat-Thu 10 am-5 pm; Dec-Feb, 10 am-4 pm. Adults $5, children $3, seniors $2.50.

Best Day at the Beach

Fire Island National Seashore

It was well after Labor Day and I shared a mid-week ferry crossing to Fire Island with a group of under-privileged city kids. Later, I came across them play-ing on the white sandy beaches—within sight of the skyscrapers of the city they had left behind—in awe of the booming Atlantic surf. Stretching for 32 miles off Long Island's south shore, this barrier island is a perfect close-in family escape, where it is fun to swim, surf-cast for striped bass and bluefish, play volleyball, or beachcomb for driftwood and shells. Ferries operate from three mainland docks between May and November, serving eight island terminals. A pleasant daytrip is the route between Sayville and Sailor's Haven. After a breezy boat ride, you can find a spot on a wide expanse of sugar-loaf beach and follow a 1-1/2-mile nature trail through a wooded area where gnarled holly and sassafras form a canopy and wild grape vines climb from the forest floor. A wooden boardwalk takes you behind the dunes and past 15-feet-tall cattails to a freshwater bog where ferns and cranberries flourish. Near the island ferry dock, a nature center has a small museum, a snack bar, ice, groceries, and umbrella rentals. You'll also find such beach essentials as a bathhouse, rest-rooms, and showers.

Fire Island National Seashore, 120 Laurel St, Patchogue, NY 11772, 516/289-4810.

Best Close-In Resort for All Seasons

Seasons Resort and Conference Center

This rejuvenated resort once was bunnyland—part of the Playboy empire, opened by Hugh Hefner in 1971. After years of decline, new owners pumped in $12 million of renovations (with another $7 million underway). The result is a year-round resort only 50 miles west of Manhattan that offers a wide range of recreational facilities, including close-in skiing. Set on 43 rolling acres of northern New Jersey, the resort has 567 guest rooms—redone in a pale-green-and-mauve color scheme. All have picture windows and terraces and/or balconies. The resort offers the upgraded rooms and amenities of a concierge floor, and has 136 suites, a number of which are equipped with sleep sofas to accommodate families. The pre-mium suite—named after Hef—has two bedrooms, an expansive living room, wet bar, wood-burning fireplace, and Jacuzzi. Recreation includes a 27-hole championship golf course (three holes were selected by *Golf Digest* as among the top 10 in the state), year-round horseback riding on mountain trails, three indoor tennis courts, and four outdoor courts lighted for nighttime play. There is a pool, a well-equipped fitness center, basketball and volleyball courts, billiards, and, nearby, what is billed as the world's largest water park. The Vernon Valley/Great Gorge Ski Area has three inter-connected mountains and 52 trails; Hidden Valley Ski Area has a rustic alpine lodge and 13 trails. Completing the resort's amenities are three eateries, a number of boutiques, a theater-style night club featuring headline entertainment, an intimate-size entertainment club, and a range of programs for children. A 55,000-square-foot, state-of-the-art conference center was added in 1991.

Seasons Resort and Conference Center at Great Gorge, P.O. Box 637, Route 517, McAfee, NJ 07428, 201/827-6000, 800/835-2555.

Earliest Think Tank

Edison National Historic Site

A motion picture pioneer. Inventor of an electronic vote recorder and stock ticker. Creator of the fluoroscope used in America's first X-ray operation. Developer of a process for extracting rubber from goldenrod plants. Credit these achievements—and many more—to Thomas Edison, more popularly known as the inventor of the phonograph and the long-life lightbulb. The prolific inventor was awarded 1,093 patents, an incredible achievement for someone whose scant formal education ended at age 12. For more than 40 years Edison lived and worked at West Orange, New Jersey, creating an "invention factory" and directing a team of 60 scientists and technicians that became, in effect, the nation's first research and development facility. The history of the man and his work unfolds with a tour of his home and the laboratory complex from which emerged the motion picture camera and an electric storage battery designed to power electric automobiles. Tours include a visit to Black Maria, a replica of the tar-paper-covered building that was the world's first motion picture studio, and the screening of *The Great Train Robbery*, a one-reeler produced in 1903 and the acknowledged forerunner of the modern motion picture. Also shown is an orientation video, *The Invention Factory*. The laboratories may be viewed by joining a one-hour guided tour. Passes to visit Glenmont, Edison's 23-room Queen Anne mansion located on a nearby 13.5-acre estate, are available at the Visitor Center.

Edison National Historic Site, Main St & Lakeside
Ave, West Orange, NJ 07052, 201/736-5050.
Laboratory tours: Mon-Sun 9:30 am-3:30 pm;
Glenmont tours: Wed-Sun 11 am-4 pm. Adults
$4.50, seniors & children $1.50.

Best House That Vanderbilt

The Vanderbilt Mansion

It was called the "Gold Coast," that stretch of Long
Island's north shore with its hilly woodland and
hidden coves chosen by prominent families in the
New York Social Register as a desirable setting for
their opulent mansions. One such home is the 24-
room beaux arts mansion built by William Kissam
Vanderbilt II in 1898 and now frozen in time as a
reminder of the lavish life-styles of the millionaires
of his day. Sitting on a 43-acre estate, with well-
tended gardens, thick woods, and terraced lawns
sweeping down to the bay, the house is filled with
original furniture, including a copy of Napoleon's
bed, rare Oriental rugs, 17th-century dining room
chairs, and a Portuguese mantel dating from 1494.
However, this is much more than simply another
well-preserved home of the wealthy. There are outdoor concerts where visitors bring in picnics and
listen to Mozart and Berlin under the summer sky.
They also can peer into the sky through a powerful,
16-inch reflecting telescope at one of the largest and
best-equipped planetariums in the country. With its
own production house, the planetarium puts on a
varied calendar of shows in its 238-seat Sky Theater
and offers a gallery of hands-on electronic exhibits
and classes in such subjects as celestial navigation,
as well as a small space museum where visitors can
touch a meteorite that plunged into Texas in 1927.
During his world travels, Vanderbilt was a great
collector, and the house contains a large exhibit of
fish, shells, and other marine specimens.

The Vanderbilt Mansion, 180 Little Neck Rd,
Centerport, NY 11721, 516/262/7888. Tue-Sat 10
am-4 pm, Sun & hols noon-5 pm.

Bully Summer White House

Sagamore Hill National Historic Site

Theodore Roosevelt is often associated with images
of rugged adventure—impetuously leading the charg-
ing Rough Riders up Kettle Hill, hunting elk in the
Badlands of North Dakota. Yet, the 26th president
also was a devoted family man, father of six. He

raised his family in the rambling, 23-room frame-and-brick house he built in 1885 in the hamlet of Oyster Bay on the north shore of Long Island. This was his permanent home and also served as the "Summer White House" during his two terms as president. "There could be no healthier and pleasanter place in which to bring up children," he said, "than in the nook of old-time America around Sagamore Hill." Today, the house and its grounds are preserved as the Sagamore Hill National Historic Site. Visitors can inspect Teddy's study with its mounted trophies, animal sculptures, and portraits of his heroes who included George Washington and his own father whom he described as "the best man I ever knew." Upstairs is the book-lined gun room where the president worked on his many writings, using a vintage Remington Standard typewriter; cleaned his guns; and entertained friends. But it is the North room that evokes images of the president's family life. Finished in a variety of handsome woods, dominated by enormous elephant tusks, and filled with paintings, flags, and hunting trophies. It is a room that is eloquently recalled by Theodore Roosevelt, Jr., who said that "it means evening, a great fire blazing on the hearth, its flickering light dancing on the flags in the gloom of the ceiling. Father, a book under one arm, poking it with a long iron trident. Mother sitting sewing in a corner of the sofa by a lamp." Adjoining a neighboring apple orchard is the 1938 Georgian house once occupied by TR, Jr. and now a museum of the Roosevelt political and family life.

Sagamore Hill National Historic Site, Cove Neck Rd, Oyster Bay, NY 11771, 516/922-4447. May-Sept daily 9:30 am-5 pm; Oct-Apr Tue-Sun 9:30 am-4:30 pm. Adults $1.

Whale of a Town

The Whaling Museum

Between 1836 and 1862 the Long Island town of Cold Spring Harbor supported a fleet of nine whaling vessels that cruised the oceans on voyages lasting between one and five years. Before the birth of the petroleum industry sounded the death knell of the whalers, the oil secured by these stalwart vessels illuminated American homes and kept its machinery running. As a reminder of these times, this museum's collection includes a fully equipped 30-foot-long whaleboat, a stout open boat that held a crew of six and was last used on a 1912-13 voyage of the brig *Daisy*. Also displayed are whaling implements, marine paintings, ship models, a diorama of

Cold Spring Harbor as a whaling port in 1850, and a permanent exhibition on Long Island's whaling industry. Scrimshaw, the sailor's art of carving on whalebone, is represented with a wonderful collection of 700 19th-century pieces. Visitors can take classes in scrimshaw (and create a trinket box), ship-in-a-bottle techniques, and maritime origami, the ancient art of folding paper to create whimsical ornaments. There are sea-chantey concerts, films on whales and whaling, and special programs such as a Christmas treat that delights youngsters, *Willy the Operatic Whale*, the tale of a whale with the ambition to sing at the Met. A popular family outing is an historic walking tour spiced with stories of the old whaling days.

The Whaling Museum, Main St, Cold Spring Harbor, NY 11724, 515/367-3418. Tue-Sun 11 am-5 pm. Adults $2, seniors $1.50, students $1.

Showiest Museum

The Barnum Museum, Bridgeport, CT

Bridgeport, Connecticut, and legendary showman and entrepreneur, the late P.T. Barnum, are inextricably entwined. The town was the winter home of Barnum's famous circus, and it was a common sight to see elephants hauling streetcars mired in mud, the circus Fat Lady sauntering downtown, and assorted clowns and jugglers patronizing Bridgeport shops and restaurants. In 1875, Barnum was elected mayor of Bridgeport, having earlier served in the Connecticut legislature. The legacy of Barnum, who died in 1891, is this museum, which was renovated at a cost of $7.5 million. It is a visual extravaganza dedicated to the impresario and his passion for the circus. Visitors learn probably more than they ever wanted to know about 28-inch-tall Tom Thumb and his lilliputian coats and carriages, as well as about such sideshow oddities as the two-headed calf and bearded lady. The story of Jenny Lind rivals that of any latter-day pop singing sensation. Barnum successfully publicized the virtually unknown singer, guaranteeing the success of the "Swedish Nightingale" before she stepped onto an American stage. Among a variety of circus props and personal memorabilia relating to Barnum, the museum contains a hand-carved model circus with 50,000 pieces and a miniature Swiss village with 20,000 moving parts.

The Barnum Museum, 820 Main St, Bridgeport, CT 06604, 203/384-5381. Tue-Sat noon-5 pm, Sun 2-5 pm.

INDEX

NOTES

NOTES

NOTES

NOTES

NOTES

TRAVEL AND CULTURE BOOKS

"World at Its Best" Travel Series
Britain, France, Germany, Hawaii,
Holland, Hong Kong, Italy, Spain,
Switzerland, London, New York, Paris,
Washington, D.C.

Passport's Travel Guides and References
IHT Guides to Business Travel in Asia &
Europe
New York on $1,000 a Day (Before
Lunch)
London on £1,000 a Day (Before Tea)
Mystery Reader's Walking Guides:
London and England
Chicago's Best-Kept Secrets
London's Best-Kept Secrets
New York's Best-Kept Secrets
Israel on a Budget
Everything Japanese
Japan Today!
Japan at Night
Japan Made Easy
Discovering Cultural Japan
Living in Mexico
The Hispanic Way
Guide to Ethnic Chicago
Guide to Ethnic London
Guide to Ethnic New York
Passport's Trip Planner & Travel Diary

Passport's Regional Guides of France
Auvergne, Provence, Loire Valley,
Dordogne, Languedoc, Brittany, South
West France, Normandy & North West
France, Paris, Rhône Valley & Savoy;
France for the Gourmet Traveler

Exploring Rural Europe Series
England & Wales; France; Greece;
Ireland; Italy; Spain; Austria;
Germany; Scotland

Passport's Regional Guides of Indonesia
New Guinea, Java, Borneo, Bali, East of
Bali, Sumatra, Spice Islands,
Underwater Indonesia, Sulawesi

Up-Close Guides
Paris, London, Manhattan

Passport's Asia Guides/Europe Guides
Japan, Korea, Malaysia, Singapore, Bali,
Burma, Australia, New Zealand, Egypt,
Philippines, Portugal, Moscow,
Leningrad, The Georgian Republic

Passport's China Guides
All China; Beijing; Fujian; Guilin,
Canton & Guangdong; Hangzhou &
Zhejiang; Hong Kong; Macau; Nanjing
& Jiangsu; Shanghai; The Silk Road;
Tibet; Xi'an; The Yangzi River;
Yunnan

Passport's India Guides
All India; Bombay and Goa; Dehli, Agra
and Jaipur; Burma; Pakistan;
Kathmandu; Bhutan; Museums of
India; Hill Stations of India

Passport's Thai Guides
Bangkok, Phuket, Chiang Mai

On Your Own Series
Brazil, Israel

"Everything Under the Sun" Series
Spain, Barcelona, Toledo, Seville,
Marbella, Cordoba, Granada, Madrid,
Salamanca, Palma de Majorca

PASSPORT BOOKS
a division of NTC *Publishing Group*
4255 West Touhy Avenue
Lincolnwood, Illinois 60646-1975